EDIB
FRAN~~CE~~

GLYNN CHRISTIAN

I believe the fastest and most reliable way to understand and to enjoy a new country, a new town, or even a new person, is through the food they eat. Everybody eats and thus, once you have some understanding of what it is they eat, why, and how they do it their way, then their personality plus the history, geography and each of the 'ologies' associated with them becomes more immediately obvious to you.

Food, and the eating of it, are certainly the best ways to discover what President Giscard d'Estaing called **la France profonde ...**

EBURY PRESS
LONDON

Published by Ebury Press
Division of The National Magazine
    Company Ltd
Colquhoun House
27–37 Broadwick Street
London W1V 1FR

First impression 1986

Copyright © 1986 by Glynn
    Christian

All rights reserved. No part of this
publication may be reproduced,
stored in a retrieval system, or
transmitted in any form or by any
means, electronic, mechanical,
photocopying, recording, or
otherwise, without the prior
permission of the copyright owner.

ISBN 0 85223 426 0

Edited by Vivianne Croot
Designed by Harry Green
Maps and illustrations by Tony
    Garrett
Editorial consultant: Rose Minette
    Sandham
Cover photograph: Robert Harding
    Picture Library/Victor Kennett

The author would especially like to
    thank the following for their help:
Catherine Manac'h of Food and
    Wine from France in London,
Simone Cointat of SOPEXA in
    Paris,
Air France,
The Press Office of the French
    Tourist Board in London,
and a legion of researchers,
travellers, drinkers and eaters
throughout France and in Britain.

Computerset in Great Britain by
ECM, London

Printed in Great Britain at the
University Press, Cambridge.

The **Local Produce Guides** in each
chapter indicate commercial crops
(mostly French varieties), although
you will come across other produce,
domestically grown or imported.
   In the **Cheese** sections,
particularly recommended varieties
are marked with a ★ .

*GLYNN CHRISTIAN is the entertaining
and innovative Food Reporter and Chef of
BBC TV's Breakfast Time and has now
made more food broadcasts than anyone
else in British TV history.*

   *His wide knowledge of ingredients and
cooking was developed during many years
as a travel writer in Europe and travelling
throughout the world; he is a Fellow of the
Royal Geographical Society.*

   *While operating a delicatessen on
London's famous Portobello Road, he
broadcast original recipes for 5 years on
London's LBC News Radio and
subsequently made 3 series for Pebble Mill
at One, including* A Cook's Tour of the
Eastern Mediterranean. *He broadcasts
regularly with Radio 2's Gloria Hunniford
and also writes for* Over 21, Living *and*
Good Housekeeping's Country Living.

   *A direct descendant of Fletcher
Christian, leader of the mutiny on HMAS
Bounty, he wrote the first biography of his
ancestor,* Fragile Paradise. *Other major
books include* The Delicatessen Food
Handbook, The Delicatessen Cookbook
and World Guide to Cheese.

Contents

Introduction

I have written in this book of journeys both old and new I have made in France, and collected the opinions, advice and experiences of French men and women, young and old. Sometimes the opinions may not coincide with what others have written, but no matter, for they are not presented as seminal but anecdotal. From knowing the circumstances in which I was told these things, and comparing your own experiences, you will develop your own understanding of France.

Even so, it will come as some surprise to most enthusiasts to learn that France's reputation for fine food is not based on long-held traditions, but on constant change, and that a general expectation of good eating is a new experience for the French.

France as she is Ate

When the Bastille was stormed in 1789 at least 80 per cent of France's population were self-sufficient or subsistence farmers. Bread and cereals were the basis of diet, as they had been since the Ancient Gauls: cabbage, broad beans, haricot beans, chestnuts and dried pulses were the main supplements. Until the end of the 19th century you were five times more likely to be nourished from vegetable proteins than from those of

meat, cheese included. What meat you might find on your plate was likely to be pork, air-dried or preserved with salt; where you were too poor to feed pigs, you raised geese, for they fattened faster, and on less feed. In most places game might augment diet; or salt cod or herring if you lived close to a trader's route; olives helped those in the south, fresh fish those on the coast. Most milk and cheese was from goats and sheep rather than the greedier cows of the north and such wild things as snails and thrushes and songbirds made welcome seasonal contributions.

From 1820 new farming techniques resulted in more productive agriculture, but it was only in 1885 that a French government could first announce that the country need no longer fear famine. Even so, not much had changed on the table; in 1885 a mere 15 per cent of the population were able to spend freely on food. The advantages were still with the minority of that privileged percentage.

The Burden of Beasts

Food as a conspicuous symbol of social position had swiftly been adopted by the new ruling class of bourgeoisie. Having axed the aristocracy, they then sublimated all ideas of equality and recreated the sumptuous meals they had so criticized before. But they *were* a minority; the Prefect of the Seine, reporting in 1849, said that of 900,000 Parisians, 600,000 were either starving or ill-fed. Yet when the restored Bourbons gave way to Napoléon III in 1851, the great kitchens of Paris responded by reaching their highest pinnacles – up to their toques in *foie-gras* and cocks' combs, truffles, lobster coral, oysters and sole. This was the Golden Age of Haute Cuisine. There was more money (untaxed) and more social competition at the top than ever. The beast of inequality gathered speed and fat as it lumbered through the naughtiness of the Nineties and into the 20th century. It took a greater beast, that of world war, finally to halt the gross parading of unequal wealth at table and to bring a more even distribution of the nation's produce.

Coke and Sympathy

The French listened gratefully after World War I when a man who had adopted the pseudo-Russian pen name Curnonsky began writing seriously about the importance of simple local and regional foods. They had been all but erased from the national consciousness for over a century, and were always beyond the means of most. Now there was not only interest but the need and, slowly, the affluence. The chickens that Henry IV had wished to see in every peasant's pot on a Sunday were available at last.

Improved transportation, especially by train, brought culinary revolution to the regions – it is still easy to find men and women in Provence who remember the arrival of the first cows in the 1920s. Trains also brought tourists; well not at first – first came travellers, who travelled to appreciate everything that was different. Tourists largely like to look, without touching or being touched by those differences. Tourism fanned into flame the crackling embers of slow change in France's commercial kitchens. Those who travelled to experience for themselves France's newly discovered enjoyment of old foods, hastened its end. It stands to reason. A chef in an international hotel in Lyon, say, must make new fish dishes – a Japanese eating

ordinary French food would have fat intoxication in only three or four days. How *do* you remain hospitable and profitable when Middle Eastern visitors won't eat pork and order Coke instead of wine, or when the British want to keep red wine for the cheese they insist on eating *after* dessert? And, perhaps even more important, how do you retain the interest of the French men and women who have travelled, and who have read, and wish for new experiences? To believe the French are shackled to tradition in food, or should be, is patronizing humbug.

Beaten by a Nose

Those changes have been fastest this last century. In

some cases the reasons are palpable. When the silk industry snagged in the 1880s, M. Faugier kept Privas and its surroundings afloat by setting up organized centres for making and distributing *marrons glacés*. When the phylloxera pest from America wiped out most of France's vines at the turn of the century, Burgundy expanded her plantations of blackcurrants *cassis* and began making a sort of liqueur from them; and the Charentes planted grass, imported Normandy cattle, and started making butter.

Fast food and the industrial canteen (15 million meals a day) have been welcomed in France too; they answer the needs of new

---

CHANGES IN THE ——FRENCH DIET——

These figures show the average consumption per head per week in the years indicated, and prove that memories of plentitude and bounty are fanciful.

Bread	1885	1983		
	5.95 kg	.98 kg		
Potatoes	1880	1980		
	1.92 kg	1.1 kg		
Meat	1840	1900	1934	1981
	384 g	730 g	903 g	2.125 kg
Milk	1967	1980		
	1.63 l	1.41 l		
Cheese	1967	1980		
	207 g	276 g		
Sugar	1840	1900	1970	1974	1980
	51 g	319 g	723 g	758 g	265 g

Percentage of income spent on food

	1950	1967	1970	1980
	46%	38%	25.6%	20.1%

INTRODUCTION

ways of life. The long lunch eaten at home and family dinners are no longer the touchstones of French domesticity or a spur to the cook. Fast food solves one problem; but it has caused others. At the 1984 Dijon Food Fair, research commissioned by disoriented modern chefs revealed a major influence of fast food centres to be the removal of that most honoured and reliable aperitif – the smell of food cooking. Modern restaurants of all kinds go to lengths to prevent customers sharing the odours, educating them to expect neither restaurants nor kitchens at home, nor food, to smell of food. This is specially true of *nouvelle cuisine* restaurants, many of which have so far lost their direction as not to put flavours on the plate either.

Fast food centres seem deliberately to serve a confusion of flavours, particularly in hamburgers, menacing any attempt by the palate to learn to like subtle, clear or simple flavours. This serving of sensation rather than flavour is now considered responsible for the inexperienced, panic-stricken or incapable chefs adopting the mantle of *nouvelle cuisine*, encouraging them to use fancy and expensive ingredients in bizarre combinations, not in competition or emulation of the fine food of the initiated chef, but to capture the attention of palates which

have been misled or ill-educated.

The Paradox of Plenty

Nouvelle cuisine is a term invented by the French writers Christian Millau and Henri Gault in the 1970s to describe something which was not new but a continuation of what Escoffier had preached earlier this century: to serve food simply and tasting of itself. But now the palette of ingredients available had become so magnified that the possibilities were limitless. The novelty of something apparently different was welcomed with relief and hyperbole by food writers, with open cheque books by tourists and the rich, and with freshly-scrubbed fingernails by thousands of YACs, Young Aspiring Chefs – well, you can't arrange three peas and a puddle of pear purée with a spoon and fork. Silver service became sliver service as everything was sliced thinly and fanned on the plate. It should have been cheaper, since there was less on the plate and chef hadn't had to buy half a beef to make a pint of stock. But it didn't work that way.

The tide has turned, not just against small portions, but because the essential commitment to presenting food tasting of itself was forgotten in the search for sensation. It is possible to sit through several courses in some of today's culinary temples, and not recognize what you have eaten, for each course has been little more than a series of warm textures, especially if it has

Curnonsky's POLITICS OF FOOD

The 'Prince of Gastronomy' believed the French food of his time had as many parties as the country's politics. His definitions of culinary creeds were written between the two World Wars but remain acute and relevant. And not just to France. *Plus ça change . . . .*
● **The Extreme Right** Rabid, reactionary devotees of *grande cuisine*. Their feet and palates were fixed firmly, and undoubtedly with aspic, in the gargantuan meals of the international 19th-century élite of royalty, nobility and *corps diplomatique*. Admirers only of Carême, stocks, sauces and garnishes.
● **The Right** Adherents of *cuisine traditionelle*, they expected their dinners to simmer lengthily over wood fires. The cook would have 'been with us' for 30 years, the wine pre-phylloxera, the *eaux-de-vie* laid down by a great-grandfather, the vegetables from their own kitchen garden, the meat, fish and poultry from a jealously guarded private supplier.
● **The Centre** Lovers of the honesty of flavour of *cuisine bourgeoise* and *cuisine régionale*, the Centrists also firmly believed in the quality of food that could be found throughout France in regional restaurants and hotels. Of course, this is how Curnonsky diplomatically

INTRODUCTION

thought of himself; indeed he was elected Prince of Gastronomes because of his almost single-handed defence of such styles of food.

● **The Left** Those who admired *cuisine sans complication*, food which could be prepared quickly and without fuss; they searched out 'little places' where the owner himself cooked and were determinedly passionate about rural and peasant foods. Great travellers, particularly in search of obscure country wines. Curnonsky wittily also dubbed them the *nomades* of gastronomy; *gastronomades*.

● **The Extreme Left** The sensation seekers. Never happy unless there was novelty and fantasy. Curious about all foreign cuisines and each strange new ingredient they encountered. Their most notable characteristic was their love of inventing new dishes. But among this group of dreamers there were true visionaries, valuable free agents who differ from political anarchists only in that they hated *bombes* – far too classic a dessert for those of their creed!

To M. Curnonsky's parties I think I must add:

● **The Don't Knows** The numberless floaters who latch on to whatever is easiest to understand or is most expensive, usually settling for the 20th-century's food *à la française,* anything a chef puts cream onto, garlic into, or serves flambéed and with a fancy name. Commercial versions of classic dishes, reinterpreted for deep-freezes and boil-in-the-bag, make them feel happiest. Duck *à l'orange* or *coq au vin* – and plenty of it – is a guarantee of their interest; with a Black Forest Gâteau to finish.

been pounded and puréed and whisked in to egg white and cream and steamed and called a *mousseline*. It seems to have become a culinary gaffe to put committed flavour in front of a client. Technique not taste rules. Have chefs forgotten their duty is to the palate, not the plate? And the much vaunted lighter sauces? Certainly it is a relief to enjoy sauces not based on strong meat stocks and which invariably taste mainly of them. But once reductions of cooking liquids which are fierce with concentrated flavour are thickened with heavily reduced cream and mounted with butter, it is stretching the English language to call them light. And nine times out of ten the flavour of the reduction has been creamed right away.

Broken Promises

For all that France has hundreds of societies devoted to its food and wine, you are much more likely to fall into a scholarly discussion of the good old days with tourists. The average Frenchmen and women know they are eating better and with more variety than at any time in their history, albeit bemoaning the changes in the customs and traditions they remember from *grandmère*. As visitors we must not impose our ill-founded and cookbook-romanticized views of French cooking on those we visit for such a short time, nor should we encourage too many wistful looks backward. How far *do* you look back? To Provence before the tomato arrived? Languedoc before the haricot came from the

New World? Brittany before wheat could be successfully grown there, or further back, before buckwheat arrived with the Crusaders? Only a fool would think things were better then.

A hamburger in Reims or a pizza sprinkled with chilli oil by the Opéra is just as much part of the French eating experience as tucking into a *cassoulet* (you'll be lucky) in the Languedoc. What is not representative of France, and never was, is whisking from starred restaurant to starred restaurant. It's a wonderful thing to do, but it isn't France. What is then? And how do you share it?

To enjoy a visit to France and to enjoy eating there you need to think like the locals, to know what they do. And this is where change has no part to play. No local willingly drives to where a guidebook tells him to do so, and most of us don't want to. In fact the France promised by most cookbooks and culinary guides simply does not exist.

The France the French Know

To search only for local or traditional dishes is to court disappointment for where they do exist they are mainly in private kitchens. To eat only in restaurants recommended by guides cuts you off from the experience of France and its food as it is today. Everywhere there are enthusiastic talented cooks and chefs who will never be famous but who are cooking honest, exciting and creative food, and are recognized as such by the locals. The key to sharing the excitement of discovery is summed up by what André Daguin said to me in Auch; to enjoy a meal you must know the fields behind the restaurant. Exactly. It is local *ingredients* you need to know about, for then you will be able to pick the restaurants, the markets and the shops that most accurately reflect them – and whether they produce traditional or new dishes they are most likely to be the most interesting.

EDIBLE FRANCE is a guide to the reality of being in France, of what to eat rather than where. Much of the information published, particularly the guides to seasonal produce region by region, has never been available in English before; indeed, some of it didn't even exist in French. Once you start to use it, you will find your own snippets of information, your own windows into France. Only through food and wine and through eating and drinking do the landscapes and the buildings, the markets and vineyards, the beaches, mountains and lakes become stitched together into a country and a people.

I hope *EDIBLE FRANCE* will help you to eat and drink better in France, and thus help you to discover the France the French know, the France the French eat.

LE SHOPPING

Shopping hours in France are leisurely. Most small food shops open early in the morning, usually 8-8.30 am. They close for a fairly long lunch hour, generally 12 noon to 2.30 pm, sometimes 3.30 pm, but they are open for business again right up to 7 or 8 pm. Almost all food shops and markets are closed all day Monday, but open on Sunday mornings to a brisk trade.

Here's a brief guide to the names of specialist shops, and what you are likely to find in them:

● *Boucherie* The classic butcher's shop sells beef, veal and lamb, leaving the *charcuterie* to specialize in pork and the *volailler* to sell poultry. But times have changed and while many butchers still do not stock pork, they frequently sell poultry and game. Many also have a *rôtisserie* roasting chickens outside the premises. In France, meat is cut with the grain, not across it.

● *Boucherie Chevaline* The horse butcher, recognizable by the horsehead sign over the door. Horsemeat is darker than beef and the higher content of glycogen gives it a sweeter taste.

● *Boulangerie* The baker shop, where bread is baked on the premises at least twice daily, sometimes more sometimes less. This is the shop to come to for *croissants, brioches, petits pains au chocolat* and the long loaf, the *baguette*.

Wholemeal bread, *pain complet/intégral*, is increasingly available in France, so are other loaves of alternative grains. Breads which keep

longer are *pain de seigle* rye bread and the round loaf, *pain de campagne*.

When touring, you may have to buy bread instead from the general shop *épicerie* displaying a *depôt de pain* sign. Under a 19th-century law every village must have at least one store either making or selling bread.

● *Charcuterie* Traditionally a butcher's shop selling only pork and pork products, but they are now expanding also, to become what was once a separate shop, the *traiteur*.

Always ask to taste the *pâtés* and *terrines* – it's a fallacy that they are uniformly marvellous. As the French do not often hang their game, *pâtés* of pheasant *faisan*, and partridge *perdreau* can be super-bland. When faced with air-dried sausage (salami), all you need to know is that the coarser the grain the sweeter and milder the flavour, and that garlic is rarely used in them as it would become rancid. *Salaisons* are small pieces of salted pork; a small hock ham is a *jambonneau* or *petit-salé*.

● *Confiserie* The confectioner's, which is either a shop in itself, or part of a *pâtisserie*. The speciality is hand-made chocolates and sweets, made on the premises.

● *Epicerie* Grocery shop, usually self-service, except when buying cheese, fruit and vegetables.

● *Fromagerie* Devoted entirely to cheese. The *fromagerie* may stupidly still refuse to use refrigeration to maintain its cheese properly. If so, go elsewhere if you find the shop hot or smelly, especially in summer, or if you are still a cheese novice.

bouchons-champagne, handy gadgets for resealing open bottles of fizz.

often the displays of oysters especially and other fish outside restaurants may be bought.

• *Traiteur* The original takeaway, where prepared dishes such as casseroles and salads can be bought. Often such shops no longer call themselves *traiteurs* but some smarter name, or they use the proprietor's name. Beware in such as *Fauchon* (Paris) or *Hédiard* (throughout France) of paying more for the label than the contents.

• *Triperie* Shop specializing in tripe, sold on its own or prepared in different sauces.

• *Volailler* Poulterer also selling game birds.

HYPER HYPER

Having haughtily ignored the idea for years longer than anyone else, the French now build the biggest hypermarkets in Europe. They are supermarket cities, where the quality of food can be as high as the speciality shops but the prices lower. There is ample space for a staggering variety of food and wine; china and kitchen equipment are recommended non-food items.

Hypermarkets usually close Sunday. If so, they are open Monday to Saturday, often up to 10 pm. Smaller hypermarkets may close for lunch. On the whole, they do not accept credit cards. But they do have exchange facilities for travellers' cheques, or there will be a bank associated with the store. Great places for the family in bad or very hot weather, as most are air-conditioned. The imminence of the hypermarket is always

indicated and advertised along whichever *Nationale* or motorway you are following; here are a few names to look out for. The big hypermarkets are always slightly out of town.

• *Carrefour* All over France. Highly recommended for quality and price.

• *Casino* There are small Casino shops in almost every village. Don't be baffled by signs for Géant Casino. This does not signify some brobdignagian baccarat, but an enormous hypermarket.

• *Champion* Specially worth a family expedition – it's one of the colossi.

• *Euromarché* The rich from St-Jean-Cap-Ferrat drive all the way to Nice to shop in their local Euromarché. Who are you to stay away?

• *Leclerc* Edward Leclerc is famed for fighting the government on petrol prices. There is a chain of Leclercs with superlative prices.

Best Buys

When you have found your supermarket, specialist shops and markets, what should you bring back that you can't get at home? Here are a few suggestions.

• *Cassoulet* Superior baked haricot beans crammed with sausage and meats.

• *Chestnut purée (purée de marrons)* Both plain and sweet with vanilla flavouring are indispensible.

• *Coffee* Beans and freshly ground coffee are much cheaper in France.

• *Marchés* Markets are the best places to buy fruit and vegetables. The vast majority will be produce of France. Good *charcuterie* and cheese stalls too, and even fishmongers. The variety and the *département* or country of origin of the fruit and vegetables is usually displayed; the most interesting *artisanale* stalls are usually found at the edges of the market.

Flowers, cheap china and kitchen tools are also for sale; this is where I buy my

• *Pâtisserie* Cakes, pastries, sorbets and ice cream are made on these premises. The standard of presentation is high, as the French housewife depends on her local *pâtisserie* for her sweet course. The French woman has never been ashamed of buying prepared foods to take home.

• *Poissonnerie* The fishmonger. The range of fish available in France is enormous, particularly shellfish. Fishmongers frequently have stalls in street markets and

Truc Stop

Indulge your kitchen with cast-iron *Le Creuset*, especially the new non-stick ones; a giant *couscoussière*, which I use for steaming large amounts of anything; the *bouchon-champagne* for re-sealing unemptied champagne bottles; marvellous knives; screw-top jars.

- *Cous-cous.*
- *Croissants, frozen.*
- *Fish pâté.*
- *Flageolet beans* Very cheap, buy them dry and by the kilo or tinned.

embossed white dinner plates can cost next to nothing with extra savings on pre-packs. Decorative plates or the scalloped green and yellow ranges from the south are sensa-

SELF PRESERVATION

Pack your (clean dry) jars with alcohol-soaked fruit during the summer holidays and they will be ready by Christmas. Try these combinations: greengages or white peaches in cognac; strawberries or raspberries in vodka or cognac; black figs in black rum; pears in gin. Peel or prick thick-skinned fruit, add just a little sugar.

Glacé fruit is expensive, but far less so than at home.

- *Graisse d'oie* Goose fat, glossy and cream-coloured and quintessentially French. Keeps for ages in the fridge.
- *Green peppercorns* Packed in brine, or dry but never in vinegar.
- *Jams and spreads* Unusual flavours like *reine-claude* greengage and *mûres mulberry*. (*Mûres sauvages* or *mûres de vonce* are blackberries.)
- *Oils* Considerably cheaper in France.
- *Olives* Rinse away the brine, repack in jars with olive oil. Flavour each one with the herb of your choice, lemon peel or crushed garlic, coriander seeds – anything. By the time you get home they will be ready.
- *Quenelles de brochet* Pike 'dumplings'; buy a tin of *sauce Nantua* to go with them.
- *Rouille* A rich sauce flavoured with saffron and hot peppers. Dollop into fish soup.
- *Smoked garlic* A speciality of Boulogne market.
- *Snails* Best value without shells.
- *Tableware* Plain white or

tionally cheap, so is the amusing pink glass tableware made by Arcopal; also crystal glasses and Biot glass (Provence).

- *Vinegar* Herb-flavoured vinegars and oils, a relatively new invention, can be made at home much more cheaply. Buy your herbs at the market, or pick them from the hills, and steep them in oil from the supermarket.
- *Wine and spirits* I tend to forego the wines and buy alcohol that can be both drunk and used in cooking – *eaux-de-vie* such as pear and raspberry (*framboise*), *kirsch*, the real blackcurrant liqueur *cassis*, and black rums. Unflavoured 40 percent alcohol *eau-de-vie pour conservation des fruits* is sold universally and is best used for drinking after soft summer fruits have macerated in it for a few months rather than as a preservative for the fruits. Add sugar to make a liqueur. Serve ice cold in iced glasses or as a mixer for wine, sparkling wine and champagne.

EATING OUT

Don't be a bore and eat only in restaurants that you have spotted in someone else's listings, or to which you have to detour for miles. Be brave and eat where and when you like. There's just one rule to follow: the only good restaurants are busy restaurants, with the possible exception of those considered fashionable, which can be dreadful.

Things to Know

To be treated seriously when you walk in without a reservation, always ask for a number of *couverts*, covers, rather than places – *vous avez deux couverts?*

- *Menu* A fixed-price meal, usually of four courses which every French restaurant must offer. There will be a choice of dishes at each course and the menus may include wine, but not coffee. Unless there is something you particularly want to try, ordering from the special menu or menus is better than à la carte. Quality is invariably good and tax and service are included. Many restaurants offer several set menus at different prices; the more expensive ones including extra courses or pricier ingredients, or wine. There may be a *menu du jour*, a set menu of the day which will generally be the freshest and best – but always look around to see what others are eating.
- *Menu dégustation*, or *menu surprise* Tasting menu. You'll be presented with a procession of small servings (chosen by the chef if it is the *surprise* menu) with the simple restriction that everyone at the table must have the same menu.

LE LABEL ROUGE

Even if you speak good French it can be difficult to shop in France, for so many of the products look so different you have no way to judge their quality. One safeguard is to look for produce with the noticeable red label, LABEL ROUGE.

The standards laid down by law for the production of anything carrying such a label are rigorous, and regularly inspected, but with the relish that the French and food writers have for scandal there is always a whisper about this or that product not conforming. At its simplest the Label Rouge means you are justified in paying a little extra for the product and can feel that little more secure. All the labels are crammed with information, but some of the advantages you are promised will be:

● *Boeuf* and *veau de lait* beef and veal. Only from the *départements* of Cher, Allier and Puy-de-Dôme. Beef will come from an animal which has been suckled by its mother for 8 or 9 months and have spent summers at grass and winters fed on grass and cereals. Not slaughtered until at least 18 months, usually over 2 years. *Charollais* beef must have both mother and father of the same breed. Milk-veal must be born at special veal-raising farms or raised by them up to no later than 15 days old. They must be fathered only by *Limousin* bulls but their mothers may be *Limousin, Charollais, Salers* and crosses of these breeds. They will be no more than 120 days old.

● *Emmental Grand Cru/Central Est* Made in every eastern *département* from the Vosges to Savoie. The Label Rouge guarantees it to be made only from milk produced from grass and hay (no silage etc), aged at least 10 weeks, and ensures standards of shape, crust, body, flavour, smell.

● *Jambon cuit* Cooked ham. Only hind-quarter meat, salted without phosphates, full muscles and meat only from one animal (not tumbled and reconstituted).

● *Jambon sec* Dry or raw ham. Dry-salting of the meat and controlled times of salting and curing.

● *Pâtés* Guaranteed percentages of the major product – 30% liver and lean meat in a *pâté de campagne,* 25% pork liver in a *pâté de foie,* and so on.

● *Saucisson sec, saucisse sèche, jésus, rosette* A guarantee that only the *noble* pieces are used, and only hard fat, with a maximum proportion of 25%. No colour or polyphosphates, coarse texture so that the quality of meat and fat can be appreciated, and controlled curing.

● *Volaille* Poultry; 90% of Red Label poultry is chicken; guinea fowl *pintade;* duck *canard* and turkey *dinde,* make up the remainder. If chickens are raised outdoors with at least two square metres of space each, they may also carry the *fermier* label. Otherwise they will have been confined but under rigourously controlled conditions of limited numbers. Diet must have been at least 70% cereal rising to 75% for the

last two weeks, and some brands fed only wheat or corn during the last week. Red Label chickens must be at least 81 days old, guinea fowl 94 days, Christmas turkeys 140 days and barbary ducks 84 days. The labels are more complicated than others and are worth checking. In order from the top they tell you:

● How long they were raised – *durée d'élevage.*
● What they were fed – *alimentation.*
● Last day of sale – *date limite de vente* – 7 days after slaughter for chickens.
● Method of raising–*type d'élevage* – ie *fermier.*
● Producer and area – *provenance.*
● Production number – *No de l'étiquette.*

Among over 100 products that have the right to sport a Red Label, there are two potatoes, La Belle de Fontenay and La Bintje de Merville (Nord) plus:

● Pink garlic *ail,* of Lautrec
● Carrots *carottes,* from Créance
● Onions *oignons,* from Auxonne
● Olives *olives* from Nice
● Green olives *olives vertes* from Picholine and La Lucques
● Black olives *olives noires,* from Nyons
● Golden Delicious apples from Haut-Diois
● Golden Delicious apples from Checy
● *Passe-crassane poires* (winter) pears from Haut-Diois

INTRODUCTION

• *La carte* Everything offered which is not on the special menu. *À la carte* dishes which are not on the inclusive menus will be more expensive. Main courses will arrive with a garnish of vegetables. Usually there will be a *plat du jour*, dish of the day, and if you are not very hungry go for this and a salad.

• *Table d'hôte* Traditionally a chance to try real home cooking. The words posted outside a farmhouse once meant 'the host's table' and invited anyone to eat with the family at a single sitting and at a fixed price. The idea caught on in many a country restaurant and simply indicated that you would be offered little or no choice.

• *Menu touristique* Generally you should look elsewhere as this is not often French food, but dull Eurofare aimed at the tourist. Yet some simple places do try, and sometimes an honest tomato salad, steak and *pommes frites* followed by ice cream will be just what you want, and the best possible value. The French do eat such things, too.

PLACES TO EAT

• *Auberge* Restaurant, usually attached to a country hotel or in rural areas.

• *Bar* Rarely serve food or coffee; when they do it will be simple dishes or sandwiches.

• *Bistro* In the provinces, a cross between café and restaurant. City bistros often rely on the romance of the name to excuse cramped space, noise and rudeness; but there's often good food to compensate.

• *Brasserie* Meals, drink and coffee anytime of the day. It was usually Alsatians, dispossessed or disillusioned by war and border disputes, who went to the cities to open such businesses and so *choucroute* and sausage are served in most. Modern Parisian versions can be a combination of American drugstores and old-fashioned *brasserie*.

• *Buffet* Usually found at stations and airports. Food and drink is available at all times, often much better than customers of BR or Amtrak would dream possible.

• *Buvette* A kiosk selling drinks, sandwiches and ice creams.

• *Café* Drinks and coffee at the bar, where prices are lower, or from a waiter. Sometimes simple meals, but snacks – *casse-croûte* – always available. *Croissants* and *brioches* in the early morning give way to *baguette* sandwiches, usually with thin slices of ham or cheese and *croque-monsier*, toasted ham and cheese sandwich. They all serve tea gladly or will make a fresh lemon or orange drink – *citron/orange pressé*. Don't be embarrassed to sit a while with only a cheap drink. Everyone else does it.

• *Cafétéria* For quick basic meals and drinks. The ones at hypermarkets are often very good.

• *Crêperie* Crêpes with sweet or savoury fillings, usually associated with Brittany. *Crêperies* can usually be found in tourist haunts. (Savoury *crêpes* often of buckwheat, sweet ones of wheat flour.)

• *Drugstore* The hot dog and other American fast foods, with simple French dishes.

• *Estaminet* small bar, often seedy.

• *Hostellerie* A restaurant, usually attached to a country hotel.

• *Libre-service* A self-service cafeteria, often part of a hypermarket.

• *Relais routiers* Motorway or main road pull-ups to refuel the lorry drivers *qui roulent pour nous*. Popular with English Francophiles. Good plain regional food, and lots of it.

• *Restaurant* For meals only.

• *Restoroute* Restaurant set near a motorway.

• *Rôtisserie* A restaurant, sometimes called a grill, which once specialized in grills or roasts; now most serve everything.

• *Salon de thé* Tea room and coffee shop, often part of a *pâtisserie*. Besides cakes and pastries, light meals on toast are often served. Haven for lone women, who may feel more comfortable here than in cafés or restaurants.

• *Snack-bar* Basic food served quickly.

• *Taverne* Usually a rural restaurant.

NORMANDY

A Heart of Butter & Cream

Normandy rather creeps up on you. There you are driving expectantly south through what you *think* is sugar beet (so few people actually *know*) and remarking on the greyness of the northern villages – and the next minute you are in England's Kent. At least that is the way it seems, for all of a sudden there is green ruralness and a thatched, half-timbered farm or cottage.

Cows who wear Glasses . . .

Lots of rosy brick is used, too, for inward-facing, seemingly fortified conglomerations of farmhouses, islands in an ocean of agriculture. Timber construction here was not chosen for cosy aesthetics but because Normandy has plenty of chalk (Pays de Caux), and little or no stone suitable for building. In any case, the black and white architecture may be neither British nor French, but one of the many relics of settlement by men from the north, Vikings, who invaded in the 10th century. Once their leader, Rollo, had

> In which we …
> ● Find spectacled cows from Scandinavian bulls …
> ● Explore the paradox of a culinary masterpiece without wine …
> ● Enjoy ancient ducks in Rouen and a unique mustard from Caudebec-les-Elbeuf …
> ● Go to Dieppe for mackerel and scallops, Honfleur for harbour atmosphere, Cherbourg for a fish market …
> ● Find whiter oysters for cooking, a menu with curried salmon …
> ● Learn of red peppers with a princess, rice puddings for kings, apples that taste of pineapples…
> ● Taste a far better butter and unpasteurized *camembert* …

extracted from the king of the Franks a dukedom for himself and grants of land for his marauders in return for some sense of peace, the new men of North Man's Land (Normandy) sailed their big-boned cattle from their old Scandinavian homes and started breeding. By perspicacious choice of cow and bull they produced the brown and white, spectacled Normandy breed, prodigious producers of fragrant milk and cream.

The renowned Norman table, set with brimming bowls of cream and slabs of thick, creamy butter is rooted in the same Dark Ages. The Vikings had relied upon bland cheeses and sweet butter as relief from the relentless rations of salted and smoked produce. As new French men, they gratefully switched to fresh fish and meats, but kept their creams, butters and cheeses. The 15th-century Butter Tower in Rouen is said to have been financed by the selling of dispensations to eat butter and cream in Lent.

Year-round Pork

It's worth repeating the still surprising cliché that an area which does not make wine should have such a reputation for its food. Few of Normandy's 'traditional' dishes are complicated. Those that are have been invented recently for demanding travellers, or Parisians too bored to eat simple food. Normandy's real food and its culinary reputation relies on that rarest of modern things, intrinsic quality – plus a climate encouraging to produce that does not require excessive flavour or bite to

A FAR, FAR BUTTER THING..

Essentially there are – or were – just two styles of butter, sweet and salted. Sweet butter can be made only from unpasteurized, sweet cream, called sweet because it has not been allowed to age and develop acidity before being churned. But today's creams are pasteurized, which kills the bacteria that would have developed the character. Modern technique replaces the heat-slaughtered goodies with a carefully controlled mixture of lactic-bacteria to reflavour the cream. The industry's name for what is sold as 'unsalted' butter is actually 'lactic' butter. Differing mixes of bacteria and differing aging periods after innoculation explain the broad variety of un-creamlike flavours found in continental 'unsalted' or 'lactic' butter. It is the discovery of these differences which so repays experiment. To my mind, Norman buttermakers add the least intrusive flavours of all, and most of their unsalted butter honestly reflects the full natural voluptuousness of rich, whipped cream. It is a revelation to use these but-

ters in baking – but they are not, properly, 'sweet' butters.

Salted butter is made savoury (after innoculation with a different mixture of bacteria) with salt, which also enhances its keeping qualities. You may or may not find unpasteurized butter *beurre non-pasteurisé,* or sweet butter *beurre doux* in markets in Normandy: the only one I know made regularly is *beurre au lait cru de Basse-Normandie* from Ste-Mère-Eglise – it is also sold in Phillippe Olivier's famous cheese shop in Boulogne. I keep some in my deep-freeze for cake and pastry making or for smearing onto hot scones with strawberry jam when I cannot get clotted cream.

The bonus of a butter search for the cook is the discovery that these butters perform differently from others. Their waxier texture is smoother in the mouth, and their slow resistance to melting and oiling makes them matchless for adding satin thickness to butter-mounted sauces, made by whisking clumps of butter into fiercely-reduced stocks.

compensate for coarseness or blandness.

Normandy is neither too hot to grow frost-sweetened root crops, nor too cold to grow delicate cherries or raspberries. Its plains and

meadows are suitable not just for dairy grazing but also for raising sheep, especially spring lambs of the salt meadows *prés-salés* of the coast. Windfall apples and pears, buttermilk and skimmed milk make perfect fodder for pigs, and there was plenty of salt from the sea to preserve their flesh before refrigeration helped develop a year-round taste for roasted fresh pork.

It's not a broad or mountainous region, so the smallest hamlet might regularly find the fish from its rivers supplemented by mussels and oysters and fish from the sea. Honfleur's merchants once even took locally-salted cod to China. Wheat and other grains grow well, both for use in baking and for feeding poultry. Britain was importing 7,000 dozen eggs a week from Honfleur 150 years ago. Thus the choice of produce has always been exceptionally wide, even if not always eaten; those root vegetables so readily puréed for modern plates were rarely used for anything other than soups and stocks until after World War II, except in times of extra hardship. But there was simply no need to make complicated dishes, even if you had the time and facilities, when boiled cream or butter could make simple food luxurious.

A New Menu

Cider and *eau-de-vie de cidre,* called calvados only when it is of top quality and from the right *départements*, have also had their distinct influence on Norman tastes. Cider is more subtle than wine in cooked dishes, and like the rest of Norman ingredients, does not need a large palette of added flavours to balance its contribution. A little onion or shallot will do, perhaps some chives.

The person I know best in Normandy is a princess, Marie-Blanche de Broglie, granddaughter of Princess Henri de Polignac of the astonishing Pommery champagne family, and latest in a formidable line of influential women. Marie-Blanche teaches cooking in the gardener's cottage of her château La Coquetterie, outside Rouen – and taught me much about the realities of modern French food. For although her family life is based on traditions and customs reflecting ancient aristocratic, social and climactic seasons, her food reflects change – indeed her school is called 'Princesse Ere 2000'. Soups and stews there are, of course, but the soup may be iced red peppers from Provence, the breasts of chicken stuffed with green beans from her own garden, and garlic cloves may be used whole as they do in Gascony – ingredients and methods which are eclectic but never eccentric.

Love a Duck

I suppose that most people come to Normandy expecting to eat good fish, which they will; to try Rouen duckling, which they should; to order *pré-salé* lamb, which they must; and to drink sparkling cider, *cidre bouché*, and calvados. Well and good, and they are the basis of some excellent times. A less considered but equally edifying pursuit is a study of Normandy's butters. Butter flavours vary, not just from area to area, but also through the treatment of the cream. A fascinating and complete background to

butter and cheese making can be found in the *Musée de Normandie* in Caen.

Before the motor car and train began shunting us inexorably towards uniformity, there was a difference between the table of Normans who lived north, and those who lived south of the River Touques. Rouen, capital of upper Normandy, and Caen, capital of lower, still offer their specialities of duck and tripe respectively. You will enjoy comparing the different merits of butter from Neufchâtel-en-Bray and Gournay and Isigny, where they credit the salty air and spray from the Atlantic for the special flavour of their butter and cheese. And there are wonderful local sights to be seen – in autumn in the Vallée d'Auge when its peculiar varieties of hard cider apples are tumbled into courtyards before pressing, and in the Pays de Bray, where 'farmhouse' cheeses are made in small tin shacks thick with humidity in the company of vital, ancient infestations of benevolent bacteria and moulds.

Yet essentially, Normandy is one of the most homogenous of regions. Although the bowls of cream have disappeared from the Norman tables you are likely to encounter, they are nonetheless the unifying touchstone, used to make acceptable anything that has come from outside.

The dairy is still the very heart of Normandy and of Norman cuisine, perhaps the only heart in France that beats the more robustly *because* of butter and cream . . .

CHARCUTERIE

As well as enjoying a rich choice of fresh meats, the Normans make a limited range of *charcuterie* from their fine pigs, fattened and sweetened on the windfalls of cider and eating apples and pears – at least those lucky enough to live on free-range farms. Normandy is rather too damp for the successful manufacture of air-dried sausages, so most of the prime cuts are eaten fresh (frozen probably), with a little included in *pâtés* and *terrines*. *Les restes* are treated with such respect as to make them nationally famous, and none more so than blood turned into black pudding. Yet, perversely, it is *boudins* from other regions and countries to which Normans often give the most adulation.

Black Pudding Axis

The epicentre of the black pudding world is Mortagne-au-Perche, also the home of those dignified giants of war and the furrow, the Percheron horses. On the first Sunday after mid-Lent (mi-Carême), the *Confrérie des Chevaliers du Goute-Boudin,* the Brotherhood of Pudding Tasters, organize an international *Concours du Meilleur Boudin.* Over three days, puddings and their makers come from every district of France and most countries of western Europe. It is a serious business, with secret recipes guarded, new fantasy shapes and new ideas paraded. The French win prizes, of course, but so do the Germans and the black pudding makers from Britain, Lancashire particularly. Over six tonnes of black pudding

are eaten during the three days, and there are black pudding eating competitions – one person ate 1.25 m of pudding in 15 minutes in 1969. Since then they keep forgetting to measure.

Where you find black puddings, you invariably find my least favourite things, large and small tripe sausages, *andouilles* and *andouillettes* respectively. If you are uncertain and want to make your mind up once and for all, then seriously confront those of Vire; they are supposed to be amongst the very best in France. There, *andouilles* often also contain veal chitterlings, and the *andouillettes* (also good from Caen where they are more robust) are usually smoked before they are grilled. Apples are a common accompaniment, sometimes puréed or sliced, sometimes in the form of cider, which may turn out to be the better idea.

If you are lucky you might find *sanguette*, which is a *boudin* made from the blood of rabbits rather than pigs. More common is good brawn, sold either as *fromage de tête* or *hure*.

FISH & SHELLFISH

The long Normandy coastline makes this region one of outstanding fish and seafood, a natural and welcoming accompaniment to its butters and creams. Dieppe and Fécamp are perhaps the most important ports commercially, but others will certainly repay a visit.

Dieppe is renowned for its young mackerel *maquereau de Dieppe* or *lisettes*, its scallops and its herrings. In history, it was the major supplier of fresh fish to Paris and famed for its relays of horses, always on the trot, which got fish packed in seaweed to Paris in less than 12 hours. This continued until the end of the 19th century when they finally converted to rail, something Boulogne had done decades earlier.

Fécamp is an important centre for making salt cod *morue* and has salted herrings to sail up the Seine to Paris since the 10th century; they have been smoked since the 13th. Honfleur seems to have been even more enterprising with such products; her merchants set up trading posts in the Far East where they exchanged their salt cod for spices. It's a charming place with 16th and 17th-century houses around the harbour and really excellent seafood restaurants. Le Havre specializes in importing products for the food industry – coffee, cocoa, sugar, spices and citrus; but if you really want to get among the buying and selling of fish of every type, Cherbourg is your place. It has a market right in the middle of town.

Sole Normande

The star of Normandy's fishy firmament is unquestionably the sole, and even here you might find it called a Dover sole or *sole de Douvres*. The competition to do something different with it keeps chefs amused and customers befuddled. Its firm flesh makes this possible, for it's one of the few fish that can stand being heated and reheated and then kept hot. To my mind, the best version of *sole normande* is the old one, simply poached in cream or in stock and served with a thick cream sauce, usually a *velouté* made with the fish stock, a *roux*, eggs and cream. Today the *saucier* may dispense with the *roux* and construct the sauce from reduced stock and cream mounted with butter. Restaurant chefs have ever felt they must add something to justify their prices, and so this basic is dramatized by mussels and prawns and mushrooms in particular; in Dieppe, or in the style *à la Dieppoise*, the mussels are creamed to flavour the sauce and prawns are used as a garnish. When you are feeling, or are, poor, lemon sole *limande* is easy on the pocket and so is *vive*, the weaver fish, highly recommended for its sole-like flesh.

In the changing climate of today's restaurants it is difficult to predict what might be offered you, or in which way it may be prepared. Apart from those already mentioned, most of the shellfish are good, and whelks and winkles *buccin* and *bigorneau* turn up unexpectedly. Limpets *patelles*, locally-farmed clams

praires, palourdes and *clovisses* turn up raw in seafood platters, the best way to start a meal, but only in a busy restaurant, to ensure freshness.

For important celebrations the Normans like turbot on the table. It may be served with a sauce *Vallée d'Auge*, in which you can confidently expect apples and cider, if not calvados as well, and cream. All Normandy on a plate, in fact. In summer, watercress from local beds, tarragon and sorrel are commonly used with both salt and freshwater fish.

MEAT, POULTRY & GAME

It's likely that visitors unfamiliar with Normandy will nonetheless know of two of its great specialities, the Rouen duckling served in a sauce which includes its blood and liver, and *tripes à la mode de Caen*. But there is another meat that is spectacularly good, and which I first ate in that most astounding of places, Mont-St-Michel, which manages to be only just in Normandy. Its bay is the mouth of three rivers, the Seine, Selune and Couesnon on the border with Brittany. There are immense expanses of salt-marsh over which the tide creeps, iodizing and salting the herbiage. Sheep and lambs which graze here develop a delicately salty flavour. These are the *pré-salés,* the salt-meadow lambs. As well as enjoying lamb simply roasted with a little garlic or onion (and no gravy), you might find it served accompanied by apples, as in *côtelette de pré-salé aux pommes. Pré-salé* may also be called *agneau des grèves* lamb of the shores. Isigny claims very special pastures.

Caneton Rouennais stuffed duckling with a red wine sauce is one of the few dishes from the classic repertoire that really may have been bad in the good old days. Its fame is based on the ruddy flesh and gamey flavour that ducks from Yvetot and Duclair develop when they are strangled or suffocated, so that their blood remains in their flesh. An unbled duck deteriorates with great speed, within hours in hot weather, but refrigeration assists here. It is proper that it does, for it was from Rouen that *La Frigorifique* set sail in 1876, returning four months later with the world's first cargo of frozen meat. Pressed duck, more a Parisian dish, is based on this Rouen recipe.

A particular feature of the two types of duck preferred – the Rouen *clair* and the *foncé* – is their long body, allowing the chef to cut attractive fillets *aiguillettes.*

There is a Normandy breed of pig, whose flesh is commonly served with cream and apples (often caramelized), or with prunes, and a race of white geese *oies blanches* to complement the numerous types of chicken around, particularly in the Vallée d'Auge. Beef is more likely to be veal if it is genuinely local.

Game was once common, particularly game birds, but when Prince François de Broglie walked me in the grounds of his wife's château, he told me that his shooting parties never expected great bags these days. Pheasant and some partridge were all they might find, otherwise it had to be pigeons or crows. Wild pigs do exist in Normandy, but they are usually on their way somewhere else; if any do remain for some time, it is because a sow has farrowed.

TRIPE
à la mode

Tripe is commonly cooked in Normandy, and in this dairying country it consists of ox stomachs, of course. *Tripes à la mode de Caen* should properly be cooked in a *tripière,* a variation of the local *marmite.* The prepared pieces of stomach are layered with onions, leeks, carrots, a good bouquet garni, cloves, pepper and a couple of split calf's feet . . . and then comes the discussion. There is a belief, supported by some practice, that the liquid should consist only of cider with a touch of calvados. This is not now common – and may not ever have been – as cider can darken unacceptably the colour of offal. It is more likely to be water with a good glass of calvados. The pot must then be sealed with a paste of flour and water and cooked, according to the books, anything from a few hours up to 48 hours, hence a further point of dispute. There is no argument about the fact that a favoured Norman time to eat *tripes* is still mid-morning, especially on market days.

In Coutances tripe is wrapped around fingers of *petit-salé* ham hock and the *tripes aux brochettes* of Ferté-Macé are worth ordering for they are packages of *gras-double* and pieces of cow or veal foot wrapped in more *gras-double* and secured with little sticks. *Gras-double* indicates the use of only three of the cow's four stomachs; *tripes* should mean that all four are employed. It is no dishonour not to cook your own. *Tripes* have always been very much food cooked by professionals for the public to buy.

FRUIT & VEGETABLES

Apples and pears dominate Normandy. Together with spectacled cows and half-timbered houses, orchards are the most common sight. The varieties of cider apple are myriad, but the best cider and *calvados du pays d'Auge*, should include the sweet *Bedan*, the acidic *Noël des champs* and *Binet rouge*, and the sweet *Doux mouen*. In other *départements* the same apples may have different names. The varieties of pear grown are more generally edible, with the *Louise Bonne d'Avranches* (September and October) and the later *Passe-Crassane* notably superior, as are the *Calville* apples.

Autumn is the time to enjoy the figs of St-Vaast-la-Hougue, where there are big auctions of dried fruit in October. Earlier, Honfleur, surrounded by orchards, has an ancient reputation for its cherries (often found accompanying duckling) and its melons. Lisieux, too, is an important centre for fruits. Berries grow extremely well in Normandy and the crop is increasing annually (especially from Caen). The varieties harvested at present give strawberries *fraises* from June to mid-October, raspberries *framboises* from July to mid-August, redcurrants *groseilles* during July, give or take a week, and blackcurrants *cassis* from mid-July to mid-August. Gooseberries *groseille à maquereau* are as often called *gades* or *gadelles*.

One of the least known harvests of Normandy is samphire *cristal-marine*, a salty, crunchy green plant

---

LOCAL PRODUCE

- **Cabbage** *choux* — Green: December to April. White: December to March. Red: Mid-December to mid-April. Dep: Manche, Calvados

- **Carrot** *carotte* — October to April. Var: *Nantaise, Amélioré, Nandor, Tancar* — Dep: Manche, Calvados.
The biggest and the best area for carrots in France: Créances and Mont-St-Michel are among important production zones.

- **Cauliflower** *Choufleur* — October to December and mid-February to May. Varied local and hybrid — Dep: Manche

- **Celeriac** *céleri-rave* — September and October. Dep: Calvados

- **Celery** *céleri-branche* — September to March. No special centre

- **Leeks** *poireaux* — October to April. Var: *gros de Rouen* — Dep: Manche – locally also

- **Lettuce/endive** *laitue/chicorée* — May to October. Var: green cabbage, iceberg, endive, *frisée* etc. — Dep: Calvados, Manche

- **Onions** *oignons* — Small production mid-July until mid-March. Dep: Calvados

- **Parsley** *persil* — Mid-November to February. December is peak time. Var: *Le Commun* – hardy and very perfumed; *Le Frisé*: vigorous and curlier — Dep: Manche
The second most important parsley-growing area of France.

- **Potatoes** *pommes de terre primeur* — Mid-June to mid-July. Var: *Orne, Ostara* — Dep: Orne

- **Radish** *radis* — May to September. Dep: Manche
In the second rung of important production zones.

- **Shallots** *échalote* — Harvested June, July, August. Long, medium long and round types. — Dep: Manche

- **Turnips** *navets* — Some primeurs, but mainly autumn. Var: *Nancy, Saint-Benoît, Jaune, Boule d'Or* — Dep: Manche

---

that grows along the coastline, and is collected mainly around Créances. It is being used increasingly with seafood by creative restaurants and can be bought preserved in bottles, but loses much of its seaside tang that way.

CHEESE

There are over 30 important Norman cheeses. Most of them of the soft, white coated style. The most renowned is *camembert* (*brie* is actually from Île-de-France, closer to Paris) and the most prolific area is the Pays de Bray. Washed-rind cheese are to be found here too, including *pont-l'Evêque*.

● *Bondard* (Pays de Bray) Its name derives from the word for a cider barrel bung, *bonde*. This is a really rich double-cream cheese (60%). Evening milk is used and it is cured for 4 months. Late autumn is the time to eat *bondard,* accompanied by a full-bodied red wine.

● *Bondon* Related to *Neufchâtel*; name refers to shape, as in *bondard*.

● *La Bouille* Invented at the beginning of the century by M. Fromage (*sans blague!*) and related to *fromage de monsieur,* a soft double cream cheese made from enriched cow's milk, cured for 2 to 3 months. Richly flavoured.

● *Bricquebec* From the abbey of Bricquebec in the Manche, a washed-rind disc weighing about 1.5kg/3lb. Mild; eaten all the year round. Not unlike *Saint-Paulin*. See **Brittany**.

● *Brillat-Savarin* Invented by Henri Androuet between the two World Wars. This triple-cream (75% fat) disc of cheese is made only by one small factory: Ets. Dubuc in Rouvray-Catillon in the Pays de Bray. A slightly sour milky flavour to it; eaten all the year round.

★ *Camembert AOC* First mentioned in 1702 but apparently perfected by Marie Harel after the Revolution with the aid of a priest who was hidden on her farm. A M. Ridel invented little boxes for it in 1880 and so enabled it to travel and become famous world-wide. Made from raw cow's milk with a 45% fat content, it is cured for at least 21 days, 6 of which are at the place of manufacture. The curd is allowed to drain naturally after being laid in 4 or 5 slices in the moulds. The body should be firm and evenly textured, but not runny and it can be eaten young when the centre looks chalky. It has a farm-like smell and a rich, rather sweet flavour. Although *camembert pasteurisé* is produced in 67 *départements* in France, authentic Normandy *camembert* is limited to a few *départements* in Normandy: Calvados, Eure, Manche, Orne and Seine-Maritime.

● *Carré de Bonneville* See *Pavé de Moyaux*.

● *Carré de Bray* A small 85g/3½oz square of cow's milk cheese; bloomy white rind and a salty rather tart flavour. End of spring to summer is the time to eat it.

● *Demi-camembert* A half-moon version of the *camembert*.

● *Demi-pont-l'Evêque* A smaller cut version of the *pont-l'Evêque*.

● *Demi-sel* A small mild cheese created in the 19th century; uncured and packed in foil. The name refers to the low salt content (1.5%).

● *Dreux à la feuille* Made

NORMANDY

from partly-skimmed cow's milk. See *feuille de Dreux* – **Île-de-France** p.99.

★ *Excelsior* A distinguished Normandy cheese. High-fat content (72%) as one would expect – it is made from enriched cow's milk – and has a mild creamy flavour. Particularly good in summer and autumn.

● *Fin-de-siècle* Very similar to *excelsior,* another double-cream cheese from the Pays de Bray.

● *Fromage de monsieur* From the Roumois area: invented at the end of the last century, a rich strong tasting *brie/camembert* style cheese; recently disappeared but now being made again.

● *Gournay* Typical Pays de Bray cheese with white-moulded rind, mild taste; small – usually only 100g/4oz. Almost a small *camembert.*

★ *Livarot AOC* One of the oldest of Normandy cheeses and more popular than any other from the province in the 19th century. It has been described as smelling like town drains running down into the sea. Made in only a limited area, the Pays d'Auge straddling Calvados and Orne, it is a washed-rind cheese, matured in a cave for at least a month after hand cutting and mixing of the curd. The cheese has acquired the slang name *le colonel* because the bands of sedge (used to keep the cheese in shape while it is maturing) are said to look like military stripes. It has a shiny reddish-brown crust coloured with *rocau* and typical sweaty feet smell, but a surprisingly delicate, sweet flavour. (*Rocau* or *roucou* is

dye from the Caribbean tree of the same name.)

● *Lucullus* A factory-produced triple-cream cheese from Normandy and the Île-de-France with a mild nutty flavour.

● *Magnum* A less mature version of the *brillat-savarin,* cured for only 3 weeks. A triple-cream cheese.

● *Malakoff* An old brand of fresh *gournay.*

● *Mignot* (Pays d'Auge) Possibly the most recently invented of the farm cheeses still made in Normandy. A thick disc of cow's milk cheese (40–45% fat) with a strong nose and a very fruity flavour. Best enjoyed in autumn and winter and usually eaten with sweet cider.

★ *Neufchâtel AOC* From Neufchâtel-en-Bray an AOC protected cheese that probably dates back to the 10th century. Made from cow's

milk it is matured for between 10 and 20 days and comes in 6 different shapes, including a heart shape (*coeur de Neufchâtel*). A farmhouse *neufchâtel* will always be presented on straw, dairy-made are wrapped in paper. The rind should be white and bloomy and the body have a mousse-like texture; smell between mushrooms and mould. It has a delicate lingering flavour, excellent with soft fruits and often eaten rather ripe. Thought to be best from August to November when

the cows are eating the rich, second-flush, late-summer and autumnal grasses.

● *Parfait* Known also as *fin-de-siècle* (qv), a typical double-cream cheese from the Pays de Bray.

● *Pavé de Moyaux* Washed rind cheese in a square or slab, spicy and strong. Perhaps the original ancestor of *pont-l'Evêque.* Also known as *pavé d'Auge.*

● *Petit Lisieux* Known also as *demi-livarot,* this is one of the oldest Norman cheeses and probably another of the ancestors of *pont-l'Evêque.* It has a 40–45% fat content and is shaped as a flattened cylinder. Strong smell, spicy flavour and best accompanied by a robust wine.

★ *Pont-l'Evêque AOC* A cheese that dates back to the Middle Ages, originally called *angelot* and then *augelot* until the 16th century, but known since the 17th century by its present name, meaning Bishop's Bridge. Today produced in 5 *départements* of Normandy. It is a rectangular cow's milk cheese (50% fat) with a washed or brushed rind, always matured in wooden boxes. The rind should be yellowish-orange to orange and the smell and flavour seem not in balance; the smell can be rather ripe, but the flavour is always surprisingly sweet. Should not be eaten runny; best from summer to winter.

● *Saint-Paulin* Famous mild washed-rind cheese. See **Brittany.**

● *Suprême* A double-cream cheese like *fin-de-siècle,* from the Pays de Bray.

● *Trouville* The trade name of a famous old farm-made *pont-l'Evêque.*

PASTRIES, PUDDINGS & CONFECTIONERY

Butter-bright *brioches* are claimed here as the invention of the people of Gournay, who make them both sweet and savoury (see also St-Brieuc, **Brittany**), but they are made wonderfully almost everywhere in Normandy. The most noticeable variation is the *gâche,* made from the same dough but baked rather flatter. (Add some raisins and you have the *kokeboteram* of Dunkerque).

You will find few *pâtisseries* or restaurants without their version of a *tarte normande,* each a variation on the theme of apples, pears and almonds and custards. Sometimes the filling will be a thick purée of apples cooked with butter, some might be baptized with calvados, some will be open, some closed, some covered with lattice or other patterns. The best time to eat them is in the autumn or winter. After the apple harvest the superlative *Reine des reinettes* will be used; but ask in September and October about apples called *Calville* – the *rouge* tastes of raspberries and is used in glorious tarts. (Having proudly been exported to the USA, the *Calville rouge* is now reimported as *Pomme de Californie.*) If you can't find a tart of the *Calville rouge,* explore markets for the *Calville blanc,* a big ivory-yellow apple whose high perfume and flavour is akin to that of pineapples.

Apples, pears and sometimes cherries, will turn up in *galettes,* which may be lots of things, but in Normandy are usually tarts or layers of filled puff pastry. Those of Dieppe and Le Havre have always enjoyed a high reputation. *Bourdelots, douillons, rabottes* and *chaussons* are all names for whole pears or apples baked in pastry, and are more likely to be found in the windows of cake and pastry shops than in restaurants.

The pectin content of apples means they lend their setting qualities to a great variety of confitures, *pâtes* (like apple curd or cheese) and jellies; *sucre de pommes* is associated with Rouen and you might well also find a *sucre des cerises.*

Chocolates flavoured with calvados are common; this is one variety of French confectionery I recommend with gusto, for somehow calvados shows through in a way few other spirits or liqueurs do. One that matches the assertiveness of calvados is also from Normandy – *Bénédictine.* Opposite the hysterically-designed building in Fécamp where it is made, a shop offers a range of flavoured confectionery, much of it chocolate-based. But check that you like the herb-medicinal flavour before you lash out money.

Worth Finding

● *Berlingots* Boiled sweets, the most important flavour of which is mint. Associated with Bayeux and Caen.

● *Le Brié* Interesting this. The wheat country behind Honfleur used to make ships' biscuits for the long-ranging fleets of that port; Le Brié is little removed from them, rather dry and long lasting. Good for dipping into coffee, cider or calvados.

● *Mirlitons* Small sweet tarts found all over Normandy, all based on pastry filled with something to do with almonds. The simplest and some would say the best, are made in Rouen, but elsewhere they are lightened with egg whites or with macaroon biscuits, another common thing.

● *Sablés* A sandy-textured biscuit considered a speciality and a treat.

● *Terrinée normande* A rice pudding flavoured with cinnamon, and also called *tergoule.* It seems once to have been made with wheat, and that was unusual enough to have made it a favourite of kings. You are most likely to find it in the Pays d'Auge.

NORMANDY

CIDER & CALVADOS

The slopes of Normandy are too fertile to grow useful grapes. So cider, apple brandy and calvados, are the locally produced drinks which accompany Normandy's rich, creamy cooking.

Good cider is easy to find, good calvados more difficult. Both come from the Pays d'Auge. The best cider will be more or less still, and labelled *cidre de la Vallée d'Auge.* If you want cider with more fizz, hunt out a *cidre bouché,* which comes in a bottle with a champagne cork, fastened with wire, as its natural fermentation is allowed to finish in the bottle.

There are three different grades of apple brandy. The lowest grade, which is *not* calvados, is made in a continuous still (as is grain whisky in Scotland), and called *eau-de-vie de cidre.* Do not be misled by the superior sounding name; it bears little relation to the wonderful fruit brandies of Alsace. *Calvados, Appellation Réglementée,* is the next quality level, distilled either in continuous stills or in the superior pot stills used in the distillation of Cognac. The cider from which it is made must come from one of ten carefully specified areas.

The most aristocratic calvados comes from the eleventh of these regions, the Pays d'Auge. *Calvados du Pays d'Auge* must be made from Normandy's best cider, *cidre de la Vallée d'Auge,* and must be double-distilled in pot stills.

Aged in Oak

Like all the best brandies, calvados can be wonderful, capturing the essence of Normandy apples in its dry, intense fruit. It is aged in oak casks, and improves enormously if it is left in these for five years or so. Look for VSOP (five years old, four of which will have been spent in barrel) and *Napoléon, Hors d'Age* or *Age Inconnu (at least six years old, five in barrel).* Incidentally, the name calvados is supposed to come from some folk memory of the wrecking of a Spanish ship called *Salvador* on the coast; well, it is only a memory ...

When you are in Normandy, you will be offered calvados at the end of a meal, but may meet it on two other occasions as well. *Café calva* is the local variant of the *café cognac,* the Frenchman's breakfast pick-me-up, a small cup of coffee, usually black, with a good slug of calvados to wash it down. Even better known, the *trou normand* (Norman hole) is a calvados drunk in the middle of a substantial meal, said to excavate more room for subsequent courses.

Less usual is *poiré,* which is best described as a cider made from pears, what we call perry. *Pommeau* is something new, made like the old *ratafias* – freshly pressed apple juice mixed with *eau-de-vie de cidre.*

Cider vinegar is also made and there is plenty of opportunity to drive, or be driven, to taste and buy direct from the manufacturer.

A very good guide to addresses in the Pays d'Auge is *Produits du Terroir,* available from Syndicats d'Initiatives or direct from CIPPA, 8 rue du 11 Novembre, 14100 Lisieux, or the Chambre d'Agriculture, 4 Promenade Mme-de-Sévigné, 14039 Caen.

MAIN CIDER CENTRES

- **CALVADOS** PAYS D'AUGE Pont l'Evêque – Livarot Cambremer – Bonnebosc
PLAINE DE FALAISE
VALLÉE DE L'ORNE Thury-Harcourt Pont d'Ouilly
- **EURE** ROUMOIS
PAYS D'OUCHE
VALLEE DE LA RISLE Pont Audemer
VALLEE DE LA SEINE Louviers Ste-Opportune-la-Mare
- **MANCHE** COTENTIN Brix – Valognes – Montebourg
BOCAGE DE ST LO Quibou – Gouvets
AVRANCHIN Villedieu – Brecey
- **ORNE** PAYS D'AUGE Vimoutiers
PERCHE Rémalard
- **SEINE-MARITIME** PAYS DE BRAY Gournay – Neufchâtel
PAYS DE CAUX Vallée de la Scie Anneville-sur-Scie
VALLEE DE LA SCIE Auffay

Bon Marché

Below is a selective list of markets plus some fairs *foires* of special interest. Check with the local S.I. for precise locations and time changes.

MANCHE

Agon Coutainville Tue, Thur, Sat; **Avranches** Sat; **Barneville – Carteret** every Sat in summer; **Beaumont-Maque** Sat; **Bréhal** Tue; **Bricquebec** Mon; **Canisy** Fri; **Cérences** Thur; **Cerisy-la-Salle** Sat; **Cherbourg** Daily (ex Sun) (fish); **Coutances** Mon; **Créances** Sun; **Ducey** Tue; **Gavray** Sat; **Ger** Thur; **La Haye-du-Puits** Wed; **La Haye-Pesnel** Wed; **Isigny-le-Buat** Mon; **Juvigny-le-Tertre** Mon, Tue after Easter and Whitsun; **Lessay** Tue; **Marigny** Wed; **Montebourg** Sat; **Mortain** Sat; **Octeville** Sun am; **Percy** Sat; **Periers** Sat; **Picauville** Fri, 29 April, 1 Dec; **Les Pieux** Fri, big market 2nd Fri each month; **Quettehou** Tue; Sartilly Fri; **Sourdeval** Tue; **St-Hilaire-du-Harcouret** Wed; **St-James** Mon; **St-Lo** Tue; **St-Martin-de-Landelles** Sat; **Ste-Mére-Eglise** Thur; **St-Pierre-Eglise** Wed; **St-Saveur-Lendelin** Thur; **St-Vaast-la-Hougue** Sat; **Tessy-sur-Vire** Wed; **Valognes** Fri; **Villedieu-les-Poêles** Tue.

CALVADOS

Argences Thur; **Aunay-sur-Odon** Sat; **Balleroy** Tue; **Bayeux** Daily pm (fish); **Le Bény Bocage** Thur; **Bernières-sur-Mer** Wed; **Blonville-sur-Mer** Daily in season; **Cabourg** Wed, Fri in winter, daily in summer; **Caen** Daily ex Mon; **Caumont l'Eventé** Thur; **Condé-sur-Noireau** Thur; **Courseulles-sur Mer** Tue & Fri; **Creully** Wed; **Deauville** Daily am; **Hérouville-St-Clair** Wed; **Honfleur** Sat; **Isigny-sur-Mer** Every 2nd Sat; **Molay Littry** Thur, Wed if hol; **Orbec** Wed, Tue if hol; **Pont-l'Evêque** Mon; **St-Jean-de-Blanc** Sat; **St-Martin-des-Besaces** Sat; **St-Sever Calvados** Sat; **Thury Harcourt** Tue; **Trévières** Fri; **Trouville-sur-Mer** Wed, Sun, daily from Easter to Sept; **Vassy** Tue; **Vire** Fri.

SEINE-MARITIME

Auffay Fri am; **Aumale** Sat pm; **Bacqueville-en-Caux** Wed am; **Barentin** Sat pm; **Blangy-sur-Bresle** Fri am, 3rd Wed of month; **Bois-Guillaume** Tue, Fri; **Bosc-le-Hard** Wed am; **Buchy** Mon am; **Canteleu** Sat am; **Caudebec-en-Caux** Sat am; **Caudebec-les-Elbeuf** Fri am (veg, food); **Criel-sur-Mer** Thur & Sun am; **Darnétal** Sun am; **Déville-les-Rouen** Sun am; **Dieppe** Tue, Wed, Thur am, Sat; **Duclair** Tue am; **Elbeuf** Tue, Thur, Sat am; **Eu** Fri am; **Fécamp** Sat, big market last Sat of month; **Fontaine-le-Dun** Thur am; **Forges-les-Eaux** Thur;

Shopping around in Caen

Where and when: **St Saveur** (Fri); **St-Pierre** (Sun); the right bank at **Cygne de Croix** (Wed & Sat); **Chemin d'Authie** (Tue & Thur).

Gaillefontaine Wed pm; **Goderville** Tue am; **Gournay-en-Bray** Tue, Fri, Sun; **Grand-Couronne** Fri am; **Harfleur** Thur am; **Le Havre** am Tue, Thur, Sat; **Lillebonne** Wed am; **Longueville-sur-Scie** Thur am; **Malaunay** Sat am; **Maromme** Sat pm; **Mont-St-Aignan** Wed am; **Montvilliers** Thur am; **Montville** Sat am; **Neufchâtel-en-Bray** Tue am, Sat am; **Notre-Dame-de-Gravenchon** Fri am; **Pavilly** Thur am; **Le Petit Couronne** Fri am; **Le Petit Quevilly** Tue, Thur, Sat, Sun am;

Rouen Tue, Wed, Fri, Sat; **Sotteville-les-Rouen** Thur, Sun am; **Ste-Adresse** Tue, Fri am; **St-Etienne-du-Rouvray** Tue, Wed, Thur & Sun am; **St-Martin-de-Boscherville** Sat am; **St.Nicholas-d'Aliermont** Sun am; **St-Romain de Colbosc** Sat am; **St-Saens** Thur am; **St-Valéry-en-Caux** Fri, Sun am June-Sept; **Le Trait** Sat pm; **Valmont** Wed am; **Verville** Tue am; **Yvetot** Wed am.

EURE

Les Andelys Mon; **La Barre-en-Ouche** Wed; **Bernay** Sat; **Beuzeville** Tue; **Bourg Achard** Mon; **Bourgtheroulde-Infreville** Sat; **Brionne** Thur, Sun; **Broglie** Fri; **Cormeilles** Fri; **La Croix-St-Leufroy** Wed; **Damville** Tue; **Ezy-sur-Eure** Sun, Thur; **Fleury-sur-Andelle** Tue; **Gaillon** Tue; **Garennes-sur-Eure** Wed; **Gisors** Mon, Fri, Sun; **Ivry la Bataille** Wed, Sat; **Louviers** Wed, Sat; **Lyons-la-Forêt** Thur; **Montfort-sur-Risle** Tue; **Montreuil-l'Argillé** Tue; **Nassandres** Sat; **Le Neubourg** Mon, Wed; **Pacy-sur-Eure** Thur; **Pont-Audemer** Mon, Fri; **Pont-St-Pierre** Sat; **Quillebeuf-sur-Seine** Sat; **Romilly-sur-Andelle** Sat; **St-André-de l'Eure** Fri; **St-Georges-du-Vièvre** Wed; **Thiberville** Mon; **Tillières-sur-Avre** Fri; **Le Vaudreuil** Sun.

ORNE

L'Aigle Tue am; **Alençon** Fri & Sun; **Argentan** Tue; **Bognoles-de-l'Orne** Wed; **Bellême** Thur; **Brouze** Mon; Easter Wed; **Domfront** Sat; **Ecouché** Fri; **La Ferté-Macé** Thur; **Flers** Wed; **Gacé** Sat pm; **Longny-au-Perche** Wed; **Le Mele-sur-Sarthe** Wed; **Le Merlerault** Wed; **Mortagne-au-Perche** Sat; **Nocé** Tue; **Passais-la-Conception** Tue am; **Pervenchères** Tue; **Putanges-Pont-Ecrepin** Thur; **Rémalard** Mon; **Le Sap** Tue pm; **Sées** Sat; **Ste-Gauburge-Ste-Colombe** Wed; **Le Theil** Wed; **Vimoutiers** Mon pm.

Ports, Beer & Champagne

" In which we ...
● Enjoy beer and herrings on the coast, and sorbets of *marc* in Champagne ...
● Discover the only vine leaves eaten in France and that champagne isn't cooked in Champagne ...
● Learn why *brasseries* always made the best *charcuterie* and how juniper flavours stews and *genièvre* ...
● Find a Little Venice growing for Britain, and try to tell the locals a thing about their sugar ...
● See an air-conditioned growth industry, sample unpasteurized butter and choose a quieter champagne ...
● Eat chocolate seafood in Le Touquet – but *pâté* almost nowhere ... "

La Champagne – the place – isn't classic France at all, not the luscious, sunny, ripe France of the posters and topless sunbathing. And neither are the other areas I've included with it here – Flanders and Picardie, Artois and the Ardennes. French is spoken of course, and they drink wine and eat garlic, but by the time Mediterranean France has pushed up to border other countries, the French have become distinctly different and, well, northern. They drink beer, and eat lots of cabbage, and pickle and smoke herrings. Most noticeably, the countryside is relentlessly flat – boring, most say as they speed south. But the great plains of northern France are precisely what have shaped its history, much of its food and all of its present prosperity. The answer lies in the soil.

A Crop of Men

From the lively ports of Boulogne, Calais or Dunkerque you can, if you wish, visit the manicured horror of the graves of thousands of young men who muddied further the dank fields of Ypres and Mons and other villages. There are more unmarked graves, too, in the older battlefields of Agincourt and Crécy. For these plains have always been the place where invading armies, from north or west, were first resisted . . . and men have ever been their greatest crop.

The north is a brighter, prosperous region today, where crops and fortunes have flourished unhindered for almost 40 years; but the crops are hardly traditional, in the way that leeks or the ubiquitous cabbage might claim to be.

Since the Revolution, the potato has been at home here. Sugar beet was established by Napoléon, and now that American strains guarantee bigger harvests, wheat. Once the north's western border, the Channel, dropped its defences to welcome armies of day trippers, today's battles are with customs officers and in the aisles of supermarkets.

Potatoes and Pigs

It is specially true in the north that regional food is what you get served in the region; for those continuously tramping armies made continuity of anything culinary impossible, and forced the area to serve what it could get, wherever it could get it. Truly traditional food will be based only on things wild – frogs and pigeons, trout or eels, herrings, and game large and small from whatever forest was left standing. And thus it is you have also quickly-made waffles and a grateful reliance on the cabbage and potato, which might have survived in frozen or trampled fields. The pig and its products, too, were sensibly important – if the winters didn't get you war did, so it behove you always to have something in the larder just in case.

In good times there was also lamb, and superlative vegetables grown in intricately irrigated areas. But it is sugar beet, of all things, that has most added to the crop of seemingly traditional foods. All across northern France there is a plethora of confectionery, pastries, breads, biscuits and cakes which celebrate the twin blessing of local sugar and wheat, and which also appreciates the additional modern bounty of Normandy's eggs, butter, cream and milk with which to mix and bake them.

As you move from the undoubted – but catholic – highspots of eating on the coast you will find extraordinary cheeses to eat with beer or juniper-flavoured spirit, and game, if you are there at the right time. You will enjoy, perhaps, visiting a vast *charcuterie* factory in Lille, the market place of Arras, and searching for the pork and lamb products of Troyes, once seat of the counts of Champagne. But you will need to work hard if you want to find out if there is still an Ardennes *pâté* that isn't simply rubbish made to look like an Ardennes *pâté*. For most of the commercially-made junk-*pâté* that is exported is made in this region, so much that it is difficult to imagine any is left behind; but it is and it is just as disgusting and dishonest here as anywhere.

Geographical Chicken

Is it possible to have food adventures in the north? Of course, but you are more assured of them if, after a nod and a visit to such places as Arras, you head for La Champagne, and if you are also very clear as to whether you are eating in starred establishments, which serve much the same food wherever you are, middle of the road places, which do the same with less style, or one of the few that makes genuine effort to reflect the area in which they are plying their trade; the real boon is that you will benefit from a wide choice of still and fizzy champagnes.

I started my travels at the top, on a Saturday evening – when I dined in the lofty dignity of the pale *boiserie* salons of *Les Crayères*, once the *hôtel-particulier* of a Princess de Polignac of the Pommery family.

Sunday morning was spent happily under the high trees of the promenade opposite Reims station, where a vast flea market offered copperware and local waffle irons and those uniquely French art-deco sets for *farine, riz, sel* and *poivre*. At one end of the promenade is *Le Continental*, a hotel with a dining room much patronized by locals. Lunch here started with a *ratafia*, of course, then a gratin of frogs' legs, and chicken in champagne, a description more geographical than of what comprised the sauce; the finale was a triumph of modern Champagne (and something now difficult to avoid) a sharp sorbet of *marc de champagne*.

A truer taste of Champagne is found on the short menu of *Le Vigneron*, just behind Reims Cathedral, where the attractions are Olivier and Hervé Liègent, father and son, their food, and what you can learn from it. Has it ever occurred to you to wonder why the French do not eat vine leaves? It must only be that there was no need to do so – yet in Champagne they *were* eaten, a clear illustration, as are the presence of *andouilles* and *andouillettes*, that life was specially hard here. The stuffing of vine leaves at *Le Vigneron* is based on lamb, a

neat package that was, even more surprisingly, fried. What happened after lunch turned a memorable occasion into an unforgettable one.

I wasn't allowed to see the bottle that came in an ice bucket, but the colour and the honeyed flavour meant I was drinking an old champagne. Is it '59 I asked? The bottle was turned to reveal the date ... 1921. It was extraordinary, a champagne from the tiny house of Frédéric Leroux that had been *en pointe* for over 50 years and degorged only two years beforehand. Its sensational colour and maderized flavour, still brightened with robust columns of bubbles, was more that of a champagne cocktail. And the full story lent even more enjoyment, for 1921 was the Victory vintage, the first sign of normality and hope after World War I, as well as being one the century's greatest vintages. Champagne needed such encouragement, for it

was also recovering from the devastation of the phylloxera blight: at its height it was not unusual for growers to harvest only enough grapes to make a single *tarte aux raisins*.

With the champagne we enjoyed bread made of untreated flour baked in wood-fired ovens and a farmhouse *cendre de champagne*. This is a rare cheese akin to a camembert but aged in wood ash, traditionally that left over from the long cooking of pigs' trotters in the style of Ste-Ménéhould. The apparently bizarre combination of champagne and cheese worked, because both, I was told, were authentic reflections of the same soil. It was all blissful until my too generous host revealed the rough diamond amidst his treasure chest of culinary gems. Once, he told me, these cheeses were aged not in wood ash but in *urine feminine*; it was particularly the custom of those who lived in Châlons-sur-Marne; they called it *fromage de cul*.

It made no difference when Hervé Liègent revealed this to have been a custom of the 13th century. I had, by now, drunk almost two bottles of Champagne's wines of one type or another; their effect was instantly doubled by the thought of what might have been done to the cheese, and by the awful similarity of the Leroux's colour to that with which it would have been done. I left shortly, abandoning a final *flûte*, to shiver my way back to Paris in an unheated first-class carriage; it was better to travel than to imbibe ...

THE CHAMPAGNE METHOD

★ Never ask for a *verre* always *une coupe* of champagne. Choose a tulip-shaped glass *flûte*. As a last resort, take a saucer with a hollow stem: the shape is supposedly based on a mould taken from Mme de Pompadour's bosom; the hollow stem was originally needed to drain off the debris which all champagne bottles contained until modern methods were perfected.

★ Champagne should *never* pop vulgarly when you open it—unless you are a racing driver ...

★ Do *not* lever the cork out with your thumb-tips: grip the cork firmly and turn the bottle.

★ Champagne will *never* fizz out wastefully if you hold the bottle at about 45° when opening.

★ Don't feel forced to drink all the champagne once the bottle is open; reseal for later with a *bouchon-champagne*.

CHARCUTERIE

The importance of beer drinking in the north is an indication of a tradition of important *charcuterie*. For it was the brewers, or *brasseurs*, who kept the best pigs, fattened on the grains of their trade, and from which were made the snacks which attracted drinkers and nibblers at any time of the day – hence our modern round-the-clock expectations of a decent *brasserie*. But the damp weather of the country meant that *saucisse*, or salami as some call it, was not commonly made; instead a distinct excellence in *pâtés* and *terrines* developed.

Today one of France's biggest manufacturers of a range of *charcuterie* is based in Lille, and there are countless others who, together with their proximate Belgian neighbours, swamp the world with a product they shamelessly call *pâté*. Some small shops still make their own *pâtés*, usually indicated by a lack of Disney-decoration and simple, uncoloured bowls and dishes. If you are a convert to the bland, fatty modern products, you have been conned if you think them simple or in any way authentic. A quick look at the table of contents will tell you that. Yet, being aware of the caveat, a good eye and nose can still lead you to honest specialities of the area. Amiens, for instance, still has a high reputation for its *pâté de canard en croûte*.

Worth Finding

● *Andouilles, andouillettes* The best-known and most reviled of pork products. Americans and the squeamish call them chitterling sausages, which means they are made from pigs intestines, sliced or layered inside more of the same. *Andouilles* are based on the large intestines, and to fill them other innards are included, such as tripe. They are boiled up in a savoury broth flavoured with cabbage, onions, potatoes or other local vegetables, but more likely to be served sliced as a cold first course. *Andouillettes* are made from the small intestines and are a common lunchtime feature in *brasseries*, where they will be freshly grilled and served with mashed potatoes and something sharp – pickled cabbage, mustards and the like. One or the other or both have at times been famed from Arras, St-Pol, Cambrai, Douai, Lille, Troyes and Armentières; but the variation of herb and spice content which once gave individuality are beyond the palates of the uninitiated – and beyond mine, for both large and small versions have an underlying sweetness that I find unnerving.

● *Boudin* Where there are pigs there are blood puddings; much rarer is a *boudin de lapin*, which is more likely to be found in Champagne; *boudin à la flamande* is served with semolina, almonds and raisins.

● *Jambon* In Reims, locally-cured hams are often baked in pastry; the more famous Ardennes hams are usually smoked and eaten raw.

● *Langues fourrées* A famed dish of Valenciennes was tongue stuffed with slices of *foie gras*, which was also called *à la Lucullus*. You might have the luck to find it.

● *Langues fumées* Smoked tongues are much more likely to be found. In Troyes they will often be sheep's tongues.

● *Pieds de cochon* Pigs' feet are big news, but no style is more famed that that of Ste-Ménéhould, over Champagne way. They are first cooked for 24–36 hours in a stock with white wine, cloves, herbs etc so that even the bones are soft enough to eat. Then they are chopped into large pieces dribbled with butter, wrapped in breadcrumbs and grilled. The real thing is not served with a sauce. (The town was also the birthplace of Dom Pérignon and is therefore a place of pilgrimage for all true champagne lovers.)

● *Petits pâtés* Small pies of pastry surrounding *pâté* mixtures, with flavourings of spice, liver and wine; the Champenoise are good at these.

● *Potje flesh/vleesch* A Flemish *pâté* of veal, chicken and rabbit, also called *terrine flamande*, something rather more spoken of than seen, in my experience.

FISH & SHELLFISH

With one third of all fish landed in France coming through Boulogne, it's no wonder hundreds of British families hover across the Channel for Sunday lunch. It's not just fish from local vessels – *rascasse* and red mullet *rouget* and *violets de Toulon* from the Mediterranean will be just as fresh. When you drive or walk over the bridge from the ferry walkway, turn immediately left and explore the fish stalls on the harbour's edge, an ideal detour on your way to the place Dalton market on Wednesday and Saturday.

The marshes of the River Somme breed especially delectable frogs (the Artois are said to be the first whom the British called 'frogs'). For the uninitiated, you eat only the fleshy back legs of frogs *grenouilles* and they are not unlike chicken wings in texture and flavour. They are popular in Champagne, and often used in a *pot-au-feu* instead of more expensive meat.

One could spend weeks travelling up and down the coast sampling each restaurant's apparently original way of serving sole, but most are simply garnished with different proportions of shellfish (noticeably prawns and mussels), mushrooms and cream. Good restaurants will do something with sorrel too.

As well as superlative sole, cod *cabillaud,* and ling *lingue* that is a revelation, it is the mussels *moules* which are a special attraction, again especially in and around Boulogne; *bouchots* are very small ones and *barbues* rather large ones. *Moules* are usually served *marinière,* steamed over a little wine with shallot, or leek or onion, but here and there you might find this done with beer. Cockles, a speciality of the Picardie coast,

trout cooked with black pepper – *au poivre bouilli. Waterzooi,* a soup of Belgian/Flemish origin, uses the same freshwater fish, but adds vegetables and cream. Beware, however, the term *waterzooi,* is used also for a chicken and leek dish.

LES BLOATERS

A surprise to most is the importance of herring *hareng* along the coast. Many simple but good bars and restaurants offer salted or pickled herrings, usually with potato, as a starter, but it is the smoked varieties I go for, especially the *bouffi* or *craquelot.* These are lightly salted and smoked, ungutted herrings, what the British would call a bloater. Around Boulogne they are smoked over oak and beech, but in Dunkerque it is said that walnut is used. Though

reputedly at their peak in October and November, when they are best served hot with a pat of butter, I've bought them and enjoyed them a lot in April and (cold) in May. Even a comparatively inland town like Abbeville has its distinctive marinade for them.

Sprats, often called *harengues de Bergues* or *haranguet,* are smoked too, and as with the herrings proper often are consumed as a snack with juniper flavoured spirit, *genièvre* – a real treat on a cold wet day.

are more likely to be called *hénons.*

In many of the busier resorts along the coast you find something called *bouillabaisse du nord,* a mixed fish stew, usually with something unnecessary like a lobster to justify the price; fish soups are also made the same way as they do down south with the fish from the rock bottom, *pêches du rocher.* A *chaudière* or *chaudrée* is a more traditional saltwater fish soup.

Inland, the fish stews are likely to be more authentic or, at least, localized; there are the *matelotes,* cooked in red or white wine and including eel, carp, perch, pike or whatever other freshwater fish has been caught. Beauvais makes good ones, and also specializes in

Eel is a special joy of the north and with the flemish influence is found *au vert* or *à la flamande,* jellied in wine and herbs; it is often cooked in beer, the acid of which balances the fattinesss nicely. Around Peronne it is made into *pâtés.*

It's worth remembering that the beautiful Vallée de la Course produces not only trout but also large-leaved watercress, and that its sharp greenness goes wondrously well with winter's great seafood treat, the scallop. But of all my memories of fish eating here, one stands out – seeing freshly-caught fish being delivered to restaurants just before they opened on a Sunday morning. Definitely worth the crossing ...

MEAT, POULTRY & GAME

Within the area almost every type of meat, game and especially poultry is raised. Traditionally, the pig used to dominate towards the west, and sheep towards the poorer eastern Champagne area, supported by a wide range of birds, from geese to guinea fowl. The modern production of beef occurs only in pockets, noticeably between Boulogne and Le Touquet, and was probably as much stimulated by the need to feed smart French tourists as anything else. Lately there has been a growing interest in goat-keeping, essentially for cheesemaking, which means that around Easter you are likely to find suckling-kid *cabri*.

Here and there, an enterprising shop or restaurateur will sell local produce or some of the small amount of boar or venison still at large. The most likely food of this kind is excellent wild duck from the Somme estuary. More important is to find and enjoy some of the styles and signature-flavours, the most noted of which is juniper berries, often in combination with beer. Equally important but harder to find is the medieval, Crusade-influenced idea of combining dried fruits with meat. *Lapin aux prunes* is relatively common, but in Flanders dried apricots might be used, the mix spiked with a little vinegar.

Although recipes for stuffed thrush, snipe etc are often mentioned in connection with the area, songbirds are no longer allowed to be shot in the Common Market and local game is quite rare.

Worth Finding

● *Carbonnade* Beef, braised with onions and beer, originally Flemish.

● *Coq à la bière* Casserole of chicken in beer flavoured with juniper or the juniper spirit *genièvre*.

● *Coq en pâte* A Champenoise speciality, which I've noticed particularly in Troyes; stuffed chicken baked in pastry. The flesh should be sliced and put back into the pastry; once the head would be left on for effect.

● *Hochepot* A soup stew usually of pigs' ears, tails etc and with other bits or other animals too; oxtail makes a very rich version. The meats must be browned in fat and flavoured with juniper berries.

● *Lapin à la flamande* Rabbit marinated in red wine and vinegar, cooked with prunes.

● *Pepperpot* An unusual Flemish combination of mutton and pork with vegetables, braised or stewed in beer.

● *Pieds de mouton* Sheep's feet, prepared in similar way to pigs' trotters and more likely to be found towards the east of the area and in Arras.

● *Pot-au-feu* Basically the same contents as a *hochepot*, but the meats are never browned. A real one is served as two dishes, first the broth and then the meat and vegetables. Regional and daily variations.

● *Tripée* Pigs' offal cooked in white wine, usually in Picardie.

● *Veau flamande* The most commonly found dish in which meat is combined with dried fruits, usually apricots and raisins or prunes.

VISITING RIGHTS

Visits to the underground caves of the great champagne-making houses in Epernay, Ay or Reims – Moët et Chandon alone have 16 miles – are unavoidable, and I urge you not to avoid several. The bas-reliefs carved for Madame La Veuve Pommery, the inventor of dry *(brut)* champagne and the great Pommery stairways and deep storage cellars cut into the chalk by the Romans will stimulate you quite as much as the cold will numb you. Only Moët will give you a sample, usually, but only one and so you still won't know the taste of a *brut sauvage*

exactly or whether to agree that only the very driest champagne shows the skill of the blender and quality of the house. *I* am certain that a slight sweetness, as with a *sec*, enhances the finesse and multiplies the savour of the wine, as sugar does to all fruit. You will have to search for a restaurant and taste the wines there, and what a treat it will be to find a sweeter and less sweet champagne, and still champagnes and red ones and pink ones … but you will usually look in vain for food that is truly from Champagne or for food to which the sparkling wine of Champagne has

FRUIT & VEGETABLES

Vegetables have saved the north again and again. Not just cabbages, which are life blood, but leeks, potatoes, beetroot, carrots and cauliflower, everything you associate with slightly chillier climates. Soups have always been basic and still do abound, often right through summer, sometimes made of a single vegetable, leek or pumpkin for instance. Just as often they are jumbled into a rich mixture; with pieces of salt or fresh pork they become the *potée*, a dish every region of France makes now for festivals, but which once might have been all you knew for weeks on end.

Picardie has been a famous region of market gardening for centuries. The biggest centre is Amiens, where the canal-irrigated gardens *hor-*

made an appreciable difference. It is daft, pretentious even, to cook out the bubbles and finesse that so much time and money has put there. It is as indefensible as cooking with Stilton or with caviar ... what's more the Champenoise only ever use still wine – if any!

Crémant wines are champagne, but less sparkling, and many think them more suitable for the morning – less noisy, I suppose.

For advice about visiting houses, routes, dates and times write or telephone:
Comité Interprofessionel du
   Vin de Champagne (CIVC),
5 rue Henri-Martin,
BP135,
51204 Epernay.
Tel: (26) 54.47.20.

LOCAL PRODUCE

● **Cabbage** *chou* — October to end December high season.
Var: round and curly
Dep: Nord, Pas-de-Calais
Lille, St-Omer and Dunkerque are major markets; but most cabbage grown here is for commercial use, *choucroute* etc.

● **Beetroot** *betterave* — Mainly an autumn crop.
Var: changing as crop increases
Dep: Nord, Pas-de-Calais.

● **Brussels sprouts** *chou de bruxelles* — Mid-November to end December.
Var: no native ones now
Dep: Nord, Pas-de-Calais, Somme
Nord is the premier production zone in France, supplying 30% of the crop. St-Omer, Lille and Aubers are market centres.

● **Carrot** *carotte* — September/October is mid-season.
Var: *Nantaise, Amelioré*
Dep: Somme, Nord, Pas-de-Calais, Aisne

● **Cauliflower** *choufleur* — Best July to September.
Var: *Malines*
Dep: Nord, Pas-de-Calais

● **Celeriac** *céleri-rave* — Maincrop September/October.
Var: *Excelsior, Neve, Monarque, Alba.*
Dep: Nord, Pas-de-Calais.
Lille and Dunkerque produce almost 20% of the national crop, which is increasing as the vegetable becomes more popular.

● **Endive** *endive* — December to March, mainly.
Var: *Zoom, Bergère*
Dep: Nord, Pas-de-Calais, Somme, Aisne
Between the Nord and Picardie 80% of the French production is grown here, although Finistère in Brittany has a much longer season. Generally grown now in air-conditioned sheds so that the requisites of dampness and darkness can be controlled.

● **Leeks** *poireaux* — September to March.
Var: many; summer, autumn and winter types.
Dep: Nord
The Nord is the biggest French production by far, but most goes for commerce, freezing and the like rather than fresh to market.

● **Lettuce** *laitue* — May to October.
Var: *frisées* curly and round, mainly
Dep: Nord

● **Onion** *oignon* — Usually harvested September.
Var: F^1 hybrids only
Dep: Pas-de-Calais, Somme, Ardennes, Aube

● **Petits pois** — May, June, July main season.
Var: dozens . . .
Dep: Pas-de-Calais, Somme, Aisne, Nord
This is 50% of the national production but virtually all is processed in some way; fresh ones from Brittany or Provence.

● **Shallot** *échalote* — Harvested June to August.
Var: *Longue* and *demi-longue*
Dep: Nord, Pas-de-Calais

● **Spinach** *épinards* — Maincrop September October.
Var: *Samos Symphonie*
Dep: Nord, Somme

● **Turnips** *navets* — Last winter and spring.
Var: *Nantais, Croissy, Milan*
Dep: Nord, Pas-de-Calais

tillonnages, prompted Louis XI to call it his Little Venice. Much of its produce is grown specifically for export abroad.

The most common vegetables are familiar to most people: cabbages, leeks •and potatoes. Cabbage is served as often as in Britain and as plainly, but is equally likely to be bathed in butter or bacon fat and flavoured with juniper berries *genièvre* a great local favourite; modern chefs wrap other foods in its leaves. The best way to eat leeks is the *flamique* of the Artois, called *flamiche* in Picardie, and often particularly confusing; in Lille for instance, *flamique* can simply be hot rounds of bread dough sprinkled with butter and brown beet sugar *cassonade,* or with just butter in Flanders. But the leek version is best and should be a purée of leeks and butter set with a little egg on a base of bread dough or, these days, of pastry. It's noticeable that although plenty of onions are grown in the region they rarely appear in the fish dishes of the coast, being considered far too strong a flavour – it is leeks you find instead.

You'll not find any particularly special potato dishes but Montdidier (Somme) is a place of pilgrimage for lovers of this South American tuber. It is the birthplace of Parmentier, who persuaded Louis XVI to patronize the potato, thereby setting a royal precedent for its eventual acceptance as a staple food.

Among the less familar vegetables grown here, haricot beans are the most important, with Soissons (Aisne) considered to grow some of the very best there are: the white or yellowish *lingot* type is harvested during September and October in the Pas-de-Calais, Nord and Aisne.

The importance given beans in the French diet is matched by an even newer industry, that of sugar beet grown on huge sheets of land. White beet sugar *vergeoise* is exactly the same as that from sugar cane, pure or almost pure sucrose, and any difference in flavour or appearance is due to the manufacturing process. What you cannot make from sugar beet is natural brown sugars and thus *cassonade,* the local brown sugar, has been flavoured and coloured with syrup from canes … but the locals won't believe you.

Fruit is grown, of course, especially apples, and is sold locally, but none is important enough to be considered a commercial crop.

And those mysterious windowless huts are not some relic of a World War, but the homes of the Belgian endive, the white blanched crisp endive, that is, if you'll excuse the expression, one of the biggest growth industries here.

CHEESE

Here cheese falls essentially into two categories: the smelly, washed-rind cheeses personified by *maroilles,* and rich, fresh cream cheeses; but recently goats' milk cheeses have started to appear. The lush grasses of the region are not really ideal for goats, as their milk and cheeses are much better for being based on the drier feed of the south. Nonetheless, many are good enough to be stocked by Phillipe Olivier in Boulogne, and that is recommendation enough. He recommends spring as the best time, and sometimes adds extra flavour and savour to locally-made *chèvres* by rolling them in, for instance, pink peppercorns.

● *Baguette Laonnaise* (Champagne) A washed-rind loaf, with very high ammoniacal nose and flavour, developed since World War II. Close relation to *maroilles* (qv). Similar cheeses are the *baguette de Thiérache, losange de Thiérache, coeur d'Arras, coeur d'Avesnes, pavé carré d'Avesnes.*

● *Barberey* A soft cheese with a tangy flavour made from skimmed cow's milk; also known as *fromage de Troyes* or *Troyan cendré.*

● *Belval* From the abbey of Belval in Picardie, a pressed disc of mild cow's milk cheese. Can be enjoyed all year round.

● *Bergues* A washed-rind cheese from the village of Bergues, close to Dunkerque. It is low fat (15–20%), and washed with beer daily. Originally an imitation of 18th-century Dutch styles, it is usually found at Monday markets.

• *Boulette d'Avesnes* A Flemish cheese made in farmhouses with buttermilk included, or industrially with *fromage blanc* and herbs, as *le dauphin (qv)*. Cone-shaped and very strong, so that *genièvre* is the recommended accompaniment.

• *Boulette de Cambrai* Herb-flavoured cheese but fresher and shaped by hand.

• *Boulette de Prémont* Richer and gentler than *la boulette d'Avesnes;* named for a village in Aisne.

• *Caprice des dieux* (Bassigny) A pasteurized cow's milk cheese, distinctively shaped to a small oval loaf. Made with enriched milk (60% fat content); delicate but characteristic flavour.

• *Carré de l'Est* A small square cheese made in Champagne (and also Lorraine) that is mild and bland; really a commerical, lesser *brie*.

★ *Cendré de Champagne* Like a small ash-covered *camembert*; the ash reduces the fat content as it matures. Only 3 or 4 farms still make them.

• *Chaource* An AOC cheese from Champagne; known since the 14th century. Made from the milk of three types of cow – the Alpine Brown, *frisonne* and *tachetée de l'Est* – it has a 50% fat content. Very white crust, perhaps with a blush of pink. Should be finely textured and not grainy, smell a little of cream and mushrooms, and taste gentle and nutty. Best in summer and autumn.

• *Chaumont* A washed-rind cow's milk cheese with a strong, spicy flavour, shaped to a tall truncated cone.

• *Coeur d'Arras* A heart-shaped version of a *rollot* from Picardie and Artois.

• *Dauphin* Another relation of *maroilles* but one which has traditionally been flavoured with pepper and tarragon since the 17th century. A high smell and flavour. Moulded into heart, shield, crescent or fish shapes.

• *Ervy-le-châtel* A soft cow's milk cheese. Bloomy rind and milky flavour; shaped to a truncated cone.

★ *Fromage d'Hesdin* A monastery-made washed-rind cheese, sometimes known as Belval, where the monastery is actually situated. Relatively new but very highly regarded by restaurateurs interested in regional food.

• *Gris de Lille* Also called *vieux puant, vieux gris* 'old stinker'. A strong, spicy, salty slab of cheese, clearly the strong man of the *maroilles* family. From Artois, Flanders and Hainaut, and best in autumn and spring.

• *Igny* Made by Trappists at the monastery of Igny in Marne. A mild, washed-rind cheese best eaten end of spring to autumn.

• *Langres* A strong, washed-rind disc from Champagne which is good from spring through autumn.

• *Larron d'Ors* Also *fromage d'Ors*, one of the least-known cheeses of the area, a low fat, washed-rind square cheese with the expected robust smell and flavour. Unusually, it is considered best in winter and spring. Ors is a village close to Cateau (Nord).

★ *Maroilles AOC* An important cheese from an area of luxurious pastureland between Hainaut and the Ardennes. Invented over 1,000 years ago at the abbey of Maroilles, it is a washed-rind cheese with the usual reddish-orange crust. The exact area of manufacture is 'the part of la Thiérache in the south of the arrondissement d'Avesnes and in the north of the arrondissement de Vervins in

FROMAGE TO GO

Phillipe Olivier is France's youngest *maître fromager*, and in his three cellars, each with a different humidy and temperature, is a selection of cheeses that even the French dream about but rarely find: *roquefort* made with breadcrumbs rather than being injected with bacteria; farmhouse-made *camembert* and *brie* from unpasteurized milk, *bethmale artisanale* from the Ariège. He also sells the only unpasteurized Normandy butter, either in bulk or packets. You simply cannot go to the north of France without visiting this exceptional shop, which now supplies a number of restaurants outside France with their cheeseboard, and you can't come home without cheese and butter from M. Olivier (43–45 rue Thiers, Boulogne).

With notice, the Boulogne Chamber of Commerce can arrange a cheese tasting for a minimal charge per head, or even better, a combined cheese and wine tasting in central wine cellars.

l'Aisne'. It should be shiny without being sticky, supple but *not* runny. The smell is definitely that of unsavoury feet but the flavour is delicious, earthy, spicy and nutty-sweet. Good in all seasons other than spring. *Goyère* is a flan made with this cheese. It is often confused with *gougère*, a cheese-studded choux pastry made both in the south of Champagne and most of Burgundy.

● *Mimolette* A Flemish cheese also called *boule de Lille* and *vieux Lille*. This was the favourite cheese of Général de Gaulle. An orange-fleshed ball related to Gouda and Edam. Its ideal age is between 15 and 16 months, but it is available younger and older. It must be aged with great care, as the rind needs regular brushing for the mites to keep their distance. A special mallet is used to determine if the cheese is properly conditioned.

● *Mont des Cats* From Godewaersvelde, close to Bailleul, this is a typical Trappist cheese, a thick pale disc with a washed-rind and lactic flavour. Made only since 1880 and commonly eaten for breakfast.

● *Quart maroilles* See *maroilles*.

● *Les Riceys* (Aube) A soft cheese made in small dairies from skimmed cow's milk. A very fruity flavour; rind coated with ashes.

● *Rollot* A washed-rind cheese from Arras area, made in a disc or heart shape and with the expected rich smell and flavour.

★ *Sorbais* A variation of *maroilles*; it takes its name from a small village in Aisne which holds an important cheese fair early in September each year.

PASTRIES, PUDDINGS & CONFECTIONERY

War has strange and lasting effects on diet. Britain's early 19th-century blockade of France encouraged Napoléon to commission the chemist Delassert finally to perfect the extraction of sugar from beet. The climate and soil of the north suit it admirably.

The most conspicuous example of lavish enjoyment of sugar is the *tarte au sucre*, also found under many local names, which is a round yeast-dough baked with a crust of sugar – a sort of sugar-pizza. Chocolate and chocolate-making seems universal, and most villages have somewhere that makes them on the premises. *Le Chat Bleu* in Le Touquet makes clever chocolate cockles *hénons*. In Champagne you will find *bouchons* chocolate moulded into champagne-bottle corks.

Confectionery is pandemic with such wondrous names as *bonbons à la sève de pin, sottises* (Valenciennes), *quinquins* (Lille), and *pailles au café* (Soissons). Pastries, croissants and open tarts of apples, prunes and pears are universal. You may find sweet *pâtes* of fruit, barley sugar *sucre d'orge* or, in Amiens, *sucre de pommes*. People in Provins may still make their *confiture de roses* and in Picardie look for *raisiné picard,* pear jam cooked with grape juice.

Of course, before either cane sugar or local beet sugar, honey was queen sweetener; that from Ste-Ménéhould went mainly to make the *nougat de miel* of Langres. Honey-gingerbread *pain d'épices,* was and is made here and so was a sort of almond bread, *pain d'amandes*.

Worth Finding

● *Bêtises de Cambrai* Mint-flavoured boiled sweets rather like humbugs. *Bêtise* means mistake, for these are supposed to have been the results of the inspired stupidity of an apprentice.

● *Biscuits de Reims* Thin macaroon-related biscuits which make a natural complementary partner to a glass of champagne.

● *Galopins/galopiau* A clear indication of local frugality, these are small pancakes made of soaked, left-over bread or brioches.

● *Gaufres* Yeasted waffles often served from stalls, properly sold just with sugar and cream, but anything goes.

● *Haricots pralinés* I've never seen these, but Soissons is famous for its beans and many other places eat them so sweetened, so they *must* exist.

● *Kokeboteram* A Flemish name for something quite ordinary in concept, a rather big brioche studded with currants. Dunkerque lays claim to it as a speciality.

● *Macarons* Almond and sugar-based macaroons; Douai makes good ones.

● *Massepain* Marzipan, a speciality of Reims.

● *Taliburs* Also sold as *rabot, rabotte* and *boulot* these are whole pears or apples baked in pastry and sold by many *pâtisseries*.

Bon Marché

Below is a selective list of markets plus some fairs *foires* of special interest. Check with the local S.I. for precise locations and time changes.

PAS-DE-CALAIS

Aire Mon, jumble sale 2nd Sun in May; **Arques** Tue; **Arras** Thur, Sat, Sun am; **Auxi-le-Château** Sat; **Avion** Thur, jumble sale 5 Sept; **Berck Plage** Wed, Sat am; **Béthune** Mon Fri; **Boulogne-sur-Mer** Wed, Sat; **Brebières** Sat; **Bully-les-Mines** Thur, Sat; **Calais** Wed, Sat, Sun; **Carvin** Sat am, jumble sale last Sun Sept; **Corbehem** Fri pm; **Courrières** Wed; **Desvres** Tue, **Etaples** Tue, Fri; **Fauquembergues** Thur; **Fléchin** Wed; **Frévent** Tue; **Grenay** Tue am, jumble sale last Sun April; **Harnes** Thur am; **Hénin-Beaumont** Tue, Fri; **Hesdin** Thur; **Isbergues** Thur, jumble sale last Sun Sept; **Lens** Tue, Fri, jumble sales 1st Mon June & 1st Sun Oct; **Licques** Mon, *Turkey Fair 2nd Mon before Christmas;* **Liévin** Wed am **Lillers** Sat; **Marquise** Thur; **Méricourt** Sat; **Montreuil** Sat am; **Noeux-les-Mines** Fri am, Tue pm; **Outreau** Mon & Thur am; **Pernes** Thur; **Le Portel** Tue, Fri; **Sallaumines** Mon am, Sat pm; **Samer** Mon, *Strawberry Fair Sun nearest 20 June;* **St-Omer** Wed, Sat; **St-Pol-sur-Ternoise** Mon; **Le Touquet-Paris Plage** Thur, Sat (& Mon in summer), Easter Mon, Whitsun; **Vimy** Sat pm; **Wissant** Wed.

SOMME

Abbeville Thur, last Wed in month; **Airaines** Fri; **Albert** Sat, 2nd Wed in month, jumble sale June; **Amiens** Daily (except Sun.) *Picardie Exhibition June;* **Ault** Wed, Sat; **Bray-sur-Somme** Thur, 1st Wed in month; **Cayeux-sur-Mer** Tue, Fri, Sun in season; **Corbie** Fri; **Crécy-en-Ponthieu** Mon; **Le Crotoy** Tue, Fri; **Doullens** Fri (fish), jumble sale 1st fortnight Sept. **Harbonnières** Tue; **Hornoy-le-Bourg** Thur; **Montdidier** Sat, jumble sale Sun before 11 Nov; **Oisemont** Sat; **Péronne** Fri (fish), Sat; **Poix-de-Picardie** Tue; **Rue** Sat; **St-Valéry-sur-Somme** Sun, jumble sale May; **Villiers-Bretonneux** Wed.

OISE

Andeville Fri; **Beauvais** Wed, Sat; **Breteuil** Wed pm, jumble sales 1st Sun July, Sun before 25 Nov; **Chambly** Wed, Sat am; **Campiègne** Wed, Sat; **Creil** Wed, Thur, Sat; *Chestnut Fair 1st Sun Nov;* **Crépy-en-Valois** Wed am; **Estrées-St-Denis** Tue pm; **Liancourt** Wed am; **Marseille-en-Beauvaisis** Fri am; **Méru** Fri & Sat am; **Montataire** Fri & Sun am; **Neuilly-en-Thelle** Fri am; **Noailles** Thur am; **Senlis** Tue, Fri am; **Ste-Geneviève** Fri am; **Verneuil-en-Halatte** Fri pm.

NORD

Armentières Fri am, jumble sale 2nd Mon Aug; **Aulnoye-Aymeries** Tue am, Sat pm, jumble sale Easter Mon; **Avesnes-les-Aubert** Sun am, Fri am (Oct-March) (fish), Thur am (veg); **Avesnes-sur-Helpe** Fri am; **Bailleul** Tue am; **Bassée** Thur & Sun am; **Bertry** Tue; **Beauvois-en-Cambresis** Thur am; **Bourbourg** Tue; **Busigny** Thur am; **Cambrai** Daily except Mon, jumble sale 1st Sun July; **Cassel** Thur am; **Le Cateau** Tue, Thur & Sat am; **Caudry** Fri & Sun am, Tue am (fruit & veg); **Denain** Tue, Thur; **Douai** Daily jumble sale 2nd Sun Oct; Dunkerque Wed, Sat, jumble sale 15 Aug. **Faches-Thumesnil** Thur & Sat am; **Flines-lez-Raches** Thur pm, jumble sale Mon (am) after 29th Sept; **Formies** Sat am; **Hautmont** Tue & Fri am; **Hazebrouck** Mon am; **Hellemmes-Lille** Wed am, Sat; **Lambersart** Tue am, Fri & Sat pm; **Landrecies** Sat am; **Lille** Daily, grand jumble sale Mon after 1st Sun Sept (midnight-1pm); **Loos** Sun am, Thur, jumble sale 1st Mon Sept; **Marcq-en Baroeul** Tue, Wed, Thur, Sat pm, jumble sale 1st Sun Sept; **Maubeuge** Sun, Mon, Wed, Sat; **Merville** Wed am; **Mouvaux** Tue, Wed, Sat am; **Roubaix** Mon am, Tue, Wed am, Thur, Sat, Sun; **Solesmes** Thur am; **Steenvoorde** Sat am; **St-Amand-les-Eaux** Wed, jumble sale 4th Sun Sept; **St-Pol-sur-Mer** Sun am; **Tourcoing** Daily exc. Sun; **Wallincourt-Selvigny** Tue am; **Wattrelos** Thur, Fri, Sun, jumble sales Whit Monday & 3rd Mon June.

AISNE

Bohain-en-Vermandois Fri; **Château-Thierry** Tue, Fri; **Chauny** Tue, Fri; **Crécey-sur-Serre** Mon; **Guignicourt** Fri; **Guise** Sat; **Hirson** Mon, Thur; **Láon** Tue, Wed am, Thur, Sat pm; jumble sales 4th Mon June; **Marle** Fri; **Le Nouvion-en-Thiérache** Wed; **Rozoy-sur-Serre** Wed am; **Soissons** Wed, Sat; **St-Gobain** Sun; **St-Quentin** Wed, Sat, Thur, Fri.

ARDENNES

Carignan Fri; **Charleville-Mézières-Théatre** Tue, Thur, Sat; **Fumay** Wed, Sat.

MARNE

Avize Thur; **Bazancourt** Fri; **Sermaize-les-Bains** Sun; **Suippes** Fri; **Ste-Ménéhould** Mon; **Vertus** Tue; **Vitry-le-François** Thur; **Warmeriville** Thur.

AUBE

Aix-en-Othe Wed, Sat; **Bar-sur-Aube** Sat am; *Wines of Champagne Fair (2 days) 2nd Sun Sept;* jumble sale Sat mid-June; **Brienne-le-Château** Thur *Choucroute & Champagne Fair 3rd weekend Sept;* **Chaource** Mon am, *Cheese Fair 3rd Sun Oct, Lily-of-the-Valley Fair May 1st;* **Ervy-le-Chatel** Fri am; **Nogent-sur-Seine** Sat Wed am; **Pâlis** Thur; **Les Riceys** 2nd & 4th Thur in month; **Romilly-sur-Seine** Mon, Thur & Sat; **Ste-Savine** Tue & Fri am; Sun am (Flowers); **St-André-les-Vergers** Wed; **Troyes** Daily, Maundy Thur (Hams), *Champagne Fair 12 to 20 June.*

HAUTE-MARNE

Bourbonne-les-Bains Wed, Sat; **Chalindrey** Thur; **Chaumont** Mon & Sun am; **Châlons-sur-Marne** Wed, Fri, Sat; **Châtillon-sur-Marne** Wed; **Dormans** Sat; **Epernay** Tue; **Orbais** Sat; **Pargny-sur-Saulx** Sun am **Reims** Daily; **St-Dizier** Wed, Sat; **Wassy** Thur.

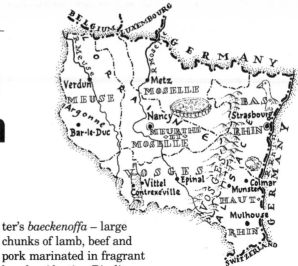

Boundaries of Tradition

Some of the most curious snippets I turned up looking at a region through its food came not from differences but from similarities. And the most intriguing questions, two of them, concern the regions which are furthest apart in France – Alsace-Lorraine and the Pyrénées. Both are bordered by other countries, but their limits have been very different over the centuries and now enclose people of diverse origin. In some cases the diversity is simply that associated with border change, but it is equally the result of refugee settlement of decimated border areas after conflict, the dispossessed moving into the deserted.

A feature of the Basque and the Pyrénéean region of France directly in contact with Spain is dishes which contain the flesh of more than one animal, or which mix meat and fish. There is the *garbure* of Gascony and the *cassoulets* of Carcassone or Toulouse; *paella* is the best known Spanish example. In Flanders, another area with historical borders different from its contemporary ones, they have a pepperpot, which mixes mutton and pork, but it is not that common. In Alsace, though, even the casual visitor can eat win-

ter's *baeckenoffa* – large chunks of lamb, beef and pork marinated in fragrant but dry Alsatian Riesling and traditionally cooked with potatoes and onions in the baker's oven while housewives did their Monday morning washing. The inclusion of beef indicates the dish to be less than a century old, and thus developed and accepted into the local ethos at the time of most identity confusion, when Alsace was swung from France to Germany four times between 1870 and 1945.

Comforting Security

I discovered *baeckenoffa* in a noisy, old restaurant by the River Ill, near 16th-century Petite France in Strasbourg. It was a place of wood and low ceilings and shared tables that felt and looked German. When my order came, it was enormous and steaming in a brown earthenware casserole. I thought there had been some mistake and that it was intended for two people. But it was indeed for one. The mixed meats and wine had created a savouriness far greater than expected from such simple ingredients, and they had

blended their individuality to the point that only differing textures allowed you to be certain which you were eating. In a properly made *baeckenoffa*, the meats are never jumbled together but given their appropriate and consistent place in the casserole; families will disagree over whether the pork should be left, right or centre, or whether it might be better if the shoulder of lamb were always in the centre – but that is the way of such dishes. Those who were clearly regulars accompanied their *baeckenoffa* with carafes of chilled red Alsatian wine, notwithstanding subzero December temperatures outside. They knew what they were doing in combining winter food with a summery-seeming wine: I enjoyably finished mine with the *tarte du jour*, of *merises* wild cherries, before starting my exploration of the pockets of junk market between the river and the cathedral.

The special element of my enjoyment was that I had eaten as traditionally as

> In which we...
> ● Eat mixed meats with chilled red wine and discover where a deposed king played sweetly...
> ● Take pretzels for tea and find how Jewish spice merchants talked amongst themselves...
> ● Decide about squirrels, taste the waters that got brewers hopping and meet the Doyen of *pâté de foie gras*...
> ● Find an artist of puff-pastry, grapple with the problem of rose-hips, enjoy beaver's tails and meet a sweetheart...
> ● Dragées through Verdun, bake a rhubarb tart, get into pickles with turnips...
> ● Discover *winstubs* and a hot tip for going cold on fruit brandies...

to wonder why we say Alsace-Lorraine instead of Lorraine-Alsace, or why they should be linked at all. Lorraine is very much bigger than Alsace, and in history has been rather more seriously French than Alsace. Joan of Arc was born here, in Domrémy. For a while it even had its own duke.

Lorraine's food is gentle, elegant even, when you move on from the soup-stew *potée* to pretty *dragées*, lots of eggy things, and sweet and savoury dishes using pastry, like *quiches*, of course. And hence come the spa waters of Vittel and Contrexéville, Baccarat crystal and Bar-le-Duc redcurrants.

The Yiddish Connection

Alsace has always been more German, and serves you *spaetzli*, ravaged tatters of noodle dough, sausages and fruit-heavy cakes. It has a reputation for Jewish influence (and thus for chocolate and *foie gras*), for wine and for superlative game. The currency of spice, cumin particularly, is explained by that Jewish presence. Jewish business men were always the merchants of Venice throughout the spice-loving colder countries of Middle Europe and Russia; until the 16th century all spice reached Europe exclusively in the trading ships of Venice. So, when the same men escaped pogrom, war or famine and crossed the Rhine into Alsace, they brought with them both the taste for and the access to spices. The question I wanted answered

ould be asked for in Strasbourg but with great ease and in the centre of what, in other cities, would be tourist-kingdom. And I had not needed to consult a specialist guide to find a restaurant serving local dishes. Here is the second mirror image this northern region has with the southern. In both, the visitor is able easily to eat those specialities and traditional foods which elsewhere are the fodder only of foodwriters' pens. Perhaps the coincidence is some manifestation of the problems of being borderline cases? Lacking any sense of continuity in culture, government or language, they defiantly opted

instead for the tangible and comforting security of identifying, and then identifying with, the food they ate. Now untrusting of modern history they stick with it.

There may be other reasons why Alsace-Lorraine and the Pyrénées alone remain areas where the casual visitor might most easily taste dishes truly of that area and which are enjoyed at home as much as in restaurants, but no one has ever offered any to me.

Sweet Lorraine

Driving or flying across the rugged, blue Vosges mountains which divide Alsace from Lorraine, you are bound was why they had stayed here? Why didn't they move further from their memories, deeper into France? It wasn't as though the towns and villages here were that much safer – Jews had been massacred in Alsace, too, although unusually the miscreants were often executed in their turn. The talking during a wine tour unravelled the reason, as I compared *vendanges tardives* in company with the 12th and 13th generations of the Hugel family who make wine in that walled masterpiece of a town, Riquewihr. Both the Alsace dialect and Yiddish have the same 8th-century German roots. Thus whatever their homeland, a new Jewish immigrant could understand and be understood here and settle into life and business without having to learn a new language or retire into a ghetto.

Pretzels for Tea

It is war that has so linked Alsace and Lorraine, uprooting them often enough to forge them inseparably in the common consciousness. They have also the Vosges as a common denominator. In summer now you can stay at the dairying farms folded into their valleys where *munster* cheese and its relatives are made. The summer woods offer the pleasure of gathering the wild berries which are made into tarts or fruit-brandies to be drunk iced in winter and, in early autumn, rich, rare mushrooms to enjoy with the game that panics ahead of you as you drive or walk. And you'll meet families out

walking, for the somewhat alpine-like hamlets, spas and health centres of 19th-century life are once again fashionable retreats from the city. The Vosges Mountains divide as much as they stitch together, for the peaks are just high enough to protect Alsace from Atlantic weather, so it is one of the sunniest areas of Fance, pleasantly warm rather than baking hot.

Alsace and Lorraine and the Vosges are not any part of the general received view of France and French food. There may be *croissants* for breakfast, but *pretzels* for tea and noisy suppers in *winstubs*, a cross between beer cellar and wine bar. Perhaps you will have a thickly creamed slice of chocolate and cherry cake, less of a catering cliché here, when the Black Forest for which it is named can be visited for the day. Alsace-Lorraine is the more refreshing because of this individuality, and more rewarding for the generosity with which you are welcome to share hospitality that is their own, rather than a posturing of *nouvelle*, chips and hamburgers. There is true tradition in food to appreciate here; but, paradoxically, the wines are like none other in the world precisely because they have no truck with tradition . . .

CHARCUTERI

The pride of every hamlet, village and town will be its *charcuterie*, for both Alsace and Lorraine cling to the old reliance on pork products, though few families now rely for survival upon a pig. Like their neighbours in Champagne, brewers *brasseurs* fattened pigs on the by-products of their brewing to make sausages and snacks to attract customers to their beer, creating some of the best *brasseries*. The combination of reliance and ancient excellence of produce means every possible variation of *charcuterie* is here, even the air-dried sausage in sunny Alsace. Most universal are the *saucisses de Strasbourg*, showing their Germanic influence by being bigger, thicker versions of the frankfurter, and thus just as likely to be seen under their other name *knackwurst*.

The complication of French, German and dialect names for most produce makes attempts at precise guidance a nightmare, so this is a region in which to use your eyes and good sense as your guide.

To my mind the most important sausages are the finely-textured ones like *knackwurst*, and *cervelas*, a name which indicates that pigs brains *cervelles* were once an important ingredient. These and all the variations upon them are likely to be spiked with pistachio nuts, whole spices, truffles and such, the variations based on individual flair and interest rather than tradition. Tongues and livers are also used as sausage ingredients, indeed there is a *boudin à la langue*, a black pudding with cubes of tongue, very common over the border in Germany. Nancy is particularly associated with black puddings, and includes in its repertoire, a soup and an omelette based upon the *boudin*.

With the abundance of both wild and commercially-reared pork, a favourite dish is *kalerei*, *fromage de tête* or *hure*, what we would call a brawn. Look for excellent *laxschinken* and *kassler*, salted loin of pork and salted cooked and smoked loin. *Schifela* is smoked shoulder.

There are *pâtés* of sorts all through the year, but come autumn and winter the range multiplies to embrace every imaginable combination of pork and game; you will even find *écureuil* squirrel. Alsace and Lorraine also have plenty of veal, thanks to their dairying. This sweet, light meat adds a sophistication and rich elegance to the *pâté* mixtures missing elsewhere. Many dishes are presented *en croûte*. And so, of course, are the *tourtes*; coarsely chopped combinations of veal and pork (usually) baked into large, pastry-covered pies and sold by the slice. Sometimes small versions will be made, not unlike lesser versions of the British pork pie. I find them tastier than most *pâtés*, and their honest farmhouse origins are often revealed in the names given them, linking them to this or that valley on one or the other sides of the Vosges. Perfect picnic and party food.

There are also hams, sometimes poached (Colmar), usually smoked and in spring combined with asparagus. *Andouilles* and *andouillettes* are found here as well, of course.

FISH & SHELLFISH

With the Rhine and its major tributary the Ill in Alsace, and both the Moselle and Meuse in Lorraine, as well as countless streams and brooks rising both sides of the Vosges mountains, freshwater fish have always played an important part in local culinary traditions. The exceptional modern restaurants throughout the region, especially in Alsace, are today tending towards lighter dishes featuring fish, and frogs' legs are served in mousses and mousselines where once they would have been gratinéed, sautéed with Riesling or found in soups. Frogs are measurably less popular than before, for the Frog Market in Strasbourg can no longer support such commerce.

You will regularly be offered salmon. In spite of stories of salmon, salmon trout and even sturgeon nosing their way so far inland, it is unlikely to be local. Instead, enjoy the countless variations offered with carp, bream, perch, tench, pike, eel and the confusingly named pike-perch or zander: respectively *carpe*, *brème*, *perche*, *tanche*, *brochet*, *anguille* and *sandre*. Butter, cream and wine will be employed, with the occasional use of an unexpected spice. It will often be cumin. Any of these fish may be found in a *matelote*, a superior stew of such fish in Alsatian white wine or a Lorraine *vin gris*, plus cream.

The abundance of trout means you might be offered a real *truite au bleu*, for which

Terrine or not Terrine?

Foie gras and *pâté de foie gras* should not strictly be found in a *charcuterie*, but in a *traiteur*, if cooked, and in a *boucherie* or *volailleur*, if fresh. But in small towns and markets, the boundaries are now blurred.

To the outsider the thought of Alsace instantly conjures up *pâté de foie gras en croûte*, and you will certainly find it here. This was probably invented in Strasbourg by Jean-Pierre Clause around 1780 for the table of le Maréchal de Contudes, governor of Alsace, who sent some to Louis XVI. Later, Nicolas-François Doyen is believed to have perfected the recipe and to have introduced truffles. It's probable that the Romans, who fattened geese with figs for *foie gras*, made a type of *pâté* and that *pâtés* of goose liver were already known in France, particularly in Périgueux. The *pâté* is properly *foie gras* in a *farce* mixture baked in pastry. Unless made with exceptional skill the pork flavour of the *farce* will draw away and dilute that of the liver. *Fois gras* or *terrine de foie gras* should be nothing but fattened goose liver. On today's budgets, therefore, you are better advised to go for a slice of nothing but *foie gras*, or as many a restaurant with a good kitchen will offer you, several scoops of their own recipe from a large earthenware pot.

Eminence Rouge

The fabled freshwater crayfish *écrevisses* have all but disappeared since the start of this century; in the 15th century they were a cheap way to feed the horde of workers who suspended the great bell of St George's in Haguenau. Lorraine has more of its *écrevisses* left than Alsace, where those you eat are more likely to have come from the Black Forest. Cooked in wine, they may be described as *cardinalisées*. The appeal has been also to poets, as this neat three-liner demonstrates:

> *Du ruisseau, l'écrevisse est l'éminence grise*
> *Qui changeant couleur, sortant d'un feu d'enfer,*
> *Prend l'habit éclatant d'un prince d'église.*

> *Out of the stream, the crayfish is an* eminence grise
> *That changes its colours, going through hell-fire*
> *To emerge in the brilliant robes of a prince of the church.*

the fish must be plunged into boiling, vinegar-spiked stock the very second it expires.

The best recommendation I can give is to take advantage of the Jewish tradition and try carp. It will often be offered with a stuffing based on ground almonds, but simpler and better is the renowned *carpe à la juive*, or *Jeddefesch* which, typical of many Jewish dishes, is prepared so that it can be enjoyed cold on the Sabbath, when cooking is forbidden.

MEAT, POULTRY & GAME

There have always been cattle here, but they were mainly in the valleys of the Vosges, and raised for their milk – and that was used for cheese. Thus neither beef recipes nor cooking with butter was common until tastes started to change about 100 years ago. Even so, rendered pork fat is as likely to be found in savoury dishes as butter. For the large Jewish community, neither was permitted, hence their special interest in raising geese for *schmalz*, or grease. But beef tongue *langue* with a Madeira sauce is considered a local triumph, and stews *à la mode alsacienne* or *suppefleisch* are not uncommon and often served with noodles. Vinegar is often used to point beef dishes, and rather than *tripes*, all four stomachs, look for dishes with *gras-double*, which indicates only the three superior stomachs are used. You might even find *estomac de boeuf farci*, a stomach filled with fat, onions and starch and boiled. I should ignore it if you do, and go instead for veal dishes, notably stuffed breast *poitrine farcie* or anything to do with calf's liver.

Pork was the mainstay of rural life, and so good was it that Ancient Rome imported much of her requirements from the peoples living on the left bank of the Rhine here. As well as the vast array of *charcuterie*, Alsace and Lorraine both enjoy fresh pork, especially suckling pig *cochon de lait*, served hot in Alsace but, more often, cold in a jelly of its own juices in Lorraine. In such an important fruit growing area, expect to find pork combined with fruits and berries, too, perhaps the famous currants of Bar-le-Duc.

Goose and Game

The two greatest – but by no means commonest – meats of Alsace and Lorraine are goose and game. The locally-reared chickens and turkeys are excellent, mainly because there is so much corn and barley grown in the area. You'll find them in cream sauces, often with wild mushrooms, morels *morilles* especially. Jewish ways of stuffing, or with casseroles containing no dairy products, are excellent, usually bright and fresh with parsley and made interesting with ground ginger. And no celebration is complete without *bouchées à la Reine* puff pastry cases crammed with chicken or ham – *brie,* it is said, for the original – in a creamy sauce attributed, as are so many elegant dishes, to the court of Stanislas.

Game, notably in Alsace, is considered outstanding even by those living in other areas of France. It runs the gamut

Cooking your Goose

Geese are fresh and ready to e▮ about the same time game makes its appearance, but, if you can bear the richness, fat-preserved goose *confit* will be around at most times of the year. The Jewish ways with goose are the best; stuffed neck *cou d'oie farci/ganshalsel* and *ragoût d'oie/gansvoresse* a stew of neck, wings and gizzards.

from wild pig *sanglier* and venison *cerf* or *chevreuil* to the pigeons of Toul and Vaucouleurs (Lorraine). *Marcassin* is the sweeter, younger wild pig; as its youth prevents it from having developed any singularity of flavour it is often indistinguishable from ordinary pork. Pheasant, partridge, (*en chartreuse* – in cabbage) and hare will all be outstanding and depending on the skill of the chef vary from simple to complicated. A *civet* is the most common way to cook all of them, and is a slow-cooked stew (properly thickened with blood but this is not now common); when game is not in season *lapin de garenne* wild rabbit will be used. Most such dishes will be cooked in local white wine, but as it is always fermented out to be bone dry it works extremely well. Equally it is a revelation to drink dry Alsatian Riesling wines from a carafe with game dishes. What red wines there are are served chilled but I think are less robust than the whites. St Hubert often appears in the name of game dishes for he was from Lorraine and is the patron saint of hunters.

FRUIT & VEGETABLES

In the 17th century, Lorraine alone grew 83 varieties of pears, 36 of peach and 33 of apples. Today there are fewer but the ways you are served them, and the other fruits of the plains, mountains and forests, are ever increasing. In summer and autumn, fruit and berries are fresh in *tartes*, strewn over and through pancakes and cakes of all shapes and sizes; then and in other season, they'll be in syrup, in chocolates, or made into *eaux-de-vie*. Dried apples, plums and pears *schnitz* are served with meat and game, or cooked fresh in autumn or winter to accompany black pudding, especially the exquisite *Reinette* apples. Pickled plums *prunes* are often served as a first course or appetizer at home. Don't be passive, expecting the fruits to come to you in menus; one of the best souvenirs is as many pots of jams, preserves and *confitures* as you can manage. Even the most ordinary supermarket offers undreamed of treasures and experiences.

Apart from the gorgeous greengages *reines-claudes*, promoted since the 15th cen-

The Bottom Line

One of my most vivid shopping experiences happened in a Colmar supermarket after a slightly too wonderful lunch. My interest in local alcohols being – how can I put it? – somewhat awakened by the lunch, I went to explore others. It was December 6th, St Nicholas was distributing gingerbread men, and much to the obvious discomfort of some elderly shoppers, *Tannenbaum* was playing relentlessly through the shop's sound system.

Disorientation heaped itself upon festive confusion, first before the jams then the fruit alcohols offered. . . . *sureau, alissier, houx, genièvre, gentiane, sorbier, épines-sapin, cumin, mûres, myr-* *tilles, pousse-églantiers, airelles* – you get the idea – elderflower, whitebeam berries, holly, juniper, gentian, rowan berries, pine needles, cumin, mulberries, bilberries, dog-rose buds, and a sort of cranberry. There were also more familiar alcohols of pear, cherry *kirsch*, peach *persicot*, quince *coing*, apricot and wild cherries *merises*. But the one which stopped further alcoholic intake that day was *gratte-cul*, translated for the excitable as rose-hip (which it is), but which actually means 'itchy-bum'. That was one cultural shock too much. Wimpishly, I bought only apricot jam, and hurried through the festively-lit snow to an overdue siesta.

tury, this is top area in France for quinces *coings*, wonderful as that oldest of all preserves, quince cheese, *pâte de coings*. The Portuguese and such call it *marmelada*, and its antiquity gives some sense to the French calling most jams *marmelade*. Bar-le-Duc is famous for its ways with red and whitecurrants, all of which are de-pipped by hand. There are many individual pockets of speciality; either broadly, such as the strawberries of Metz, or specifically, such as the *toupie*, a pear unique to Colmar.

It would be hard to miss altogether the region's most famous vegetable, cabbage, either as *choucroute*, or as a garnish to some cooked dish. It might be red, green or white, with or without chestnuts or other goodies, but it will be there. In winter, of course, it is essential to the *potée* and *pot-au-feu*; any difference between the two is purely of interest to academics, for both are rich mixtures of meat and local vegetables in broth, and no single ingredient affects the result enough by inclusion or omission to render either worthless of enjoying.

In the north of Alsace you'll find the hop fields and barley fields which succour the breweries. So it's here you are more likely to find hop shoots *jets d'houblon*, perhaps in a soup. Long white radishes, very dark red beetroot, cucumbers or *morilles* in a cream sauce are all indigenous but relatively unexported. Spinach appears a lot; one *bouillon* combines it with eggs, raisins and spices in a clear reminder of the eastern origins of many of Alsace's people. The mix of influences is clearly illustrated in the little town of Stosswihr, famous for its painted easter eggs but also for *brou de noix*, made by soaking green almonds in *eau-de-vie* in the sun with cinnamon, anis, nutmeg and sugar, once the products only of Araby.

After the cabbages, the most generally encountered vegetables are the onion, used liberally in more than the onion tart served so universally as a starter, and the potato. Lorraine was growing it and incorporating it into *potées* by 1665, a good century before Parmentier was nagging Versailles.

Horseradish *raifort* is a favourite condiment, a suitably wild flavour to serve with the fabulous game. Equally likely to be wild are dandelion greens *pissenlits* for spring salads, or sorrel *oseille* and nettle *ortie* for spring soups. Those who stay in the chalets of the Vosges may find both fruit and vegetables have been collected from nature; most beguiling are the wild mushrooms of autumn, sometimes in spring too, or the elusive wild strawberries *fraises des bois*. In Alsatian Hoedt, it is sophistication that brings brief annual fame. Its asparagus, cut from beds of 800 ha/1,600 acres and most often served with local hams, is typical of the cosmopolitan influences of this seeming backwater. It was introduced by the town's pastor – who had come from Morocco – in 1873. There is a small monument to him on the old presbytery, as well there might be.

LOCAL PRODUCE

Vegetables

- **Asparagus** *asperges* — Start of April until end of May.
  Dep: Haut-Rhin, Bas-Rhin.

- **Cabbage** *chou* — September to April.
  Var: every type, red, white and green; Dep: Haut-Rhin, Bas-Rhin.
  Best *choucroute* variety is *blanc d'Alsace/guintal*.

- **Cucumber** *concombre* — February until October.
  all under cover Dep: Meuse, Moselle, Meurthe-et-Moselle.

Fruit

- **Apple** *pomme* — September until December.
  Var: mainly foreign Dep: Haut-Rhin, Bas-Rhin.

- **Cherries** *cerises* — June until last days July.
  Var: *Montmorency* (clear juice) Dep: Haut-Rhin, Bas-Rhin,
  Chattelmorelle (coloured juice) Meuse.

- **Plums** *prunes* — Mid-August to start October.
  Var: local ones, mirabelle and Dep: Bas-Rhin, Haut-Rhin,
  quetsch especially also Moselle, Meuse, Meurthe-
  greengages *reine-claude* et-Moselle, Vosges.
  Almost all mirabelles and
  quetsches are used for
  confectionery, conserves and
  distilling.

CHOUCROUTE

Cabbage as a King

Steaming yallery-greenery, glistening with newly-forbidden fats, jewelled with spices and topped with dribbling slices of pink-grey sausage and hunks of pork, *Choucroute* is essentially salt-pickled cabbage, what we know better perhaps as *sauerkraut*. It is thinly sliced and layered with salt when there is plenty – for the times when there is not. Some authors suggest its popularity throughout Northern France is dropping alarmingly, but a quick turn through a village High Street will quickly dispel this. *Choucroute* may not be being made at home as much, or eaten in restaurants so often, but it is sold in huge amounts to be enjoyed at home. And not just in Alsace or Champagne – you'll find it steaming fresh in markets in Paris and Bordeaux, *traiteurs* and *charcuteries* all over France organize special *choucroute* nights, and it is a mainstay of many a *brasserie*, for beer is a proper accompaniment. Even Colmar itself organizes *choucroute* days in September, presumably to remind people of it as summer disappears. If you've never eaten it, thinking it heavy, salty, sour and fatty, do not continue to desist. For even though it can be all those things, and like most of the best northern dishes, belongs to the mists and grey skies of autumn and winter, it is usually lighter and more delicious than you can imagine.

Choucroute garnie indicates the pickled cabbage has been drained, washed and cooked for several hours, and will be served piled with a variety of meats and charcuterie, commonly a thickly-sliced sausage (it would be *knackwurst* in Strasbourg or Colmar), pickled (salted) pork and fresh belly of pork. The reality is infuriatingly more complicated – and infinitely more fun. For some will use goose fat and some oil or lard, some will cook the cabbage in stock, others will use beer or, and this is the most common, dry white Alsatian wine. Whatever is used, one of the few agreed points is that the *choucroute* should be cooled until the liquid has all but disappeared. Onion, usually used very sparingly in *choucroute*, may be increased and some will use juniper, some coriander seeds, some both. Some cooks will include vegetables, others cook them separately, but a firm tradition is always to serve potatoes *en robe de chambre*, baked or steamed, very floury and dry potatoes in their skins. And when it comes to the *garnie* part, well, anything can appear. Black pudding might be here, some tongue there, different sausages or parts of the pig or some *confit* of goose. There have been garnishes of snails; and in a reliable restaurant a *choucroute* with smoked fish is light enough to be perfect summer food.

And then there is *choucroute royale*, in which a bottle of champagne or Alsatian *crémant* is poured through the dish just before it is served. To me this is crass beyond words, an insult to the wine. Cook *choucroute* in champagne if you must – the *champenois* and anyone who actually likes champagne wouldn't – but *don't* pour it in after cooking.

Turnip in a Pickle

Rather harder to find are *navets confits*, salted turnips used in the same way as pickled cabbage. Even fewer people make this at home, and only few shops now sell it, but they are one of the highlights of my discoveries, and worth pursuing. Jean Hugel, of the Riquewihr winemakers, told me how he remembered it being made. Only white turnips were used: each was impaled on a spike and turned against a blade to cut it into a single long thread. These were layered with salt, juniper and pepper in stoneware jars, and left for three to four weeks, with the liquid and scum formed by the fermentation removed regularly. Each time you ate some, the linen cloth and weighted wooden lid which fitted inside the jar, and together kept out the air and prevented putrefaction, had to be changed.

Navets confits turns up in unexpected places, humble and grand. I was introduced to them by M. Hugel as an accompaniment to the superlative pheasant, baked inside a *farce* of its legs, I ate at the Auberge du Schoenenbourg in Riquewihr. 'That,' he said of the combination, 'is all Alsace on a plate.'

CHEESE

The celebrated *munster* dominates the scene in this region on both sides of the Vosges mountains. The few other cheeses available are also made from cow's milk and have the usual yellow-orange to red coloured rind typical of washed cheeses.

● *Fromage blanc/Bibbeleskas.* Fresh cheese used in cheesecakes and tarts. Also eaten with horseradish and herbs.

● *Gérômé* and *Gérardmer*. The same cheese type as *munster*, but made only the Lorraine side of the Vosges mountains. *Gérômé* is a corruption of the longer name.

★ *Gureyin.* A domestically-made *fromage fort* fermented in a crock until creamy and yellow. In the Pays Messin (Lorraine) you may find it in markets or village shops.

● *Munster AOC.* A well-known cheese made in farms high up on the Vosges slopes of both Alsace and Lorraine. Originally of monastic origin (Munster is a contraction of the Latin *monasterium*) it has been in existence since the Middle Ages. Faithful to tradition, *munster* is made with rennet-curded milk, put into moulds with neither washing nor mixing; it drains slowly and matures for 21 days (14 for a *petit munster*). *Munster fermier* is best eaten in summer and autumn when the cows are out to pasture on the thick grass of the Hautes Chaumes which adds particular savour to the cheeses. The commercially-made dairy cheeses, *munster laitier*, are much the same all the year round. The cheese, a flat disc in shape, has a smooth surface varying in colour from yellow-orange to red and has the typical strong washed-rind odour. Mild when very young, it becomes spicy with a sweet, rich flavour as it matures.

★ *Munster au cumin à l'anise.* A farm-made *munster* flavoured with cumin seeds or anise (sometimes caraway) seeds. When you buy *munster* cheese, you sometimes get a small sachet of cumin to sprinkle on it as you eat.

● *St-Rémy.* A factory-made cow's milk cheese from Lorraine; square in shape and weighing about 200g/8oz. It has a smooth, light red-brown rind, very strong smell and somewhat spicy flavour. Best eaten from late spring through to autumn.

● *Thionville.* A processed cheese, made from *mattons*, a Lorraine-made whey cheese; see *mettons* (Burgundy).

★ *Oelenberg.* Made in the traditional way by Trappist monks in the monastery of Oelenberg in Alsace; a mild, lactic-flavoured cheese with a smooth, light yellow rind.

QUICHE SERA SERA

When Elizabeth David first wrote of them, a *quiche* was a delicate, pale and trembling thing, a simple savoury custard of cream and eggs and a little bacon, baked in pastry and served lukewarm on every upwardly-mobile pine table. Today the word is used for anything savoury in pastry without a lid, even in France. The battle for its proper use is lost. Although more associated with Lorraine, the name *quiche* seems to be based on the Alsatian word *kuche*. Be that as it may, the *quiche* was indeed once just cream and eggs baked with a little bacon in puff pastry, justifying by this last detail the description 'Lorraine'. Once onions, cheese and other ingredients were added to the custard mixture, you had a *féouse*. The *féouse* was basically simpler and cheaper, often a flavoured, flour-thickened white sauce on a bread dough base, and thus clearly related to *tarte flambée/flammekueche*. Today, *féouse* is considered archaic, and *tarte* is more commonly used – or would be if *quiche* didn't sound better. The appearance of the *bouchée à la Reine* – white sauce with chicken or ham in puff pastry cases – at the court of 18th-century Nancy, was not a culinary breakthrough but a refined regal combination of the topping of a *féouse* and the puff pastry base of a *quiche*, two established dishes of the people, which explains the alacrity with which those *vol-au-vents* were universally accepted. Few celebrations, even today, are complete without them.

PASTRIES, PUDDINGS & CONFECTIONERY

To hear some, you'd think nothing sweet or delicious or frothy was ever baked here until Louis XIV sent his father-in-law, King Stanislas of Poland, off to Nancy to be Duke of Lorraine. But Alsace and Lorraine needed no regal patronizing, for the abundance of milk and cream also meant butter if you wanted, the plains grew wheat for flour, and you had to do something with all the luscious fruits of summer, that cascade from trees, bushes and vines.

Fruit pastes, jams and *confitures*, spirits and liqueurs were all embraced, as they were invented, as ways to use the harvest and enjoy it later. Bar-le-Duc became famous simply because its people bothered – and do still – to individually extract the great pips from red and white currants before they cooked them up. Everyone else cheats by making jellies, so they can strain out the pips after the cooking.

Pastry is featured because the region has the ingredients, and because it claims the invention of puff pastry. Well, Claude Lorraine the painter is given the credit, but he may have brought back the idea from the time he spent in Italy. He started working life as a pastry-cook there in 1613. It is a claim with substance, and there is little of the coun-

Stanislas the Sweet

The most famous duke of Lorraine was dethroned Stanislas of Poland, father-in-law of Louis XV. He was a minor king with a major interest in food. Life at his ducal court in Nancy and at his Fontainebleau look-alike château at Lunéville was one of culture and cooking. He is credited with the creation or perfection of *madeleines* and the *baba au rhum,* and *bouchées à la Reine,* to show he was not only sweetness and light.

A·D·R·I·N·K·E·R'S·G·U·I·D·E

Wines of ordinary Alsace AC quality should usually be drunk young. Alsace wines of *réserve* quality, made in good years, benefit from bottle age. *Vendange tardive* and *sélection de grains nobles* wines should be kept for a minimum of five years.

The Last Decade
1984 Light, of no great quality. Not for keeping.
1983 Excellent, potentially long-lived vintage. Particularly good Riesling and Tokay (Pinot Gris) should be kept at least five years. Ordinary wines are already drinking well.
1982 A large crop. Most needs drinking up.
1981 Good wines, though some a little low in acidity. Best wines still holding on.
1980 Small, light crop. Riesl-

ing the only success. Drink if certain of quality.
1979 Elegant, attractive vintage. 'Réserve' wines still showing well.
1978 Excellent 'réserve' wines, still very drinkable.
1977 Avoid.
1976 Superb, especially Rieslings. The best wines are still young.
1975 Good, typical vintage, but most wines are not ageing fast.
1974 Poor. Avoid.

Previous greats
Late harvest or 'réserve' wines from 1973, 1971 and 1967 will still be worth trying. Drink older wines only on recommendation.

Spirits & Liqueurs
Alsatian *eaux-de-vie,* colourless fruit brandy can be made from practically any fruit,

and the best are exquisitely perfumed – see fruit and vegetables. But more unusual is *marc de gewürztraminer*; made when the debris left after pressing Gewürztraminer grapes is turned into wine and then distilled. This fiery, chocolate-flavoured spirit is the perfect restorative after an autumn visit round the vineyards but like all white spirits must be served freezing cold into a cold glass to be appreciated.

Lorraine produces very much the same range of spirits as Alsace and, less commonly, *ratafias* of many fruits, combinations of the fresh fruit and a related or neutral *eau-de-vie. Ratafia de noyau* is made from the kernels of peaches and apricots and thus has an almond-like flavour. Good *marcs,* too.

ALSACE LORRAINE

ter claim there is with *brioches*, for instance. Because poultry is important, there are meringues: as honey was abundant, *beignets* may still be served with this natural sugar rather than a syrup of refined beet sugar. There are some specially unusual names amidst cakes and confection-ery for you to find – *biberschwanz de Haguenau*, beaver's tails, *cailloux de Rhin* Rhine stones, and the like.

═Worth Finding═

- *Baba* Another reputed invention, or intervention, this time by Duke Stanislas himself, by the simple expedient of dipping some rather dry *kugelhopf* (most of it is) into syrup. Now made rather lighter and more yeasted, often with rum in the syrup (*baba au rhum*) and served with fresh fruit and cream.
- *Bredle/petits fours à l'Alsacienne* Rich, buttery little biscuits brought out on every special occasion, and so named in French because they were cooked in a special, small oven – *petit four*.
- *Bretzel/pretzel* Sweet and savoury pretzels of every size are a visual trademark of Alsace and Lorraine.
- *Bergamotes* Square sweets made with honey, which are reckoned to taste like a local pear of the same name; associated specially with Nancy.
- *Chocolates* There are many reasons for good chocolate here. Jews from Spain who settled in Alsace brought knowledge of this New World luxury to the rest of Europe. With the later proximity of sugar beet fields plus the abundance of fruits, liqueurs and spirits . . . how could they go wrong? They didn't. There are special specialities, like the *carreaux en faïence* of Sarreguemines, but each *chocolatier* has something to recommend.
- *Crêpes Alsaciennes/pfannekueche*. Yes, pancakes, but not thin bitsy *crêpes*. The ones I ate were always enormous, flat and thick, smothered with berries from the Vosges, fresh or preserved, and with rivers, or mountains, of cream. There are savoury ones, too; *schankelas* are small ones, made with ground almonds to accompany creamy desserts.
- *Dragées* Sugared almonds have been made in Verdun since 1220 at least, and have been commercialized since 1660. The almonds were always imported – mainly from Spain and Italy; today the hard crisp case may also enrobe nougatine, chocolate, liqueurs or an almond paste.
- *Kaffeekrantz* Briochebased, large or small iced confections to enjoy with coffee.
- *Kugelhopf* Although almost certainly not originating in the region, this yeasted cake with a hole in the middle has become one of its icons. It's also found as *kuelhopf, gugelhupf, kugelhopf, kougelhopf* and more. With or without raisins and a surface scattering of flaked almonds, it is best baked in earthenware rather than metal moulds.
- *Lebkueche* Sweet gingerbread biscuits made from a recipe of considerable antiquity, the name coming from ancient German for sweet *leb*. Thick, thin, soft, crisp, iced or uniced, they are usually tongue or heart shaped. Large *hertzlebkueche*, decorated with flowers of icing, were once more important. Men sent them to sweethearts, who found their names iced upon them plus a verse and a small piece of looking glass, so she could see herself in her lover's heart.
- *Linzertorte/Tarte à la Linz* A sweet tart of pastry which should include almonds and *kirsch*, be filled with jam, and covered with a lattice-work of pastry. Raspberry, cherry, strawberry or redcurrant confections are the most popular and authentic fillings.
- *Macarons (des Soeurs)* Macaroons have been made in Lorraine since at least the 12th century. After the Revolution in 1789, dispossessed nuns went into business making them, hence the suffix.
- *Mendiant* Also called *bettleman*, this is a terrific cake/dessert, made from stale *brioche, kugelhopf,* or breadcrumbs, mixed with egg, spice, *kirsch* and cherries or apples. Extremely good served warm with custard. A big brother of the *gâches* of Normandy.
- *Mirabelles* These fêted goldyellow plums are made into numberless examples of sinfulness. In Metz they are preserved in a very rich sugar syrup, in Strasbourg they are crystallized, and they and other such plums as the quetsch may also be stuffed (*fourrée*), either with a mixture based on ground almonds or with a purée of themselves.
- *Tartes* One of the simplest but most special joys of Alsace and Lorraine, particularly so in summer. Rhubarb, believe it or not, is enormously popular in Alsace. The rhubarb is usually drained of liquid by being cut and sprinkled with sugar before baking. As well as the expected apples and pears, you'll find cherries *cerises* and wild cherries *merises*, every type of plum and all the berries of the mountains, bilberries and blackberries, whortleberries and blueberries. Raspberries and strawberries too.

Bon Marché

Below is a selective list of markets plus some fairs *foires* of special interest. Check with the local S.I. for precise locations and time changes.

MEUSE
Bar-le-Duc Tue am, Thur, Sat; **Bouligny** Wed pm; **Commercy** Mon, Fri am; **Ligny-en-Barrois** Tue & Fri; **Stenay** Fri am; **St-Mihiel** Sat am; **Tronville-en-Barrois** Thur am; **Vaucouleurs** Sat am; **Verdun** Tue & Fri, Wed.

MEURTHE-ET-MOSELLE
Audun-le-Roman 1st & 3rd Wed in month; **Baccarat** Fri am; **Blamont** Fri am; **Bouxières-aux-Dames** Thur & Fri pm; **Crusnes** 10th & 25th of month; **Custines** Tue am; **Dameslevières** Fri pm; **Dombasle-sur-Meurthe** Thur am Giraumont 10th & 25th (pm) of month; **Herserange** Wed am; **Joeuf** Fri am. Tue &, jumble sale 1st week June; **Liverdun** Tue pm Longuyon Fri am, *Gastronomic Fair 1st Sept Sun*; **Longwy** Tue, Thur & Sat am; **Lunéville** Tue, Wed, Thur, Sat; **Moutiers** Wed am; **Nancy** Daily exc Sun; **Pagny-sur-Moselle** Thur am; **Pont-à-Mousson** Sat, jumble sale 25 Aug; **St Nicholas-de-Port** Fri am; **Saulxures-les-Nancy** Fri am; **Tomblaine** Mon am; **Tucquegnieux** Thur pm; **Valleroy** Fri am; **Varangéville** Wed am (veg); **Villerupt** Tue & Fri to 11 am (veg).

MOSELLE
Algrange Fri, jumble sale begin Sept; **Ars-sur-Moselle** Fri am; **Audun-le-Tiche** Thur am, Sat pm, jumble sale May; **Behren-les-Forbach** Sat; **Bitche** Tue, Fri; **Boulay** Wed, Fri; **Bouzonville** Tue (pigs, veg); **Château-Salins** Thur am, *Quiche Fair 1st Sat Sept*; **Clouange** Tue, Fri; **Créhange** 1st & 3rd Fri in month; **Creutzwald** Thur am; **Dieuze** Mon, Fri am, jumble sale 1st Fri Oct; **Faréberswiller** Thur am; **Forbach** Tue, Fri, jumble sale Sept; **Freyming-Merlebach** Wed, Thur am; **Guénange** Tue & Sat pm; **Hagondange** Tue am & Fri;

Hayange Tue, Thur, Fri pm Sat; **L'Hôpital** Sat am; **Maizières-les-Metz** Thur; **Metz** Daily exc Sun; **Moussey** Wed; **Moyeuvre Grande** Wed, Thur, Sat, jumble sale June/July; **Ottange** Thur; **Petite Rosselle** Wed, Thur; **Phalsbourg** Fri; **Puttelange-aux-Lacs** Sat; **Sarralbe** Thur; **Sarreguemines** Fri am; **Sierck-les-Bains** Tue; **Stiring-Wendel** Wed, Thur, Sat; **St-Avold** Tue, Fri; **Thionville** Tue, Sat, Thur; **Woippy** Tue am, Fri, *Strawberry Fair last but one Sun June*.

Shopping around in Strasbourg
Where and when: **Neudorf, bd de la Marne, pl de Bordeaux** (Tue); **rue Ste-Marguerite, ancienne Halle de Corbeau** (Wed & Fri); **Neuhof, Pont-de-Kehl, Montagne Verte, pl J-Macé, Polygone** (Fri); **Neudorf, pl de la Marne, Robert-sau, pl de Bordeaux** (Sat).

VOSGES
Arches *Pastry Fair June;* **Bains-les-Bains** Fri am; **La Bresse** Sun am; **Bruyères** Wed am; **Charmes** Fri am; **Châtel-sur-Moselle** Fri am; **Contrexéville** Tue & Fri am; **Darney** Fri am; **Epinal** Wed, Thur, Sat; **Fraize** Fri am; **Gérardmer** Thur, Sat am; **Golbey** Thur pm; **Liffol-le-Grand** Thur am; **Lamarche** Fri; **Mirecourt** Sat am; **Moyenmoutier** Thur am; **Neufchâteau** Sat am; **Monthureux-sur-Saône** 2nd Mon of month, *Pudding Fair 2nd Sun Oct;* **Plombières-les-Bains** Fri (Oct to April), Tue, Fri & Sun (May to Sept); **Rambervillers** Thur; **Raon-l'Etape** Sat am;

Remiremont Tue & Fri am; **Saulxures-sur-Moselotte** Wed; **St-Die** Tue, Fri am; **Thaon-les-Vosges** Thur am; **Thillot** Sat am; **Val d'Ajol** Sun am, *Andouille Fair 3rd Mon in Feb;* **Xertigny** 2nd & 4th Thurs of month; **Vittel** Wed, Sat am, *Frog Fair, 1st fortnight April.*

BAS-RHIN
Andlau Wed; **Barr** Sat; **Benfeld** Mon am; **Bischheim** Fri; **Bischwiller** Sat; **Bouxwiller** Mon; **Brumath** Wed; **Chatenois** Wed; **Dambach-la-Ville** Wed, Sat; **Erstein** Thur am; **Fegersheim** Thur; **Haguenau** Tue (pigs), Fri; **Hochfelden** Tue; **Illkirch-Graffenstaden** Tue am; **Lauterbourg** Tue & Fri; **Marmoutier** *Onion Market* 2nd Sun Sept; **Mertzwiller** Thur; **Molsheim** Mon am (pigs); **Mutzig** Fri am; **Niederbronn-les-Bains** Fri; **Obernai** Thur; **Pfaffenhoffen** Sat (pigs); **Reichshoffen** Thur am; **Rhinau** 1st & 3rd Tue of month; **Rosheim** Tue, Fri; **Sarre-Union** Fri am (pigs); **Saverne** Thur (pigs), Tue, Sat (veg); **Schirmeck** Wed; **Sélestat** Tue, Fri; **Seltz** Thur & Wed (pigs); **Soultz-sous-Forêts** Tue (pigs); **Strasbourg** Tue, Wed, Thur, Fri, Sat; **Vendenheim** Mon (pigs) Wed; **Wasselonne** Mon (pigs); **Wissembourg** Tue, Thur (pigs), Sat; **Woerth** Wed (pigs).

HAUT-RHIN
Altkirch Thur; **Bartenheim** Fri; **Bergheim** Mon; **Colmar** Thur, Sat; **Dannemarie** Sat am; **Guebwiller** Tue & Fri am; **Ingersheim** Wed am; **Kaysersberg** Mon; **Lapoutroie** Fri; **Lutterbach** Wed, Sat (fruit); **Masevaux** Wed am; **Mulhouse** Tue, Wed, Thur, Sat; **Munster** Christmas Market, 15 days before Christmas; **Brisach** Fri am, 1st Tue of month; **Orschwir** Thur am; **Ribeauville** Sat, *Wine Fair last Sat & Sun July;* **Riquewihr** Fri; **St-Amarin** Mon am; **Ste-Marie-aux Mines** Sat; **Thann** Sat, Wed am; **Turckheim** Fri, *Wine Fair Aug;* **Willer-sur-Thur** Thur; **Wittelsheim** Thur, Fri am; **Wittenheim** Fri am.

Saints, Saracen Wheat & Pancakes

There's only one proper way to reach Little Britain from Great Britain, *Bretagne* from *Grande Bretagne*. Go the way of the ancients and nobles, directly by sea, with your head filled with stories of magic and mystery, of King Arthur and Merlin, and the Corsairs, those good pirates, who robbed only on behalf of others. The precedent you follow is remarkable.

Apple v. Grape

Other than over-using words like fresh and simple, it has been virtually impossible for anyone to define the Breton table. The most accurate view I found was from Gault Millau who say that although it ranges from the *galettes* of grain and iodized potatoes of the extreme west through commercial market gardens on to the creamy lavishness of Rennes in the east, Brittany actually divides into only two culinary regions: the northern coast, *Haute-Bretagne*, which is influenced

by the cider-based cuisine of Normandy, while the south, *Basse-Bretagne,* is allied to the wine-based food of the mouth of the Loire. It makes sense, especially when you know that Normandy and Brittany have always squabbled over who claims Mont-St-Michel in the north and that Nantes in the south was considered part of Brittany until bureaucracy took it to one side and said it should now consider itself in Loire-Atlantique. It also makes sense that the cuisine of these two neighbours should have seeped along their proximate coasts, mingling only on the eastern border in Rennes. West of Rennes and in the wooded wilderness that divides the two coastal areas, fashion and style seem to have made few inroads.

In between remained most independently Breton, for here there was little chance for most men or influence to reach. Grains and vegetables were more particularly the

basis of diet; cider, wine and cream were much the same, nice when you could get them. It is that last, cream – and butter from it – which must be the single ingredient that might be considered a unifier. Yet there can never have been much cream left once the better-keeping butter had been made, for Brittany has virtually no historic tradition of eating or of making cheese.

Yesterday Today

The strongest modifiers of Brittany's food have been the climate and the landscape, ever more relentless and wind-torn as you travel westwards towards the Atlantic. Fully to appreciate how rugged life remains even today, visit one of the offshore islands, an island like l'Île de Seine, off the southwestern tip, Pointe du Raz. Here beneath the lighthouse which lords it over the single square kilometre of the island, the rule which once dominated

> ## In which we …
> ● Learn of iodized potatoes and how Crusaders went against the grain …
> ● Taste the dumplings of ancestors, and fight about *brioches* …
> ● Find a lard with shallots and decide on a lobster dish's origin …
> ● Look for vintage sardines, test a northern *bouillabaisse,* fish for spring whitebait and sail to stone-tethered sheep for a salty treat …
> ● Enjoy an upmarket lardy cake, look for a bread of oats and cream, and drown in wells of love …

all Brittany's coasts remains the only way to survive: *'La mer aux hommes, la terre aux femmes . . .* the sea is men's work, the land is women's.' While men fish or hunt seabirds or gather things which live in shells to make stews, women hack with shovels and picks at the poor thin layer of sand and guano. Not much will grow but grain of one sort or another, and potatoes that taste of iodine because of the guano at their roots and the spray on their leaves.

On the mainland, grain was the only reliable staple and remained so here longer than in other regions. Pork and other meat was too valuable to eat more than once a week, or as salted accompaniment to something else, wherever you lived. On the coast you could hardly rely on daily fish with such unreliable seas at your

doorstep. So the grain crops needed to be hardy, reliable and warming, like the crops of Scotland and Wales and Ireland. This means barley, oats, rye and, once the Crusaders began returning, Saracen's wheat (buckwheat, *sarrasin* or *blé noir*), actually grass seeds rather than a true grain. These are all good crops for poor land, but none of them contains enough gluten in its flour to make a light, yeast-risen loaf, and so they were made into the most ancient and universal of foods, grain porridges *bouillies.* Sometimes the porridges were made extra thick and boiled in a cloth to make savoury or sweet puddings, the *fars* and the *noces.* Only in Brittany are they still part of today's diet.

Visitors driving quickly through to some other region may be able to taste these, especially such savoury

boiled puddings, as the *kig ar fars,* more of a buckwheat dumpling, and glimpse through it the culinary world of all our ancestors. But *bouillies* and *fars* took time to make and cook, and neither was a substitute for bread. So the Breton household made *galettes,* large pancakes, and when buckwheat arrived from the Middle East, it became the favourite.

Toujours Galette

Originally these large, griddle-cooked pancakes were simply made to bulk out, as bread would have, simple food – eggs, salty bacon or a little meat, a few vegetables. As wheat became more generally available, towards the end of last century, white and wholemeal wheat flour began to be used to make sweet pancakes, a treat for better times and another way to use cream. Today *galettes* have become the symbol of Brittany. There seems nothing savoury that cannot be served in or on a buckwheat *galette,* and nothing sweet that is not good with wheaten pancakes. In Rennes, they eat *galettes* with *tripes.* The current interest in eating fish has made Brittany a foodlover's must, but to be honest there is as much criticism of holiday resort junk food as there is elsewhere. Its market gardens provide superb vegetables, even though the great majority are for canning and freezing, and the survival of old yeast-raised cakes, especially on the north coast, makes an adventure even of wandering from *pâtisserie* to café … .

CHARCUTERIE

It is the central regions of Brittany that produce superlative pork flesh, and thus the best *charcuterie*.

The range is as broad as you will find anywhere, enhanced by local entrepreneurs as much as by modernism and copying. The products with the best reputation come from opposite ends of the charcuterie business (but the same end of the pig) – *andouilles/ andouillettes* and hams *jambons*. But for a guaranteed reflection of true Breton taste and cooking, it must be the baked combinations of meat – usually pork – and vegetables to which you should turn your palate's attention. You might, for instance, find *haricots rouges* puréed with sausage meat and salt pork. Some of the really famous *pâtés* – of horse and of cormorant – seem to have disappeared from Concarneau, among other places, but you can still get *pâté de lièvre*.

════Worth Finding════

● *Andouilles* Large slicing sausages made of the large intestines and other pieces of the innards of pigs. If you like both the idea, and the flavour, those from Guéméné, Auray, Ancenis and Carhaix are known to be the best.

● *Andouillettes* Grilling sausages made from the small intestines, usually served hot with onions and potatoes. Quimperlé has a reputation for such sausages.

● *Boudin noir* and *boudin blanc* Black and white puddings. These are a great tradition in inland Brittany. In Rennes where the *blancs* include the town's famous poultry, you are likely to find them served with haricot beans or, naturally, apples. In Brest they may be made with cream. My favourite, and another taste of antiquity, is the *boudin aux pruneaux* associated with Dinard and Beauséjour, worth visiting also just for its name, which means 'nice stay'.

● *Caillettes* Rissoles or faggots, often with a mustard sauce.

● *Casse* A terrine of ham baked in a caul, often that of calf but also chunks of veal baked with other bits in an earthenware pot called a *casse*.

● *Jambon* There are many locally-produced hams, and it's likely you will find them cured with some proportion of *eau-de-vie de cidre*. The most famous Breton ham is from Morlaix, where butter, and thus baking, is also outstanding.

● *Lard* There are three *lards* here. Basically you have pork fat or bacon (not our lard, which is *saindoux*). The next most general is *lard recet*, a rendered mix of salt-pork fat and shallots. Either one, but especially the latter, is important to Brittany's most famous soup made with buckwheat. The third, *lard Nantais*, is a dish of pork chops cooked with wine, most often a Muscadet, on a bed of almost every type of edible offal.

● *Terrine* Seemingly a catch-all name, but used most for baked combinations of meat and vegetables.

FISH & SHELLFISH

Brittany has more important fishing ports than any other port of France and, after Boulogne, the biggest. There are few places on the wind- and sea-tortured coastline that do not make some contribution to the haul. The largest ports are St-Malo, Douarnenez, Loctudy, Lorient, Port de Keromen, Quibéron and Concarneau.

The catch is varied enough

════Worth Finding════

● *Anguilles* Eels. The rivers of the Côtes du Nord and the Loire at Nantes are the most obvious sources. Might be grilled or served in cream; sometimes smoked and grilled over apple wood or soaked in milk and sautéed in butter, which they are prone to do in Lamballe.

● *Brochet* Pike. Found everywhere and the most likely of fish to be served *au beurre blanc* but it will also be pounded with cream and eggs and shaped into *quenelles*.

● *Cabillaud* and *morue* Cod and salt cod. St-Malo is the most important for either. The related ling is known recognizably as *lingue* but also as *julienne*.

● *Carpe* Carp. From the Côtes-du-Nord particularly, and also the Loire and Nantes. Usually grilled, often on skewers. The roes *laitances* may be found combined with tuna in an *omelette bretonne*.

● *Civelles/pibales* Tiny eels, deep-fried like whitebait or served in omelettes. Fished from the river weeds in March to keep a serious eater enthralled for weeks. Anything in shells is marvellous, including scallops, winkles, whelks and, of course, oysters. Two great attractions are, for the rich, lobster *homard,* and for me, clams *palourdes,* particularly when they are stuffed. The continuing row about the origin of *homard à l'Armoricaine* has three protagonists: one group which feels it is a recipe from Brittany (Armorica); a second that says it was simply invented by someone who came from St-Pol-de-Léon in the region;

and a third who maintain that it is all a dreadful misunderstanding and that it was first called *à l'Américaine.* It seems likely that the inventor was Pierre Fraysse from Sète in Languedoc. After working in Chicago he opened a restaurant in Paris called *Peter's.* He modified a dish from his own region, which used oil and tomatoes, substituting whisky for *eau-de-vie* and flattering his guests by calling it *à l'Américaine.* Subsequently gastronomes such as Briand and Montagné, perhaps in praise of the lobster rather

than its sauce, determined it should be *à l'Armoricaine.* This seems silly to me, for nothing based on oil and tomatoes could possibly be thought Breton. In any case, I'm not convinced this is what should be done to the fine, sweet flesh of any lobster.

Sardines in Oil

Don't leave the region without buying and trying Brittany's most important contribution to the tea tables and picnics of the world – sardines in oil.

One of the most important sardine-preserving centres

and April. Although a speciality of Nantes, they are found throughout Brittany.

● *Coquilles St-Jaques* Scallops. More than half the French catch comes from St-Brieuc, where they have only been redeveloped as a catch since 1960.

● *Crabe* or *tourteau* Crab. Served many ways but only St-Malo has a tradition of serving cold boiled crab with mayonnaise.

● *Grenouilles* Frogs. Found most places, served with *sauce poulette,* a rich cream sauce with wine and mushrooms.

● *Homard* Lobster. Even if you solved the problem of where or what *homard à l'Armoricaine* is or should be, they wouldn't sell you one cheaply, even in places where it is common, such as Concarneau, Quiberon, Roscoff and the mouth of the Loire.

● *Huîtres* Oysters. A very special speciality of Brittany. Belon are the best known and get their special flavour from the rich mixture of fresh and sea-water which swirl together at the mouth of the Belon river. As is common, the oysters are not actually

bred here but come only to be flavoured and fattened for 8–10 months. Other important centres are Cancale, Auray, Prat-Ar-Coum. Oysters from Lannilis are said to have the saltiest flavour. The large oyster park between Pointe de Pardic and the Îles-St-Quay takes its seed oysters from the Morbihan, as do most of France's famed types. There is little to see for the tourist, for the action is underwater most of the time. Paimpol is another good oyster centre. (See **Bordeaux** for more oyster information.)

● *Lotte* Monkfish or angler fish. Sweet firm-fleshed fish with lobster-like flavour; also called *baudroie.*

● *Morue* See *cabillaud.*

● *Mulet* The grey mullet, usually served roasted or grilled, sometimes on skewers, and also with *beurre blanc.*

● *Ormeaux* Abalone. In Dinard made into a *ragoût* with Muscadet, or put into the unusual *civet de pêcheur,* fish in red wine.

● *Oursin* Sea urchins. A speciality of St-Brieuc, where the roe is eaten spread on garlic bread.

● *Poulpe* or *minard* Octopus. Easily found, but no common method of preparation prevails.

● *Raie* Skate. Most often served classically with *beurre noir,* browned or burned butter, and capers.

● *Sardines* Fished almost everywhere and specially important at Quibéron and Douarnenez where there are over 50 canners. Fresh ones are grilled, of course, but also put into soups – and may even turn up in cream, it being Brittany. Connoisseurs will look for cans with date marks, for vintage sardines in oil are a rare treat, indeed. Gravier Aîné Cie is a revered brand. All must be 1 year old before sale, improve another 6 years in the tin and must be turned every 6 months.

● *Thon* Tuna. There are two types, *thon blanc* and *thon tropical.* The *blanc* is the most likely one to be found fresh and you could find it baked, marinated or, most unexpectedly, combined with carp's roe in an omelette. The *tropical* is usually frozen, and the fishermen of Concarneau make this one of their specialities.....

today is Concarneau, and in its *Musée de la Pêche* you can see the original glass containers used for sardines in oil. On the last Sunday in August there is a festival commemorating the time when sardines were the sole life-blood of the port, an opportunity to see folklore in the streets.

For both sporting and culinary pleasure, it is important also to turn your attention inland, for Brittany is equally a paradise of freshwater fish, the Côtes-du-Nord alone having almost 2,200 km/1,400 miles of trout streams, 126 km/80 miles of fishing canals and hundreds of reservoirs, ponds and pools. There's every famous type of fish, excluding it seems, the shad, but including salmon.

Salt and freshwater fish are generally simply cooked – grilled mostly, or poached – and served with cream or sauces with cream and butter in them. In the south-eastern regions of Morbihan and Ille-et-Vilaine, where they border the Loire regions and are close to Nantes, the voluptuous *sauce beurre blanc* will be more noticeable, but not necessarily more memorable.

Beware of any salt cod *morue* dishes unless you are certain you like it.

Brandade de thon is a curiosity, and must be a relatively new one, for it is a mixture of tinned tuna fish and the local haricot beans, clearly influenced by Italy's *tonno e fagioli*. It's nice, but once I was presented instead with tuna accompanied by Russian Salad in a distinctly individual mayonnaise, which seemed also to have come from a tin. *And* it was served in a scallop shell! *Caveat emptor...*

Cotriade

BOUILLABAISSE DU NORD

Of all the fish dishes, I suppose there is only one you really should try more than once, *cotriade*. Like the better-known *bouillabaisse* of the south, this is a fishermen's soup, originally made by them from their share of the catch. Variety of fish is more important than the exact ingredients, but a balance between oily coarse fish and firm white fish is the ideal. It always includes potato, but sophisticated ingredients like wine, *eau-de-vie de cidre* or saffron are the fancifications of food writers. Cream is commonly used to finish it, and in summer sorrel is a delicious addition. Although traditionalists don't include any shellfish, the bright gleam of mussels is becoming quite common. As with *bouillabaisse,* don't waste your money on any version which contains delicate langoustine or lobster, and even if served it, do not use *rouille* – well, you can, but it will no longer be *cotriade.*

GARLIC
AND SHALLOTS
AND ONIONS

An old culinary rule used to be that garlic *ail/aulx* started popping into pots only once you crossed the River Loire, and that the further south you went, the more was used. That remains broadly true today, but now that France imports so much garlic from abroad – mainly South America – it is used more generally. But don't be confused or put off simply by the amount used in any dish – the further south you grow it, the sweeter and milder garlic becomes. That is why the Languedociens use it in whole cloves and why they'll cook chicken and lamb with handsful. Thus, if you've had provençal-style food that lost you friends because of garlic contents, it either was not truly provençal or the garlic had probably come from another area, and gave a much stronger taste than the recipe actually demanded. Even onion should not be recognizable in a true provençal dish.

Onions *oignons* remain the great standby of the north and as far south as the Lyonnais; generally the French do not use them as lavishly as,

MEAT, POULTRY & GAME

The obvious importance and attraction of Brittany's seafood should not divert the visitor from the undoubted attractions of its other products. In 1689, Madame de Sévigné was asking for *'une aile de ces bonnes poulardes de Rennes*. Strictly speaking *aile* means wing, but the word is often used to mean breast in poultry cooking, with *aileron* used for the wing proper. Whatever part you eat, they are excellent, for there is more to French poultry than the *poulets de Bresse*. Cooked in white wine, often with prunes, the local breed is called *coucou,* and has eggs with a rather yellow shell. Other parts of Brittany produce other types.

☆☆☆☆☆☆☆☆☆☆☆☆☆☆☆☆☆☆☆

for instance, the British. So, with fish, for example, it is more likely that leeks *poireaux* are used. And if not leeks, then the shallot *échalote.*

Shallots are actually a distinct member of the onion family with a mild flavour something between onion and garlic. They come in a variety of shapes and sizes, including a long, wine-flushed one which is astonishingly sweet and found only in the south. They are *not* spring onions or small pickling onions, and none of these is a substitute for them, whatever cookbooks say. Garlic is rarely used in the same dish with shallots; but if you cannot get shallots, some mild onion and a touch of garlic will give a better, sweeter and more authentic solution than simply substituting onion.

☆☆☆☆☆☆☆☆☆☆☆☆☆☆☆☆☆☆☆

You should find a number of pigeon dishes in inland places, and farm-raised ducks, especially *canetons Nantais.*

With such a reputation for *charcuterie,* there is a lot of pork. *Porché* is a soup-stew of trotters, skin and bony pieces of pig, cooked with sorrel overnight in the village baker's oven.

With so much dairying, there are plenty of veal dishes, noticeably more than of beef. The most important meat is *pré-salé* lamb, raised on salty marshes of fields exposed to sea breezes, both of which Brittany has a surfeit. You should eat this as plainly as possible, ideally as a roasted leg – *gigot de pré-salé* – with or without haricot beans. If you ever see roasted forequarter or shoulder *épaule* of *pré-salé* you may more easily understand what all the flavour fuss is about; shoulder is also as likely to be stewed and served with artichokes.

Perhaps a place to experience this is the Île d'Ouessant, a short sail into the Atlantic west of Brest, where the small sheep have to be tied together and tethered to stone walls as protection against the strong, salt-laden winds which so flavour their feed. It is the epitome of the Breton maxim of work, for only the women tend the sheep.

Game is not very varied. Hare *lièvre,* and wild rabbit *lapin de garenne* are probably tops and both are used for *terrines* and *pâtés.* If you find local wild duck *canard sauvage,* make the most of it. That from La Brière has a reputation.

FRUIT & VEGETABLES

I harbour two enduring pictures associated with Brittany. One is of Roscoff – or Onion – Johnnies, Bretons on bicycles with the new crop of onions flung over the handlebars. The other is of narrow Breton roads jammed with the tractors and anger of farmers protesting about the derisory prices received at dutch auctions for their artichokes and other produce, which was then sold at high prices in cities around France and Europe. Both are seen less today, the first as a result of what farmers did about the second. Dynamic leadership organized the growers against their exploiters, then ensured access to newly-created markets abroad by providing their own transport – the Brittany Ferries.

A lot of produce you see cultivated in the fields of Brittany is not for fresh consumption but for canning, freezing or drying. Haricot beans, *petits pois,* spinach and brussels sprouts are the most important, I suppose. Other products flourish although they are not native to the area; garlic in North Finistère, cider apples in Ille-et-Vilaine and South Finistère, apples and pears generally and, rather surprisingly, *marrons* in Redon. This centre in Ille-et-Vilaine takes its chestnuts very seriously, serving them with potatoes, with sausages and, of course, with its buckwheat *galettes.*

Although the haricot bean is linked insolubly with the culinary view of Brittany, this has only been so since the *ancien régime*. Before the haricot, the broad bean *fève* was the staple. According to Gault Millau there are two distinct garnishes called *bretonne,* one just of beans, the other a white sauce with finely sliced leeks, onion and celery but *definitely* no beans, an old sauce for things white – poultry, eggs and fish. Other beans here include the native *coco paimpolais,* and the *chevriers* haricots dried a special way to keep their fresh green look, a technique perfected at Arpajon in the Essonne, and where there is an annual beano, *foire aux haricots. Chevriers* must not be confused with *flageolets.*

Beans and virtually every other vegetable grown here and elsewhere turn up in the expected *potées* and *potages* of the region, including a delicious pumpkin *potiron,* and thick *mitonnée,* of onions, bread and milk. Such heavy, simple food is rarely the lot of the visitor to enjoy.

Rennes is interesting for the summer eater. Asparagus has been officially encouraged as a crop since 1585, and her artichokes have been famous for quite as long, eaten raw, quartered and fried or boiled and served with a cream sauce. Best of all are the *petit gris*: not snails, but tiny melons of perfumed pink flesh, a delicious complement to the fruit from the extreme opposite end of Brittany, the strawberry of Plougastel. It was here in about 1800 that M. Fréziers brought back plants from Chile and Virginia, crossed them with European varieties and began the modern love affair with the fragrance and flavour of

LOCAL PRODUCE

● **Artichoke** *artichaut*	Mid-May until October.
Var: *Camus de Bretagne*	Dep: Finistère, Côtes-du-Nord.

With 65% of French production, and rising, Brittany dominates Europe.

● **Bean** *haricots à écosser*	Harvested August/September,
Var: *Coco paimpolais*	but sold semi-dry until November.
	Dep: Grown only around Paimpol.

Unique to Brittany, this bean has a speckled pod and white seeds. A *écosser* means 'in the pod' or 'to be podded' and these are a hybrid product, a semi-dry bean but remaining in the pod. They can be podded and further dried or used as 'almost fresh'.

● **Cabbage** *chou*	Mid-January/mid-March.
Var: *Winter king*	Dep: Finistère, Ile-et-Vilaine.

Reds and whites grown locally

● **Carrot** *carotte*	Primeurs start in October,
Var: *Nantaise, Nandor*	season continues until following May.
	Dep: Finistère, Ille-et-Vilaine.

● **Cauliflower** *choufleur*	Peak, January to May.
	Dep: Finistère, Côtes-du-Nord, Ille-et-Vilaine.

70% of national production comes from Brittany, and there is always one variety or another being harvested throughout most of autumn, winter and spring.

● **Chicory** *endive/witloof*	October until April.
Var: *Zoom, Bergère*	Dep: Finistère.
● **Cucumber** *concombre*	May to October.
	Dep: Finistère.

BRETON BUCKWHEAT

Haute Bretagne gave the world the buckwheat galette, called a *gaoff* when it is at home. Traditionally, they were made only with buckwheat but in these feebler times, wholemeal or white flour may be added. Make your own with a couple of eggs, half a litre of milk, 450g/10oz buckwheat flour and 100g/4oz melted butter. Fry in butter in a large pan, better still on a griddle.

strawberries. Before then, they were as boring as many of the modern British varieties have become.

Angelica *angélique* is candied, and mint is used in *berlingots,* but on the whole herbs are not an important part of traditional Breton cooking. Modern chefs, of course, use their perfumes more readily. The only dish generally mentioned is chicken *à la Nazairienne,* from St-Nazaire, with tomato, tarragon and cream sauce.

- **Leeks** *poireau*
Var: *Briand tardif, Armor*

December until April.
Dep: Ille-et-Vilaine.

- **Lettuce** *laitue/chicorée*
Var: White and green cabbage types plus icebergs increasingly now.

May until December, with icebergs May/June and September/December.

- **Onion** *oignon*
Var: *Rosé de Roscoff*

Freshly dug end July to start October.
Dep: Finistère

- **Potato** *pommes de terre nouvelles/primeur*
Var: *Duke* from Paimpol region is exclusively for British market; *Ostara, Brittany Prince*

Mid-May until end June.
Dep: St-Malo, Paimpol, St-Pol de Léon.

- **Shallot** *échalote*
Var: long, medium and roundish types: the medium length ones are most productive, the long ones the sweetest and best for cooking; Britain usually gets the round ones . . .

Freshly dug June and July, stored for year-round use.
Dep: Finistère.

Brittany grows 70% of France's production; but these are very different from the wine-red and white, long shallots of the south, which are less commercialized, and one of the few onion-y things delicate and sweet enough to include raw in food.

- **Spinach** *épinard*

May/June and October.
Dep: Finistère, Morbihan.

The biggest producers in France; 33% of the total crop.

- **Strawberry** *fraise*
Var: *Belrubi, Gariguette Favette, Kid Gauntlet, Gorella* (good)

May until mid-September.
Dep: Finistère (Plougastel).

- **Tomato** *tomate*
Var: *Marmande, Montafanet, Quatuor*

May until end November.
Dep: Finistère and around Rennes.

CHEESE

The washed-rind cheese holds its own in Brittany. *Saint-Paulin,* the best known, is quite typical. Virtually no other varieties of cheese are produced.

- *Campénéac* A typical Trappist or Saint-Paulin style cheese, *except* this one is made by nuns. Rather new on the scene; although very smelly gratifyingly mild of flavour.
- *Crémet Nantais* A fresh cow's milk cheese from Upper Brittany with mild creamy flavour, often eaten as a dessert with fresh fruit or compôte.
- *Fromage du curé* A factory-made, washed-rind cheese with strong nose and taste. Invented by a *curé* from Nantes in the 19th century; also called *Nantais.*
- *Meilleraye de Bretagne* Large, tangy, washed-rind Trappist cheese you can buy by the portion.
- *Nantais* See *Fromage du curé.*
- *St-Gildas-des-Bois* A soft triple cream cheese with bloomy white rind. It has a faint smell and a creamy flavour. Beaujolais is a suitable accompaniment.
- *Saint-Paulin* The daddy and mummy of all the washed-rind cheeses of this type, also the mildest. Made year round from pasteurized milk in Brittany and elsewhere.

PASTRIES, PUDDINGS & CONFECTIONERY

St-Brieuc on the favoured northern coast claims the invention of the *brioche,* one of the most perfect of all amalgams of butter and wheat flour. It is a claim hotly disputed by neighbouring Counouaille, by the people of Brie (who reckon *brioches* are so called because they once contained their cheese), and by the inhabitants of Gournay in Normandy. The very name would seem to give the claim to the *St-Briochains*; or is that *why* they claim it? There are long brioches called *cornes* in Nantes and *cornics,* a sort of croissant in Douarnenez. The most interesting though is *kouign'amann.* The name is dialect for cake and butter. It is a yeast dough folded and rolled about butter and sugar – an exceptionally upmarket version of English lardy cake.

Just as famed and far easier to find made well, perhaps because it is simpler to make, is *gâteau breton,* a rich pound cake which should include almonds and dried fruits. According to Gault Millau, it was invented only last century in Paris, as was the *Paris-Brest,* a ring of choux pastry sprinkled with almonds and stuffed with cream. Both have been convincingly embraced in the interest of profit and tourism and why not? *Quatre-quarts,* though, seems a more authentic thing, a classic pound cake of equal weights of eggs, butter, flour and sugar. In late summer look for *gâteau aux figues fraîches.* Although almost all of Brittany ripens

wonderful figs, this cake is specially associated with St-Briac.

In the extreme west and centre of Brittany, where both soil and weather combined to defeat the growth of the old strains of wheat, other grains have fought and defied the elements, particularly nutty buckwheat, *sarrasin* or *blé noir.* You are most likely to meet it as a *galette,* indeed it would be difficult not to do so, but these are usually savoury. It is more unusual to be confronted with *far breton,* a *bouillie* or porridge of buckwheat (or of oats *avoine*), sweetened with dried fruits, raisins or prunes usually. *Noce* is always a sweet version (boiled in a cloth like the original British suet puddings) so it may be sliced for serving. *Far*

breton is most easily met with in the south-western Pays de Léon. *Fars* of other types, and even *far breton,* might well be savoury, as is the *kik am gaz.*

Now that there is more wheat available, bakers have increased the palatability of some of the lumpen breads once made with alternative grains, notably *pain de seigle* rye bread, *pain d'antan* mixed wheat and rye flour (called maslin in Britain) and cooked very slowly and my favourite, the naturally sweet *pain d'avoine,* oaten bread. Of course the Bretons have long appreciated the affinity of oats and cream and many places make oat bread with cream, *pain d'avoine à la crème.*

Most cream is used as is or is made into butter for baking, but there are many puddings based on milk curds, including junket *jonchée.*

Dol-de-Bretagne makes a sweet, light pickle of pears for dessert, *poires au vinaigre.*

Worth Finding

• *Berlingots* Peppermint boiled sweets especially made in Morbihan.
• *Craquelins* Basically a rather dry biscuity thing, but also found stuffed with apple or cherries.
• *Crêpes dentelles* Literally 'lace pancakes'. The superthin, crisp, rolled pancakes made commercially in Quimper since 1897 are quite the best crunchy accompaniment to frozen or creamy or fruity desserts.
• *Crêpes (de froment)* Wheatflour pancakes, white or wholemeal, almost always served sweet, and sold from *crêperies* virtually everywhere, with cream an obligatory accompaniment.

• *Maingaux, mingaux, mingots* The epitome of highsummer sumptuousness. Today it is whipped cream or a very light cream cheese with raspberries, strawberries or cherries; but once a complicated mixture of creams of different ages to give a desired slight sharpness.
• *Mamgoz* Associated with Quimper, these are apples baked with jam and butter.
• *Puits d'amour* 'Wells of love'. Seductive pastry shapes stuffed with summer's soft fruits, especially strawberries. There'll be a lake or mountain of cream nearby, too – or perhaps some *maingaux. . . .*

Bon Marché

Below is a selective list of markets plus some fairs *foires* of special interest. Check with the local S.I. for precise locations and time changes.

FINISTÈRE
Brest Mon, Fri; **Carhaix-Plouguer** Sat; **Châteaulin** Thur; **Concarneau** Mon, Fri; **Crozon** 4th Wed of month; **Douarnenez** Mon, Fri, Sat; **Le Faou** Sat; **Guerlesquin** Wed; **Huelgoat** 2nd & 4th Thur of month; **Landerneau** Sat, 1st Mon each month; **Landivisiau** Tue (auction of animals for slaughter); **Lesneven** Mon; **Loctudy** Tue; **Morlaix** Sat; **Ploudalmézeau** Mon; **Pont-Aven** Tue; **Pont-l'Abbé** Thur; **Quimper** Wed, Sat (cattle); **Quimperlé** Fri; **Rosporden** Thur; **St-Pol-de-Léon** Tue.

CÔTES-DU-NORD
Binic Thur; **Broons** Wed; **Callac** Wed; **Châtelaudren** Mon; **Corlay** Thur; **Etables-sur-Mer** Tue; **Guingamp** Sat; **Lamballe** Thur; **Jugon-les-Lacs** Tue, Fri; **Lancieux** Tue; **Lannion** Thur; **Lanvollon** Fri; **Lézardrieux** Fri; **Merdrignac** Wed; **Paimpol** Tue; **Plancoet** Sat; **Pléneuf-Val André**

Tue, Fri (June – Sept); **Plestin-les-Grèves** Wed; **Pleouc-sur-Lie** Thur; **Ploubalay** 1st & 3rd Mon of month; **Plouha** Wed; **Pontrieux** Mon; **Quintin** Tue; **Rostrenen** Tue; **St-Brieuc** Wed, Fri & Sat; **St-Cast-le-Guildo** Tue, Fri, (June to Sept); **St-Quay Portrieux** Mon, Fri; **Trégastel** Mon; **Tréguier** Wed (pigs); **Uzel** 1st & 3rd Wed of month.

MORBIHAN
Allaire Fri; **Auray** Fri, 2nd & 4th Mon; **Baud** Sat; **Elven** Fri; **Gourin** Mon; **Hennebont** Thur; **Josselin** Sat; **Locminé** 3rd Thur of month (breeding cattle); Mon pm (beef cattle); **Lorient** Wed & Sat; **Malansac** Fri (only in chesnut season); **Malestroit** Thur; **Muzillac** Fri; **Ploermel** Mon, auction every Tue.

ILLE-ET-VILAINE
Bain-de-Bretagne Mon; **Betton** Sun am; **Cancale** Daily; **Dol-de-Bretagne** Sat; **Domagne** Mon; **Fougères** Sat, Fri am (cattle); **Grand-Fougeray** Thur; **Guerche-de-Bretagne** Tue; **Loheac** 2nd Sat of month; **Louvigne-du-Désert** Thur; **Maure-de-Bretagne** Thur; **Médrèac** Tue; **Melesse** Thur; **Mordelles** Tue, Wed; **Noyal-sur-**

Vilaine Tue; **Pipriac** 1st Tue of month; **Pleurtuit** 2nd Wed of month **Redon** Daily; **Rennes** Daily; **Sens-de-Bretagne** Mon; **St-Brice-en-Coglés** Mon; **St-Just** Thur Oct & Dec (chestnuts); **St-Malo** Tue, Fri, (St-Malo town), Mon, Thur, Sat (Rocabey); **St-Méloir-des-Ondes** Daily (potatoes in summer, cauliflower in winter) Fri (pigs); **St-Ouen-des-Alleux** Wed (catte); **St-Servan-sur-Mer** Tue, Fri; **Tinténiac** Wed; **Vitré** Mon.

Wandering around in markets is the best way to discover what makes the heart of a region beat. I don't want to load you down with so much information that you are unable to respond spontaneously to what you find or to make your own memorable mistakes, but here are a few tips and useful words.
● *Braderie* A kind of huge jumble sale, held annually or more often and lasting for a day or as long as a month. Think of all those authentic kitchen things *d'occasion*, as used by *grandmère*, even if it is not your own.
● *Comice* Not a Pear Fair but an agricultural show.

MARKET WISE

● *En gros* Wholesale; you'll want *detail* retail.
● *Forain* **Un marché forain** is an itinerant market, so you may meet it several times in one region. **Une fête foraine** is a funfair.
● *Marché au cadran* A traders' auction conducted against the clock by tight-lipped, ruthless wholesalers. Incomprehensible but worth watching at a distance. Don't join in.
● *Poulain* Don't be fooled by assonance, association and expectation that this has anything to do with chickens; a

poulain is a colt. *Foires aux Poulains* are regularly held.

Remember that not all markets take place in les Halles or la place du Marché.You may be directed to a *cité, lotissement,* or *Z.U.P. (zone d'urbanisation priorité),* all of which indicate a large housing estate or new town development. They too have their regular market days. What could be less *touristique*? Also keep it in mind that France has many religious and public holidays, and market days that clash with these may be postponed or brought forward. Check with the local *Syndicat d'Initiative.*

A Mushrooming Tradition

Bed of the royal river, *le fleuve royal*, playground of the *ancien régime* and Garden of France, the Loires are a combination of the fabulous and the commonplace. It is strangely comforting to know, as you wander through the great galleries and gardens of the magnificent châteaux, that outside is the region of Muscadet and Sancerre wines, of familiar logs of goat cheese from Ste-Maure, of strawberries, and of Golden Delicious apples that someone will slice to make a caramel-rich upside-down tart. But this familiarity of the table can mislead visitors into dismiss-

ing the food of the Loires as predictable and uninspired. How wrong they are, for this very predictability is the Loires' proud insignia of authenticity and of tradition.

Buried Treasures

The most common style of sauce, other than the velvet-warmth of *beurre blanc*, is of cream and mushrooms, regarded by many as stateless *à la francaise* food. But this sauce is centuries old and, far from being any reflection of boringness, is an illustration of how the region's food so impressed its visitors it was relentlessly copied and devalued, famil-

iarity breeding an ill-deserved contempt. Those mushrooms have been a specialized local crop ever since men hewed caverns into the hills to carve building blocks for the châteaux, and then used the caverns' darkness as a new source of income.

If you plan only to see the châteaux and then to move elsewhere for culinary pleasure, I should reconsider and stay much, much longer, exploring the modern Loires' food and the perfumed red wines with names of châteaux, Chinon for instance. For although a new epithet, its reputation as Garden of France is well deserved, something I more than proved when I stayed once in medieval Loches, well off the château route.

The streets, markets and ancient bent-walled buildings of Loches are a great place for the culinary roman-

for King Charles VII. It must have been easy if the markets of Loches were only half as good as I found them now.

Public Executions

Even well inland, as Loches is, the tight, noisy market

> In which we ...
> ● Share a mistress's comforts, squabble in markets and steam in seaweed ...
> ● Find a regal affinity and learn the truth about Loire-abiding recipes ...
> ● Sorrow for missing vegetables and learn not to reject *rillons* ...
> ● Discover saffron gardens, a birthplace of dispute and what was hatching in Amboise ...
> ● Unpeel a Châteaubriand mystery, local pears with a Down Under connection and an undercover tart ...
> ● Join arguments about sandy biscuits ...
> ● Draw *pistoles* and make a *divertissement* to a rhapsody in Blois ...
> ● Learn the Roman way with honey cakes and just where the men are most *doué* ...

---

tic. There lived Agnès Sorel, first of the great royal mistresses of whom we know who made a career of giving a king the comforts that queens, crowns and ermine could not. Her speciality was ministering to the stomach, and she is said to have created salmis of woodcocks *bécasses* and *petits timbales*

smelt of the sea, with a choice of oysters and wet, bright fish, fresh enough to seem slumbering rather than dead. Pungently competing for the nose's attention were the open-sided trucks selling goat's cheese from the Touraine, rich *camemberts* from Normandy and farmhouse *brie* from the Île-de-France.

Beyond them were parked the more colourful sellers of sausages and hams, black and white puddings, *andouillettes* and the local passion, *rillettes*, most vendors wearing the black, wide brimmed hats and startling neckerchiefs of Bretons and Auvergnats.

I was cooking to earn my board at the time and was quickly taught the secret of shopping in markets – to adopt the discipline of shopping with no list other than of the number of guests that must be satisfied. Lists for shopping pinch the imagination and close the eyes to what is on display. Once I had started, my confidence quickly grew enough to compete with the locals, feeling the breasts of the live chickens and squabbling with the best of them as I protected my turn to be served. I poked and pried at boxes of snuffling brown-furred rabbits, pigeons, ducks and guinea fowls *pintades*. It was only the eyes of the chickens I managed to avoid, so we had chicken for dinner. But I lacked the confidence to take them home privately to wring their necks or chop off their heads, and had to have them executed for me there and then, much to the amusement of the locals. They (the chickens) were delicious, stuffed with black pudding and local apples.

We began that meal with a whole fish cooked in seaweed so fresh that only the clinging remains of a vermouth marinade needed to be added to the casserole. Steamed in a distillation of the sea and studded with salty-fresh oysters warmed in cream and the seaweed's juices, it made us believe we were dining on the sea's edge.

We ended with a confection of ice cream and sorbet from M. Couturier of rue de la République, a master *glacier*. Had you imagined there would be a guild of master ice cream makers? There is, as part of *Les Maîtres Pâtissiers de France*, and you can find them in most towns and villages of any size, displaying their badge on the window. Each has his or her specialities, and M. Couturier names some after Agnès. But that night we ate his *Pompadour*, pear and *poire William* sorbet inside rasperry ice cream on a meringue base, a fruity affinity of regal magnificence I had not imagined. And neither would Agnès, for the growing and eating of vegetables and fruits had little real significance in her time.

Regal Dearth

When Catherine de Medici came later from Italy to marry the heir of King François I, she added a few vegetables including artichokes to the gardens and encouraged a lighter touch to the food she found. She was not tampering with the food of France, barely even with the food of the Court. Her chef's pretty concoctions were for special occasions, for parties and fêtes; most courses of most aristocratic and courtly meals were still of flesh. Meat was the main meal of the rulers: grains and cheeses and whatever grew that was edible, that of the ruled.

Just as Catherine's contributions to the foundations of

haute cuisine have only little place in the history of French food, the glorious châteaux of the Loire Valley contribute the thinnest threads of gold to the fabric that wove itself into France. But the château of Villandry at least offers a glimpse of a true picture of that past life, through the tiniest culinary chink. Villandry is not set in a manicured hunting park and I cannot remember anything of its rooms except for the views from them of descending terraces of Renaissance knot-gardens, the lowest of which is a kitchen garden *potager*. It has been restored to its 16th-century state, planted only with vegetables and fruit trees that were contemporary, and thus fascinating for what is not there, most noticeably potatoes.

What a shame Monsieur (Louis XIV's brother) and his catamites, or the huntress Diane de Poitiers, or the inventive Agnès Sorel and their glittering friends did not know the pleasure of squashing the floury body of baked or roasted potatoes into the juices from the haunches and ribs and skewers of game and game birds and poultry. I feel much more sorrow for them for that lack than I feel envy of them living in the gilt salons of those hunting-lodge châteaux. Just think of those smoky fires, and the draughts, and the stone floors – and all that meat and no potatoes.

CHARCUTERIE

The Touraine precisely, and the Loires generally, offer a singular opportunity to decide what you really think about *rillettes,* which claim this as their home. The name is a diminutive of the rarely used *rille*. Not that this will make any difference, for diminished or otherwise, *rillettes* are either an unctuous, spreading essence of sublimity (to their devotees) or a bland, stringy and pallid paste (to everyone else). After much consideration in the establishments of Tours and about, I have come down fairly heavily on the side of the dissenters.

You, or rather they, make *rillettes* by taking moderately fatty pork – neck is considered best – reducing it to small pieces, and cooking it with the addition only of salt over gentle heat for many hours, stirring as often as practical. To even out the texture, the exhausted meat is further harried into threads by being pulled apart with two forks. To the true enthusiast the fork is still new-fangled, and there are only inimitable throat sounds and operatic appeals to heaven at the mention of how factories *whisk* the stuff. Other than salt, no seasoning is allowed (more's the pity). To me the exercise is pointless, for the interminable cooking emasculates whatever flavour may have been present in the threads of meat, and I have never spread *rillettes* upon bread without thinking the flavour to be that of overboiled, underseasoned meat.

Rillettes or *rille d'oie*, the same product but made from goose, and *rillettes de lapin de la garenne,* made from wild rabbit, are even more highly considered. As some measure of excellence for the basic product, the suffix *de Tours,* plus some indication that the product was actually made in that city, usually works. But there is no legal protection of the claim. All of Anjou makes *rillettes;* Blois, Vendôme and Saumur are regularly mentioned for theirs.

Be careful not to reject *rillons,* thinking they are chunky *rillettes. Rillons,* often called *grillons* else where, are pieces of pork cooked in fat until most of their own fat is rendered and they are very crisp and crunchy; Tours makes them well, too, and Vendôme does the same with ham *jambon.*

The Orléannais has an ancient reputation for its *pâtés,* but the disappearance of most (not all) game on four legs and recent legislation banning the taking of most on wings means the varieties are reduced considerably. Only the old or the intrepid attempt today to make the famous *pâté de Pithiviers* stuffed with whole larks. Most reliable for a taste of genuinely wild local produce is probably that of

hare *lièvre.* The Sologne and the Gâtinais and the Beauce alike have some reputation for *pâté* and there is some chance of it being of venison *venaison.* The most famous *pâté* centre must be Chartres. It is said that a hare *pâté* offered to Attila the Hun so calmed his warriors that they settled here peaceably to become farmers in the Beauce.

If you have just one stop you can make in the area, and you are enamoured of *charcuterie,* I think you should choose Tours. There you can lunch with more assurance upon *rillettes* and *andouilles* or *andouillettes.* You will then be a man or woman who knows what they like.

After that, or instead, I should head for Nantes, which does everything well, or for Le Mans in the Maine, where white pudding *boudin blanc* of onions, eggs, fat, herbs and spices is usually grilled. That I recommend. Tripe, too, is a popular dish, and often it will be just the choicest of stomachs, the *gras-double,* and will come finished with much cream. (Neither is *charcuterie,* but there are more ways to enjoy eating large amounts of fat than *rillettes.)*

Worth Finding

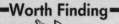

- *Lard Nantais* Sometimes *petit lard;* pork rinds, liver, lungs and flesh prepared in small pieces and, usually, served with pork chops.
- *Jambon* Ham. Amboise hams are specially delicious.
- *Jambonneau* Small cone-shaped ham, usually just the

hock. Perfect for picnics. Also served boiled with potatoes, cabbage and chestnuts.
- *Saucisses au muscadet* Porky sausages with a modicum of wine included and sometimes served with a chestnut purée *puřee de marions/châtuignes.*

FISH & SHELLFISH

For me, a valley presupposes the presence of water somewhere in its twisted lengths. But until I first drove into the Loire Valley while researching my book on delicatessen foods in 1978, I had no idea of quite how much there was throughout the *départements.* For as well as the Loire and its best-known tributaries – the Cher, Indre, Vienne and Loir – there are a good half dozen more streams of note, plus the countless lakes of the Sologne, the puddles of the *marais* you find here and there, and the man-made *étangs.* Thus the inhabitants have a special regard for freshwater fish, of which they have not just the fullest range but also a wide repertoire of ways to prepare them.

Freshwater Fish

As with meat, simple cooking was traditionally favoured. So a *friture* or mixed fry-up of perch and gudgeon *goujon* and tench *tanche* is basic. When shad *alose* arrives with spring, often as early as February, it may be stuffed with sorrel *oseille* and baked or, in special restaurants and private homes, served with *mousserons,* the most delicate of wild spring mushrooms, fresh and bright. Yet it is as likely to be simply served with plain butter, or with *beurre blanc,* the sauce which most perfectly combines the contradictory sources of the finest foods – art and science. You might find pike *brochet* in *quenelles,* but it, too, is just as likely to be roasted with plain butter.

THE LOIRES

Loire salmon is not extinct as it is claimed, but not very common. Remember it will be fatter and tastier for being caught nearer the sea, as salmon does not feed in freshwater.

After *beurre blanc* or plain butter, mushrooms and cream are probably the most common ingredients of sauces, nudged into individuality by the use of this or that local white wine, or wild mushrooms. It is a shame if you make the mistake of thinking such dishes the result of modern influence or to be 'international' cooking. But of course, they will only be simple honest reflections of local food if the establishments cooking them are the same. It is easy to dismiss as a modern affectation the offer of shad or pike with chives, but this is a proper and local way, owing nothing for the current Michelin fashion for replacing parsley with chives willy-nilly.

In the Beauce, and perhaps elsewhere, the same mistake may be made when these and other fish are offered with saffron, but saffron is, surprisingly, a crop of Boynes in that region.

Most books, and everyone you ask, of course, say the banks of the *fleuve royal* are the real birthplaces of *matelotes,* stews of fish in wine, that may or may not be finished with cream. Eels and lampreys were once the basis of the Loire version. The latter is less common these days, but in Chinon they have a distinguished method of frying it in walnut oil. Eel is perhaps the most popular of the freshwater fish, and as well as in *pâtés,* braises and casseroles,

it might be found served with prunes. (I cannot imagine why there is so much antipathy towards eating eel, shared sometimes by me, for it has the cleanest, clearest flavour and succulent juicy flesh.)

In March and April Nantes celebrates the appearance of *civelles* or *piballes,* minute elvers which are cooked whole in omelettes or made into a sort of *pâté.* They are delightfully nutty and have none of the large-eyed horror of whitebait. Although not a major fishing port, Nantes was once the most important commercial port, certainly in the 18th century, when sugar, rum and spices were imported from Africa and the Americas. Many of the industrialized food products of Nantes and neighbouring Lower Brittany are based on the older requirement of producing victuals for the crews of the merchant navy.

There are small fishing ports along the coast of Loire-Atlantique of course, whence come scallops *coquilles,* oysters *huîtres,* lobsters *homard* and a variety of crabs. There are mussels, too, but they are more a speciality of the coast of Vendée, with L'Aiguillon-

sur-Mer as the acknowledged centre.

Mussels have been cultivated around here since at least the 13th century. Its bay is protected from the fiercest Atlantic winds by the Île-de-Ré, and irrigated by sweet water from the land. It takes two or three years before the mussels are big enough to sell, and it is estimated that there must be more than 6,000 *bouchots* wooden posts on which they are raised. Naturally the area uses them every which way, including the *mouclade* associated with the Charente-Maritime. This is an upside-down *éclade,* in which the mussels are grilled *on* a bed of pine needles rather than under them (see **Bordeaux** p.120).

La-Tranche-sur-Mer, has mussels and oysters too, raises beef in the *marais* and, according to Gault Millau, claims its potatoes are the best in the country. You may see men slashing their way dangerously through the river growth from boats in the *marais de Goulaine.* They are not fighting off killer eels but harvesting *souche,* a tough swamp grass which makes terrific litter for animal stalls.

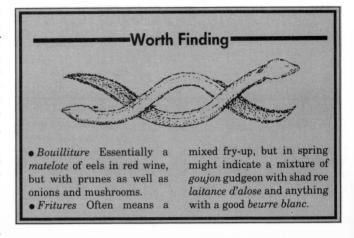

━Worth Finding━

● *Bouilliture* Essentially a *matelote* of eels in red wine, but with prunes as well as onions and mushrooms.
● *Fritures* Often means a

mixed fry-up, but in spring might indicate a mixture of *goujon* gudgeon with shad roe *laitance d'alose* and anything with a good *beurre blanc.*

MEAT, POULTRY & GAME

You need little more than the operatic trumpets of Rameau in your car to summon up thrilling tableaux of past days as you drive through the Maine or the Orléannaiss. Skeletons, or in some cases, whole limbs, of a countryside dedicated to *la chasse* are still easy to find. These are forests, elegant and light in an unmistakeably French way. Meat, its hunting and eating, was the basis of life for court and country. But except for small pockets of hare *lièvre* some quail *caille* and perhaps partridge *perdreau* and the deer of the lake-laced Sologne, the natural game which even 20 years ago made this area of France's most reputed hunting has gone, or gone elsewhere, or is artificially reared, like the pheasants. But to complement or replace hunted meat, there are luscious domesticated alternatives. Even they have roots in the past. Not everyone enjoyed earning their dinner on horseback. Not everyone had a horse.

Veal and beef are amongst the best, grown succulent and fat enough to be served simply. For the pasturage, particularly of the Touraine is so rich that dairying animals are uncomfortable and goats overwhelmed. A small part of Normandy's Perche, the Petit Perche, juts into the Loires and produces beef you'll often find deliciously braised. Cholet is perhaps more generally known for beef; Montsoreau and Saumur are more associated with excellence of veal.

Veal is just one of the specialities of Le Mans, a most

Fois Gras Canard

The charming village of Palluau-sur-Loire, about 25 km/15 miles from Blois, is where Cathérine and Didier Urso make and sell recommended fattened duck livers. They are the only people for hundreds of miles who do so and their shop, *Le Canar-dière,* is on Place de L'Eglise, in the shadow of a mainly 16th century castle restored lavishly by Paco Rabanne. The ducks are fattened in the château's old stable block. Their livers are cooked with as great care as they are and also made into pâtés. Take home *confits, confits de gésier* giblets, or *gressons,* cubes of duck fat not quite rendered down, and wonderfully wicked on hot toast.

interesting centre for flesh eaters; its race of chickens, *poulets gris,* traditionally fattened on the local produce of wheat and milk, are particularly worth seeking. Capons *chapons* were the most highly prized, but these are not popular with our EEC masters and may no longer be found. La Flèche was the biggest supplier of chickens to the *ancien régime,* but it was at Amboise that the western world's first incubator for artificially rearing chickens was installed – in 1496. It was a surprise to me to find in several books, but in no restaurants, reference to *oeufs en meurette,* the Burgundian dish of eggs in a red wine sauce, being enjoyed here. Still Burgundy is only across the border, and turkeys and guinea fowls are also reared here, so I suppose they do everything possible with eggs. Chicken is also likely to be called *géline.*

Worth Finding

• *Filet Châteaubriand* Châteaubriant is a town in Loire-Atlantique of some renown for its beef. Châteaubriand was an author born in St-Malo. Either name, but properly that of the man, is given to a thick piece of prime, centre-fillet steak. But before World War II even the Savoy would serve it as a piece of fillet steak grilled between two thinner slices (of sirloin I was told).
• *Haricot de mouton* A braise or stew of mutton and vegetables which should *not* contain haricot beans, for it is both a recipe pre-dating the arrival from America of these beans and a vulgarization of its old name, *halicot,* from the verb to cut small. But many restauranteurs avoid disappointment and argument by including beans.
• *Poulet/géline Lochoise* Poultry with the sauce associated with Loches, of onion, cognac and double cream.
• *Poulet aux chipolatas* Chicken stuffed with small sausages.
• *Gouguenioche* A pie of chicken and eggs you may find in Vendée.

All the poultry, and the wild ducks taken from the river banks, can be found cooked in red wine, but the singular herb-flavoured red wines of Bourgueil and Chinon make extremely interesting *daubes, civets* and every other kind of stew, including *coq au vin.*

Vendée, especially its *marais* marsh, drained to become pasturage centuries ago, produces excellent beef and incidentally, snails; those of Lucon are the most famed.

Lamb and mutton of the *charmoise* breed are the product of Montmorillon, and the coast of Vendée will offer good *pré-salé* lamb in spring. Château-Gontier (Mayenne) is perhaps more for those interested in the living animal: it is the registration centre for pedigree *bleu du Maine,* a breed of sheep distinguished by steel grey markings on their legs and face. In the Beauce, Châteaudun is a major sheep raising centre and mutton market. Of pigs, the *craonnais* are of the oldest repute.

Indre-et-Loire includes Ste-Maure, famous for goat's milk cheeses and walnut oil. Only here are you likely to be offered kid *cabri* at spring time, or a *gigot de chèvre,* for its pastures are already drier and more suitable, like that of Poitou.

FRUIT & VEGETABLES

The countryside close to the rivers of the Loire is riddled with the man-made caves, originally the birthplace of the walls of 15th and 16th-century châteaux but now the site of a gigantic cultivated-mushroom industry, a commercial undertaking, incidentally, which has existed since at least 1600. The expression, *de Paris* associated with mushrooms means they are cultivated, for originally Paris was virtually the only market for what was then a luxury. Langeais and Chênehutte-les-Tuffeaux are places to look for mushroom caves. Saumur is one of the most important centres for drying them. In Marboué (Beauce) the bigger heads are stuffed with snails and baked with garlic.

The wild and cultivated marvels of the garden of France are beyond listings, for lists suggest inevitably some

LOCAL PRODUCE

Vegetables

● **Artichoke** *artichaut*	April until October. Dep: Maine-et-Loire, (Angers), Vendée (Sables d'Olonne).
● **Asparagus** *asperges*	April until June. Dep: Loir-et-Cher, Maine-et-Loire.

After the Gard, Loir-et-Cher is second biggest grower; markets include Saumur, Chinon, Orléans, Blois, Selles-sur-Cher.

● **Cabbage** *chou* Var: *Tête de Pierre, Roi d'Hiver*	September until February. Dep: Loire-Atlantique, Vendée, Maine-et-Loire, Loiret, Sarthe.
● **Carrot** *carotte*	July until following May. Summer crops May until July.
● **Cauliflower** *choufleur*	Mid-October until May. Dep: Loire-Atlantique, Vendée, Maine-et-Loire, Indre-et-Loire.
● **Celery** *céleri-branche*	End April to July covered. Mid-August to November open air. Dep: Loire-Atlantique, Maine-et-Loire.

Grown covered and in open air: Tours has a celebrated *celeri violet.* Nantes, Angers and Saumur important market centres – biggest overall grower in France.

● **Courgette** *courgette* Var: *Diamant* (field) *Seneca* (covered)	mid-June until Mid-October. Dep: Loiret, Vendée.
● **Cucumber** *concombre*	May until August. Dep: Loiret, Loire-Atlantique, Maine-et-Loire, Loire-et-Cher, Indre-et-Loire, Vendée.

The Loiret is France's biggest producer: 14% of national crop: Orléans, Nantes and Angers are biggest markets.

degree of finite knowledge. This is impossible when a region too glibly associated only with the broad bean *fève* includes also the Beauce, one of France's granaries (Châteaudun is its centre) and the Gâtinais, famed for walnuts, honey, saffron and mushrooms, and Orléans, maker of the world's best wine vinegars, pickles and mustard. It was Orléans, not Dijon, that stimulated a huge increase in the French mustard crop in the 1940s.

The Loire Valley is where St François de Paul created the *Bon Chrétien* pear 500 years ago – it is said to have disappeared from French markets, but survives in Australasia, I believe. In 1849, the Comice horticultural gardens in Angers developed the *Comice* pear, and if you are in Amanlis in September its own summer pear *Beurre d'Amanlis* should be ready. The better known Williams is ripe about mid-August and is finished by end September. The huge *Louise-Bonne* pear is a speciality of Les Essants.

Whence, too, came the queen after whom the French call their greengage *reine-claude*. Claude, wife of François I, was born in Romorantin in the Sologne, home of excellent apples, of strawberries and, for those who look, the medlar *nèfle*. Strawberries, incidentally, are often served in red wine hereabouts.

Reinettes little queens, are a French variety of apple considered as good as the British Cox; the Loire grows a number of local strains, including the *Reinette d'Orléans* – and plenty of the superb *Reine de reinette*, queen of reinettes, considered one of the world's best apples and thought to have come first from Britain. Azay-le-Rideau has rather special apple orchards. Upside down apple cakes or tarts are commonly found. They are known sometimes also as *tartes renversées* or *solognotes*, and appear sometimes in an expected variation using pears rather than apples. Use good Golden Delicious apples or Cox's to make this as special at home as the original.

Olivet is another pear centre, and makes those bottles of Williams *eau-de-vie* with a whole pear inside. There are great cherry orchards too, as in Vineuil, but her cherries, mainly *guignes,* tend to be used to make *guignolet* (cherry brandy), and the real fame of Vineuil is her asparagus.

Dried plums *prunes* turn up in any number of sweet or savoury dishes, but not perhaps as much as they used to do. Tours was once known as a city of towers *tours* for there were dozens, where plums (originally from Damascus, i.e. damascenes, hence dam-

---

● **Fennel** *fenouil*	Autumn-ish. Dep: Maine-et-Loire.
A traditional crop of the Loire valley.	
● **Leek** *poireau* Var: *Briand, Artaban, Malabare* (giant winter variety)	All year round. Dep: Loire-Atlantique, Vendée, Maine-et-Loire.
Loire Atlantique is biggest producer in France after the Nord.	
● **Lettuce** *laitue/chicorée* Var: round batavia, curly endive etc.	Covered from March. Open air from June to autumn. Dep: Loire-Atlantique, Maine- et-Loire, Vendée.
Amongst France's most important production zones.	
Cabbage and iceberg varieties	Main season April until September. September to November has almost no crop. Dep: Loire-Atlantique, Loiret, Maine-et-Loire, Vendée.
● **Onion** *oignon*	All year, but mainly August– May. Dep: Loiret, Maine-et-Loire.
● **Radish** *radis*	All year round. Dep: Loire-Atlantique, Maine- et-Loire, Vendée.
By far the most important production zone in France.	
● **Shallot** *échalote* Var: short and long varieties, including *Grise* and *Jersey*	Harvested June and July, available all year round. Dep: Maine-et-Loire, Vendée, Loiret, Loire-et-Cher.
● **Tomato** *tomate* Var: *Beefsteak*	Mid-April until mid- November. Dep: Loire-Atlantique, Maine- et-Loire, Loiret, Vendée.
● **Turnip** *navet* red/white and violet/white	February until October. Dep: Loire-Atlantique, Loiret.
Loire-Atlantique is one of 4 biggest producers.	

sons) were dried and stored for winter use. Blois also dries its golden plums *mirabelles* into prunes and calls them *pistoles* (as does Brignoles in Provence because their shape and colour is reminiscent of old gold coins). Expect lots of sorrel *oseille* in spring and early summer, with freshwater fish generally, or specifically, in an *omelette beauceronne* combined with bacon and potato. Sorrel may also be cooked with chestnuts. The *prepons* is a sweet melon, cardoons *cardons* are popular, pumpkin, amazingly, is eaten in pies, and the Touraine has a peach/apricot they call *alberge*. Although not used noticeably, saffron *safran* is an unexpected harvest of Boynes (Loiret); it takes more than 200,000 of the hand-picked stigmas from the saffron crocuses to make 500g/1 lb, hence the astronomical expense. Saumur, like many wine centres grows luscious strawberries and Cholet makes many of hers into jam.

Fabulous Fungi

If you miss the asparagus of spring, you might better wait until autumn when wild mushrooms, especially from the forest of Orléans abound. *Cèpes* and other types of *bolets* predominate but the forest breeds excellent parasol mushrooms *courmelles/coulemelles*. Summer visitors may be compensated for unseasonal dampness by the earlier appearance of the apricot-perfumed *girolles/chanterelles*. Vilainer-les-Roches is the traditional centre for making the wicker paniers into which you gather them or send your harvests of fruit to market.

LOCAL PRODUCE

Fruit

● **Apple** *pomme* Var: *Reine de reinettes, Clochard, Belle de Boskoop*	Harvested September to mid-November for selling September to July. Dep: Maine-et-Loire, Loiret, Cher, Loire-Atlantique, Sarthe, Indre-et-Loire, Deux-Sèvres.

A very important crop, which also includes English, American, even Japanese varieties; except, of course, the 'Golden' and granny smith.

● **Currants** *cassis* Var: *Noir de Bourgogne*	July. Dep: Maine-et-Loire, Loiret Cher, Sarthe, Loire-Atlantique.
● **Hazelnuts** *noisettes*	Main harvest October to November. Dep: Loiret, Indre.

From July you can buy green *noisettes,* our cob nuts; the dried ones are mainly sold for chocolates and biscuits but as the Loiret, together with the Dordogne, produces 50% of French crop, there should be some around in the shell *en coque* for you.

● **Melon** *melon* Var: *Charentais*	May/June until September. Dep: Deux-Sèvres, Loire-Atlantique, Vendée.
● **Pear** *poire* Var: *Beurre Hardy, Comice, Passe-Crassane* (winter) *Williams*	Harvested from end-August to mid-November, sold August to April. Dep: Maine-et-Loire, Loiret, Sarthe, Indre-et-Loire.
● **Raspberry** *framboise*	Mid-June to mid-July. Dep: Loire-Atlantique.
● **Strawberry** *fraise* Var: mainly *Belrubi*	April until early August. Dep: Loire-et-Cher, Maine-et-Loire.

Based in the Loire Valley and the Sologne but very much aimed at the Parisian market: centres include Angers, Saumur, Romorantin, Vallée du Cher, Contres, Soings.

══════Worth Finding══════

● *Bourdaine* A pie of apples and preserved plums *confiture de prunes,* mainly encountered in the Maine.

● *Cassemusse Brioche* stuffed with fresh goat's milk cheese eaten with fresh fruit or grapes, especially in Ste-Maure.

● *Chouée* A great favourite in Angoulême, green cabbage tossed in masses of butter.

● *Cotignac* Quince cheese, one of the world's oldest sweet treats, sold in the Orléannais in wooden boxes. It was believed by the ancients to cure almost everything, especially hangovers and associated alcohol-related discomforts.

● *Datrée de choux* Cabbage, which should be the small green *piochon/piochou,* mixed with mashed potatoes and bathed with *beurre blanc.*

Angers has a broccoli named for herself, Sully-sur-Loire harvests the oriental *crosnes,* tiny tubers, Nantes and Angers grow *macres* water chestnuts, Chemillé grows enormous amounts of mint and camomile for vermouth. Le Mans has a local hazelnut *culroux* (redbottom), a local chestnut *nouzillard,* and also grows the important walnut variety *franquette.*

Nut oil is every bit as important and famous here as in the Dordogne; Tours makes it well, and so does Ste-Maure.

In short, the orchards and gardens that stretch either side of the Loire and its tributary rivers fairly bristle with opportunity for good eating. With its own good butter and cream, and that of neighbouring Normandy and the Charentes, with which to make lakes of *beurre blanc,* only those who are slow of learning, or too fast of driving, will fail to eat well.

CHEESE

Farm-produced goat cheeses abound in the green valleys of the Loire: some are mild, like *chavignol,* others far more goaty, such as the distinctive *pyramides.* Although *chèvres* predominate, you can also find a good selection of small flavoursome cow's milk cheeses in the valleys, the *olivet* being perhaps the best-known.

★ *Bondaroy au foin* From the Orléannais of soft cow's milk cheese with a tangy flavour that is cured for five weeks in hay-filled bins.

● *Chavignol-Sancerre* (Berry and the Sancerrois). A small flattened ball of mild, *chèvre* eaten as a dessert. It does not become a *crottin* (q.v.) until quite black and brown.

● *Crezancy-Sancerre* Similar to *chavignol,* a mild goat's cheese from the southern Loire area.

★ *Crottin de Chavignol AOC* A cheese with a reliable regional tradition and flavour, this has been made by the peasants of Sancerre since the 16th-century. It is now AOC protected. Made from full-cream goat's milk, these cheeses are small, white or ivory in colour and have a fine white mould. Best from March to November, the characteristic taste getting stronger with age. It is a favourite snack, may be grilled or marinated in white wine. Made in most parts of Cher and in small areas of Loiret and Nièvre (Burgundy). These cheeses were not called *crottin* until 1829, and the origin is a supposed reference to a small oil lamp with the same shape. When they are allowed to age and become black and horrid they are then the *crottin* referred to in the dictionary – horse droppings.

● *Entrammes* A typical unpasteurized washed-rind, cheese made in the monastery of Entrammes in Maine which made the original *Port Salut.*

● *Frinault* (Orléans) A small, strongly flavoured disc of cow's milk cheese, best in summer and autumn. 50% fat content. The *frinault cendré* is cured in boxes of wood ash for four weeks, which creates a waxier flavour and texture.

● *Gien* A *chèvre* or *mi-chèvre* made only on farms in and around Gien in the Orléannais region. Nutty flavoured; may also be cured in plane leaves or ashes.

● *Graçay* A recently-invented goat cheese from the Arnon valley; truncated cone weighing about 500g/1lb with dark blueish coating and dusted

with powdered charcoal.

● *Laval* Made by Trappists at the monastery of Laval in Maine, a washed-rind disc of cow's milk cheese. The body should have lots of tiny holes; pale rind and sharpish somewhat unexpected flavour.

● *Levroux* A Valençay-style cheese made around the fortified town of Levroux.

- *Ligueil* and *Loche* Commercially made *chèvres,* similar to a *Ste-Maure.*
- *Montoire* A fruity flavour to this small *chèvre* from the Loire valley shaped into the classic truncated cone. *Troo* is a variety.

★ *Oléron* A pure white fresh sheep's milk cheese from the Île d'Oléron. Mild creamy flavour and 40–45% fat content. Made in whatever shape and size attracts on the day. Mainly available in spring.

★ *Olivet bleu* (Orléans) Small disc of blueish skinned blue cheese; cured for a month in chalk caves of Olivet. It has a full but not sharp flavour and is made form cow's milk.

- *Olivet cendré* An *olivet* matured in wood ashes, and thus lower in fat (40%).
- *Pannes cendré* Low fat (20%–30%) cheese of skimmed cow's milk from the Orléanais. Strong flavour after curing three months in wood ashes. Seen mainly in late summer and autumn.
- *Romorantin* See *Selles-sur-Cher.*
- *St Benoist* or *St-Benoît* From St-Benoît-sur-Loire a farm-made disc (about 350g/14oz) made from partly skimmed cow's milk. Perhaps of monastic origin, but the pale rind has not been brushed or washed; fruity flavour.

★ *Ste-Maure Fermier* (Touraine) A popular *chèvre* with a goaty smell and strong taste. Cylindrically shaped and made on the farm, this cheese has straw running through it, said to indicate where the cheese broke and was stuck together again after unmoulding.
- *Ste-Maure laitier* A commercially produced version of the *fermier* with no straw. Often called a 'log'. *Verneuil* is another brand name.

- *Sancerre* A commonly used catch-all name for such *chèvres* as *chavignol, crezancy* and *santranges.*
- *Santranges-Sancerre* A tangy goat's milk cheese produced on farms in and around Santranges in Berry; shaped like a small flattened ball.

★ *Selles-sur-Cher* Said to recall the sweetness of life in the valleys of the Loire and Cher (which enjoy a fine climate), this is one of the well-known goat's milk cheeses that are covered with powdered charcoal. Lightly renneted curd is placed in moulds – unbroken curds are the secret to this cheese – and it is then salted and coated with ash and left to mature for 10 to 21 days. Mild in flavour it is best enjoyed from the end of spring until autumn. Protected by an *appellation contrôlée* the manufacture of these cheeses is limited to a few départements of Loire-et-Cher, l'Indre and Cher.

Also known as *Romorantin.*
- *Tournon-St-Pierre* A mild, nutty chèvre from Tournon, made on the farm. Tallish trimmed cone, and good in summer.
- *Valençay fermier* A mild goat's milk cheese produced on farms in the Loire area. Shaped as a low truncated pyramid, dusted with charcoal; best eaten from late spring to autumn although locals also macerate it in crocks for use in winter.
- *Valençay laitier* Known also as *pyramide,* a well-known goat's milk cheese made commercially all year using frozen goat's milk curds and powdered milk. A strong nose and slightly rancid taste. *Levroix* is the same thing; *chabris* is a brand name of commercial *valençay* and *levroux.*
- *Villebarou* A cow's milk cheese from the Loire that is fast disappearing. Distinguished by its appearance – a thin flat disc not wrapped but sitting on a plane leaf.

A DRINKER'S GUIDE

As a rule, drink all Muscadet, Sancerre and Pouilly Blanc Fumé as young as possible: avoid bottles over three years old. This holds true, too, for all other basic dry Loire whites; only Vouvray and Savennières will repay keeping. The very best Chinon and Bourgueil will last for 10 years; most reds will not improve after 5. The best sweet white Chenin Blanc wines, from a good vintage, can last a lifetime.

The last decade
1984 Average: beware high acidity in young wines. No great sweet wines.

PUDDINGS, PASTRIES & CONFECTIONERY

When it comes to the end of a meal, you've probably read it already, in the Fruit and Vegetable section, for with such luscious abundance of almost every fruit you don't have to try hard to find delicious and simple puddings.

It is the *tarte* that rules, with enough variations of pastry and of fillings to keep you amused differently each day. Lamotte-Beuvran in the Sologne is the home of the tarte *Tatin*, the upside down caramelized apple pie that bears the name of the hotel-keeping sisters, *les demoiselles Tatin*, who made it famous.

As you might expect, local prunes *pruneaux* feature quite as much in *tartes* as fresh fruits, sometimes whole, sometimes as rich purées, or stuffed with almonds or other dried fruits. Prunes soaked and then simmered in wine are a special favourite and are usually served teamed with one or other of the dairy products so featured – cream, cream cheese, junket *jonchée* or thicker curds *caillebotte*.

Gâteau de Pithiviers

Almonds have a special role here, for they flavour one of France's most famous pastries, that of Pithiviers and which is called just that or *gâteau de Pithiviers feuilleté*. The filling is *frangipane,* an almond pastry cream additionally flavoured with rum, and this is one case where I did bother to travel to the eponymous town to try a speciality and where just being there enhanced the flavour, I'm sure. Puff-pastry is seen in *millefeuilles* as specialities in almost every pastry shop.

Plenty of honey traditionally found its way into cakes in the past and still does in *pain d'épices* gingerbread. Interestingly, the idea of putting honey into cakes is only a few centuries old; when the ancient Romans and Greeks spoke of honey cakes, they meant cakes which had been soaked in a honey syrup, as they still do in Greece and the Middle East. Honey also flavours a number of sweets, of which *rigolettes* are probably the ones most worth trying.

Blois, already mentioned for its *pistoles* has also a reputation for chocolates and, unusually, makes a chocolate cake con brio – *gâteau chocolat de Blois*. When you get to the borders of this large area you find other influences creeping in, especially that of Brittany into Anjou. Pancakes and *crêpes* become more common, filled, naturally, with fruits.

And then there are the biscuits. Nantes invented the *petit beurre* biscuit. Illiers, (called Combray by Proust) is famous for *madeleines* and regardless of what Nancy thinks its claim is, Illiers seems to have made *madeleines* since the Middle Ages; it was one of the stops on the long pilgrimage to Santiago de Compostela in Spain, the sign of which journey was a scallop shell, and the shape of these biscuits remembers that. Sablé-sur-Sarthe argues with all of Normandy about who invented those other almost universal biscuits the *sablés*. The choice everywhere will probably calm most argument, but should you want a single centre in which to eat pastries, cakes and confectionary, the craftsmen of Le Mans have the Gault Millau accolade of being specially gifted *doué*.

1983 Good, large harvest. Excellent sweet wines to keep; other wines make good drinking now.
1982 Large, ripe crop which lacked acidity. Neither red nor white wines will keep, with the exception of a few good Vouvrays and Bourgueils.
1981 A small harvest of good wines. Nearly all are ready.
1980 Quality only average. Most fading fast.
1979 Not a year that suited the Loire. Drink with caution.
1978 Quite good for sweet wines; average elsewhere. Drink soon.
1977 Mean year. Drink only under duress.

1976 Excellent sweet wines. Seek out: they are just beginning a glorious life. Some Bourgueil is still magnificent.
1975 The very best Chinon and Bourgueil will still be worth trying. Some good lightweight sweet wines.
1974 Avoid.

Previous greats; (for the best sweet Chenin Blanc wines only) 1969, 1964, 1961, 1959 and 1947.

Spirits & Liqueurs

Anjou makes an *eau-de-vie* and *marc* plus spirits and sweet liqueurs from its many fruits, so do all the *côteaux* of the Loires.

Bon Marché

Below is a selective list of markets plus some fairs *foires* of special interest. Check with the local S.I. for precise locations and time changes.

LOIRE-ATLANTIQUE
Bernerie-en-Retz Fri; **Châteaubriant** Wed; **Coueron** Thur, Fri; **Donges** Thur; **Guémené-Penfao** Fri; **Loroux-Bottereau** Sun, *Wine Fair 1st Sun Mar;* **Nantes** Daily especially Sat; **Rezé** Tue, Fri, **Savenay** Wed; **St-Brévin-les-Pins** Thur, Sun; **St-Etienne-de-Montluc** Fri; **St-Nazaire** Daily exc Mon, *Onion Fair 15 Sept;* **St-Sebastien-sur-Loire** Tue, Fri; **Trignac** Wed; **Vallet** Sun, *Wine Fair 3rd week Mar.*

MAYENNE
Ballée Wed; **Château-Gontier** Thur & Sat am; **Cuille** Thur; **Fougerolles-du-Plessis** Fri; **Gorron** Wed; **Lassay-les-Châteaux** Wed; **Laval** Tue & Sat am; **Mayenne** Mon; **Montsurs** Tue; **Port Brillet** Tue; **Pré-en-Pail** Sat; **Renazé** Fri; **Villaines-la-Juhel** Mon.

SARTHE
Allonnes Sat; **Aubigné Racan** Sat; **Beaumont-sur-Sarthe** Tue; **Bonnetable** Tue; **Bouloire** Tue; **Cérans Foulletourte** Tue; **Conlie** Thur; **Coulaines** Thur & Sat am; **Ecommoy** Tue; **La Ferté-Bernard** Mon; **La Flèche** Wed, Sun; **Fresnay-sur-Sarthe** Sat; **Loué** Tue; **Le Lude** Thur; **Mamers** Mon; **Le Mans** daily except Mon, Fri most important; **Marolles-les-Braults** Thur; **Noyen-sur-Sarthe** Sat; **Parcé-sur-Sarthe** Thur; **Sablé-sur-Sarthe** Mon, Wed; **Savigné-l'Evêque** Thur; **La Suze-sur-Sarthe** Thur; **St-Calais** Thur.

EURE-ET-LOIR
Arrou Fri; **Auneau** Fri; **Authon-du-Perche** Tue; **Bonneval** Mon; **Brezolles** Wed; **Brou** Wed; **Chartes** Wed, Thur, Fri, Sat; **Châteaudun** Tue, Thur, Sat; **Châteauneuf** Wed; **Dreux** Sun, Mon, Fri; **La Ferté-Vidame** Thur; **Illiers-Combray** Fri; **Janville** Wed; **Maintenon** Thur; **Nogent-le-Rotrou** Sat; **Senonches** Fri;

St-Remy-sur-Avre Sat; **Toury** Wed; **Voves** Tue.

LOIRET
Beaugency Sat; **Châtillon-sur-Loire** Thur; **Courtenay** Thur; **Gien** Sat am, Wed am (poultry); **Malesherbes** Wed; **Montargis** Wed am, Sat; **Orléans** Tue, Wed, Thur, Sat; **Puiseaux** Mon: **St-Denis de l'Hôtel** Sun am, *Cheese & Junk Fair 1st Sun June;* **St-Hilaire-St-Mesmin** Mon, Wed & Fri (May to Sept), daily in cherry season; **Sully-sur-Loire** Mon; **Tigy** *Asparagus Fair 3rd Sun in May.*

CHER
Aubigny-sur-Nère Sat; **Baugy** Fri; **Bourges** Daily; **Châteaumeillant** Fri; **Culan** Wed; **Dun-sur-Auron** Sat; **Graçay** Thur; **Henrichemont** Wed; **Mehun-sur-Yèvre** Wed; **Sancerre** Sat; Tue (Mar to Nov); **Sancoins** Wed; **Savigny-en-Sancerre** Thur; **St-Amand-Montrond** Wed, Sat; **St-Florent-sur-Cher** Fri; **St-Germain-du-Puy** Thur; **Vailly-sur-Sauldre** Fri; **Vierzon** Tue am, Wed, Sat.

INDRE
Argenton-sur-Creuse Tue, Sat; **Bélabre** Fri; **Le Blanc** Sat, Wed; **Buzancais** Fri; **Châteauroux** Sat, Mon (cattle); **Châtillon-sur-Indre** Fri, Sun; **La Chatre** Sat; **Cluis** Fri, Sun; **Issoudun** Wed, Sat; **Levroux** Mon, Fri; **Luant** Wed; **Mézières-en-Brenne** Thur; **Neuvy-St-Sepulchre** Fri, Sun; **Neuilly** Fri; **St-Benoit-du-Sault** Thur; **St-Gaultier** Fri; **Tournon-St-Martin** Tue; **Valençay** Tue; **Villedieu-sur-Indre** Wed.

INDRE-ET-LOIRE
Amboise Wed (glass), Fri, Sat, *Melon Fair 1st Wed Sept;* **Azay-le-Rideau** Wed, *Wine Fair last weekend Feb, Apple Fair last weekend Nov;* **Bléré** Fri, Sat, *Melon Fair 2nd Fri Sept;* **Bourgueil** Tue, *Wine Tasting 2nd Tue Sept, Chestnut Fair 4th Tue Oct;* **Celle Guenand** Wed, *Melon Fair 1st Sun Sept;* **Chambray-les Tours** Thur, Sun; **Chinon** Thur, Sat, Sun; **Joué-lès-Tours** Sun, Wed, Thur, Fri; **Ligueil** Mon; **Loches** Wed; **Montlouis-sur-Loire** Thur, *Wine*

Fair 3rd weekend Feb; **St-Branches** *Onion Fair 2nd Wed April, Melon Fair 29 Aug;* **Ste-Maure-de-Touraine** Fri, *Cheese Fair 1st Sun June;* **St-Pierre-des-Corps** Tue, Wed, Fri, Sat, Sun; **Tours** Daily (poultry Wed & Sat), *Garlic & Shallot Fair 26 July;* **Vouvray** *Wine Fair 2nd weekend Aug.*

LOIR-ET-CHER
Blois Daily, Sun am; **Contres** Fri; **Droué** Tue; **Herbault** Mon; **Mondoubleau** Mon; **Montoire-sur-le-Loir** Wed; **Montrichard** Mon; **Neung-sur-Beuvron** Tue; **Romorantin-Lanthenay** Wed, Sat; **Salbris** Thur; **Savigny-sur-Brave** Tue; **Selles-sur-Cher** Thur; **St-Aignan** Sat; **St-Amand-Longpré** Thur; **Vendôme** Fri.

MAINE-ET-LOIRE
Angers Daily; **Avrillé** Tue; **Beaufort-en-Vallée** Wed; **Beaupreau** Mon; **Candé** Mon; **Chalonnes-sur-Loire** Tue, Fri; **Champigné** Tue; **Châteauneuf-sur-Sarthe** Fri; **Chemillé** Thur; **Cholet** Tue, Wed, Thur, Fri, Sat; **Combrée** Fri, Sat; **Fontevraud l'Abbaye** Wed, Sat am; **Jallais** Fri; **Lion d'Angers** Fri; **Montjean-sur-Loire** Thur; **Montreuil-Juigné** Fri; **La Pommeraye** Mon; **Les Ponts-de-Cé** Fri; **Pouance** Thur; **Rochefort-sur-Loire** Wed; **Romagne** Mon; **Saumur** Sat, Tue, Wed am, Thur; **Segré** Wed.

VENDÉE
Aizenay Mon; **Beauvoir-sur-Mer** Thur; **Challans** Tue, Fri; **Chantonnay** Thur, Sat; **Châtaigneraie** Sat; **Coex** Sat; **Les Epesses** Fri; **Les Essarts** Wed (eggs & butter), 1st Wed (poultry); **Fontenay-le-Comte** Sat; **La Gaubretière** Mon; **Les Herbiers** Thur; **Luçon** Wed, Sat; **Montaigu** Tue, Thur, Sat; **Moutiers-les-Mauxfaits** Fri; **Notre-Dame-de-Monts** Sun am; Thur, Sat; **Les Sablés d'Olonne** Daily in summer; **St-Gilles-Croix de-Vie** Tue, Wed, Thur, Sat; **St-Hilaire-de-Riez** Thur, Sun **St-Jean-de-Monts** Daily at beach, Wed, Sat; **St-Michel-en l'Herm** Thur; **Talmont-St-Hilaire** Tue, Sat; **La-Tranche-sur-Mer** Tue, Fri, Sat & Sun in season; **Vendrennes** Wed (butter).

Not My City – But Yours

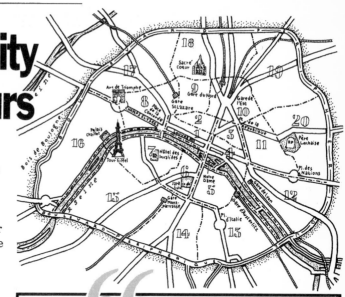

On countless visits to Paris I learned, as millions of others must have done, that the pleasure of seeing a famous painting, revisiting a favourite royal apartment, or simply of sailing on the Seine is only complete if you blend it into contemporary life rather than viewing it as an obligatory set lesson in history or tourism. People rarely go home to boast of seeing the Eiffel Tower or the Mona Lisa; it is taken for granted. The memories they share are of discovering a sumptuous new ice cream flavour or a creamier pastry, being told to take home a jar of **Fauchon's** passion-fruit syrup to store for an instantly-made sorbet, of **L'Ecluse** wine bars where you may learn of fine clarets by the glass and *foie gras* by the slice, of serendipity in a Russian tea shop which serves cheese scones, of going to a cookery class given by a princess. For any one of these meant they had slipped under the skin of Parisian Paris, and were no longer onlookers.

There is something else about Paris. As capital and seat of kings it has more than its own glory to reflect. It must dutifully mirror the produce of all the ancient or forgotten fiefdoms and king-

> **In which you will discover...**
> ● Kitsch for kitchens and a street of chopped liver ...
> ● Virgin choices, ice-cream queues on an island and the best cookbook shop in France ...
> ● Bread that is Art, haunted bars and cookery lessons with a Princess ...
> ● Madeleine glitz relief and Maxi-Minim's snacks ...
> ● Grand Mother Goose's bargains and a Paradise of tableware ...
> ● Engadine amid Abbesses ...

doms within France's modern borders. Transport, commerce and nationalism make this more likely than ever, and the interested and discerning may, through Parisian markets, shops and restaurants, build up a culinary portrait of the country. This is why I have here

broken the even mosaic of this book, and devoted this section more to the discovery of Paris than to the Île-de-France which surrounds her.

Your Own Routes

The guidelines I have chosen are based on my beliefs and

experience – that food is the best and most universally interesting way to discover any city. So, I have taken 11 of the central *arrondissements* of Paris, combined them to make six areas, and produced a guide to their most important or interesting food-related establishments, from open and covered markets to department stores, from tiny tea shops and butchers to antique shops, cheese shops, bakers and ironmongers.

The maps accompanying each section are purposely simple so you may, say, after reading the guidance given, work out a route for yourself either to cover it all, or to pander to your special interests. Restaurants are fairly limited, purposely; there is an ocean of advice on the subject and you probably already have a guide, and enough sense to paddle your own canoe.

Comparisons

One tip for those not enamoured of cities, who are speeding through to elsewhere, or who are marooned in Paris by time or funds: take advantage of the huge range of regional foods offered here to learn, and to prepare yourself for journeys elsewhere in the country. For comparison is the finest way to learn anything and you can't compare without some basis. Also, be bold. The addresses I have given are but a framework upon which to build your own adventures.

Turn left or right, linger longer or hurry past. It is not my Paris I want you to discover, but yours . . .

MARKET PLACES

In the *arrondissements* guide I've indicated some of the markets, but below is a checklist for the market researcher in a hurry.

3e arrondissement
Enfants Rouges
(covered)
39 rue de Bretagne
open 8am to 1pm and 4 to 7.30pm
Sundays 8am to 1pm

5e arrondissement
Maubert
(uncovered)
place Maubert
open 7am to 1.30pm Tuesday, Thursday
and Saturday

Monge
(uncovered)
place Monge
open 7am to 1.30pm Wednesday, Friday
and Sunday

Port-Royal
(uncovered)
bd Port-Royal beside the Val-de-Grâce
hospital
open 7am to 1.30pm Tuesday, Thursday
and Saturday

6e arrondissement
Saint-Germain
(covered)
between rues Lobineau, Clement and
Mabillon
open 8am to 1pm and 4 to 7.30pm
Sundays 8am to 1pm

Raspail
(uncovered)
bd Raspail, between rues du Cherche-
Midi and de Rennes
open 7am to 1.30pm Tuesday and Friday

7e arrondisement
Saxe-Breteuil
(uncovered)
place Breteuil, where ave de Saxe meets
ave de Ségur
open 7am to 1.30pm Thursday and
Saturday

RUNGIS AND THE MARKETS OF PARIS

The transferral of the Parisian wholesale food market – *Les Halles* – from central Paris to Rungis, just beside Orly airport was as devastating to Parisians as losing a vital organ: *Les Halles* was the 'stomach' of Paris and for a while there was a feeling of starvation, or at the very least unfamiliar gnawing hunger pains. But the new freedom of movement in the ancient central streets, the creative developments above and below ground, and the obvious success Rungis has made in maintaining traditional choice and freshness of produce has finally won the hearts and stomachs of the suspicious Parisians.

For the visitor, however, it means the demise of one of the great Parisian experiences: you can no longer share onion soup early in the morning with men who have already done a hard day's work (probably unloading the onions). Rungis is one of the largest wholesale markets in the world, and does not have

8ᵉ arrondissement

Europe
(covered)
rue Corvetto, between rues de Maleville and Treilhard
open 8am to 1.30pm and 4 to 7pm
Sundays 8am to 1pm

10ᵉ arrondissement

Porte St-Martin
(covered)
31 and 33 rue du Château d'Eau
open 8am to 1pm and 4 to 7.30pm
Sundays 8am to 1pm

St-Quentin
(covered)
85 onwards bd Magenta
open 8am to 1m and 4 to 7.30pm
Sundays 8am to 1pm

Alibert
(uncovered)
rue Alibert to rue Claude Vellefaux
open 7am to 1.30pm Thursday and Sunday

18ᵉ arrondissement

La Chapelle
(covered)
rue d'Olive
open 8am to 1pm and 3.30 to 7.30pm
Sundays 8am to 1pm

Ornano
(uncovered)
bd Ornano between rues Mont-Cenis and Ordener
open 7am to 1.30pm Tuesday, Friday and Sunday

Crimée
(uncovered)
4 to 30 bd Ney
open 7am to 1.30pm Wednesday and Saturday

Barbès
(uncovered)
contre-allé of bd de la Chapelle, opposite Lariboisière Hospital
open 7am to 1.30pm Wednesday and Saturday

Ney
(uncovered)
bd Ney between rues Jean-Varenne and Camille-Flammarion
open 7am to 1.30pm Thursday and Sunday

Ordener
(uncovered)
rue Ordener between rues Montcalm and Championnet
open 7am to 1.30pm Wednesday and Saturday

PARIS EN CUISINE

This small company offers a dozen ways to get under the skin – and behind the green baize doors – of culinary Paris. In a series of demonstrations, visits or walking tours – mainly during summer – American enthusiast Robert Noah offers the chance for you to combine the breads of *Poilâne* and cheeses of *La Ferme St-Hubert* with fine wines; to watch demonstrations in such renowned kitchens as those of the Beauvilliers; to learn about chocolate at *La Maison du Chocolat*, pastry at *Millet* and sugar work with the acclaimed M. Tholoniat. You can devote your time to bread; to visiting a market (including Rungis) with a chef; to touring restaurant kitchens; to tasting wines with top *sommeliers* or to actually cooking, during one-week courses in restaurant kitchens.

If you are venturing further afield, Robert Noah can also arrange classes at the National School of Pâtisserie in Yssingeaux (Auvergne) or with great chefs such as Michel Guérard, Bocuse or Boyer, among others.

Telephone in advance or write for the brochure to:
Robert Noah,
Paris en Cuisine,
78 rue de la Croix-
Nivert,
75015 PARIS
Tel: Paris 4250.04.23
(Telex 680461)

much time for the casual rubbernecker. If it is high on your agenda though, contact Robert Noah, American foodie of *Paris en Cuisine* (qv); he arranges a limited number of early morning visits. Frankly, you might find that you are only seeing rather more of what is everyday in the street markets of Paris.

In central Paris alone there are over 80 markets, covered and uncovered, for you to find and enjoy; some 70 of these are food markets, *marchés alimentaires*. Some are permanent, some are peripatetic; you'll most enjoy those stumbled upon serendipitously. If you are a marketomane, contact the Mairie de Paris (tel: 276.49.61) for their special free leaflet (in French), *Les Marchés de Paris*. Even with the leaflet, it is better to check with your hotel first.

Of course, it's not all food. Don't forget the flower market on the Île-de-la-Cité or the fabulous flea market *marché aux puces* at Clignancourt, still with sensational treasures and junk and some delicious steamy bistros and restaurants where you may listen to a Piaf imitator as you eat your *moules*.

DEPARTMENT STORES
Les Grands Magasins

It's tons of fun to find speciality shops and to see and taste new things – but unless you go to something more ordinary as well, you've not actually been to France, and you remain a tourist; what's worse, a tourist with airs. Markets are a start, and a very good one, but they aren't always in the next street, and even if they are, you may have hit the wrong day or time. What do you do? Make sure you know where the department and chain stores are.

France's provincial towns have kept their department stores, deliciously fading though some of them are. A quick swing through their food department shows what people like to cook, eat and drink locally, the china, glass and cookware show how fashion conscious they are, and the clothes and furniture indicate the inroads 'designers' have or have not made.

Most universal, and most definitely not to be missed, are the self-service chains of *Prisunic* and *Monoprix*. (Self-service is *libre-service*.) They sell marvellous plates, cups, glassware, provençal pottery, super French crystal and kitchen gadgets at ridiculously low prices – important to remember if you are unable to raid a hypermarket (qv). Most have excellent food departments if you are self-catering, or simply want

something to munch on your way past. Good for basics to bring home, too – jam, coffee, oil etc.

Most visitors go to *Galeries Lafayette* and *Au Printemps* and think they've done the department stores. No, they have not. *Monoprix* and *Prisunic* are all over Paris and they really are worth making time for. Here are some others worth tracking down:

● **Bazar de l'Hôtel de Ville,** *55 rue de la Verrerie, 4e Quincaillerie* is probably my favourite French word. It means hardware and ironmongery, and BHV is renowned for the most complete range possible. Good book section and kitchen goodies, too.

Another big branch at *119 rue de Flandre, 19e*.

● **Au Bon Marché,** *38 rue de Sèvres, 7e* Two great buildings divided by the rue du Bac; called the *doyen de nos grands magasins* by Gault Millau. A specially good food department on the ground floor of *Magasin 2*.

● **Galeries Lafayette,** *48 bd Haussmann, 9e* Main shop; also *Tour Montparnasse, 17 rue de l'Arrivée, 15e* Important and influential for fashion and style – in everything.

● **Au Printemps,** *bd Haussmann, 9e* Main store; other branches: *République, 63 rue de Malte, 11e; Nation, 21 cours de Vincennes, 12e; Italie Cen-*

tre Commercial Galaxie, pl d'Italie, 13e; Ternes, 30, ave des Ternes, 17e. This last is one of the most interesting; it has an excellent food department but behind and beside it is one of the best permanent food markets in Paris, and ave des Ternes has outstanding branches of the chain stores, bars, cafés, restaurants, *traiteurs* and *charcuteries* of note.

● **La Samaritaine,** *rue du Pont-Neuf, 1er* Two huge buildings with some amazing internal architecture that lurches you back to the days when nice men wrapped parcels with brown paper and string which came never-endingly from hidden spools. You can buy *everything*, living or dead, and there are amazing views of all Paris from the 10th floor of *Magasin 2*, but the terrace there is closed from October to March. Especially exciting when they have their sales, but I'm mad about it anytime.

● **Aux Trois Quartiers,** *17 bd de la Madeleine, 1er* As its position might lead you to expect, very traditonal and classic in atmosphere, especially in its twinset and tweed clothes. It feels somewhere between London's Harvey Nichols and Harrods; and has a nice tea salon on the 4th floor where you can lunch lightly and, usually, elegantly.

ARRONDISSEMENTS 1, 2 & 3

The Tuileries, Louvre and Palais-Royal, Comédie-Française, Les Halles, Bibliothèque Nationale, Bourse, Archives Nationales and Temple.

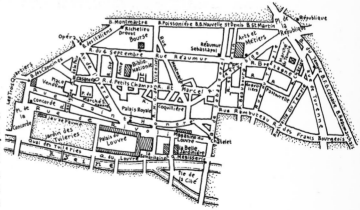

It's too easy to saunter through the Tuileries, gasp at the Impressionists in the Jeu de Paume, hit the highspots of the Louvre and then head back to the place de la Madeleine: so I've started you at the other end of these *arrondissements* – as you explore the culinary attractions you'll find the cultural and civic sites listed above in somewhat reverse order. When you finish, though, you'll have seen some of the crustier side of Paris, perhaps explored a food market or two, found where *Les Halles* used to be and, I hope, be more in a frame of mind to view the Louvre and Palais-Royal as grand but living houses rather than just as museum buildings. You'll enjoy what they have to show much more – the *Musée des Arts Décoratifs*, entered from the rue de Rivoli, is a stunning collection of authentic rooms from every period of French domesticity, grand and otherwise.

This part of the route starts at the upper eastern corner of the 3e *arrondissement* (métro: **Temple** or **République**). Much of it is through areas which are not at all grand, but in which the 'old Paris' is still visible.

● **Brocco,** *180 rue du Temple, Pâtisserie* and tea salon; amazing art-deco temple, marble walls, high painted ceiling, superb façade shows off excellent cakes and pastries – *charlotte aux poires, tartes aux framboises.* Go for the decor and be doubly pleased that the goodies are good too.

● **Souche Laparra,** *157 rue de Temple* Cutlery; very good value and craftsmanship in silver and silver plate of all styles.

● **Comptoir du Chocolat et des Alcools (CCA),** *108 rue de Turene* Alcohols and chocolates; dark, foreboding shop with old-fashioned displays and surly salespeople, excellent prices for quality wines and fine chocolates compensate. There is a minimum purchase required, about £15.00.

● **Confroy,** *34 rue Saintonge* Bakery; wholewheat *baguettes* and every other grain-bread baked in a wood-fired oven, modest assortment of pastries including almond *tartelettes* and prune turnovers; nicely restored interior. Highly recommended for quality.

● **Cannelle,** *10 rue de Bretagne* Natural products; interesting *artisanale* soaps, oils and herbs, also biscuits; extravagant display window.

● **Bassaguet Morin, Charcuterie Fine,** *17 rue de Bretagne* Prepared food; small square room filled with delicious things – eggs in smoked salmon aspic, pork in aspic, cooked meats, well prepared *pâtés* and salads.

● **J. Durand,** *25 rue de Bretagne* Pastry and ice cream; strawberry tarts overflowing with fruit, beautifully decorated coffee and walnut cake, boxes of sweets and miniature cream puffs, *Père Duchesne* almond tart: enormous weekend queues.

● **Cours des Halles,** *29 rue de Bretagne* Produce; lovely fruit attractively presented.

● **Marché des Enfants Rouges,** *39 rue de Bretagne* Small covered market of 20-30 stalls; 3 fishmongers, butchers, fruit and vegetable stalls. Fishmongers sell salt cod *morue,* spider crabs, tiny live crabs, smoked fish kebabs. Coffee shop **Le Café Torrefié** at *35 rue Charlot* in the market has two kinds of arabica, robusta and roasts on premises. Teas also.

● **Caves de Bretagne,** *40 rue de Bretagne* Opposite market entrance. Beers, *cidre bouché,* wines and spirits from all over France. *Fauchon* luxury tinned and bottled goodies. Good range of champagnes and calvados also. Friendly.

➤If you turn up *rue Picardie* or the streets either side of the Mairie, you'll find the covered *Marché du Temple.*◄

● **L'Oustal,** *68 rue des Gravilliers* Prepared foods and regional products from Auvergne and the Rouergue; tiny shop with specialities produced on farms including *confit de canard* preserved duck, *marrons glacés,* sausages, homemade *fouace* (*brioche* with candied fruit). Whole cured hams hang from the ceiling.

PARIS

- **Ambassade d'Auvergne,** *22 rue du Grenier-St-Lazare* Restaurant; rustic and warm with exposed beams; consistently good regional food; start with cabbage and bacon salad, then try one of the daily specials like duck stew or *cassoulet* with lentils, accompanied by wine from the area, perhaps a St-Pourçain.
- **Durand,** *147 rue St-Martin* Grocery: worth a detour for the belle-époque decor – the front window is framed by a milkmaid painted on tiles and the interior is colourfully tiled as well, with marble work surfaces; stocks essentials like eggs, tea, jam and also goat cheese and walnut bread from *Poilâne* (qv).
- **Duthilleul & Minart,** *14 rue de Turbigo* Professional clothing; uniforms for butchers, bakers, chefs and waiters; excellent source for aprons and dishtowels and some of the natural fibre garments can be quite chic out of their normal context.
- **Central Union,** *28 rue de la Grande-Truanderie* Gifts; super-creative modern kitsch objects which look like something else, but enormous good humour and French style.
- **Jounna,** *45 rue Montorgueil* Butcher; narrow shop with high marble altar in the front displaying meat on one side and poultry on the other.
- **Montorgueil Cuisine,** *49 rue Montorgueil* Prepared food; divine odours will lure you in; food simple but tasty; try the roast pork and sample some of the salads.
- **Stohrer,** *51 rue Montorgueil* Pastry and chocolate. Stand opposite to appreciate the building: business began in 1730. Tall display cases stacked high with *bonbons* and pastries – the *Ali-Babas* are a house speciality, as are buttery *pains au chocolat* and sparkling strawberry tarts; delightful original decor with Louis XV-era ladies cavorting on the walls and ceiling.
- **Rue Montorgueil Market,** *80 onwards rue Montorgueil* Gutsy, noisy and sometimes bloody remnant of the days when *Les Halles* was just across the street. Americans living in Paris tend to be sniffy about it, but *they* can afford to shop at *Fauchon* or the markets of the Left Banks. Visitors may be astonished at the butchers, for instance, but they should be entranced, knowing that here, along with *rue de Montmartre*, they will be more in touch with Paris than the Beaubourg centre, slick (and virtually uncleanable) though it is. Chefs from some fairly smart restaurants shop here daily, so it's good enough for me.
- **Lair,** *98 rue Montorgueil* Regional products from Auvergne; a small branch of the chain of shops distributing locally-cured Auvergnat ham, sausages and farm cheese. The place for a terrific *cantal, laguiole* or, midweek, fresh auvergnat cheeses. Extraordinary *charcuterie* from exotic pieces of the pig.
- **P. Capron,** *100 rue Montorgueil* Bakery and pastry shop; huge croissants, pretty apricot and strawberry tarts. Small square pound cake, *le Weekend*, a speciality.
- **Comptoir Landais,** *52 rue Montmartre* Southwest regional products; *foie gras, confit*; try *croustades*, apple or prune, in tissue-paper thin pastry with fly-away tops. Individual or party-size.
- **Detou,** *58 rue Tiquetonne* Speciality ingredients; important shop for *pâtisserie* ingredients packaged in bulk – chocolate, flour, candied violets, bags of salted nuts, boxes of biscuits; also sell smoked salmon roe and pickled herring, along with a good selection of wine and champagne in modern part. Good prices.
- **La Bovida,** *36 rue Montmartre* Restaurant supplies; spices in bulk, aluminium moulds in many shapes and sizes, dishes, glassware and cooking vessels.
- **A. Simon,** *33 rue Montmartre* Restaurant supplies; wine glasses by the dozen, huge lucite salad bowls, stainless steel or silver-plated cutlery, china in myriad patterns, all restaurant quality at wholesale prices; must buy in quantity. Also at *36 rue Etienne Marcel*, over the road.
- **Big-Gel,** *30 rue Montmartre* Frozen food; only large quantity packages – 5kg/12lb boxes of crayfish, 2kg/4½lb bags strawberries (all stemmed, good for making sorbet).
- **Foie Gras Luxe,** *26 rue Montmartre* Commercial prepared foods; raw *foie gras* or mixture of duck and goose livers. Known for prosciutto, Bayonne ham, *rillettes*, Ardennes smoked ham, inexpensive *choucroute*.
- **Les Vins de St-Chinian,** *18 rue Montmartre* Wine; huge vats at the back of the shop with hoses for refilling your own bottles with their dry red wine; other vintages by the case; tinned foods – *cassoulet* and *confit d'oie*.
- **M.O.R.A.,** *13 rue Montmartre* Restaurant supply store since 1814; portable ovens and professional size food processors; fantastic range of moulds and cake pans and almost everything else, including books and video tapes of cooking demos.
- **Marguerite Dorlin,** *11 rue Montmartre* Fish market; large shop, good quality and an interesting variety of fish – skate cheeks, sabre, baby salmon.
- **Pietrement Lambret,** *8-10 rue Montmartre* Poultry and meat, mainly wholesale; an old-fashioned operation selling chickens and hams from a large open shop, raw *foie gras*, year-round, fresh or imported depending on season.
- **Labeyrie,** *8 rue Montmartre* Speciality foods; *foie gras* raw, *mi-cuit* or conserves, *mushrooms*, truffles under distinctive red, gold and black label; deluxe tinned foods are not as good as expected.
- **Quatre Saisons,** *4 rue du Jour* Houseware; pitchers and decanters, glass domed cheese platters, canisters and kitchen gadgets;

lots of pine furniture, too.

● **Battendier,** *8 rue Coquellière* Prepared foods; renowned since the early 1800s and favoured by everyone from the Napoléons to de Gaulle. Fresh Colmar *foie gras, charcuterie, andouillettes* and *boudins noir* black puddings; also excellent *plats du jour* to take away or enjoy on the few pavement tables outside.

● **Le Pavillon Baltard,** *9 rue Coquellière* Alsatian restaurant; numerous varieties of *choucroute*, most famous for their fish version.

● **Vattier,** *14 rue Coquillière* Restaurant; oyster bars fill the sidewalk between *Vattier* and *Battendier*, outdoor tables, oysters on bed of ice in front; a better place for oysters and shellfish than anything else.

● **Alsace aux Halles,** *16 rue Coquillière* Alsatian restaurant; oysters and *choucroute* in a quaint looking half-timbered place; the proliferation of restaurants in *Les Halles* dates from era of the old market.

● **Petit Quenault,** *56 rue Jean-Jacques Rousseau* Speciality ingredients; chocolate of every kind and bitterness in bulk (1kg/2¼lb blocks), dried wild mushrooms, nuts (500g/1lb minimum), fruit and herb vinegars, nut oils. *Mi-cuit foie gras* towards end of year.

● **Dehillerin,** *18-20 rue Coquillière* Cookware and kitchen equipment heaven; huge selection of *everything* – individual tart moulds in every size, every conceivable shape and design of dessert moulds, copper bowls and balloon whisks; go early in the day if you want a civil reception and don't expect advice.

● **Boucherie Coquillière,** *32 rue Coquillière* Butcher; meat neatly presented with the usual plastic roses, a chance to compare French *Charollais* beef with Angus from Britain.

● **Oriental,** *32 rue Coquillière* Take-away food; hot spring rolls to munch as you go; smells so good you can't walk past.

● **Au Bain Marie,** *20 rue Hérold* Tableware, culinary memorabilia; great, small and unusual items suitable for gifts – fish bone plates, bird-shaped lemon squeezer, egg cups and fantasy salt and pepper shakers; antique asparagus plates and menu holders; extensive collection of antique linens, books and fascinating old menus upstairs.

● **La Langouste,** *8 pl des Victoires* Old-fashioned supplier of live fish, crayfish and lobsters from own tanks; frozen shellfish also sold. Open in morning *only* for collection of orders.

● **Au Panetier** *(Lebon), 10 pl des Petits Pères* Bakery; lovely old shop; ceramic murals of parrot theme gives character and sense of another era; strawberry tartlets and onion turnovers, wood-oven bread including poppy seed *pavot* and pepper *poivre*.

● **Lucien Legrand,** *1 rue de la Banque* Wine specialist; the decor hasn't changed for two generations. Excellent selection of inexpensive regional wines plus spirits, port etc of great age. Confectionery and spices too.

➤Detour into the covered shopping area **Galerie Vivienne** (one entrance is up *rue de Banque* past *Lucien Legrand*) to step back into another time.◄

● **Willi's Wine Bar,** *13 rue des Petits-Champs* Restaurant and wine bar; light meals, salads, hot daily specials with unmatched selection of Côtes-du-Rhône. Cheerful, chic and sometimes snobby in spite of – or because of – the English owner. At least the staff speak your language. There is another branch at *18 rue des Halles*.

➤For a scenic shortcut to *rue de Richelieu*, take *rue de Beaujolais* (just down from *rue Vivienne*) and go through the *passage de Beaujolais*, up the steps on the right. There are many restaurants back there and it is quiet.◄

● **Tachon,** *38 rue de Richelieu* Cheese shop; unprepossessing established specialists with

unusual and fine farmhouse cheese. Labels give fascinating information. *Epoisses* is particularly good here. Nearby neighbourhood speciality food shops and fruit and vegetable stands make this detour most enjoyable.

● **Chez Pauline,** *5 rue Villédo* Restaurant; absolutely classic French food, including regional and seasonal favourites in a setting that is almost a cliché of what you expect a bistro to be. Tons of fun.

● **Boucherie Ste-Anne,** *64 rue Ste-Anne* Butcher; offal, rabbit, young duckling (not just duck by any other name); milk-fed veal is the real speciality.

● **Aux délices de Paris,** *64 rue Ste-Anne* Prepared food, grocery; fruit, milk, eggs, the usual salads and *quiches*, ethnic specialities – spring rolls from a Vietnamese chef, taramasalata and stuffed vine leaves from a Greek.

● **Grandmère l'Oye,** *7 rue de La Michodière* Tiny shop specializing in *foie gras*; raw to make your own *terrines*; formed into cylinders or in *terrines*; cooked *mi-cuit* (the best); and in conserve (tinned). Thought to be among the cheapest in Paris; small wine selection. No credit cards taken.

● **Jean Gabart,** *14 rue de La Michodière* Bakery; fantasy shaped loaves in display cases flanking door; individual lemon curd tarts and huge fluffy meringues in window; sandwiches and a few essential groceries like eggs and milk.

● **La Tour de Jade,** *20 rue de La Michodière* One of the best Chinese-Vietnamese restaurants in one of Paris's oldest buildings; economical set menu, large selection *à la carte*, first class take-away too.

● **Paul Corcellet,** *46 rue des Petits-Champs* Condiments, exotic food; always something new at this shop. Wondrous jams (including green tomato), fruit vinegars, flavoured mustards, unusual rums and liqueurs, house wines and champagnes. I defy you to walk out empty-handed.

● **Maison des Foies Gras,** *9 rue Danielle-Casanova* Slices of *foie gras* from the *terrines* in the window, cans of *pâté de foie gras*, and in season fresh truffles and *foie gras*; they also sell chocolates, *bonbons*, liqueurs. Open until 11pm, including Sundays, also for fruit, cheese, cooked dishes.

● **Boucherie Bernard,** *19 rue Danielle-Casanova* Butcher; large selection, not necessarily the best quality, but not expensive; good *charcuterie* and salads.

● **Flo Prestige,** *42 pl du Marché St-Honoré* Prepared food; imaginative and tasty dishes of class – for which you may pay accordingly; also offers pastry, ice cream and wine. Associated with *Brasserie Flo* one of the best and most authentic in Paris.

● **Potron,** *20 pl du Marché St-Honoré* Fish shop founded in 1795; huge tiled room with beautiful fish fanned out on shaved ice so fresh they seem still alive – many are, in tanks.

● **Marché St-Honoré** The large market halls are nearly deserted due to an impasse with the municipal administration; I hope it is a temporary situation, but the few remaining merchants queried were not encouraging.

● **Chédeville et Bourdon,** *12 rue du Marché St-Honoré* Commercial butcher and prepared foods; substantial *choucroute* and hearty potato salads, Corsican sausages and recommended *andouillettes*; they supply *terrines* and *pâtés* to **Maxim's** and other restaurants.

● **Le Rubis,** *10 rue du Marché St-Honoré* Wine bar, restaurant; the 'local' bar for this neighbourhood has been invaded by the young smart set; simple meals of tripe, sausages, black pudding etc, sandwiches and snacks anytime; interesting wine selection.

● **Au Jardin d'Espagne,** *8 rue du Marché St-Honoré* Fruit and vegetables; large fresh produce shop; attractively arranged.

● **Au Ducs de Bourgogne,** *4 rue du Marché St-Honoré* Burgundian products; smoked duck breast, *andouillette, croustades*, regional wines and liqueurs.

● **Jean Danflou,** *36 rue du Mont-Thabor* Alcohols; unique – and hard to find; at the left rear corner of the courtyard, go up to the 1st floor and ring the bell; a small tasting room to try the full range of *eaux-de-vie, marcs* and cognacs of great distinction. No obligation or pressure to buy, but you will.

● **Le Soufflé,** *36 rue du Mont-Thabor* Restaurant; a bit touristy but isn't that what you are? The soufflés are very good, which is the important thing.

● **W.H. Smith & Son,** *248 rue de Rivoli* Bookshop but not like the one in your High Street. Light meals and traditional teas upstairs under the eaves; food book section with menu dictionaries and guides to French regional food among the cookbooks; extensive array of guidebooks, too.

➤While in the *rue de Rivoli*, find time to explore the marvellous department stores: **La Samaritaine** between *rue de l'Arbre* and *rue de la Monnaie*, **Magasins du Louvre** on the *pl du Palais Royal* and **La Belle Jardinière** between *rue du Pont Neuf* and *rue des Bourdonnais*.◀

● **Arcasa,** *269 rue St-Honoré* Houseware; small, carefully chosen array of crystal, tableware, china and linens; furniture upstairs – good for gifts.

● **Godiva,** *237 rue St-Honoré* Belgian chocolates; a treasure cave of foil-wrapped *bonbons* twinkle under crystal chandeliers in large glass display counters; expensive but appreciated.

● **Seladoux,** *215 rue St-Honoré* Pastry shop; a window full of sparkling fruit tarts and fresh cakes that is hard to pass.

● **Bossu,** *310 rue St-Honoré* Prepared foods; buy a snack to munch on the street or your whole dinner, soup to sweet.

● **Aux Beaux Fruits de France,** *304 rue St-Honoré* Produce; neat, orderly artful displays of perfect fruit and vegetables.

● **Ferme St-Roche,** *203 rue St-Honoré* Cheese; good selection of farmhouse cheeses, especially *chèvres*; homemade pasta, too.

● **La Galerie des Vins,** *201 St-Honoré* Wine; under new management and just refurbished, specialist for rare vintages; glasses and corkscrews.

● **Gargantua,** *284 rue St-Honoré* Prepared foods and bakery; known for giant croissants and pastries, enormous array of prepared salads, roasts, desserts; good *charcuterie* and a few tables for a quick meal.

● **Verlet,** *256 rue St-Honoré* Coffee and tea salon; a mecca for serious lovers of coffee or tea for here you can buy the lot. Tea or coffee will also be blended to your taste and you can get a light meal. A goodie for the enthusiast, stimulating to the amateur.

● **Delamain,** *155 rue St-Honoré* Wonderful old bookshop which moved here from the Palais Royal in 1880; pretty glass canopy over the door and a small selection of French cookery books among the treasures.

● **Antiquités pour la Table,** *170 galerie de Valois* Under the arcades of the Palais Royal is an extraordinary trove of dinner services, glassware, tea and coffee sets, from the 1800s to the 1950s. You can bargain, find missing pieces, buy huge or small services and generally have a marvellous time.

● **Louvre des Antiquaires,** *pl du Palais Royal* Antiques market; a well organized self-administered alliance of about 250 reputable antique dealers displaying their treasures in a renovated former storage hall of the Louvre; of particular culinary interest is *l'Herminette* – tureens and terrines, tools and scales, on the ground floor; other shops offered Moustiers and Quimper (Brittany) pottery, Rose

Medallion porcelain, pewter plates and steins, crystal and silver decanters, antique silver cutlery and beautiful old wooden platters, bowls and implements. Not cheap but convenient – and warmer than the flea markets in the winter!

- **Maison Micro,** *144 rue St-Honoré* Greek products and ingredients; drums of olives and capers, sacks of lentils, pistachios, chickpeas, olive oil, Greek wine.
- **Porcelaine Blanche,** *108 rue St-Honoré* Tableware, bistro crockery, terrines and pie moulds, Limoges seconds – mostly in plain white, of course. Has a clone in London's Notting Hill Gate.
- **Clément Blanc,** *90 rue St-Honoré* Butcher; huge commercial operation with shop open to public as well; if you are there about 7am or 4pm you'll see deliverymen in their bloodied, white hooded coats carrying in whole sides of meat.
- **Le Temps Retrouvé,** *6 rue Vauvilliers* Old linens, lace tablecloths, blouses and slips; old dinner services, silver flatware and glasses, too; mainly 19th-century rather than classic antiques.
- **Papeterie Moderne,** *12 rue de la Ferronerie* Signs; marvellous minute place for stationery freaks; crammed with all sorts of signs that are part of Parisian daily life – butcher's tickets, cheese tickets with names of common cheeses, innumerable others including WC 'mixte' and the perennial *chien méchant* (beware of the dog). Great souvenirs.
- **Forum des Halles,** *rue Ste-Opportune* Shopping centre; cavernous and variable but worth an expedition if you have time on your hands and comfortable shoes on your feet. Look for FNAC for an extensive selection of cookery books at low prices, the museum shop for reproduction porcelain plates, and Habitat, the great British export.

ARRONDISSEMENTS: 4 & 5

Pompidou Centre, Marais, Hôtel de Ville, Tour St-Jacques, Jewish Quarter, Place des Vosges, Bastille, Notre Dame – Île-de-la-Cité, Île-St-Louis, the Quais, Latin Quarter, Sorbonne, Polytechnique, Musée de Cluny, Musée National d'Histoire Naturelle, Panthéon.

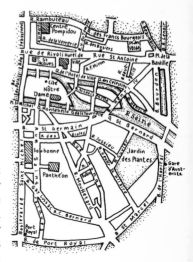

All seafood lovers should touch their cap at the Tour St-Jacques, in the place St-Jacques on the border with the 1ᵉ *arrondissement* – for this was the gathering point for the tens of thousands of pilgrims who annually walked in penance wearing scallop shells to the shrine of St James at Santiago de Compostela in Spain, for whom the first travel guide was written and for whom *coquilles St-Jacques* were considered cheap and easy nourishment.

Domestically, these two *arrondissements* include the single - but - special - friends households of the fast refurbishing Marais, the student hangouts of the Latin Quarter and the great silent town houses of Île-St-Louis and of the President himself; thus the food available is particularly wide ranging. You can eat *falafel* in pitta or salt beef and cheesecake, watch the breaking of the bread at Notre Dame, queue for the best ice cream of your life in rue St-Louis-en-l'Île, shop in expensive places for antiques or oils, dawdle down the slope of the rue Mouffetard market or, find one of the best cookbook shops in France which will send you regular newsletters on request.

- **Laurence Roque,** *69 rue St-Martin* Tableware and china; tablecloths, tablemats and everything else in every imaginable colour, design and cloth – it seems. Tea things and pine furniture confirm the British origin of lots of the wares.
- **Bazar de l'Hôtel de Ville,** *55 rue de la Verrerie* See **Department stores** p.74.
- **Lescen-Dura-Eurocave,** *63 rue de la Verrerie* Wine paraphernalia – grape presses, casks, corks, bottles, glasses, corkscrews, wine coolers and a wide range of wine racks; volcanic rock to balance the humidity if your *cave* is too damp.
- **A la Ville de Rodez,** *22 rue Vieille-de-Temple* Products from the Auvergne; as well as the expected hams, *fouace* (sometimes with *cédrat* amongst its glacé fruits) and *cantal* cheese, here will be more homely things, *salaisons* and *andouillettes* and other internal piggy bits.
- **Tout au Beurre,** *45 rue Vieille-du-Temple* Pâtisserie; shop through the window for your choice and don't overlook the chocolates. The luscious *praline noire* comes highly recommended.

● **Maison des Colonies,** *47 rue Vieille-du-Temple* Coffee merchant; a spacious shop with wooden floors and excellent, inexpensive range of coffees from almost everywhere, plus blends. The teas are just as varied and include both classic mint, jasmine and rose plus modern mango, blackberry and the like; honey, jam, biscuits. Building was once the home of the ambassadors from Holland.

● **La Cave de Gambrinus,** *13-15 rue des Blancs-Manteaux* Wines and beers, particularly specializing in the latter. There are perhaps 400 types from over 30 countries. To help there are suggested assortments by country or type. Very interesting wines, liqueurs and spirits, too.

➤ *Rue des Rosiers* is the ancient centre of Jewish life in the Marais, and remains so. The quarter is typically confusing with wonderful buildings on winding streets. If touring is getting too much, head for number 27 or number 7 for sustenance, or to number 4 for no-nonsense relaxation. ◀

● **Le Roi du Falafel,** *34 rue des Rosiers* Exotic grocery; a reminder that Jews have their roots in the Middle East. Olives, nuts and everything else from that part of the world. Things to try include *falafel*, hot cakes of chickpeas or beans in a pitta bread with salad, now almost the national dish of Israel.

● **Finkelsztajn,** *27 rue des Rosiers* Pastry shop specializing in central European goodies, but with a Madagascan proprietor; poppy seed loaf, fruit filled *pavés*, strudels. And have they got a cheesecake for you!

● **Jo Goldenberg,** *7 rue des Rosiers* Restaurant and delicatessen – a real Jewish community centre; chopped liver, salt beef, cheesecake (it's not *so* Orthodox, you understand) and a lovely noisy place to go for Sunday lunch, whatever your faith.

● **Hammam Saint Paul**, *4 rue des Rosiers* Nothing to do with food unless you have overeaten, but a wonderful old-fashioned steam bath and sauna with a restaurant overlooking the plunge pool. Men Thursdays and Saturdays; women Wednesdays and Fridays. Beauty treatments plus healthy food. A buried treasure unearthed for you . . .

➤Now that you are here, you might like to detour to the *rue de Sévigné* and the *Musée Carnavalet*, 400 years of Parisian history in Madame de Sévigné's house. A little further up at *5 rue de Thorigny, 3e* is the *Hôtel Salé*, home for Picasso's collection of Picassos. The *hôtel* was built by M. Aubert with the proceeds of his salt tax collecting for Louis XIV – hence the name.◀

● **Felix & Arthur and Dattes & Noix,** *2 and 4 rue du Parc-Royal* The first is an ice cream parlour, the second a *salon de thé*, both owned by the same brothers and both remarkably creative; ice creams and sorbets in one and excellent cakes, salads and savoury goodies in the other. Chic in a Marais sort of way, too.

● **L'Arlequin,** *13 rue des Francs-Bourgeois* Glassware; 19th and 20th-century glasses, tumblers and storage jars. Good place to poke about in to find something you didn't know you wanted.

➤Good poking about too in some of the shops of the arcades of *place des Vosges*, built in the 17th century for Henri IV's royal spectacles and surrounded by magnificent town houses – look for the *trompe l'oeil* brickwork.◀

● **Clichy,** *5 bd Beaumarchais* Tea salon, *pâtisserie* and chocolates – frescoed views of the Marais right beside the Bastille. Painted by M. Bugat who also gets praise for his croissants and pastries and his lavish chocolates and seasonal window displays.

● **Brasserie Bofinger,** *5 rue de la Bastille* The oldest and one of the most wonderful belle-époque restaurants in all Paris, Specializing in Alsatian food, like a *brasserie* should, but also outstanding seafood and good house wine. You can order until 1am every morning. A favourite of Jean Cocteau.

● **Caves des Pyrénées,** *25 rue Beautreillis* Wide range of wines from all over France but particularly the lesser known ones from the southwest and Pyrénées, with such names as *Tursan* and *Irouleguy*.

● **Au Cheval du Marais,** *32 rue St-Antoine* Horse butcher; marble fronted purveyor of richly coloured horse flesh for roasting, stewing, frying and braising, plus, less expectedly, the 'other parts' – tongue, heart and so on. Regional non-horse products include *cassoulet* and *confit d'oie*.

● **Poissonnerie de la Bastille,** *51 rue St-Antoine* Splendid fish shop with inspired art nouveau tiling of traditional Breton fishing scenes. You might find samphire, kebabs with five types of fish, sea urchins and live eels. It's a delight to talk to the staff who take pleasure both in their surroundings and their excellent produce.

● **Les Fils Peuvrier,** *43 rue St-Antoine* Dairy; spotless white tiled shop selling cheese, butter, cream, *crème fraîche* and eggs. The *chèvres* are usually excellent. It has a slight atmosphere of yesteryear.

● **Caves St-Antoine,** *95 rue St-Antoine* Wines and spirits; vast but cramped emporium specializing in clarets, but with grand names from every region plus *vins de pays* bottled on the premises. Terrific selection of beers, too.

➤Here you should cross the border into the 11e – actually you simply turn left out of *rue St-Antoine* into *bd Richard Lenoir* to the *Marché de la Bastille*, but only on Thursdays and Sunday mornings.

It's a huge neighbourhood market with over 150 stalls of noise and banter. Mainly fruit and vegetables but look for **Pierre Lucien** whose homemade cream cheeses sit dripping in pottery moulds, for the mushroom stall which had *girolles* and *petits rosés* in July but overflowed with varieties 'n autumn, fish-stalls and butchery and *charcuterie* sellers with sausages galore from the regions, At the Bastille end Arab traders predominate. If your French is good, look for M. Chamillard **'A La Poule d'Or'**, who actually produces the poultry he sells live. He expects to turn over 15,000 eggs on Sunday as well as rabbits, quails, really good homemade *pâtés*, ducks, geese – the lot sold with humour and lots of advice and recipe tips. You'll really feel you are in France here.◄

● **Suba,** *11 rue de Sévigné* Hungarian *charcuterie*; the place to buy a supply of both hot and sweet paprikas, whole or ground, so you can make your own flavours. Hungarian wines, meats and sausages and unusual savoury strudel rolls. Not open Sundays.

● **Pâtisserie St-Paul,** *4 rue de Rivoli* A young artist in pastry, butter, cream and chocolate who opens early each day Wednesday to Sunday. His *baccarat de Chantilly* is layers of chocolate and whipped cream; and his *quatrequarts* or pound cake is baked with apples.

● **Confiserie Rivoli** *17 rue de Rivoli* Sugared almonds *dragées* of some variety and in many packagings, plus sweet regional specialities, such as *calissons d'Aix* to look at.

● **Izraël (Le Monde des Épices),** *30 rue François-Miron* Speciality and exotic foods; in business over 50 years and overflowing with sacks of nuts, grains and pulses. Imported tinned specialities, especially from the Middle East (you may find Egyptian white truffles – relatively tasteless but cheap and good for impressing others). Prepared foods and baskets for sale.

● **La Poussière d'Or,** *11 rue du Pont-Louis-Phillipe* Secondhand tableware, linens and laces of the best quality plus tea sets, glasses and food related items.

● **Au Pain du Sucre,** *12 rue Jean-du-Bellay* A sugar shop; an enormous array of sugars of all sorts, colours and flavours, plus fantasy shapes. Chocolates, *dragées*, honey and fruit jellies *pâtés de fruits*, too; A real sweetie . . .

● **Le Jardin en l'Île,** *8 rue Jean-du-Ballay Charcuterie*; specialities from Gascony, wines from the southwest and a big selection of *pâtés* and *terrines*. Tinned things include wild piglet casserole *civet de marcassin*, but few of these are worth the money.

● **La Tropicale,** *4 rue Jean-du-Ballay* Ice cream shop, part of a small group; 45 flavours with summer and winter specialities. Expect to queue in busy times. Not open until 1pm.

● **Brasserie de l'Île-St-Louis,** *55 Quai de Bourbon* Another Alsatian *brasserie* of excelling reputation and excellent situation to revive the visitor. Nothing warms like hot *choucroute* in winter, or refreshes like chilled, bone-dry Alsatian riesling in summer.

➤*Rue St-Louis-en-l'Île* is one of my favourite Parisian streets, not least because it is the local for some of the most exclusive addresses in town yet retains a High Street feel. Bakeries, cheese shops, *traiteurs* and antiques, with glimpses of the Seine down the side roads. Some shops work the old way, with Monsieur doing the work and Madame sitting hawk-like at the cash register. After 9pm the *Angelis* restaurant (no 31) has jazz, and you can't get much more Parisian than that.◄

● **Lecomte,** *76 rue St-Louis-en-l'Île* Cheese shop; very good with the rich creamy fresh cheeses of the Île-de-Paris, *bries, fountainebleaus* – that sort of thing. Excellent *chèvres* in spring. Every cheese matured on the premises.

● **A l'Olivier,** *77 rue St-Louis-en-l'Île* After over 150 years in the rue de Rivoli this speciality oil shop is re-established here. Truly fabulous smells assail you as you discover virgin olive oils, sesame and nut oils, and every other type of oil; plus fruit vinegars, essential oils for aromatherapy – and super-succulent Breton sardines in olive oil. Best present ever for elderly relatives . . .

● **Aux Fruits de France,** *72 rue St-Louis-en-l'Île* Fruit and vegetables; fairly reliable place to find whatever is special and in season in the regions if you are cooking for yourself, or are interested.

● **Boucherie Mon Gardic,** *44 rue St-Louis-en-l'Île* Butcher; prize-winning *andouillettes, poulets de Bresse,* happy veal *veau de lait fermier* (with certificates to prove it) and free-range guinea fowl *pintadeau.* Small family-run establishment you can trust.

● **Les Panetons,** *47 rue St-Louis-en-l'Île* Bakery; a fabulous range of breads including ryes with walnuts and raisins. Savoury tarts and *quiches,* cheesecake, fruit tarts and pretty creations; *Arabella* is red currants on sponge base topped with meringue.

● **Lefranc,** *38 rue St-Louis-en-l'Île* Cheese shop; farmhouse *bries* and other wonders are aged in the 17th-century cellars beneath this shop. I like to watch the aristocratic men who carefully choose two or three cheeses as their contribution to their nearby lunch and dinner tables. Excellent selection of *chèvres*.

● **Berthillon,** *31 rue St-Louis-en-l'Île* Best ice cream in Paris and some of the longest queues; think of a flavour and it will be there, especially seasonal fruits, which may alternatively be made into sorbets. I like the bittersweet chocolate ice cream and the *marron glacé* – what's better is some of each. Also sold around the corner at **Restaurant Cadmios** (*17 rue des Deux Ponts*) and at **Le Flore-en-l'Île** (see below) your feet need a rest.

● **Haupois,** *35 rue des Deux-Ponts* Bakery; considered one of the best in Paris for traditional breads. Small loaves offer the chance to experiment. Super cakes and the expected *sablés, florentines* and so on.

● **Le-Flore-en-l'Île,** *42 quai d'Orléans* Tea-shop and café; a corner site overlooking Notre Dame where you can sit and dawdle over a Berthillon ice or a cup of tea – or both. Classical music soothes, too.

● **Lerch,** *4 rue due Cardinal-Lemoine* Alsatian baker; *kugelhofs* year round, wondrous fruit tarts according to what is seasonal and traditional gingerbreads for Easter and Christmas.

● **Boulangerie Courtois,** *18 bd St-Germain* Bakery; good *baguettes,* and the fruit charlottes are recommended by the locals.

● **Aux Produits de Bretagne et des Pyrénées,** *42 bd St-Germain* Regional produce; business must boom, for this shop is closed from June to mid-October. When open it is a tumble of wonders of exceptional quality, especially for air-dried hams, fresh sausages and *confits.* Cider from Brittany.

➤*Place Maubert* is the scene of a busy and good market on Tuesday, Thursday and Saturday mornings. The high presence of police does not mean dishonest traders – the President lives just around the corner at *22 rue de Bièvre*; number 33 is Yorgantz, a Russian-Armenian piano bar (!) with blinis, stuffed aubergine, kebabs . . . When the market isn't there, the high-class locals are still served well. In one corner at 31 and 35 are Vietnamese shops with exotic herbs, vegetables and fruits, oriental teas, dried squid, betel leaf; at number 35 there are also cooking utensils and cookbooks. In between the two is a Vietnamese restaurant if you want to try before you buy. Directly opposite is:◄

● **Charcuterie St-Germain,** *47 bd St-Germain* Charcuterie, *traiteur*; really superb selection of made-up dishes plus individual savoury tarts and *quiches, croques-monsieur* and genuine-looking *flamiche*, the leek tart from Picardie.

● **Than Binh,** *18 rue Lagrange* A branch of one of the Vietnamese food stores on Place Maubert.

● **Madam Bardon,** *Box 11, Quai de Montebello* Recommended by Patricia Wells *(Food Lover's Guide to Paris)* for old French cookbooks if you can cook in that language. Not usually there Sunday or Monday.

● **Gilbert Jeune,** *5 pl St-Michel* Books and records; you may have to search a little over several floors but there are plenty of cookbooks and food-based-books in this huge shop; very good records, too.

➤*Rue de la Harpe* is tourist-orientated and sometimes pushily so with constant admonitions for you to eat here or there. Mainly Arabic or Greek, nonetheless it's fun and the pastry shops are better and more authentic than the restaurants.◄

● **Au Gargantua,** corner of *rues de la Harpe* and *Huchette* Another spot for oversized croissants and sandwiches plus terrific speciality bread, salads and prepared foods.

● **South Tunis,** *17 rue de la Harpe* Ethnic pastry shop; perhaps the most authentic of the many syrup-dribbling and sometimes brightly-coloured pastries here. The ones using rosewater or orangeflower water syrup and an almond or pistachio filling are the most voluptuous.

● **Piccadilly Pub,** *92 bd St-Germain: le pub Anglais à la Parisienne* but I thought you'd like to know where it was . . .

● **Au Gourmets de Cluny,** *86 bd St-Germain* Pâtisserie and cafe; good apple turnovers and they seem to like to do unusual coloured things with meringue.

● **Au Canard Laqué,** *70 bd St-Germain* Oriental restaurant

– could be the place to have a French Chinese take-away. Good barbecued pork and crisp duck.

➤*Rue de la Montagne-Ste-Geneviève* is a nice neighbourly street with a touch of the east as you enter at one end but a more solid French regional ambiance at the other.◄

● **La Triperie des Carmes,** *2 rue de la Montagne-Ste-Geneviève* Offal from head to toe; M. Léonard prides himself on being able to bone a calf's head in 5 minutes and on personally buying and preparing everything displayed. The only man I know who seems to *fondle* tripe, liver, feet and, well, the dangly bits . . .

● **Jean-Baptiste Besse,** *48 rue de la Montagne-Ste-Geneviève* Wine shop of clutter but magnificence; provided M. Besse survives still (he opened the shop in 1932), he will find you treasures and specialities of great and small wines (perhaps a Château-Chalon), armagnacs and cognacs.

● **Apple Tart,** *50 rue de la Montagne-Ste-Geneviève* Bakery; a localised clientèle enjoys crusty breads and fruit flans and tarts from this small shop.

➤*Place de la Contrescarpe* is close to the Ecole Polytechnique and thus a popular student hang-out. Swing through it and *rue Rollins* to *rue Monge*, one of the best local haunts in Paris.◄

● **King Henry,** *44 rue des Boulangers* Beers and spirits, and very proud of holding the record, they think. More than 500 brands of beer for sale and at least 200 of whisky and all the liqueurs and 'funnies' you've heard of but never seen.

● **Au Ducs de Gascogne,** *31 rue Monge* Charcuterie and *traiteur*; part of nationally franchised chain of shops specializing in Gascon produce. All the goose and duck products including *foie gras* are actually from their own stock rather than imported. Some nice tinned sauces and one of the places to get genuine *magrets* which can only come from ducks fattened for their livers. Excellent recipe sheets.

● **M. Grivet,** *28 rue Monge* Pâtisserie and baker; specializes in stocking sweet specialities from the regions – *pruneaux d'Agen, grisettes de Montpellier, poutous de Béziers, castilles de Perpignan* etc – fascinating but most of them are boringly similar and based on almond. Best go for his own chocolates unless you are writing a thesis.

● **Au Cochon d'Auvergne,** *48 rue Monge Charcuterie*; an attractive shop that tries hard to have a good range of regional produce – one of the few in which I've found goose rillettes *rillettes d'oie*.

● **Mon Kraemer,** *60 rue Monge* Cheeses; large shop with marble counters and unmistakeable but not unpleasing odour. Lots of raw milk *fermier* cheeses from the regions, plus *fromage frais*, jams and honeys.

● **Morin,** *70 rue Monge* Pâtisserie; I liked the bavarois best, especially the blackcurrant *cassis* and the raspberry *framboise*. Other goodies to tempt include hand-dipped chocolates.

➤Wednesday, Friday and Sunday mornings you'll find a market in *place Monge*. Stall 61 sells particularly good whole rye breads from the Vendée, but they are not the sort of thing to pop into a suitcase. *Le Villefranche* on Place Monge features Niçoise specialities.◄

● **Pharmacie,** *74 rue Monge* Herbal pharmacy; over 2,000 medicines available, most seeming to be laxatives, antirheumatic or slimming – or a combination. Interesting display details medicinal properties of herbs.

● **Comptoir du Chocolate et des Alcools,** *84 rue Monge* Discount alcohol and chocolates; part of chain. Liquor is now better than the chocolates and regular promotions and gift packs are usually excellent – and genuine – value. Perhaps the place to buy more expensive spirits – cal-

vados, armagnac and the like. Minimum purchase required.

➤*Rue Mouffetard* has been a stronghold of *le petit commerce* and a food market since the 14th century. Once closely associated with horse trading and in the 19th century street of artisans, its partly cobbled climb is changing again as small shops and cafés become discos and boutiques and tourist traps. Yet there is tremendous atmosphere, and as Paris constantly changes, the Greek, Spanish, Brazilian, Lebanese and Martiniquais restaurants (at the Contrescarpe end) merely reflect this. Make sure you have enough time to explore the side streets and discover far more than can be listed here. Much of the criticism of produce or service is simply part of the Parisian act. But as a visitor, do you care? It's village life.◄

● **Traiteur Ara,** *106 rue Mouffetard* Arabic and Eastern specialities with specialities home made by the Turkish-Armenian owner. Cheeses in oil, *labna, poutargue,* Russian and Turkish wine and raki.

● **Le Moule à Gâteau,** *111 rue Mouffetard* Pastry shop chain that usually turns up in busy market streets. Everything baked with butter and everything sold by the portion. Good and honest, and much preferred by me to the overdecorated, glazed creations of smarter looking places.

● **Les Panetons,** *113 rue Mouffetard* Modern bakery; range of breads of different grains plus savoury tarts and *quiches*; the watercress one is excellent. Fresh pasta too.

● **Poissonnerie A. Rault,** *125 rue Mouffetard* One of the biggest of the fish shops and thus varied enough to keep you fascinated for ages.

● **La Briocherie de St-Médard,** *158 rue Mouffetard* Butter bakery; specializes in *brioches*.

● **Le Village Africain,** *2 rue de l'Arbalète* Exotic grocery; intriguing range of African fruit

and vegetables and such exotica as powdered shrimp, dried fish and *gnagna* – that's right, *gnagna*. . .

● **Le Fournil de Pierre,** *6 rue de l'Arbalète* Bakery – part of an acclaimed group specializing in wholemeal breads *pain complet*, but also makes a 7-grain loaf and very good spinach pies.

● **Coutellerie,** *102 rue Mouffetard* Knife shop; a proud survivor of rue Mouffetard the way it was. An Auvergnat family-run shop with a full range of knives from Laguiole in the Aveyron.

● **Aux Vrais Produits d'Auvergne** Regional produce; enormous selection of air-dried sausages and outstanding hams hang from the ceiling. So much else to sell, including fascinating cheeses, that both produce and customers spill onto the street.

● **La Cave du Languedoc,** *42 rue Daubenton* Wine shop; although stocking a good range of southern wines, there is much else of interest here.

● **La Tuile au Loup,** *35 rue Daubenton* Provençal gifts and books; handicrafts, ceramics and such – plus books about the region and its products. Good for gentle research before you head south.

● **Quincaillerie,** *24 rue des Patriarches* Ironmongers; an Aladdin's cave of economical cookware, reasonably priced pottery bowls, casseroles, cheese moulds, baskets and the like.

● **Les Délices d'Aphrodite,** *4 rue de Candolle* Greek restaurant and *traiteur*; fun place that really bustles at lunchtime, plus everything you need for Greek cooking.

● **Porcelaine Blanche,** *119 rue Monge* Tableware; seconds, ends of ranges and overstocks are the best bargains amid crockery, cutlery and glassware of style and standards.

● **La Ferme du Périgord,** *3 rue des Fossés-St-Marcel* Regional specialities from the Périgord including *confits* and truffles in season.

● **Jadis et Gourmande,** *88 bd de Port-Royal* Sweets and chocolates of almost every kind, from caramels to peppermints, and wonderful fruit jellies including quince *coing*. Chocolate is made into fantastic things. Great for nicely-packed, pricey presents.

● **Le Verre et l'Assiette,** *1 pl Alphonse-Laveran* Exceptional book shop; the only shop in France to combine collections of food and wine books. With more than 2,000 titles, a regular newsletter and very helpful attitude they are a major source of support to food writers and enthusiasts and deserve every franc you care to spend.

● **Aux Cornets de Murat,** *22 rue St-Jacques* Pastry shop; lovely stained glass panels, large selection of *petits fours* (decorated bite-sized cakes), many other cakes.

● **La Ferme Villier,** *202 rue St-Jacques* Grocery; not just a general store, but picturesque and well maintained.

● **Charcuterie Laurent,** *204 rue St-Jacques* Marvellous 1900s decor with mirrored walls, converted gas lamps; full of hams and sausages, *pâtés*, prepared dishes, cheese, wine – you can buy a picnic or a whole meal.

● **La Brûlerie,** *2 rue des Fossés-St-Jacques* Coffee; the divine scent of fresh roasted coffee will lure you in; also jams, teas and biscuits.

● **Ferme Ste-Suzanne,** *4 rue des Fossés-St-Jacques* Cheese shop and restaurant; small store with a large classic selection, a collection of antique curd ladles adds atmosphere; the restaurant offers a simple and tasty menu of cheese specialities.

● **Boulangerie Moderne,** *16 rue des Fossés-St-Jacques* Bakery; anything but modern in decor or content, the bread and pastries are based on traditional recipes and techniques; don't miss the delighful painted tile ceiling.

➤ *Rue Clotaire* leads to the Panthéon. ◄

ARRONDISSEMENTS 6 & 7

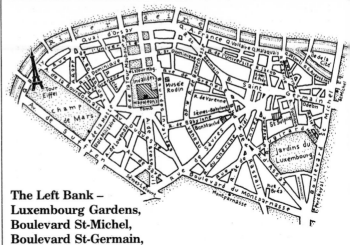

The Left Bank – Luxembourg Gardens, Boulevard St-Michel, Boulevard St-Germain, Ecole des Beaux-Arts, Invalides, Napoléon's Tomb, Musée Rodin, Eiffel Tower.

You'll find three famous cooking schools close to the Eiffel Tower in the 7e, presumably because here you'll also find some of the most expensive food shops and markets in all Paris and *no-one* dare spoil the produce there. Or perhaps it's because no-one can afford to eat regularly in **Le Drugstore** or on the glittering terraces of the cafés either side of ever-fashionable Boulevard St-Germain, that locks the sometimes selfconscious 7e into the livelier and more literate 6e. White Russians seem still to rule, Napoléon's Empire is striking at **Le Récamier** and names like **Petrossian, Christian Constant, Barthélemy, Lenôtre** and **Poujaran** supply the *ton* with luxurious or perfect foods, and the observer with entertainment and a bittersweet taste of the life lead by politicians, aristocrats and Americans in Paris.

The 6e seems more public and has better places to eat and drink. Indeed **Le Procope** is where coffee was first sold in Paris in 1686. Oscar Wilde ended his life in **Hotel le Bélier** and its bar is a terrific place to toast his turn of phrase. Picasso lived it up in the **Café de Flore** and Hemingway gave readings at **Aux Deux Magots**, where Sartre was a regular. Now the public idolise those of the fashion world based hereabouts, and its leaders are to be seen at **Brasserie Lipp**, but only at *certain* times and at *certain* tables.

Definitely not to be missed is **Poilâne** the baker, if only because someone described the place as being 'where art meets baking'. Very Left Bank, that.

● **Comtesse du Barry,** *1 rue de Sèvres* Speciality food store; famous for mail order of *foie gras, magret de canard, terrines*. Other stores at *13 rue Taitbout 9e, 88 rue Mozart, 16e*.

● **Vigneau Desmarest,** *105-107 rue de Sèvres* Caterers; everything is beautifully presented but pricey. Handmade ravioli and pasta, *pain Poilâne*; the *charcuterie* is their pride.

● **Eurasia,** *52 rue de Sèvres* Oriental market with takeaways. Breaded prawns, spring rolls, pot stickers.

➤ There is a very good street market on Tuesday and Friday on *bd Raspail* between *rue du Cherche-Midi* and *rue de Rennes*.

Rue du Cherche-Midi dates back to the 15th and 16th century when *cherche-midi* meant someone who begged for food at midday, the time of the day's main meal. Antique shops and discount designer shops at lower end; upper end by Sèvres-Babylone very trendy – and pricey. ◄

● **La Tropicale**, *128 rue du Cherche-Midi* Ice cream shop; takeaway cones 1-3 scoops; honey and pine nuts, *miel et pignons*, blackcurrant *cassis*, passion fruit *fruit de passion*. The shop in the 4e has places to sit.

● **Belusa**, *86 rue du Cherche-Midi* Tea salon which doubles as an antiques shop; good selection of teapots and curiosities. Large choice of teas including apricot and almond. Light lunches. *Tarte canadienne* is walnuts and maple syrup.

● **L'Eté Indien**, *102 rue du Cherche-Midi* Tea salon with marble-topped tables and original prints. *Tartine de chèvre:* ice cream includes pear *poire* and pistachio *pistache*.

● **Casa Pascal**, *15 rue d'Assas* Economical china, mainly French and mainly white; an opportunity to buy things we don't make, such as pierced dishes for radishes.

● **Petit Bacchus**, *13 rue du Cherche-Midi* Wine shop with daily tastings of 3 wines. Small restaurant specialises in excellent ham and *rillettes*. On Saturday afternoons in autumn and winter, winemakers are often there.

● **Mère Clos**, *13 rue du Cherche-Midi* Butcher; owned by Alain Testu whose awards line the blue and white tiled walls. *Prêt-à-cuire* ready to cook includes *canard aux pêches* duck with pea-

ches, *rôti florentine* lamb, and guinea fowl dishes.

● **Poilâne**, *8 rue du Cherche-Midi* Boulangerie set in a 14th-century Gothic abbey and probably the best known in France. Owned by Pierre Poilâne, who is famed for his bread designs, of which the most famous is the cluster of grapes. It is rumoured that Salvador Dali commissioned him to make a bedroom out of bread after he saw a bread chandelier hanging in M. Poilâne's office. The wheat used in baking is grown and milled to M. Poilâne's secret specifications. The sour-dough bread is baked around the clock in wood-fired ovens, in kitchens hewn from rock 500 years ago. It is now flown all over the world. Look for the 2kg *pain de campagne*; apple tarts, and *pain aux noix* walnut bread. Closed Sundays.

● **Soleil de Provence**, *6 rue du Cherche-Midi* Foodstore; packed with vats of olives and oils. Flower oils, sweet almonds oil, soaps, jams, *vin d'orange*. Organic honey from Paul Tardieus in Provence. Closed Sundays.

● **Hélène Fourner-Guérin**, *25 rue des Sts-Pères* Antique shop specialising in 18th century porcelain from Strasbourg, Rouen and Sceaux; Delft tiles and 18th century faïence.

● **Debauve et Gallaix**, *30 rue des Sts-Pères* Chocolate shop; began life as a pharmacy until M. Gallaix, believing they were a beneficial tonic, began to manufacture chocolates in 1818. Black squares of praline and croquettes of bittersweet chocolate. The shop is protected by the Beaux Arts society.

● **Interfruits**, *27 rue des Sts-Pères* Specialising in exotic fruit arranged in wicker baskets.

● **The Twickenham**, *70 rue des Sts-Péres* Pub-style bar offering over 20 beers; *confit de canard*.

● **Le Bélier**, *13 rue des Beaux-Arts* Hotel where Oscar Wilde met his end. Restaurant overpriced but visit the bar for an

apéritif and drink with the spirit of the 90s . . .

➤ Down *rue Mabillon* you'll find the covered St-Germain market, surprisingly warm and neighbourly and with generally high standards of produce, knowledge and welcome.

The *rue de Seine* is specially noted for its art galleries and art supply shops. ◄

● **Tabac de L'Institut**, *21 rue de Seine* Wine bar, oldest establishment in the quarter. Wine by the glass and sandwiches served in tiny bar at rear.

● **La Palette**, *43 rue de Seine*, Bar; popular with the local artists. Excellent coffee and sandwiches made with *pain Poilâne*.

● **Fournil de Pierre**, *64 rue de Seine* (also corner of *rue de Sèvres* and *St-Romain*) Boulangerie; excellent tarts and choice of 4 pizzas daily. Bread by kilo. Also good cheese and *charcuterie*. Pierre Desnon founded *Europ-Assistance*.

● **La Table d'Italie**, *69 rue de Seine* Italian food store; sandwiches and pizzas to eat at counter. Good spot for lunch after visiting Buci market or Latin Quarter. Homemade pasta and a complete selection of Italian hams and cheeses.

● **La Specialité du Café**, *54 rue de Seine* Coffee shop with a range of freshly-ground coffee including Brazilian. Jams sold.

● **Boulangerie Boudin**, *6 rue de Buci* Boulangerie; known since 1950 for *fougasse*, made with puff pastry instead of bread dough, and its cheesecake.

● **Vieille France**, *14 rue de Buci* Pâtisserie; good *chocolat de maison*, *merveilles* – puff pastry with honey and jam, *tamousse roquefort, palet cognac*.

● **Bonbonnerie de Buci**, *12 rue de Buci* A *maître pâtissier;* tea salon upstairs. *Mousse aux pommes* sold with caramel coulis; Black Forest cake *forêt noire*.

● **Boutique Layrac**, *25-27 rue Buci* Traiteur and catering service where prepared foods can be bought. Best just to look!

● **Aux Vrais produits d'Auvergne**, *32 rue Buci* Charcuterie; specialising in products from Auvergne, one of 10 such shops throughout Paris. *Tomme fraîche d'Auvergne, confits*, walnut bread.

● **Le petit Zinc**, *25 rue de Buci* Restaurant open until 3am; 1900s decor and trendy clientèle. Southwest and Aveyron cuisine including *choucroute de poisson*.

● **Taverne de Nesle**, *32 rue Dauphine* Bar; best mug of beer in Paris award in 1977; over 400 beers from around the world. Zywiec from Poland, Tsing Tao from China, Macabé from Israel.

● **Le Mauritius**, *39 rue Mazarine* Restaurant serving food from the Isle of Mauritius: samosa, *brunjani* (fish).

● **Charcuterie Coesnon**, *30 rue Dauphine* Charcuterie run by the Coesnon family from Normandy. Fifteen varieties of black pudding *boudin noir; boudin blanc* and *andouillettes*.

● **Charcuterie du Pont-Neuf**, *12 rue Dauphine* Charcuterie; winner of *Concours National du Boudin Blanc* white pudding; *Andouillettes de Troyes*.

● **Antiquarius**, *33 rue Guénégaud* Restaurant filled with turn-of-the century antiques and hung with giltframed portraits. Good red wines of Provence and a bargain menu.

● **Axis**, *18 rue Guénégaud* Shop specialising in whimsical *objets d'art*; bistro ashtrays and gloveshaped vases.

● **L'Ecluse**, *15 Quai des Grands-Augustins* Wine bar that lets you sample superb bordeaux by the glass, first of this group. Gas lamps and belle-époque posters. Good for a late-night snack; *foie gras* with Sauternes; *filet d'oie* and St-Emilion.

● **La Cannelle**, *53 Quai des Grands-Augustins* Victorianlooking restaurant operated by daughter of Raymond Oliver, sister of Michel (qv 7ᵉ).

● **L'Attrape-Coeur**, *9 rue Christine* Restaurant; 1930s style, serves until 1am; *foies de volaille tartare* and *daube de porc et aubergine*.

● **A la Coeur de Rohan**, *59-61 rue St-André-des-Arts* Nonsmoking, country-style tea salon with classical music and the occassional live concert. *Scones au fromage!*

● **Allard**, *41 rue St-André-des-Arts* Restaurant and bistro awarded *Les Lauriers du Terroir* for exceptional regional cuisine.

● **La Tchaika**, *9 rue de l'Eperon* Russian tea salon with matching foods, next door to *Maison du Livre Etranger*. Caviar, Borscht, bitter chocolate cake, *fromage blanc torte* – German cheesecake.

● **La Lozère**, *4 rue Hautefeuille* Restaurant doubling as tourist information centre for the Lozère, serving its excellent dishes and *charcuterie*, including *saucisse de Lozère*.

NB No 15 was where Charlotte Corday stabbed Jean Marat in his bath tub.

● **Le Procope**, *13 rue l'Ancienne-Comédie* Café and restaurant, dating back to 1686, the oldest in Paris. It was here that a young Sicilian, Franceso Procopio dei Coltelli, who had arrived in the city to seek his fortune, began selling the new beverage – coffee. A gold plaque commemorates its most notable patrons – Voltaire, Diderot, Rousseau, Ben Franklin, Danton, Marat, Robespierre and Bonaparte. More interesting historically.

● **La Pinte**, *13 carrefour de l'Odéon* Bar with over 50 beers. Usually crowded, sometimes rowdy – or is the word hearty?

● **Brûlerie de l'Odéon**, *6 rue Crébillon* Coffee shop selling 15 freshly-ground coffees, plus the complete range of Fortnum and Mason teas.

● **Brûlerie Caumartin**, *71 rue Crébillon* Coffee shop with an excellent *cachel gris* – a blend of Costa Rican, Venezuelan and Colombian beans. One of the best pure Colombian coffees in Paris.

➤*Rue Monsieur-le-Prince* combines two great French enthusiasms: the orient (and its food) and the cinema; quite an experience.◄

● **Chez Maître-Paul**, *12 rue Monsieur-le-Prince* Restaurant; awarded *Les Lauriers du Terroir*. Small rustic interior. Wines from the Jura and excellent *morbier* and *vacherin* cheeses.

● **Polidor**, *41 rue Monsieur-le-Prince* Unpretentious homecooking in art-deco surroundings.

● **Nam-Long Produits**, *48 rue Monsieur-le-Prince* Oriental food shop selling Chinese, Japanese and Vietnamese products. Exotic fruits, rice alcohol and ginger liqueur; rice bowls and spoons.

● **Edouard Charles**, *38 rue Vaugirard* Liquor store with over 80 kinds of armagnac dating back to 1939. Those from the lower Armagnac region are a speciality. Also products from southwest France.

● **Pons**, *2 pl Edmond-Rostand* tea salon; an aristocratic, old world place specialising in China teas. Perfect after wandering through the Luxembourg Gardens.

● **Estrella**, *34 rue St-Sulpice* Coffee shop whose owner refuses to blend beans. Colombian, Kenyan.

● **Chez Georges**, *11 rue des Canettes* Bar with reputation for 'typical' bistro atmosphere but popular only with tourists.

● **Guy**, *6 rue Mabillon* Brazilian restaurant; *Feijoada* – the national dish – served Saturday lunchtime.

● **Ferme Ste-Helene**, *18 rue Mabillon* Épicerie and cheese shop with excellent variety. *Chèvres fermiers, bries, coulommiers*.

● **La Foux**, *2 rue Clément* Restaurant with a reputation for good Saturday luncheons. Lyonnais dishes in the winter, provençal during summer.

● **Miaid**, *9 rue des Quatre-Vents* Wine store which used to be a *crémerie*; 1850 decor has been retained. Specialities: Château Pech-Redou, Côteaux de la

Clape, 1900 Port Greyhound Colheita.

● **Brasserie Lipp,** *151 Bd St-Germain* Fashionable designer brasserie (See p 89.)

● **Aux Deux Magots,** *64 Bd St-Germain* Famous brasserie and bar with a literary and philosophical history. (See p 89.)

● **Café de Flore,** *172 Bd St-Germain* Equally famous brasserie and café. (See p 89.)

● **L'Appartement,** *21 rue Jacob* Antique shop; 19th-century tableware and cutlery; furniture and linen. Afternoons only.

● **Tiany Chambard,** *32 rue Jacob* Antique shop specializing in art-deco and from the '30s, '40s and '50s. Tableware. Afternoons only.

● **Maison Rustique,** *29 rue Jacob* Bookshop, specializing in gardening and 'how to' books on beer and cheese. Plant and vegetable books. French language only.

● **Culinarion,** *99 rue de Rennes* Kitchen shop specializing in moulds, and decorative objects. Pricey.

● **Porcelaine Blanche,** *112 bis rue de Rennes* Tableware shop; one of a chain of Paris stores, specializing in white porcelain. Bistro plates, café au lait bowls, terrines; prices between 15–30% below average.

● **FNAC,** *136 rue de Rennes* chain store whose book section contains one of the largest and most comprehensive collections of food and wine books.

● **Au Beau Viandier,** *25 rue du Vieux-Colombier* Belle-époque butcher; decorated with championship awards. *Prêt-à-cuire* a speciality; *rôtis de veau avec farcie* (pistachio, anchovy, apricots).

● **Les Arêtes,** *165 bd du Montparnasse* Fish restaurant; fisherman's *pot-au-feu*, salmon, oysters.

● **La Closerie des Lilas,** *171 bd du Montparnasse* Restaurant and brasserie which draws film stars and the BCBG (bon chic, bon genre). An old haunt of Henry James and Hemingway.

Piano bar, brasserie reasonable, restaurant overpriced.

● **Arts Populaires-Tea Pot,** *7 rue Bréa* Kitchen shop, three stores in one. Two specialize in kitchen and tableware.

● **Galerie Michel Sonkin,** *10 rue de Beaune* Antique shop specializing in folk objects of wood. Bread stamps (from when villages and families put their seal to bread loaves), wooden butter moulds.

● **Tan Dinh,** *60 rue de Verneuil* Restaurant specializing in Vietnamese cuisine with a dash of French. Excellent wine cellar. *Poulet au patates douces et cardamome* and sweet and sour veal.

● **Newman & Newman,** *40 rue de Verneuil* Antique shop which supplies dates and history for all its collection. Silver coffee sets, menu holders, crystal and table linen.

● **Mazot Meyer,** *32 rue de Verneuil* Antique tableware dealers with a collection of 19th-century asparagus and artichoke plates, pitchers and platters.

● **Porcelaine,** *22 rue de Verneuil* Tableware shop; Pillivuyt porcelain with some spectacularly brave and bright designs. Cheese and candy-making kits. Stainless steel and bronze flatware.

● **Les Glénan,** *54 rue de Bourgogne* Restaurant whose American chef Marc Singer won *Les Lauriers de Terroir*, the Gault Millau award for exceptional cuisine.

● **Pradier,** *37 rue de Bourgogne* Pâtisserie which has as its slogan 'all pâtisserie made with butter' and the taste confirms it. Also handmade chocolates and very good savoury pastries. Closed most of summer.

● **Dubus,** *175 rue de Grenelle* Boulangerie specializing in *fougasse.*

● **Barthélémy,** *51 rue de Grenelle* Cheese shop patronized by the famous, including Giscard d'Estaing. Tiny, chaotic and very much 'in'. *St-Maure de Pussigny, cantal de Salers, chèvres fermiers, vacherin du Mont d'Or,*

beurre cru à la motte de la vallée de la Douve (Cotentin).

● **Surface,** *16 rue St-Simon* Tile shop specializing in Italian decorator and hand-painted tiles.

● **Dîners en Ville,** *27 rue de Varenne* Antique tableware shop, particularly pieces produced 1880-1930. Glasses, carafes, barbotines, whisky flagons, silver.

● **L'Herbier de Provence,** *80 rue du Bac* Shop (one of 7) selling herbs, spices and candied peel, all kept in huge sacks and sold by the pound. Honey, oils, olive oil, soap of Marseille.

● **Baucia,** *76 rue du Bac* Italian food shop dedicated to a small village in Cremone. *Panettone perugina (brioche au beurre* with raisins), *salami de cremone, cicillo* (mild milanese cheese shaped like a pear).

● **Lenôtre,** *44 rue du Bac* Pâtisserie and caterer, part of the Lenôtre empire which includes five Paris shops, a school and an out-of-town factory. Chocolate is a speciality; *concorde* is a meringue filled with chocolate mousse.

● **Christian Constant,** *26 rue du Bac* Pâtisserie and tea salon which also make some of the best chocolate. Attracts the BCBG clientèle to its white contemporary rooms. Nineteen teas, with either acacia honey or five different sugars.

● **Lefèbvre Fils,** *24 rue du Bac* Tableware shop; 18th-century *trompe l'oeil* serving dishes in the shape of plates of olives, cabbages, etc. Faïence.

● **Boucherie d'Orsay,** *20 rue du Bac* Butcher specializing in *veau fermier.* Once owned by a Mr. Boring!

● **Dominique,** *19 rue du Bac* 'Old Russia' restaurant; *blinis* with caviar, *tartes au fromage.*

● **Jean Saffrey,** *18 rue du Bac* Ice cream shop where funseekers buy made-to-order busts of Marilyn Monroe, or Giscard d'Estaing. An off-the-freezer-tray President Mitterand will set you back 150F.

- **Florence Rousseau,** *9 rue de Luynes* Antique shop selling serving dishes, barbotines for asparagus and oysters, silver sugar tongs and spoons.
- **Au Bon Marché,** *38 rue de Sèvres* **Department store** (see p.74).
- **Le Récamier,** *4 rue Récamier* Empire-style restaurant frequented by government ministers. Outdoor dining, too. Burgundian cuisine (*oeufs en meurette*) and one of the best wine cellars in Paris.
- **Peltier,** *66 rue de Sèvres Pâtisserie,* frozen fruit, soufflés, mango-flavoured charlotte; excellent croissant.
- **Maison du Fromage,** *62 rue de Sèvres* Cheese shop, supplies grand restaurants. All cheeses are cave-aged. Rare *fermiers* such as *livarots* and *reblochon; beaufort.* Raw cream butter from the Charentes, usually.
- **Marché Breteuil,** *ave de Saxe,* from *ave de Ségur* to *pl de Breteuil* Market selling fish, produce, cheeses, flowers and some clothing. One of the moving markets, here Thursday and Saturday. It's a nice street to wander in.
- **Marie-Blanche de Broglie Cooking School,** *18 ave de La Motte-Picquet* Cookery school run by an ebullient French princess of the Pommery family, with courses in English, French and Spanish. Classes are held in Marie-Blanche's Paris apartment or at her château in Normandy; recommended.
- **Le Petit Boulé,** *18 ave de La Motte-Picquet* Russian tea salon owned by the Petrossian family. Piroski, blinis, tarama on toast, chocolate cake; also sells *foie gras,* honey and teas.
- **Marie-Ann Cantin,** *12 rue du Champ-de-Mars* Cheese shop with two cellars – one lined with damp rocks to keep cows cheese moist, and a less humid cellar for goats cheeses. Nearly 100 seasonal cheeses and a good selection of farm goats cheeses. Daughter of Christian Cantin who has famed cheese shop in 15e.

- **Le Cordon Bleu,** *24 rue du Champ-de-Mars* The famous classic cookery school recently bought by Cointreau. Courses given in French with afternoon demonstrations.
- **Dubernet,** *2 rue Augereau* Food store specializing in products from the Landes; *Foie gras au torchon, chichons d'oie, cous d'oie farcis, cassoulet.*
- **Pantagruel,** *2 rue de l'Exposition* Family-run restaurant specializing in cuisine of the southwest. During the game season (October-February) chef Alfred Israel serves up a classic venison stew. *Soufflé aux oursins* during November and December.
- **Marché rue Cler,** *ave de la Motte-Picquet* to *rue St-Dominique* Expensive street market in an upmarket area. Look for *moussaka* or *coulibiac* at *Charcuterie Gorin* at no 40, and the Italian market *Davoli* at no 34, which has exceptionally good produce. The market has more space than most and lots of residential Americans who are grateful for this.
- **Leonidas,** *39 rue Cler* Chocolate shop; Belgian chocolates are sweeter than French; *noix blanches à la créme fraîche.*
- **Rôtisserie du Champ-de-Mars,** *36 rue Cler* Volailler specializing in seasonal game birds *poulets de Bresse, Loué, Périgord, Nantais, canards de Barbarie, Nantais* and *croisés.* Bresse turkeys at Christmas.
- **Poissonnerie du Champ-de-Mars,** *145 rue St-Dominique* Very special fishmongers, specializing in langoustes, lobsters and trout, all direct from their own salt and freshwater tanks.
- **Viandes du Champ-de-Mars,** *122 rue St-Dominique* Butcher; *poulets de Bresse, canettes de Barberie* and excellent beef and tripe.
- **Pâtisserie Millet,** *103 rue St-Dominique Pâtisserie,* caterers and tea salon, owner M.

Millet and pastry chef Dennis Reffel are both *Maîtres Pâtissier.* Millet is also president of the Union of Pastry Chefs. Chocolate made for sale throughout France. Double-filled *pain au chocolat, kiwi* or *fruit de passion* charlottes. All perfection.
- **Gisquet,** *64 rue St-Dominique* Boulangerie dating back to 1900, decorated in earthenware tiles and pottery. Large round country loaves.
- **La Varenne Ecole de Cuisine,** *34 rue St-Dominque* Cooking school founded in 1975 by British cookbook writer Anne Willan. Special one-week courses during the summer and Easter holidays.

Demonstrations open to the public between 2.30 and 5.30pm Monday to Friday, and 10am to 12.30pm on Saturdays. All in French and translated into English.
- **Petrossian,** *18 bd La Tour-Maubourg* Internationally-acclaimed speciality food shop where for over 50 years the Petrossian family has been supplying Parisians with caviar, gathered three times a year from Astrakhan and the Caspian Sea. Branch in New York, too. Smoked salmon, truffles, *foie gras,* vodkas – everything rare and expensive and stylish.
- **Poujaurin,** *20 rue Jean-Nicot Pâtisserie* and *boulangerie;* becoming noticeably famous for organic bread, especially the *baguettes. Gâteau basque,* pizzas, gingerbread, and lovely pastries. Southwestern influence, so worth finding – and watching for the future.
- **La Maison Chavinier,** *39 ave Rapp Pâtisserie; madeleines, gâteau basque* and *pain de seigle aux raisins* all baked in a wood-fired oven.
- **Puyricard,** *27 ave Rapp* Chocolate shop; handmade chocolates arrive twice weekly from Aix-en-Provence; *chocolats fourrés* and *calissons d'Aix.*

And now you're off to the Eiffel Tower . . .

BRASSERIES

Brasseries are great places for soaking up atmosphere as well as resting the feet and eating and drinking without busting your budget. Below are a few to be found in the *arrondissements* covered in this guide to Paris.

- **Gus** *157 rue Montmartre 2ᵉ*
- **Le Vaudeville** *29 rue Vivienne 2ᵉ*
- **Chez Jenny** *39 bd du Temple 3ᵉ*
- **Bofinger** *5 rue Bastille 4ᵉ*
- **L'Ile-St-Louis** *55 quai de Bourbon 4ᵉ*
- **Aux deux Magots** *64 bd St-Germain 6ᵉ* Hemingway used to read his poetry here and Jean-Paul Sartre was a regular. Serves 25 different whiskies. Open daily to 2 am.
- **Café de Flore** *172 bd St-Germain 6ᵉ* Another artistic haunt. Picasso came here almost every night after World War II. His table is second from the front door. Albert Camus. Simone de Beauvoir and Jean-Paul Sartre (when not *chez les magots*) were regulars.
- **Lipp** *151 bd St Germain 6ᵉ* Designer *brasserie* favoured by Yves St Laurent and other famous couturiers, as well as President Mitterand (in the evening).
- **Lutetia** *23 rue de Sèvres 6ᵉ.*
- **Lowenbrau** *84 ave des Champs-Elysées 8ᵉ.*
- **L'Alsace** *39 ave des Champs Elysées 8ᵉ*
- **Le Grand Café** *4 bd des Capucines 9ᵉ*
- **Taverne Kronenbourg** *24 bd des Italiens 9ᵉ*
- **Flo** *7 cour des Petites Ecuries 10ᵉ.* Food definitely worth queuing for.
- **Terminus Nord** *23 rue de Dunkerque 10ᵉ*

ARRONDISSEMENT 8

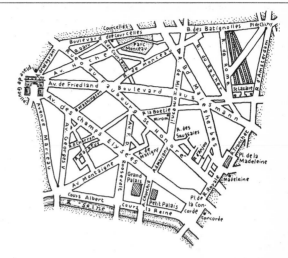

Arc de Triomphe, Champs Elysées, Elysée Palace, Faubourg St-Honoré, Grand Palais, Petit Palais, Place de la Concorde, St-Lazare, Madeleine.

High fashion has now come down to the pegs in the rue du Faborg St-Honoré, but the Elysée Palace and the grand mansions of the American and British Embassies ensure they, and the food shops thereabouts, don't have to drop their prices. Rue Daru is a touch of Russia, the best Danish and German foods can be found, and on the eastern borders are **M. Androuet** and **La Ferme St-Hubert**, renowned cheese shops.

For truffles and *foie gras*, dinner at Maxims, tea-times of elegance, breathtaking silver and glass for tables, caviar on toast, and anything else luxurious, you simply never leave the 8ᵉ. Yet the great boulevards carved through medieval Paris last century left pockets of thin streets and high contrast. You'll easily find your own culinary routes once you've touched bases

with these highlights. I specially like the tangle of small shops and streets named after international cities between Boulevard Malesherbes and the Gare St-Lazare.

- **Boutique Danoise,** *42 ave de Friedland* Crystal and housewares; glorious glass and massive crystal bowls in simple designs with clean modern lines; also sleek leather furniture.

Flora Danica, *142 ave des Champs-Elysées* Restaurant; four kinds of herring plus *gravad-lax*, smoked eel or salmon; apple, almond or prune pastries and delightful Danish specialities – take-away, too. Upstairs is the more expensive *Copenhague* which has a Danish Table or *smorgasbord*.

- **Peter,** *191 rue du Fbg St-Honoré* Exclusive tableware and cutlery; solid silver or silver plate with handles of precious things or of plastic to suit dishwasher. China and serving pieces too.
- **Maison du Chocolat,** *225 rue du Fbg St-Honoré* Chocolates; luscious chocolate cakes and *tourtes*, exceptional quality chocolates made on the premises; even the shop seems to be chocolate-coated.
- **Lambert,** *260 rue du Fbg St-Honoré Traiteur, épicérie;*

select grocer and fruiterer with the best of whatever is available. *Poulets de Bresse*, farmyard turkeys, quality game and hot spit-roasted chicken.

● **A la Ville de Petrograd,** *13 rue Daru* Restaurant and *traiteur;* a log façade evokes its namesake; sample fresh caviar, smoked salmon, blinis, coulibiac and borscht in the dining room or take some home; appropriately situated facing the gold domes on the Russian Orthodox Church.

● **Daru,** *19 rue Daru* Russian *traiteur*, grocer and casual restaurant, features speedy service and smoked fish, stuffed aubergine, shashlik, caviar, blinis and coulibiac; all may be taken away.

➤Go down *rue de Courcelles* and through the gilded gates onto *ave Van Dyck*, which gives access to *Parc Monceau*. Here you have a glimpse of Parisians at leisure. The best ice cream cones are from the *gaufrette* stand near the entrance from *bd de Courcelles* on your left.◄

● **Cernuschi Museum,** *7 ave Velasquez* Art museum; filled with oriental treasures.

● **Boissier,** *11 bd de Courcelles* Confectionery and pastry; jam and biscuits; individual chocolate meringue cakes and éclairs; lavish display window overflowing with chocolate covered cherries and cherry drops. Also at *46 ave Marceau.*

➤Walk on to the *place Prosper Coubaux* and down *rue du Rocher*, a market street with many attractive food shops.◄

● **Daire,** *71 rue du Rocher* Honey; superb variety of flavours plus honey spice cakes, honey confectionery and good jams and jellies.

● **Nissim de Camondo,** *63 rue de Monceau* Museum; a preserved townhouse with lovely paintings and furniture.

● **Marché de l'Europe** A new covered market in a modern building but still unfinished. Not worth making a special detour for at the present – but the sur-

rounding streets have lots of bakers, *traiteurs*, butchers and cafés to keep you busy and entertained.

● **Puiforcat,** *131 bd Haussman* Tableware; extravagant displays of sensational settings. Many designs reproduced from the original 19th-century collection of M. Puiforcat, which is now in the Louvre. Crystal goblets and fragile china, ornate silver holloware, silver decanters and vacuum bottles. *The* place for important wedding or anniversary gifts.

● **René-Gerard St-Ouen,** *111 bd Haussmann* Bakery and café – they call themselves sculptors in bread; windows filled with fantasy bread creations – animals, bicycles and baskets; light meals served in the informal café, *quiches*, salads, omelettes and desserts.

● **L'Esprit et le Vin,** *65 bd Malesherbes* A true Mecca for the wine lover; wine accessories; tasting glasses, wine decanters, coolers and corkscrews; gift boxes of glasses; silver and crystal claret jugs; top hat ice buckets.

● **Vernet,** *65 bd Malesherbes* Bakery and tea salon; cheese-wrapped frankfurters served on rich home made rolls, croissants filled with chicken and ham, cheese cocktail biscuits, fruit tarts, chocolate macaroons.

● **Augé,** *115 bd Haussmann Épicerie;* luscious fresh fruit complements speciality ingredients and a well-chosen range of ancient and modern wines and spirits. Once *the* place to go for polar bear steaks or elephant trunks, or anything else intrepid.

● **Bonbonnière St-Augustin,** *85 bd Haussmann* Confectionery; bon-bons and nougats in pretty gift baskets, marzipan, chocolate nut clusters; teas and biscuits also.

● **Au Lys Royal,** *13 rue de la Pépinière* Confectionery; marzipan tennis balls and good bitter chocolates in leopard-print boxes.

● **La Cigogne,** *61 rue de l'Arcade Pâtisserie;* some *charcuterie*. Alsation specialities include puff pastry pretzels, cinnamon kugelhof by the piece, *strudels* – and lovely, real sausages, *choucroute* and smoked tongues.

● **Bougnat Boutique,** *5 rue de l'Isly* Restaurant; regional food; farm cheese, wines and regional products from Auvergne; excellent lunchtime platters of cold *charcuterie* or hot heartiness.

● **Lenôtre,** *3 rue du Havre* Confectioner, baker and *traiteur*; renowned for quality and creativity; cordial-filled chocolates; prepared foods, stylish and appetizing – avocado and prawn salad with raspberries. Daily specials such as chicken in aspic with multicoloured salad garnish; select your own croissants and rolls. Also *44 rue du Bac 7ᵉ*.

● **Porcher,** *30 rue Tronchet Traiteur*; salads and *tourtes*, roast chicken and spring rolls to carry away; they preserve their own plums in alcohol.

● **La Carpe,** *14 rue Tronchet* Kitchen supplies; several styles of knife rests to avoid washing up between courses; bar ware, kitchen equipment and small appliances.

➤ Go back up *rue Tronchet* to where it intersects *rue Vignon*. A walk down *rue Vignon* is a feast; even-numbered shops are actually in the 9th arrondissement, but are included here. ◄

● **La Maison du Miel,** *24 rue Vignon* Honey; more than a dozen kinds including thyme, lavender or acacia honey. Yogurt or granola biscuits and honey spice cake.

● **Tanrade,** *18 rue Vignon* Famous for over 200 years; superb jams and jellies, the best *marrons glacés* (in winter), excellent honey, chocolates, teas and confectionery (including 50 flavours of bonbons).

● **Fournil de Pierre,** *21 rue Vignon* Extraordinary bakery owned by the man who set up EuropAssistance. Each day a different savoury bread is featured, *brie* or onion, for instance. Chocolate or raisin *brioche,* walnut bread, chewy triangular wheat rolls and breads, assorted biscuits, chocolate chip and almond.

● **Ferme St-Hubert,** *21 rue Vignon* Cheese shop and restaurant, justly famed as one of the best; owned by the bearded and avuncular Henry Voy, who is on hand to give advice. Raw milk farm cheeses matured on the premises, but all types of French cheese represented. Tasting by reservation. Cheery restaurant next door proposes cheese dishes for every course including *roquefort soufflé,* cheesecake, *raclette,* cheese fondue, *camembert* croquettes and generous cheese platters. Home made *chèvre à l'huile.* Sell own cheese book and excellent reference chart.

➤ While you are on the borders of the 1e and the 8e, stay there and take the chance to look at the classic department store, **Aux Trois Quartiers,** *17 bd de la Madeleine.* ◄

● **Fauchon,** *26 pl de la Madeleine.* Glittering Mecca for one-stop luxury shopping. Totally reliable for *foie gras* and excelling *foie gras de canard.* Syrups for sorbets, dried mushrooms, very cheap wild rice, and eccentric jams – jasmine blossom for instance. Masterful fruit and vegetables and intoxicating *traiteur* for upmarket snacks and picnics. Bakery and coffee shop, but you must pay for pastries before you choose, irritating if your french is not good. Go. Even if you are poor . . .

● **Marquise de Sévigné,** *32 pl de la Madeleine* Chocolates, *salon de thé;* devastating chocolate cake and rich, reliable, macaroons; pralines are recommended as take-away chocolates.

● **Hediard,** *21 pl de la Madeleine* Refurbishment right opposite **Fauchon** means sharp competition. Pistachio and pine-kernel oils, famous jams and jellies made in own kitchens, (recipe

book too), extraordinary range of flavoured vinegars and oils, and just about everything else. Very good wine shop plus smart restaurant upstairs with elegant food.

● **Maison de la Truffe,** *19 pl de la Madeleine Traiteur,* fruit shop specialising in truffles. Fresh and preserved truffles, especially for Christmas of course. *Foie gras;* made up dishes of quality.

● **Créplet-Brussol,** *17 pl de la Madeleine* Cheese shop; a touch of the farm and market in mid-Paris. Excellent selection of *chèvres,* farmhouse butters, *roquefort* pastries, cheesecakes.

● **Caviar Kaspa,** *17 pl de la Madeleine* Caviar shop and restaurant; downstairs buy caviar, smoked sturgeon, smoked salmon, eel, *gravadlax.* Exceptionally smart restaurant upstairs serves 4 types of caviar in various portions on thick blinis with melted butter and sour cream. Flavoured vodkas. Bar for single diners. Wondrous wicked escapism.

● **L'Ecluse,** *15 pl de la Madeleine* Wine bar and restaurant; everyone still learning about food and wine should know about this chain. Vintage wines by the glass, *foie gras* by the slice.

➤ *Marché de la Madeleine* If you need relief from the glitz of the Madeleine, head to the top of the *place* and this tiny, secret market entered from *11 rue Tronchet* or *7 rue de Castellane.* There's a fish stall, butcher, fruit and veg men, lovely old fashioned creamery and cheese shop plus a Lebanese shop selling middle eastern goodies. *La Tonkinoise* is a very simple Vietnamese restaurant and a Chinese snack bar and takeaway with just a few high stools to sit upon. I love the place for putting my feet on the ground, or for putting together an economical lunch. But should I be telling you this . . . ◄

● **Au Vase Etrusque,** *11 pl de la Madeleine* Super-classy china, crystal and porcelain, Meissen and limited editions.

● **Odiot,** *7 pl de la Madeleine* Upmarket cutlery, crystal and porcelain in the elaborate French style; some of the cutlery patterns are pre-Revolution . . .

● **Au Verger de la Madeleine,** *4 bd Malesherbes* Fruits and liquor; a formidable selection of wines and whiskies; fuzzy green almonds in summer, strawberries in winter, fresh truffles, too.

● **Betjeman and Barton,** *23 Bd Malesherbes* Teas; everything for the perfect Anglophile tea party; selected teas individually blended, but also kettles and tea cosies (tut-tut), Wilkin jams, chutneys, bacon and special sausages. More for Americans than ex-patriot Brits.

● **Maison du Whiskey,** *20 rue d'Anjou* Whisky specialist; an array of sparkling decanters fills the window; inside are mini-decanters in the shape of golf balls, bar ware and a huge selection of whiskies, malts, Irish, Canadian and bourbons. Some are very old, but what counts is when they were *bottled* – they change little out of the cask.

● **Lotus d'Or,** *5 rue de Surène* Confectionery; chocolates, home made caramels, fruit jellies, sugared almonds and irresistible mints in replica antique biscuit cannisters. A branch of the **Confiserie Rivoli,** *17 rue de Rivoli.*

● **Le Savio,** corner of *rue Boissy-d'Anglas* and *rue de Surène* Bar, tearoom and bakery; pristine *petits fours* and shimmering fruit tartlets, chicken or ham stuffed croissants, *quiches,* sandwiches; food all day at the bar.

● **Jadis et Gourmande,** *27 rue Boissy d'Anglais* Confectionery; specializes in fantasy form chocolates, bow ties for Father's Day and plaques to replace greeting cards with birthday wishes; jams, teas and gift baskets. Every type of caramel, fruit jelly and *bonbon.*

➤ Cross the street and continue down until you find *Cité Berryer* on your left through the archway under the *Hotel d'Aguesseau.* On Tuesday and Friday mornings it's a noisy, bustling market place. Since the designated main entrance is *rue Royale*, the mailing address of all the following places is *rue Royale*. ◄

● **Caves de la Madeleine,** *25 Cité Berryer* (Stephen Spurrier) Wine academy and shop; wine classes and tastings, often held in English; helpful and genial staff in the burgundy-coloured shop; at the other end of the passage is Stephen Spurrier's restaurant, the *Moulin à Vent,* and his wine bar, the *Blue Fox,* which serves light meals.

● **Villeroy & Boch,** *23 rue Royale* Tableware famous and expensive, botanical design dishes and cookware beautifully displayed with shelves of glittering glass.

● **Ladurée,** *16 rue Royale* Pastry shop and tea salon of mirrored Louis XIV distinction, overseen by the cherubim on the ceiling. Equally heavenly cakes, pastries and specialities – filled *brioches* and *royals,* chocolate or coffee almond biscuits.

● **Christoflé,** *12 rue Royale* Elegant cutlery and glass, from soup tureens to nut crackers in plastic, porcelain or silver. Established since 1850 but very aware of trends and fashions.

● **Lalique,** *11 rue Royale* Crystal showroom, mostly decorated pieces; the wine glasses and glass plates are exquisite.

● **Maxims and Minims,** *76 rue du Fbg St-Honoré* Two extensions of the renowned and still highly rated art nouveau restaurant in *rue Royale*. One is a specialist food shop selling almost anything that can have a Maxim's label upon it, plus reproductions of ashtrays and so on. Some of the prices have far too many numbers in them but the quality is generally faultless. Gault Millau say the vintage sardines are among the best. *Minims* is something .between a fast-food bar and nouvelle-cuisine snackery. Great style and not bad choice or prices, but the whisper is it may not have long to go . . . perhaps it's that silly name.

● **Boucherie de la Présidence,** *15 rue Montolivet* Lively, stylish butcher a few yards from the Elysée. Specially good veal and poultry which you can also buy roasted; pristine meat counter.

● **Boulangerie des Saussaies,** *12 rue des Saussaies* Bakery and restaurant; fresh individual veal *pâtés* in puff pastry; hot daily specials served at the stand-up counter; good bread and *palmiers.*

● **Orfèvrerie Ancienne,** *18 rue de Miromesnil* Antique silver tableware; sparkling array of antique holloware and cutlery.

● **Corne d'Or,** *23 rue de Miromesmil Traiteur* and groceries; attractive salads, stuffed tomatoes and *pâtés* displayed in the window, plus *quiches,* wine.

● **Jean Luce,** *30 rue la Boétie* Gifts, china and glassware – order your monogrammed dinner service, French cutlery, classic or modern or something simpler.

● **Boucherie Miromesnil,** *29 rue Miromesnil* Butcher; top quality Normandy beef; neat rows of chickens and chops, and sawdust on the floor; sells a few *pâtés* and vegetables.

● **Bonbonnière St-Honoré,** *28 rue Miromesnil* Chocolates and confectionery; display windows filled with sugared almonds, *dragées,* rich nut clusters and a pyramid of jams.

● **Au Petit Montmorency,** *5 rue Rabelais* Top-class restaurant; long known for their fine *foie gras de canard*; the restaurant now sells it to take away.

● **Dalloyau,** *101 rue du Fbg. St-Honoré Salon du thé* a success for almost 190 years; pastry, prepared foods, the best croissants in Paris to enjoy in the upstairs tea room. *Mogador* and the best of the classic *gâteaux, opéra* etc. Fine jams, mustards and other specialities.

● **Little Pig,** *23 ave Franklin D. Roosevelt* Grocery, *traiteur;* very popular prepared dishes of meat, fish or poultry, some to eat cold, some to reheat. Pig's trotters, seafood, sausages, salads, fruit and wine, too.

● **Boulangerie St-Philippe-du-Roule** *73 ave Franklin D. Roosevelt* Bakery, restaurant; crusty *baguettes* and chewy macaroons, home made ice cream; *quiches,* pizza and *pâté.*

● **Le Val d'Or,** *28 ave Franklin D. Roosevelt* Wine bar and restaurant; a good place to stop for a glass of beaujolais and a plate of country ham and sausage; more substantial meals featuring daily specials available in the downstairs dining room.

● **Meurisse,** *49 bis ave Franklin D. Roosevelt* Chocolates; small bright confectionery with chocolate covered nougatine, chocolate nut discs sandwiched with chocolate cream.

● **Lamazère,** *23 rue de Ponthieu* Restaurant; famed for once having a 1kg/2lb truffle; outstanding for such treats as *cassoulet* and *confit*; light meals in the bar until 2am; *foie gras* and fresh truffles may be bought 'to go'.

● **Boutique Tong Yen,** *7 rue de Ponthieu* Take-away Oriental dishes; home delivery or you can enjoy your meal in the restaurant around the corner at *1 bis rue Jean Mermoz.*

● **Catalin,** *12 Champs-Elysées* Confectionery; on the lower level of the shopping arcade *Galerie Élysées-Rond-Point;* incredible fantasy marzipan creations shaped like cheese, rolls and bread, fruits and vegetables, marine life, baby chicks and big red lips. Traditional chocos, too.

● **Spécialités de France,** *44 ave Montaigne* Regional products and confectionery; sweets from all parts of France, glacé fruit, plums and cherries in alcohol, raspberry liqueur, honey. The President takes gifts from here when he travels – well he would, wouldn't he?

● **Fouquet,** *22 rue François - 1er* Speciality foods; nicely gift-boxed assortments of their own mustards and condiments, preserves and teas; handmade chocolates. Unusually they have marmalades among the jams and *confitures;* good fruit syrups, too.

ARRONDISSEMENTS 9 & 10

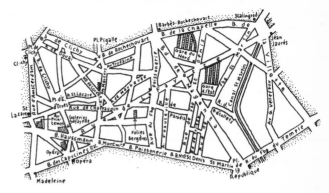

- **Faquais,** *30 rue de la Trémoïlle* Speciality foods; particulary good coffees, roasted daily, or you can buy green beans. Jams, *foie gras, confits de canard,* outstanding oils, teas, wines, spices; quite simply one of the best in town.
- **Nicolas,** *27 rue Marbeuf* Ultra classic crystal, cutlery and porcelain, with a famous sale from mid-January to mid-February.
- **Torréfaction Marbeuf,** *25 rue Marbeuf* Coffee and tea of the highest quality, both pure and blended, plus regional jams and honeys.
- **Vignon,** *14 rue Marbeuf Traiteur;* one-stop shopping – roasts, all stuffed and tied, veal with wild mushrooms or paella to heat up, prepared vegetables and salads, fruit, cheese, wine, desserts.
- **Cave de Georges Duboeuf,** *9 rue Marbeuf* Wine; the King of beaujolais – but others too; most of the wines are bottled under his own label; sampler boxes of 6 splits or 8 half bottles of different beaujolais wines.
- **Maison d'Allemagne,** *45 rue Pierre-Charron* German *brasserie* and *traiteur; frankfurters* and *cervelas* and *bockwurst, sauerkraut* and potato salad, lots of beer and delicious pastries.
- **L'Ecluse,** *64 rue François-1er* Wine bar and restaurant; one of the four moody spots to enjoy fabulous bordeaux wines by the glass and/or to eat wondrously but sparingly. A great chance to check out, say, a sweet sauterne with a slice of good *roquefort* or simply to sip a vintage you'll never afford by the bottle. Open until 2am.
- **Maison du Caviar,** *21 rue Quentin-Bauchart* Restaurant; toy with caviar or smoked salmon and blinis until 2am or take their specialities home and do it there.
- **Le Fouquet's,** *99 ave des Champs-Élysées* Bar and restaurant; in the same spot since the Champs Élysées was a muddy country lane; a good place to stop and watch *le monde* go by.

Opéra, Casino de Paris, Folies-Bergères, Porte St-Denis, Porte St-Martin, Gare du Nord, Gare de l'Est, Canal St-Martin.

Here's a challenge for your culinary nose to lead you towards real exploring, to inspect the underside of Parisian high-life and haute-cuisine. For beyond **Galéries Lafayette** and **Au Printemps** on Boulevard Haussmann, the swagger of the Opéra and the famous theatres, north of the swirling boulevards and east of the railway stations, is working-class life.

You quickly leave behind places familiar, yet the sights to be seen are more fascinating just for that. All has once been more fashionable and so there are abrupt surprises – some of the best and oldest confectioners in Paris, a magical Indian food shop, startling offers and Utrillo vistas in narrow rue des Martyrs, Oriental jewish shops, plus the most concentrated array of china, crystal, glass and a poster museum in a street nicely named de Paradis. **Schmid** is the best Alsatian *charcuterie,* **Grandmère l'Oye** sells the best *foie gras.* As ever, the streets around railway sta-

tions are vivacious with competition and emotion, but they are blisters of intrusion . . . and there is the Canal.

Do you know about the Canal St-Martin, which bisects the 10ᵉ as it starts its watery way to Belgium? Once you cross it, pleasure spots and historical buildings must be of your own imagining, although there are details of Louis-Philippe lettering on shopfronts and elegant balconies to appreciate. It is vast, dilapidated and quietly self-sufficient, lived in by artisans and shopkeepers and immigrants, and an illustration of what is found in the provinces rather than what is expected in Paris. Maigret feels right at home.

From the high arched footbridges over the canal, you'll look down on barges with potted palms and televisions and checked curtains, especially by the *Pont Tournant* which opens every half hour. The 9ᵉ and 10ᵉ are not the places for the usual touring, and conspicuously expensive or scanty clothing would be stupid. To me the atmosphere is finely balanced between welcome and challenge; I feel I must not gawp or comment or take arty photographs, if any. Yet it *is* photogenic, and it's raunchy here and *triste* there, but the welcome in the cafés and bars is only as honest and sincere as you are. Of course, it's like working class neighbourhoods anywhere – they've seen a lot of living, but not a lot of tourists . . . thus, I've not noted the neighbourhood shops and bars and stalls across the canal. Those who will be interested, will be capable of finding them on their own.

● **Léonidas,** *13 rue Auber* Belgian chocolates; you can choose both the pretty gift boxes and the assortment which goes into them.

● **Zagori,** *6 rue La Fayette* Although looking mainly like a self-service sweet shop, it's more important. You must sample their ice creams and sorbets, made for many of the grand restaurants; only real fresh ingredients are used and if you want to thrill a French host or hostess, ice cream cakes or *vacherins* can be made to order.

● **Galeries Lafayette,** *40 bd Haussmann* **Department store.** (See p 74)

● **Au Printemps,** *64 Bd Haussmann* **Department store.** (See p 74)

● **Brûlerie Caumartin,** *71 rue de Caumartin* Coffee roaster and restaurant between the two-buildings of *Au Printemps.* Very high reputation for pure coffee and blends; you can try one if you eat here.

● **Baggi,** *38 rue d'Amsterdam* Ice cream; simple surroundings for the oldest ice cream makers in Paris, father to son for over 130 years. Plain, direct flavours of ice cream and sorbet, or elaborate confections of the two in cakes or sundaes; *Caresse* combines hazelnut, cognac and walnut; *Williamette* is pear and blackcurrant sorbet. Often as many as 50 flavours in summer.

● **Androuet,** *41 rue d'Amsterdam* Cheese shop and restaurant; M. Androuet is revered in France for his knowledge and influence and books. The cheeses are sensational, and upstairs you can eat a variety of menus with cheese in every course, from triple creams to blues, for instance. I'm not really sure that is the way to enjoy cheese, to be honest.

● **Bonbonnière de la Trinité,** *4 pl d'Estienne-d'Orves* Mainly chocolates; one of three shops with a reputation for old-fashioned respect for the customer and the product. Chocaholics swear by the blocks of *supra-bitter* or *supra-amer*, really dark and intense, in thick plain slabs or stuffed with everything imaginably wicked. Honeys and teas.

● **Pierson,** *82 rue de Clichy* Speciality foods; the great speciality is olive oil of many flavours, more or less acidic, or as fruity as you like. Nut oils, too, plus poultry from the Landes, teas and, most important, sardines in olive oil.

● **Shah et Compagnie,** *23 rue Notre-Dame-de-Lorette* Indian food and supplies – riveting example of ethnic food shop, including fresh exotica imported direct. Spices and spice mixtures, unusual rices. The more you buy the less you pay.

➤ *Rue des Martyrs* isn't very touristy, yet it is classically Paris. A narrow winding street with peeps of *Sacré-Coeur* over rooftops like Utrillo paintings. As you climb towards Pigalle, *filles de joie* in tightly belted raincoats ogle from doorways. ◄

● **Charcuterie Lyonnais Terroir,** *58 rue des Martyrs* Supposedly the best source of lyonnaise *charcuterie* in Paris. You should be able to sample a true *rose de Lyon,* and burgundian specialities from *jambon persillé* to pike *quenelles.* Stock changes according to season.

● **Molard,** *48 rue des Martyrs* Cheese shop; charming, marble-lined shop with display of cheese-making pots and moulds (not for sale). Usually a good variety of

chèvres, homemade yogurt and *crème fraîche.* One researcher found sheep's milk ricotta.

● **Beaubois,** *10 rue des Martyrs* Pâtisserie and baker; recommended for its sour-dough bread *pain au levain* and savoury tarts.

● **Bourdaloue,** *7 rue Bourdaloue* Another 'olde-worlde' sort of place with their own confectionery and chocolate, ice cream and sorbets to complement the range of cakes and pastries. Flavoured macaroons, apple *chaussons* and a *pain de gênes,* an almond pound cake. A few tables for tea or coffee.

● **Fouquet,** *36 rue Laffitte* One of two shops specialising in confectionery of the utmost quality. Everything is special but particularly raspberry drops, caramels and exceptional glacé fruits, although, as usual, these look better than they taste. Everything is prepared here. On another site is prepared the special and recommended vinegars. Other condiments, preserves, jams, champagne.

● **A la Mère de Famille,** *35 rue du Fbg-Montmartre* Confectionery and *confitures* are the prizes for finding this, the oldest confectioners in Paris. Wonderful dried fruits from the best areas of France, chocolates, *marrons.*

➤ *Rue Cadet* makes a fascinating detour, it's full of food shops and stalls, a butcher selling pale *pré-salé lamb* in spring, fishmongers and the start of a Jewish orthodoxy, and surprise . . . especially when you wander back and along *rue Richer* to see the *Folies-Bergères* building on your way to lunch at *Brasserie Flo.* ◄

● **Poissonnerie Moderne,** *2 bis rue Cadet* Fish shop; specialises in Mediterranean fish, reflecting the sort of people who live here. You could find *rascasse,* red and grey mullet, tuna and salt cod.

● **Mon Porc,** *18 rue Cadet* Charcuterie and butcher; they cure their own hams on the premises; *rillons* and *andouilles.* Fresh *foie gras,* available most of the year, one of their specialities.

● **Le Dessert Fin,** *24 rue Cadet* Exceptional cake shop; Bavarois of fresh fruits and whipped cream are their great pride – the passion fruit is my favourite. But marvellous *gâteaux* of all sizes and flavours. A find.

➤ Intriguing *rue Richer* has Tunisian Kosher shops (truly) and at no. 51 a kosher shop selling Adolphe Burgers – *think* about it . . .

Rue de Paradis is *the* street for china and glass, French and imported at every price range. But before you spend time or money, there are two little known museums I earnestly recommend: ◄

● **The Baccarat Crystal Museum** (no. 30) is combined with a vast and impressive shop selling everything from magnificent chandeliers to glasses and animal sculputres. The fascinating museum has crystal dating to 1823 and ancient glass blowing instruments.

● **The Musée de la Publicité** (no. 18) There are extraordinary art nouveau mosaics in the passage and stairway to this exhibition mainly of poster art – Picasso for Cocteau etc. Shops selling posters, too. Don't miss it. Some of the recommended shops are:

● **Limoges Unic,** *56 rue de Paradis* Villeroy and Boch, Lafarge and others as well as a wide range of Limoges.

● **Le Potier d'Etains** Specialises in pewter; silver and faïence.

● **Editions Paradis,** *29 rue de Paradis* Famous marques of crystal like Baccarat and Lalique, figurines by Tallec, Lyadro and Wiertasca.

● **Arts Ceramics,** *15 rue de Paradis* Traditional china and silver, reproduction faïence; good for gifts..

● **Limoges Unic,** *12 rue de Paradis* Another branch, but specialising in more formal designs of the great names of china and porcelain.

● **Tholoniat,** *47 rue du Château-d'eau* M. Tholoniat fashions sugar into every imaginable shape with consummate artistry, and there is a good variety of rich classic cakes. But look carefully at those chocolates famed for their luscious centres, and then look away – many are fashioned to represent the, ummm, droppings of this or that animal. It's a comment on what is thought of his competitors rather than of his own chocolates, I believe.

● **Marché du Château d'Eau** On the corner of *rue du Château d'eau* and *rue Bouchardon,* opposite the local mayor's office. This old, covered market is a genuine flavour of the way things used to be, but may be too much for some – especially the sight of produce being washed in the communal fountain. But it does survive as a protest against too much progress and if the locals like it, who are we to criticise or patronize? Open Tuesday to Saturday, closed 1–4pm and on Sunday mornings.

● **Schmid,** *76 bd de Strasbourg* The most important and busiest Alsatian *charcuterie* in Paris. Wonderful *choucroute* and all the sausages and *salaisons* you can imagine to go with it. Naturally enough, the fruit tarts of spring and autumn are terrific. Their other branch at *3 bd Denain* has less selection but you can actually eat there.

● **Marché St-Quentin** On the corner of *bd Magenta* and *rue Chabrol,* this covered market has recently been restored, and has one of the Wallace fountains which used to grace most of Paris as a focal point. An hour or two spent here tells you much of what is happening in Paris. For the choice ranges from fabulous Atlantic and Mediterranean fish to Asian take-aways including samosas, health foods, Corsican ewes' milk cheese, a *triperie, volaillier* with every imaginable bird, marvellous vegetables, regional *charcuterie,* wine, a café – and frozen foods.

● **Aux Délices de la Table,** *63 rue Chabrol* Speciality foods; strangely out of place luxury food shop with produce from *Fauchon* including wines and spirits, chocolates and teas.

● **Mauduit,** *12 bd Denain and 54 Fbg St-Denis* Really marvellous food to 'eat here or take away', mainly prepared at the second address. Confectionery, chocolate, pastries or something more substantial. The Denain address is somewhat belle-époque and has an upstairs tea salon.

➤ Now, here you can walk on to the *Canal St-Martin* and cross it to do some real exploring.

If you do, head for the revolving bridge and the *Café du Pont Tournant* on *rue de la Grange-aux-Belles,* and watch this extraordinary world go by through fabulous 19th-century etched glass windows.

Otherwise, head up to Montmartre by *rue de Dunkerque,* which is brash and touristy beside *Gare du Nord,* and thus with the advantage of good cheap eats and cheap hotels; once over the junction with *boulevard Magenta* it narrows and becomes neighbourly. You'll find plenty to interest you, including: ◄

● **Grandmère l'Oye,** *57 rue de Dunkerque* Small shop specializing in *foie gras,* fresh and cooked, but which doesn't accept credit cards as their prices are considered lowest for value in Paris. Other goodies too – caviar, dried wild mushrooms, truffles. *Le Figaro* has called it and its sister shop 'The Berthillon of *foie gras*'; it *is* nicer to buy it here than from the glittering palaces of the 8e.

● **Sarazin,** *70 rue de Dunkerque* One of several good confectioners and pastry shops in the street; nice fruit tarts and *feuilletées,* super presents, stuffed bonbons *bonbons fourrés.*

● **La Corniche,** *corner of bd de Rochechouart* Friendly Tunisian café-restaurant to enjoy mint tea and something *à la carte* or from a set menu; *brik à l'oeuf,* good couscous and the like.

ARRONDISSEMENT 18

Pigalle, Montmartre, Place du Tertre, Sacré-Coeur, Clignancourt

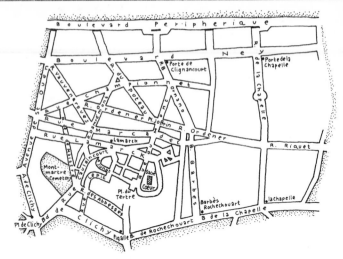

I can't think of a better autumn morning I've spent anywhere. The sparkling, cleaner air and sudden, high gaping views down to the Seine dismissed the steep-stepped routes that make and mar Montmartre. A street-fair enlivened further both the bohemian casualness and my enjoyment of picking over fresh *cèpes* and *trompettes de la mort* from overflowing panniers, and it assisted the weaker to walk past the dribbling stacks of heads, legs and haunches of venison and boar. The fair's gallic disorganisation melted the crowd into one: for while men with bag pipes and girls with clogs jigged regional dances in the streets, pop music blared from lamp-posts; someone had forgotten to close the streets and cars hooted and drove cursing through the ribboned troupes. With two slices of nut-and-caramel filled *engadine* from *Le Moule à Gâteau*, the sun on my back, and a wonderous array of fish and cheese, meat, poultry, game, *charcuterie* and confectionery to explore, it was *pas de problème*.

The drama of Montmartre's setting forces new views upon you on even the shortest walk. They are as potent as the paintings, even amid the coachloads of gapers, and still infect hundreds of artists with the belief that they can emulate the imagery of their Impressionist predecessors. You can judge their success, and those who buy the works, in the Place du Tertre. But it is

you who will have a finger – feet? – on the more valid pulse of Montmartre when you potter down rue du Mont-Cenis to the markets of rue du Poteau and rue Duhesme. If you've only a short time in Paris but want to balance the might of her monuments and art with some modern reality, this is probably the best place to do it. And you can combine the area with the *Marché aux Puces* at Clignancourt. There are other antique and junk markets, but you need to see this once at least. There are bargains in small things for kitchens and in bigger pieces, if you look carefully.

● **Le Wepler,** *14 pl Clichy* Seafood restaurant, specialising in oysters, but also such regional specialities as *confit de canard* or *andouillette*. Daily until 1.30am.

● **Pettier,** *14 ave de Clichy Boulangerie;* traditional shapes and types of loaves plus walnut bread.

● **Cochet,** *20 ave de Clichy Pâtisserie; palmiers,* sorbets, chocolates and excellent *petits fours*. Closed Wednesdays.

➤ The area where *rue Lepic* meets *avenue de Clichy* is a busy mixture of styles and cultures. At the corner of the two thoroughfares is *Moulin Rouge* surrounded by sex shops, shops catering for transvestites, and fast food shops. The district has always been favoured by artists and theatrical people – a plaque at *45 rue Lepic* commemorates where Vincent van Gogh and his brother once lived. It is now a shop called *Triperie*, one of a number of small designer shops which, along with 50s retro and funky clothes boutiques, are concentrated here. A large Arab and North African community has settled around Clichy, which has meant an influx of exotic foods into the shops and market. Don't be sniffy and look only at the high-class shops – the supermarket on the left as you walk up is really terrific – and *cheap* for snacks, mineral water to sip, and toiletries. ◀

● **La Poularde,** *10 rue Lepic* Old poultry market with glass and wooden counter where poultry is cut to order. *Poulets de Bresse* delivered Wednesday and Friday, venison in season; barbary duck, guinea fowls, quails eggs.

● **Lux Bar,** *12 rue Lepic* Local bar with marble-topped tables and tile mural of belle-époque Montmartre. Also serves food.

● **Caves Lepic,** *19 rue Lepic* Wine shop with both *petits vins* and *grands crus*, and especially good bordeaux.

● **Broquère,** *22 rue Lepic* Île de la Réunion specialities; converted from an old *grainerie*. Plantains and okra, vanilla pods, peanuts, exotic syrups, pink peppercorns (*baies roses*, actually not pepper but Florida Holly).

● **Les Petits Mitrons,** *28 rue Lepic Pâtisserie*; old-fashioned *tartes* and *tourtes*, home made jams and preserves, *cherry clafoutis* and cucumber and *mint tourte*.

● **Via Domani,** *79 rue Lepic* Household shop with special lines in ultra-modern Italian and French-designed tableware and furniture.

● **Da Graziano,** *83 rue Lepic* Restaurant situated on the site of one of three remaining *moulins* on the hill. Three doors away is the famous *Moulin de la Galette*. Tables in the garden. *Carpaccio* and *panserotti* are specialities.

➤ One of the finest art-deco metro signs can be found at Metro Abbesses. An art-deco water fountain scintillates in the cobble-stoned and chestnut-lined *Place Emile-Goudeau*, a walk up *rue Ravignan*. *Abbesses Market*, *rue des Abbesses* Street market stretching from the corner of rue Lepic to metro **Abbesses**. ◄

● **Au Cochon Rose**, a butcher/ caterer *fabrication artisinale* does business from a two-storey wooden house painted with a pink pig. Fresh pasta from sidewalk pasta machine at the *épicerie*.

● **La Boutique au Fromage,** *48 rue des Abbesses* and **Chez Claude,** *50 rue des Abbesses* sells every type of clam as well as ready-to-heat *escargot* prepared in butter.

● **Letellier-Volaille,** *57 rue des Abbesses* resembles a hunting lodge where stuffed partridges and quails are traded beneath the stuffed heads of deer and boar. Beautiful *coquilles St-Jacques* with corals, as well as tuna

and live crabs are available at **Poissonnerie de la Butte** on the corner of *rue Lepic*.

● **Le Moule à Gâteau** sells every one of its butter-made cakes and pies by the slice.

● **L'Assommoir,** *12 rue Girardon* Restaurant named after Emile Zola's first realistic novel and full of the owner's cats – most of them china – plus a collection of African and Oceanic masks. Specializes in haddock, turbot and *magret de canard*.

● **Vineyards of Montmartre,** *rue des Saules* Vineyard, of all things, producing a wine which is sold off once a year at a charity auction held at Hotel de Ville. Around 36F a bottle. A grape harvest festival in October.

● **Caves de Nîmes,** *7 bis rue Tardieu* Wine shop selling 160 kinds of *crus d'appellation* and 40 champagnes. Cheese platters on wicker prepared to order. Cahors St-Didier '78; Crozes hermitage '77; Pinot Noir Bourgogne. Closed Wednesdays.

➤ Now find *Place du Tertre*, teeming with artists good and bad, the stunning views of Paris from the Butte and Sacré-Coeur Cathedral; plenty of places to eat and snack, but it's better to go on away from the crowd. ◄

● **Beauvilliers,** *52 rue Lamarck* Smart and expensive restaurant which draws a very Parisian crowd and is filled with more flowers than any other establishment in the city. Specialities include *rogonnade de veau aux truffes et à la crème de marsala*.

● **Ferme Poitevine,** *64 rue Lamarck* Cheese shop; *munster fermier* and *camembert*. Recommended *charcuterie*, too.

● **La Gourmanderie,** *110 rue Lamarck* Foie gras speciality shop, offering new concept in eating; *foie gras* and *plats de jour* can be eaten on the premises or taken away. Large wine selection.

● **Sadier,** *43 rue Ramey* Classic *charcuterie* and caterers in the *Champenois* style; interesting range of champagnes and wines.

● **L'Epidaure,** *78 rue Labat* Tea salon offering vegetarian food made with natural products. Closed Tuesdays.

● **Meneau,** *59 bis rue du Mont-Cenis Boulangerie* specializing in health foods prepared by Abel Meneau and sold throughout Paris. *Pain de campagne biologiques,* cakes *diététiques,* wonderful almond macaroons. Closed Sundays. Honeys include raspberry *framboise*.

● **Cave du Mont Cenis,** *60 rue du Mont Cenis* Wine cellar; casks of wine are stacked outside on the pavement before bottling; special offers chalked on board. *Vieille Armagnac 1942*.

● **Pâtisserie René Raveau,** *81 rue du Mont Cenis* Classic *pâtisserie; Ganache* chocolate cake and the *gâteau maison* (chantilly and chocolate-topped caramelized *crème*) are specialities. Said to be one of absolute best of this style in Paris.

➤ *Rue du Poteau* is a busy working-class market street where every shop sells vegetables, fruit, meat, poultry, prepared foods or flowers. Shops in the surrounding streets are devoted strictly to food and food-related products. ◄

● **Fromagerie de Montmartre,** *9 rue du Poteau* Cheese shop offering almost 250 cheeses including *pérails fermiers* (cow or sheep). Corsican cheese, chantilly cream, bite-sized *fromage frais* covered with herbs, raisins, cinnamon, walnuts etc. Heart-shaped cheese moulds and fresh pasta also sold.

● **Charcuterie du Montmartre,** *11 rue du Poteau* Charcuterie; *plats à emporter* like *canard a l'orange* and stuffed zucchini. Whole glazed hams.

● **M. Billard-Produits Régionaux,** *12 rue du Poteau* Shop selling Breton products; *Kouingaman, far breton* and *crêpe froment (fait maison)*. Full selection of sausages and *terrines*.

● **Lair,** *23 rue Lepic* and *23 rue du Poteau Charcuterie;* specializing in food from the Auvergne.

- **Jandré,** *76 rue Duhesme* A *Maître de France pâtisserie*; peach and pear charlottes.
- **Market rue Duhesme,** Street market between the corner of *rue du Poteau* and *rue Ornano.* Many merchants still wear blue smocks. Serenaded by street musicians, vegetables, fish, poultry, cheese, meat, flowers, and some clothing are for sale. The *saucisse Bretonne* and *saucisse fumée Bretonne* sold at *Produits Regionaux Debeaux, 62 rue Dehesme* have both won 1st prize des-Côtes-du-Nord. Closed Sundays and Monday afternoons. Good fish at no 63 and cheese at 72, *Jean Barthélémy avec les Mauriciens.*
- **Soldacongo,** *53 rue Dehesme* 'Seconds' shop; reject, out-of-stock and overstock china. Coloured earthenware.
- **La Pêche Bretonne,** *8 ave de la Porte-de-Montmartre* Fish shop which also supplies many fine restaurants. Mediterranean and Atlantic fish; fresh frogs' legs, *bouillabaisse.* Closed Mondays and Tuesdays.
- **Lechaudel,** *52 rue Darémont Triperie;* tripe in muscadet, madeira, tomato, *lyonnaise* or *savoyarde.* All kinds of tongue and liver and a full assortment of *abats* – giblets and offal. Closed Wednesday mornings and Saturday afternoons.
- **Fougasserie,** *159 rue Marcadet Boulangerie;* specializing in *fougasse* with *lardons,* with cumin.
- **Aux Ducs de Gasgogne,** *123 rue Caulaincourt* Speciality shop; own brand *foie gras* products from Gascony (no imported livers used). Shops located throughout Paris. Wines from the region; *petit ragoût d'oie, salmis de pintade, médallion de foie gras.*
- ➤ From *rue Caulaincourt* walk up rue Junot where the building at no 13 with its tile murals is a homage to *dessinateur* François Poulbot. Further on is *rue Girardon,* a delightful residential street lined with chestnut trees. The houses are of painted brick, an unusual sight in Paris.

Walk up *rue Tourlaque* to Le Fusains (at no. 22), an artists colony set in a maze of 16th-century buildings. Classic and modern sculptures are set in the flowering overgrown gardens. ◄
- **L'Escargot de la Butte,** *46 rue Joseph-de-Maistre* Restaurant dedicated to *escargots.* They're also painted on the building, featured on posters and celebrated in sculpture. Closed Mondays.
- **Schmid,** *199 rue Championnet Charcuterie* specializing in food from Alsace; *choucroute, saucisson de foie.*
- **Chuet,** *28 ave de St-Ouen* Corsican products; proprietor Henri Chuet receives deliveries of *broccio* cheese from Corsica every 15 days. Charcuterie includes *prisuttu, figatelli, lonzo, coppa.*

Bon Marché in the Île-de-France

Below is a selection of markets in the towns around Paris. Unless otherwise stated, the markets are open daily, except Mondays.

ESSONNE
Arpajon Fri; *Bean Fair 19-22 Sept;* **Bièvres** Wed am *Strawberry Fair 3rd Sun June;* **Brétigny-sur-Orge** Thur, Sun am; **Brunoy; Corbeil-Essonnes; Dourdan** Wed & Sat am; **Draveil** Tue, Thur, Fri, Sun am; **Etampes** Sat, Tue am; **Longjumeau** Wed, Thur, Sat, Sun am; **Massy** Tue, Fri, Thur, Sun am; **Montgeron; Palaiseau; Ris Orangis** Wed, Thur, Sat, Sun; **Savigny-sur-Orge** Tue, Thur, Fri, Sat pm, Sun am; **St-Geneviève-des-Bois; Vigneux-sur-Seine; Viry-Châtillon** (ex Sat pm) **Yerres.**

VAL-d'OISE
Argenteuil; Arnouville les Gonesse Tue, Wed, Thurs, Sat, Sun; **Beaumont-sur-Oise** Tue, Thur, Sat am; **Bessancourt** Tue, Fri am; **Enghien-les-Bains** Tue, Thur, Sat am; **Ermont; Garges-les-Gonesse; Gonesse** Tue, Thur, Fri, Sun; **Groslay** Thur, Sun am; **Montmagny** Wed, Fri, Sun, *Pear Fair 2nd week Oct;* **Montmorency; Monsoult** Tue, Fri am; **Pontoise** Tue, Thur, Fri, Sat; **Sannois** am Tue, Wed, Thur, Sat, Sun; **Soisy-sous-Montmorency** Mon, Wed, Fri, Sun; **St-Brice-sous-Forêt** Tue, Thur, Fri, Sun; **Taverny** Tue, Fri am; **Villiers-le-Bal** Tue, Fri, Wed, Sat.

YVELINES
Achères Fri am, Wed, Sat; **Celle-St-Cloud; Conflans-Ste-Honorine; Essart-le-Roi** Tue am, Fri; **Freneuse** Mon, Thur, Sat during asparagus season; **Maisons-Laffitte** Wed, Sun am; **Mantes-la-Jolie** Wed, Sat am, *Onion Fair 1st Wed Dec;* **Marly-le-Roi** Tue, Fri, Sun; **Maurepas** Wed, jumble sale Sat (Oct); **Meulan** Mon, Fri am jumble sale 18th Sept; **Plaisir** Tue, Fri am; **Rambouillet** am Wed, Sat, Thur; **Sartrouville** am Tue, Thur, Sat, Sun; **St-Germain-en-Laye** Wed am, Thur, Fri, Sat, am Sun; **Velizy-Villacoublay; Versailles; Vesinet; Viroflay.**

SEINE-ET-MARNE
Bois-le-Roi Thur, Sun; **Brou-sur-Chantereine** Tue, Sat; **Champagne-sur-Seine** Thur, Sat; **Coulommiers** Wed, Sat, Sun; **Crécy-La-Chapelle** Thur, Sat, Sun; **Fontainebleau** Tue, Fri, Sun; **Gretz-Armainvilliers** Tue, Fri; **Guignes** Fri; **Jouy le Chatel** Wed, Thur; **Lésigny** Wed, Sat; **Meaux** Tue, Thur, Sat; **Melun** Wed, Sat, Thur, Sun; **Montereau-Fault-Yonne** Wed, Sat; **Moret-sur-Loing** Tue, Fri, Sat, Sun **Nemous** Wed, Fri; **Ozoir-la-Ferrière** Wed, Sat, Thur, Sun; **Pontault-Combault** Tue, Wed, Fri, Sat; **Provins** Sat, Thur, **Roissy** Wed, Sat; **Villeparisis** Wed, Fri, Sun.

As befits the cradle of France, this is the home of the cheese voted king – *brie de Meaux*. All the other cheeses made in the area are either variations of this round, flat, white-moulded variety, or are soft, creamy cheeses, some enriched further with double cream.

● *Boursin* Famous flavoured soft cheese, commercially produced, with a high 70% fat content. Also made in Normandy.

Charlemagne, Henry IV and by Queen Marie Leczinska who used it in her famous *bouchées à la reine*. Made from raw cow's milk, the white crust should be slightly pigmented with red or brown, the body a firm pale yellow – supple but not runny and the flavour farmy and rather nutty. Best from July to March – but difficult to look after well in high summer. The most highly regarded is from Meaux itself. Made in

● *Chèvru* An ancient farmer's cheese that keeps well, cured on beds of fern for a month. Very similar to *brie de Meaux* in flavour and may be called a *fougère* or *fougèru*. Very delicious dinner party food.

● *Coulommiers* Increasingly produced in factories, a smaller type of *brie de Meaux* on a bed of straw (usually plastic!). Sometimes made extra rich at 50% fat content.

● *Délice de St-Cyr* From St-Cyr-sur-Morin, a triple-

ÎLE DE FRANCE CHEESE

● *Brie de Coulommiers* Also known as *brie petit moule*; related to *brie de Meaux*, it is rather rich and sharp and sometimes used to make cheese croquettes. Best autumn to spring. Weighs about 1kg/2lb or more. NB *not* a *coulommiers* (qv).

● *Brie laitier* Commercially produced in the Île de France and in other parts of the north; weighs 2-3kg/4-7lb. Made of pasteurized milk of differing fat content, and the quality varies enormously. In France you should only eat the next 3 types:

● *Brie de Meaux fermier* Officially voted 'King of Cheeses' in 1815 by the 143 negotiators of the Congress of Vienna, who reorganized Europe after the Napoleonic Wars. This cheese has an ancient and distinguished history. It was appreciated by

the *département* of Seine-et-Marne and as well in nearby *départements* of Burgundy, Champagne and the Loire.

● *Brie de Melun AOC* Another *brie* protected by an AOC this is perhaps the oldest of them all. Produced in small dairies but in the traditional manner and cured twice as long as other *bries*. Made from raw cow's milk and very like *brie de Meaux* (qv), but a little fruitier and earthier to the nose. Smaller too at about 1.5kg/3lb. Best July to March. May also be eaten fresh *(frais)* or sprinkled with charcoal *(bleu)*.

● *Brie de Montereau* A very fruity flavour to this *brie* made in traditional small dairies. Also known as *Ville-St-Jacques* and more the shape and size associated with Normandy *camemberts*.

cream cheese (75% fat) with a mild, somewhat nutty flavour, excellent with light fruity wines.

● *Explorateur* Commercially made triple-cream cheese with creamy flavour and 75% fat content.

● *Feuille de Dreux* Made from partly-skimmed cow's milk, a low fat (30-40%) cheese with a strong fruity flavour related to *brie de Melun*. An ancient household cheese, wrapped in 6 chestnut leaves.

● *Fontainebleau* Fresh cheese curds mixed with whipped cream and thus an immature triple-cream cheese. Eaten with sugar as a dessert, but needs to be chilled. Phillipe Olivier sells it, so you can bring it home from Boulogne; but it's simpler to make your own.

● *Ville-St-Jacques* See *brie de Montereau*.

A Brother-hood of Committees

Life at the domestic tables of Burgundy must be dreadfully confusing. The region eats and drinks under the burden of as many opinions as there are people, and under the scrutiny of more brother-hoods, societies, circles, guilds and the like per village and town than anywhere else in the world. *Les Chevaliers du Tastevin* have become an inter-national institution; others are relentlessly local – the Chevaliers dedicated to protecting and eating *pauchouse*, the *Confrérie de l'Escargot*, *Les Chevaliers des Trois Cèpes* and the like. The epicentre of this earnest scholarliness is Dijon.

I went there in early November, knowing only that the city's name was on a lot of mustard and that the dukes of Burgundy had been envied for their kitchen. I travelled by slow stopping train northwards from Lyon,

with the Saône on my right, and the grey skeletons of the last vintage on my left, through Chagny and Châlons and other towns with nothing but names to tell of their connection with wine. From trains you see little of the real life of a village, smell neither tang of acrid black tobacco nor the rich air of buttery baking, hear no hiss of a coffee machine, enjoy no sudden turn into a bright market or quiet shop where even old friends are addressed as Monsieur and Madame. At least on this route I knew they were there, for I had once driven open-topped through the harvesting villages. Now my backyard view from the carriage completed the picture, for behind the tall, bright-tiled village houses I discovered gardens growing herbs and tightly-staked tomatoes, with next door here an ill-tempered goat

bullying with yellow teeth a hedge, and there in the next, the last reddened apples on an old tree waiting their turn for the table.

Distinguished Bodies

The reason for this seemingly unseasonal visit is one which I urge all admirers of French food to copy, a visit to the Dijon Food Fair; and you can now get to Dijon from Paris by TGV in 1½ hours. It is different from most fairs, being for the public rather than for the trade. For two weeks families from Dijon and *la toute France* cram the hall to taste *saucisses* new to them, compare oysters from Brittany with those of Aquitaine, eat in restaurants from other regions, try old and new gingerbreads from Mulot et Petitjean, and to sniff at specialities from the featured guest country. Few internationally-known brand names are there, not even of

> **In which we...**
> ● Go above the salt and below stairs in a palace...
> ● Learn of wet nurses and dry hams in the Morvan...
> ● Explore a lotte of confusion and see where boiling wine changed our life...
> ● Taste the produce of a fisherman's pouch and try to get an invitation to a genuine pig-out...
> ● Are told not to expect fireworks in Chambertin and learn how to lose heart...
> ● Enjoy the cream of the currant crop and perhaps a Japanese rarity, and cut into a *gaude*...
> ● Find which cheese should have holes, and which cheese isn't a cheese...
> ● Buy gingerbread and are introduced to a rock which should not be eaten...
> ● Meet unusual women and learn of one's connection with a monastery...
> ● Go to a fair and taste all day...
> ● Visit the town that cuts the mustard...

vine, and thus it is an excellent opportunity to compare the products of champagne houses never seen in Britain and the US. Or perhaps to taste the wines of Arbois or of new plantations from the south.

The Dijon fair is also the meeting place of distinguished bodies with long names; exceptionally learned and interesting culinary papers are delivered by *États Généraux de la Gastronomie Française et de l'Alimentation de Qualité*. Members of the press belonging to equally over-named societies come from all over France to hear what they have to say, and to attend the only other functions to which the public is not privy, the judging of alcohols and the awarding of the year's new ribbons by *La Commanderie des Cordons Bleus de France*.

A Hearty Kitchen

If the food or the fair becomes too much to digest easily then you should return to the centre of town and the duke's palace. Fully to appreciate its golden symmetry, delay your expedition until late in the evening, then circle the site so that you approach it by one of the arch-ended, narrow streets that empties into the subservient low semicircle of shops on the place de la Libération. Dramatically, the floodlit palace floats at eye level across a broad rise of cobbles, a grand country house come to town, with undertakers and gingerbread shops for its gardens and fountains. Only when you return the next day will you appreciate the irony of building such a palace around the lop-sided Tower of Philippe le Bon.

Included in the palace is the *Musée des Beaux Arts*, housing the best art collection in France after the Louvre and mercifully open on Mondays when everything else is closed. Once you have walked to find favourites on the walls and appreciated some fine contemporary furniture in the grander rooms, return to the ground floor and to the room considered by many as the heart of Burgundy, the 15th-century kitchens of the palace. There is talk that the dukes entertained there, but a few minutes imagining the heat from the fires that burned under the six open chimneys should show this was no place for velvets and breeches. No, I think the meaning behind this view is that the dukes were here so overwhelmed by the food their fabulous wealth and power could command that their culinary hospitality was an important part of the influence they wielded. The kitchen became a symbol of Burgundy in a way it did nowhere else, perhaps explaining that rash of opinions and brotherhoods. Currency was given to the belief that in Burgundy everyone ate and drank like a duke. Of course, that simply wasn't the case.

Committee Cheese

The Burgundians are largely descended from bluff Vikings, the sort who came overland rather than by sea. They found things fairly well organised, thanks to the legacy of the Romans – decent vines, good grain crops and access to the produce of the north, east, west and south via river and easy land. The essentials of the Burgundian table today are much the same. The wine you know about, although almost no-one can claim to understand the finessing of vineyard names on the bottles' labels. And today Burgundy grows three times more wheat than she can eat. With this long tradition of grain there is generally an excellent range of *pâtisserie* and of bread; the number of bread types is increasing according to a local baker, as the French demand more wholewheat and mixed grain loaves. In the Morvan, pigs remain virtually free-range, but the other crop, of wet-

nurses for Paris, is today harder to find.

Freshwater fish, small game, poultry and snails all played their part in the Burgundian diet of the less privileged majority, but the basic was that of most of France, a porridge, or *bouillie,* of whatever grain was available. Often it was millet, for this gives more bulk when cooked than any other grain but this was universally replaced by maize when it came from the Americas. Today *bouillies* are eaten only by the old, but through choice rather than necessity.

The Burgundian's easterly neighbours, the Francs-Comtois have none of that culinary competitiveness. The very name of the region means Free Country and a palpable independence has been enhanced by extraordinary community spirit – and more committees. The cheese-makers formed themselves into co-operatives before the end of the 13th century to make communal cheeses, the fruits of the mountains, in *fruitières.* The motto of winemakers some centuries later was: We Are All In Charge.

A Pinch of Salt

Franche-Comté, often confused with Jura, which is only its southern *département,* appears to have borrowed a number of foods from other countries – they have there a fondue of cheese like the Swiss, their *gaude* of cornmeal is often served like *polenta,* their *bresi* is thinly sliced air-dried beef, like that of the Alps, and such *vins*

jaunes yellow wines as Château-Chalon taste like sherry. They serve a cheese flan *flamusse,* and ramekins of cheese, with apparent ignorance of those of Burgundy. But it is as well if any such similarities you notice while visiting are kept to yourself, for in the Franche-Comté they *are* Francs-Comtoises.

You may, however, laugh as much as you like at the ineptitude of central governments and at royal madness in Arc-et-Senans (Doubs). Here you will find the extraordinary semi-classical buildings of the *Saline Royale,* Royal Saltworks. Built in the late 1770s, it planned to provide huge quantities of salt by the evaporation of water from local saline springs over fires stoked by wood from the forest of Chaux. But almost immediately, the salt level of the spring was found to be lower than thought, there wasn't nearly enough wood, and other more economical methods of making salt were mastered. The restored buildings and works are well worth seeing, and then you can go off to older, smaller, nicer Salins-les-Bains, a spa with salt mines and wells you can visit.

Fun of the Fray

You will find much to intrigue you in Burgundy and Franche-Comté. Where it is most interesting you are most likely to find some supporting organisation in the background. There are enough in Franche-Comté for there to be a *President des Sociétés Culinaires de Franche-Comté.* The men and

CHARCUTERIE

women who bring their country produce to the narrow streets and huge covered market between Dijon's rue de la Liberté and Church of Notre Dame, will belong to one or have a relative in *La Cousinerie de Savigny-les-Beaune,* or supply something special to a *rôtisseur.* Thus anyone with French who enjoys a good argument on the relative merits of one chicken against another or the amount of garlic that should be in the butter of the snails prepared in Auxerre is in for a wonderful time. It's even more interesting because here, far more than in Lyon, supposedly famed for the influence of women on its food, I found successful and respected women in the food business, like Madame Porchevet, who has managed to winkle supplies of Cîteaux out of the monks who make it. Or Louise Mirbey, chef-patronne of *Auberge du Vieux Moulin* (Aubigny – 70140 Pesmes), and President of the *Association des Restauratrices-Cuisinières.*

I can't guarantee you'll always eat wonderfully in Burgundy or Franche-Comté, but I can guarantee you'll have much fun doing it. You'll meet more enthusiastic shopkeepers, with handwritten labels in red ink on everything, more eccentric opinions and more newly-invented specialities than anywhere else in France. The best way to cope with it is to do as the Burgundians. Form a committee of people who agree with you. You'll be welcomed to the fray...

As with most foods, Burgundy and Franche-Comté have absorbed the best ideas from neighbouring regions and adapted them to their superior produce. Even with such abundance, they make and enjoy *boudins, andouilles,* and *andouillettes* in Arnay-le-Duc, Chablis, Clamecy and Mâcon. I like to snack wickedly on *grillons* and *grattons* which are pieces of bacon or salt pork cooked until crisp and frizzled; they are also found in *galettes.* Sausages are great spe-

cialities, both air-dried *saucissons,* such as *rosette du Morvan,* and fresh or smoked *saucisses* which are usually enjoyed hot. The garlic ones – *à l'ail* – may be cut up to fatten a soup of cabbage and onion, and there are others flavoured with cumin.

Exceptional hams are a great boast of the area, especially those from Morvan and Luxeuil in Franche-Comté. Ham is often enjoyed hot, braised, with a cream sauce or as *saupiquet.*

Worth Finding

● *Bresi* Thinly sliced cured and air-dried beef, usually eaten as is, but sometimes put into *potées.*

● *Jésus de Morteau* Morteau is an important centre of *charcuterie.* The *jésus* or *jésu* is a dried salami type of sausage, one of many using the name and all from the East of France. It is said to be so called because it, or this style,

is 'the best in the world'.

● *Judru* This *saucisson sec* is made in the end of the large intestine of the pig and has been famed for centuries. The meat is chopped rather than minced and macerated in *marc de bourgogne.* Originally made only in Chagny, where the pigs' erstwhile diet of acorns and vipers gave the flesh a special flavour.

FISH & SHELLFISH

In this region of rushing streams, of brooks and rivers, I find myself thinking of Louisiana: her Cajun craw-fishers are descended from 17th-century French immigrants and the Acadienne swamps now produce 85% of the world's harvest of *écrevisses* freshwater crayfish. There are persistent whispers that most *écrevisses* sold in France are actually Acadienne, imported through necessity in the same way as snails and *foie gras*. But considering the amount of fresh water available and the comparatively few visitors who patronize Franche-Comté, I feel more certain of getting a genuine local crayfish here than anywhere else in France. Just as well, for what is more luxurious than the rich sauce of puréed crayfish tails, cream and wine named after the epicentre of crayfish eating, Nantua, just across the way in Savoie?

In Burgundy and Franche-Comté you can dine confidently, assured of the best of virtually any freshwater fish you would expect to find inland. Rainbow trout is superb universally, and especially from the Cure and Cousin in the Yonne, from the Doubs in Franche-Comté and at Gray and Dôle, where Louis Pasteur began his experimenting by boiling wine. Smaller, quieter restaurants may offer the rare chance of a genuine *truite au bleu*.

Pike *brochet* is also found poached in white wine, for those stories of the bones being difficult are a little over-dramatic. You will find carp, eels, perch and tench (*carpe, anguilles, perche* and *tanche*) *en meurette* among other ways, but not the rare char.

The snail most often eaten throughout France is the *petit gris* (helix aspersa), which is specially common on vineyards. It fattens itself through summer, when it is but a waning one, for it is one of the few culinary specialities of national importance not protected by AOC legislation. Thus, even in Burgundy, your *escargots de* psyche, for their custom of disappearing into the earth in winter and emerging in summer was linked ritualistically with life and death. Only one festival associated with such

A RITUAL

OF SNAILS

known as a *coureur* or runner, then becomes a *dormeur* or sleeper when it burrows under the ground to hibernate in winter. It is at this time that the snail is considered tastiest, and this is when snail hunts are, or were, common. Not very sporting.

In the chalkier regions of eastern France there is a bigger, fatter, juicier snail, the Burgundy snail, *escargot de Bourgogne* (helix pomotia). In the culinary world it is a star, *Bourgogne* might be any species – what's more they may come from Turkey, and might well have arrived prepared and frozen.

The high general regard the French seem to give snails is less than a century old. Although the Romans cared enough to provide artificial rain for the snails they raised, the French regarded them as food for the poor, or for hard times. But they have long been part of the national customs survives in Burgundy, at Bassou near Auxerre, an important centre for snail preparation still.

All French snails are becoming rarer as a result of the increased use of agricultural chemicals, especially in vineyards, and the disappearance of hedgerows. Even though laws prohibiting the gathering of Burgundian snails during their breeding season (April 1st to June 30th) have been passed, the

● *Écrevisses à la nage* Often called a *nage* of this or that. *Nager* means to swim and so these dishes are always crayfish, whole or just tails, in an aromatic liquid, not sauce, of wine and herbs, sometimes with cream or butter or both.

● *Meurette* Burgundian red wine sauce used for almost everything and excellent on eels, carp, perch and tench.

● *Pauchouse,   Pochouse, Pochou* One of the region's most famous dishes and still found easily. It is a stew of freshwater fish, a variation on the *matelote* of the north of the region. The essentials are eel and burbot (classically from the Saône or Rhône), white wine, onion and garlic. Some recipes will include bacon or salt pork, cream or *marc*; old ones insist that only carp, eel and pike should be used. Several villages claim the invention, and some say the word is a dialect corruption of *pêcher* (to fish), others that it is a corruption of a word for a fisherman's pouch. Certainly   Verdun-sur-le-Doubs is one of the sources; inevitably they have a *Confrérie de la Pauchouse*.

omble chevalier, which is cooked more simply and anyway is more likely to be found in adjoining Savoie. Butter, cream and wine, onions, mushrooms and garlic are all used extensively; but it may be a surprise to find *lotte* on the menu. This is not the monkfish or anglerfish of the deep ocean, but an abbreviation of *lotte de rivière,* which is burbot.

Naturally, with so much water around, frogs are common, and commonly eaten, especially in Franche-Comté where among the many famous soups is one made from *grenouilles*.

number actually harvested is remarkably small and few restaurants, anywhere, are able to offer the genuine product. Thus 95% of all snails consumed in France come from Germany, Hungary, Czechoslovakia,   Poland, Yugoslavia, Greece, Turkey, North Africa or South-East Asia. Many of those countries have been forced to cut their quotas dramatically, some because drought has reduced their reserves, some because France is attempting to control the condition of snails arriving at the borders. Most are shipped live but often over 25% are dead on arrival, with many of the survivors diseased. Frozen ones avoid this, but are often tough and tasteless through bad feeding and worse processing. The combination of a shortage in France and reduced supplies from abroad is increasingly changing the role of the edible snail – reversing it indeed. The food of the poor may soon be the food only of the rich.

The average French person eats   600–800g/1½–2lb of snails a year at present. A study of old cookbooks reveals the taste for snails with garlic-laden butter is very modern. Butter with a *touch* of garlic and a lot of parsley was considered the way really to enjoy the flavour of the snail, and when I was served an   omelette   of   butter-smothered snails at a cognac distillery outside Jarnac, I understood why, and enjoyed the delicious nutty flavour of snails for the first time in my life. It is said in fact that the flavour is rather of *eau-de-vie,* or of cognac itself if they are genuinely local snails. A white wine is the best accompaniment if the garlic is restrained.

Amongst the myriad different ways of preparing snails, one of the most unusual is the *cargolade* of Languedoc-Roussillon, in which they are grilled over charcoal, and here is where you are equally likely to find them combined with a little salted   ham/*petit   salé,* anchovies or nuts. Elsewhere wild   mushrooms,   cream,

herbs, anis and tomatoes will feature; sausage is part of Provence's *à la suçarelle* style where you suck the snails from their shells. On the west coast, Angoulême is the most renowned centre; indeed people here are known as *cargouillards,* said to move as slowly as the *cargouilles* which they stuff and put into *ragoûts*.

Many modern restaurants eschew shells, and so also do some old ones, notably the fabulous-looking *Escargot Montorgueil* in Paris. Here they serve up to seven varieties of snail, and also create delicate gratins and casseroles. With fascinating mirrors and painted ceilings it's one of the most evocative restaurants in Paris and quite as old as it looks; it's equally famed for an almost professional lack of interest in you.

MEAT, GAME & POULTRY

The great *charollais* cattle from Charolles produce the most famous meat of the region, to the outsider. The appeal is more to the breeder and producer than the eater for the flavour of the huge amounts of flesh each animal produces is pretty inferior. But if you like looking at beef on the hoof, St-Christophe-en-Brionnais is the biggest market centre for them. There is a variation called the *charolles-nivernaise,* and for more flavour the animals of Bezail and l'Auxois repay investigation. Any of them should be found grilled over *sarments* (vine cuttings). Naturally, with so much dairying throughout Burgundy and Franche-Comté, there is veal, usually served simply with cream-based sauces. Because so much grain is grown almost every type of poultry bird is bred; they are particularly likely to be teamed with cream plus a seasonal green, anything from dandelion to tarragon.

Virtually unobtainable outside France is the *poulet de Bresse* which has an *appellation contrôlée* of its own; first time, eat it as plainly a you can to appreciate the flavour; *à la crème* is a favourite.

Burgundy's game, which runs the gamut from *sanglier* wild pig and *marcassin* wild piglet, to venison, hare, pigeon and pheasant is exceptionally good. What's bagged from the forests of Morvan at least equals the superlative quality of that from Alsace; certainly it's a persuasive reason for being here in autumn and winter rather than in sum-

---

Worth Finding

- *Boeuf bourguignon* This is what it's called when you are *not* in Burgundy, where it is *boeuf à la bourguignonne,* which is beef in a *sauce meurette.*
- *Chaudrée de lièvre* A hare stew flavoured with wine from Jura; more likely to be found in Franche-Comté.
- *Coq au Chambertin* The ultimate *coq au vin,* but to be authentic only fresh young wine should be used, so don't expect fireworks and don't pay huge prices; a white wine alternative might be *poulet au Meursault.*
- *Ferchuse* You may like to avoid this, a *ragoût* of lights, that is, lungs, heart etc.
- *Fondue bourguignonne* Actually Swiss, a cheeseless fondue where pieces of steak are cooked in boiling oil at your table.

- *Galimafrée* Sounding Elizabethan, this is a Morvan roast shoulder of mutton stuffed with bacon and mushrooms and served with vinaigrette.
- *Jambon persillé* Once served only at Easter, today it is perfect summer food, provided a decent ham is used. Should be generous chunks of ham in a parsley-packed jelly of white burgundy.
- *Lapin rôti* Although implying a rabbit roasted simply, this is almost always one of the many ways the Burgundians find of combining their mustard and their rabbits, often by covering the rabbit with a mustard coating or sauce.
- *Petit-salé aux pissenlits* Simple, peasant food celebrating spring, the classic combination of salt pork and

young dandelion greens.
- *Potée* Hearty vegetable/pork soup/stew found in most areas, made local by the variety of vegetables; you might also find it here including oxtail *queue de boeuf* which makes it even more to the British taste.
- *Saupiquet* The first dish I ever ate in Burgundy and something you should certainly order if you see it. Classically it should be slices of excellent Morvan ham, with a creamy sauce based on a classic *espagnole* or brown sauce with extra butter, vinegar, pepper and, sometimes, juniper berries. Great when it is great, but the balance of creaminess and sharpness is not easy to achieve. Gault Millau point out that where it was once famed throughout France, it is now underrated.

Egg-Bound

With so much poultry about, and so much grain to feed them upon, you are bound to find eggs offered often. Indeed, some spots have fancy names for simple dishes which turn out to be ham and eggs. Eggs turn up whisked into creamy sauces but are also featured as protein alternatives, hence that most famed Burgundian dish, *oeufs en meurette,* poached eggs in a robust thickened sauce of young local red wine, as important

here as haggis to a Scot.

Eggs combine with milk and cream in a number of savoury dishes; they are sometimes mixed into the cheese fondue of Franche-Comté; they set the Burgundian cream and bacon flan called *fouée,* first cousin of the true *quiche*; they go into *gougères* and *galettes* and the *crépiau* (a dialect name for pancakes). But they are most commonly and deliciously used in omelettes, classic with bacon

or salt pork but also with the simplest of local vegetables, herbs and greens, even cabbage. The *omelette nivernaise* of summer will probably combine ham and sorrel *oseille.* More famous is the dramatic *omelette au sang* made with pig's blood; it's sometimes called *omelette bourguignonne.* Hard-boiled eggs are served with local hams, and are enjoyed with spring-fresh dandelion greens in the Morvan.

mer. *Lapin de la garenne,* wild rabbit is a great local favourite. Towards the south, where more goat's milk cheeses are made, you will find roast kid *cabri* around Easter. Although pigs are raised universally their flesh is more likely to be found in *charcuterie* of some kind. Look for delicious *tourtes* which are which are rather like a *pâté* baked in pastry, pie-shaped rather than loaf-shaped, and *petit-pâtés,* a sort of small hot pork-*pâté* pie. But in Franche-Comté, break a leg to get invited to a *repas du cochon* which should be a progression from *boudin, fromage de tête* and *andouilles* to chops and roasts of pork . . .

An important flavour difference between the meat cooking of Burgundy and that of Franche-Comté is the type of wine used. The wines of Arbois and the sherry-like Château-Chalon of the Jura lead a distinct individuality to Franc-Comtois cooking.

POULETS DE BRESSE AOC

Contender for title of best chicken in the world, the White Bresse breed has white skin, flesh and feathers, smooth grey or blueish legs with four toes and a red wattle – any variation, even of feather colour means the bird may not be sold under an AOC label. Famous for centuries, fraud and substitution meant that some control of their production was mooted as long ago at 1591. It was only in 1936, however, that their production zone was first defined and it took until 1957 to agree legally on how they must be raised.

The most important centres within the 400 square

km/250sq mile are Bourg and Louhans, whence Fernand Point went to Vienne to become famous. Seven breeders supply day-old chicks to some 1,000 farmers, who may raise only 500 at a time. The birds spend 35 days as chicks and then must be free-ranging, on grass, for 9 weeks in the open air. Their feed must be nothing but cereal, with corn predominating, and skim milk. Even the weight of each bird before and after dressing is defined and, although there are *poulets, poulards* and *chapons,* they are usually collectively referred to as *poulets de Bresse.* AOC of course.

Dindes and Dindons de Bresse AOC

The parvenu turkey from the New World has found a little paradise for its time on earth here, too. Much less common than the chicken, but just as revelatory to enjoy as long as you can trust the chef.

FRUIT & VEGETABLES

Any talk of the fruit or vegetables of Burgundy brings to mind a strange contrast of favourites – the ancient crop of *cassis,* and the modern one of *crosne du Japon.*

Cassis blackcurrants were recommended medically in Burgundy centuries ago, but were as likely to be administered as an infusion of the leaves as in a decoction of the berries. In the heady days of 18th-century 'vapours', their reputation for efficacy was further enhanced and by 1750 the Dijonnais were encouraged to begin serious planting of the bushes, first at the Château Montmuzard. The gradually increased crops inspired another *cassis* medicine, that of berries macerated in alcohol. In 1841, they perfected *crème de cassis,* made by crushing berries into vats of alcohol, filtering the result and sweetening it, according to what are said to be secret techniques, but which use ordinary old sugar. If you are going to make some yourself, and there's no reason why not, use one part of currants to three of plain *eau-de-vie* and don't sweeten until you've drained off the mash. As you can imagine, there is both alcohol and flavour in that mash, so strain out the pips and include it when you cook up, or cook down, some *pâte de cassis,* made just the same way as an apple or damson cheese.

The quick success of the *crème* meant even more bushes were enthusiastically planted throughout Côte-d'Or, often between the grape vines. Thus when phylloxera

---

LOCAL PRODUCE

Vegetables

● **Cabbage** *chou pommé*	Dep: Côte-d'Or,
● **Carrot** *carotte*	August to mid-November Dep: Saône-et-Loire, Côte-d'Or
● **Cauliflower** *choufleur* Early varieties, mainly for export	Around June Dep: Côte-d'Or, Saône-et-Loire
● **Celeriac** *céleri-rave*	Harvest in summer, stored for winter Dep: Côte-d'Or
● **Cucumber** *concombre*	Midsummer crop Dep: Saône-et-Loire
● **Fennel** *fenouil*	Autumnish, but stored Dep: Rhône, Ain, Haute-Savoie
● **Lettuce** *laitue/chicorée* Var: from curly endive and batavia down to round lettuces	Variable according to type Dep: Saône-et-Loire
● **Onion** *oignon*	Mid-June harvest starts, sold next April Dep: Côte-d'Or
● **Radish** *radis*	Spring to summer Dep: Saône-et-Loire
● **Shallot** *échalote*	Freshly dug mid-summer, stored for use all year Dep: Côte-d'Or

The second-largest production zone after Hérault.

Fruit

● **Blackcurrants** *cassis* Var: *Noir de Bourgogne, Royal Naples*	July, usually Dep: Côte-d'Or Saône-et-Loire
Cherries *cerises* Var: *Bigarreau, Marmotte de l'Yonne*	June to mid-July Dep: Yonne June–July (variable)
Raspberry *framboise* Var: *Rose de-Côte-d'Or*	Dep: Côte-d'Or, Yonne

One of the few French varieties of raspberry grown commercially; has wonderful aroma.

---

destroyed the vines later in the century there was still a crop to produce income. The popularity of *crème de cassis* dropped dramatically during and after World War II, said to be a result of using saccharine instead of sugar. Miraculously, Mayor Felix Kir, who was also a canon of the church, announced his favourite drink to be a dilution of *crème de cassis* with chilled white burgundian wine of the *aligoté* grape. He was seen introducing 'his' drink to Russian leader Nikita Khrushchev, Pope John XXIII, and any other dignitary who happened to be present contemporaneously with a reporter, photographer or cameraman. The Kirs,

SOME LIKE IT HOT

Although Dijon is the spiritual and historical home of the mustard which bears its name, Dijon on most mustard jars now simply indicates a style of mustard and may be used by any mustard maker in France who meets the *appellation contrôlée* laws.

All mustard is made from black mustard seeds *brassica nigra* or brown mustard *brassica juncea* or some mixture, which are initially ground into a mustard flour, coarse or fine. This has negligible smell and no apparent taste when first put onto the tongue; but contact with water releases the oil and the bite. Exactly what is done to this mustard flour is what determines each style of mustard. To become *moutarde de Dijon* it is mixed with unripe grape juice but other styles will use wine, cider, beer, a mixture or just plain water. The strength depends on how much mustard flour is used in proportion to the liquid and whether or not any other solids such as sugar or other flours are included. The most difficult part of the operation, particularly if you want a hot mustard, is conserving the oil which evaporates at temperatures of 40°C.

Most of the mustard eaten in France (90%) is Dijon-style but the mustard seed is no longer exclusively grown in that region, although it grows very well there, discovered, they say, when Roman troops scattered seeds by the roadsides as they tramped backwards and forwards through the three parts of Gaul.

Mustard making was important in Dijon as long ago as the 13th century when the seeds were aged and ground with cloves, and cinnamon – but not allspice as some will tell you, for this had not yet come from the New World. The firm of Grey-Poupon established in 1777 further enhanced the city's reputation by developing a recipe which used white wine; today the company's shop at 32 rue de la Liberté is owned and operated by Henri Poupon, a descendant of the financial partner of M. Grey, the inventor.

Milder mustards are indicated by such labels as gentle *douce,* yellow *jaune,* brown *brune,* green *verte* and violet *violette.* Flavoured mustards are *moutardes aromatisées* or a *moutarde aux aromates* if there is some complication of flavouring; if something simpler is used the label is likely to tell you as in *moutarde aux fines herbes* or *moutarde à l'estragon.*

Moutarde à l'ancienne is almost always relatively mild and made with coarsely ground seeds, which process inhibits the release of some of the mustard oils. But in such a huge market, over 50,000 tonnes eaten in France alone each year, manufacturers will say and do almost anything to attract your attention. For a truer taste of ancient days, I think you have to go to Elbeuf, for some of M. Tabouelle's authentic *moutarde forte* (see **Normandy**)

Bouillie for Them

In Franche-Comté there was a long delight in barley broths, now declined. But it is there, rather than in Burgundy, you might be offered a form of *bouillie,* the thickened porridge of grain meal which was the major sustenance of the region for aeons. The Francs-Comtois call it *gaude,* and make it of cornmeal, cooked with water until very thick and served with milk or cream, perhaps wine. It may be sugared and served as a sweet, or left to cool, cut into squares and fried, like the *polenta* of Venice. The closest you are likely to get to anything remotely like the warm, thick goo of *bouillie* is *fondue,* made from mountain cheeses, and proper to the Franche-Comté via Switzerland, but certainly incorrectly described as *fondue bourguignonne* (qv).

Once the reliable 19th-century strains of American wheat came to Burgundy, which had always had supplies but which now grows three times as much as it eats, the Burgundians slowly turned their backs on such food in favour of more plentiful and varied breads, and still pride themselves today on the range baked there.

drink and man, were a gift from God to the growers: one of the most needed, and most successful, marketing ploys of the age.

Beware when buying that you are indeed buying an alcohol rather than a sugar syrup (the label will tell you) and don't be boring but go also for other flavours of the same idea. *Vedrenne Père et Fils* of Nuits-St-Georges make a sensational *crème de fraise des bois* wild strawberry, remarkably true to flavour as the fruit is not cooked in any way; its alcoholic strength is high at 20% but *crèmes* can be 16% or less, which also makes them cheaper.

The Japanese artichoke *crosne,* properly *choro-gi,* was introduced to Paris from Japan in the 1880s via Crosne in the Essonne (Seine-et-Oise). Fashionably taken up in those days of orientalia, it survives as a delicious curi-

osity only in pockets now. Sully-sur-Loire in the Loiret is one pocket. St-Seine-l'Abbaye in the Côte-d'Or is another. They are a slightly waxy, small root, sometimes confused with jerusalem artichokes – *topinambours*; the only other place I know that cultivates them regularly outside Japan is the market gardens around Wellington, New Zealand.

There are less exotic but equally delectable specialities – the asparagus of Auxonne, red and white haricot beans, the cherries of the Yonne, aniseed and hop shoots *jets d'houblon* – but there is also a huge, broad and general variety of more common vegetables and fruit. Most were once enjoyed primarily in the soups of one sort or another found in every region, but just as universally are now served lightly, elegantly and individually.

CHEESE

This is a cheese-lover's heaven. Champagne's cheeses naturally blend with those of Côte-d'Or giving more types of *chaource* and washed-rind cheeses. The rest of Burgundy makes a farmyard of cheeses, mainly *chèvres,* but some cow's milk or a mixture, the *mi-chèvres.* In Franche-Comté, you find two famous styles of cheese, *gruyère* and *cancoillotte,* both of which require some explanation.

Gruyère is a word commonly misused, particularly in France, where it has become a generic name for all the great, cooked mountain cheeses which we are more likely to associate with Switzerland – *emmental, gruyère, comté* and *beaufort.* Worshipped as 'the fruits of the mountains', these cheeses are made in a *fruitière.* If it were not confusing

---

enough to people who don't know which cheese has the holes, a French *gruyère* does have a considerable number of holes, which a Swiss one should not have. I would avoid all known words and go for *comté* or *beaufort* as they are so rarely seen outside France. The Comtois use them for cheese-wine *fondues*, of course!

And there is *cancoillotte*, a leser version of *fromage fort*, fermented leftovers. To be exact it is not really cheese at all, for the basic ingredient is *mettons*, which is made by heating whey, to solidify all the protein not already coagulated, that is, all the protein in milk which is not casein. Some sources say that farm-wives make their *mettons* by heating curds, but I find this rather unlikely, for the point of both *mettons* and *cancoillotte* is the thrifty use of a whey that would otherwise be wasted or fed to animals.

Although long, this is not an exhaustive list, especially when it comes to *chèvres*, but these are names you are most likely to see.

★ *Bleu de Gex* or *Haut-Jura AOC* Blue cheese from the highest pastureland of the Jura, where exceptionally varied flora give the milk of the *montbéliarde* cows a unique flavour. It is made by hand in traditional ways from raw milk; progressive salting gives both body and crust a special texture and an uneven marbling of blue-green which often clump together. Recommended season is May to October, for then you know the cows have grazed on the best of the fresh herbage of the Haut-Jura. This blue has such subtlety of flavour it is recom-mended that you eat it before other cheeses if you have a choice.

● *Bressan* (Bresse, Pays de l'Ain) A soft, truncated cone of medium-flavoured goat's cheese, which is best in sum-mer and autumn, and which sometimes is a *mi-chèvre*.

● *Bresse-bleu/Bleu de Bresse* Commercial blue cheese cre-ated in 1950 and based on *saingorlon* itself created to copy the soft blue gorgonzola of Italy. An unaggressive fla-vour and nice creaminess from its 50% fat content.

● *Bouton-de-culotte* See *Mâconnais*

● *Cancoillotte* (Franche-Comté) *Very* ripe *mettons* (qv) heated with brine then mixed with butter and eaten warm on bread or toast. Sometimes garlic, white wine or other fla-vourings are used. Beware of greyish look, this cheese keeps for only a short time.

● *Cendre d'Aisy* (Montbard – Côte-d'Or) A soft cow's milk cheese in disc or truncated cone shape. Cured in *marc* for two months or so then stored in wood ash. Mild smell until cut; very strong flavour. Sometimes called *Aisy cendré*.

● *Charollais* (Charolles, Bur-gundy) Goat or cow's milk, or a mixture. Hard, nutty cheese commonly used for *fromage fort* when aged.

● *Chèvreton de Mâcon* Horrid small buttons of *chèvre* stored for use in winter, when they are grated into *fromage fort*. Dark brown and brittle with an appalling smell, and only likely to be found in real spe-cialist shops or in small town markets. Who had the nerve to eat the first one?

★ *Cîteaux* (monastery of Cît-eaux, Côte-d'Or) A really deli-cious rich but unaggressive washed-rind Trappist cheese still made by monks. Their abbey remains the only reli-able source but Mme Simone Porcheret (18 rue Bannelier, Dijon), France's only female *mâitre fromager,* manages to have a few each week of what the monks can spare. A treat.

★ *Claquebitou* (Beaune) Fresh soft goat's milk cheese flavoured with garlic and herbs. Mainly domestic but some enterprising goat keep-ers may sell to you direct – look for signs as you drive in the area.

★ *Comté* or *gruyère de comté AOC* (Franche-Comté) Made for over 1,000 years and Deservillers is possibly where *gruyère* was created. The man-ufacture of *comté* is concen-trated in the *massif* of Jura but spreads throughout Fran-che-Comté. Only milk from the *montbéliarde* and *pie rouge de l'Est* cows may be used. A cooked, pressed cheese, matured 3 months (minimum) to 10 months. It should be almost odourless but have a nutty, fresh taste whether young or matured and may be enjoyed all year round. NB A local *gruyère* may almost be the same cheese, but uses different milk.

● *Dornecy* (Nièvre) A fairly uncommercialized *chèvre* or *mi-chèvre* made in and around the town of the same name, weighing just over 200g/8oz; although very goaty, the smell should be light.

● *Ducs* (Yonne) A commercial *brie/camembert* type cheese in a cylindrical shape made from pasteurized cow's milk.

● *Emmental français* Although mainly a product of Haute-Savoie, this French version of the Swiss cheese

L·A G·O·U·G·È·R·E
A·N·D
L·E·S G·O·U·G·È·R·E·S

Although a speciality of both the Aube in Champagne and the Côte-d'Or and using only the *gruyères* of Franche-Comté, *gougère* is specially associated with, and found all over, Burgundy. It is simply a choux pastry studded with cubes of a *gruyère* of some type. Today it is often made very small as an elegant warm accompaniment to drinks, but in any case, shape or style *gougère* is an excellent accompaniment to red or white wines, and may be served in place of cheese before a pudding course.

If you are driving into Burgundy from Champagne, Sens is one of the first important culinary centres and is recommended for its version, but it is the town of Tonnerre that claims its original invention.

It is important not to confuse *gougère* with the *goyère* of northern France, which is a tart made with *maroilles* cheese or with *gouerre*, which is a potato and cheese cake.

Do it yourself using your favourite *choux* pastry recipe studded with roughly chopped *gruyère*; at a pinch Dutch *gouda* will do. Never use grated cheese. Drop the paste onto a lightly greased baking

with the holes has been made here since the early 19th century, when German-Swiss cheesemakers immigrated. Aged cheeses are thought best November to May, but young ones are enjoyed all year round.

★ *Epoisses* A small round cow's milk cheese regularly washed with *marc*. Develops a penetrating smell and powerful flavour. Often kept in ashes over winter or used in *fromage fort*. M. Jean Gaugny of *Laiterie de la Côte* in Brochon (Gevrey-Chambertin) makes good ones and is also responsible for developing *L'ami du Chamertin* which is *époisses* washed in Chambertin. Lucky thing!

● *Fromage fort* Not often marketed; essentially old or overripe cheese mixed with butter, sometimes with leek water, sometimes with *marc* or with herbs, and then sealed in a pot, with occasional stirrings, for several months. It may explode; if I eat it, I do. Eaten on bread or toast with a little onion or garlic, and the truest example of an acquired taste I know.

● *Les Laumes* A brick of cheese washed with water, coffee or wine. Eaten freshish after three months, or aged, when it becomes extremely spicy and strong. Best in autumn and winter.

● *Lormes* (Nièvre) A *chèvre* or *mi-chèvre* of classic truncated cone shape with thin, blueish rind and strong flavour. Look for it in Lormes or around Clamecy.

● *Mâconnais* or *Chevreton de Mâcon* (St Pierre de Cruzille in Sâone-et-Loire and mountains of Mâcon area) Small (50g/2oz), rather firm *chèvre* with only faintly goaty flavour but which may also be eaten very fresh when it is rather creamy. May be a *mi-chèvre* or all cow's milk; these are available and good all year round. When stored over winter they become dark brown and rank. These are then called *boutons de culottes* used for *fromage fort*.

● *Mamirolle* (Mamirolle dairying school, Franche-Comté) A washed-rind loaf of pasteurized cow's milk, that is rather richer in flavour than might be expected.

● *Metton* (all Franche-Comté, but especially Besançon) Essentially a tasteless nugget of whey cheese, made by boiling whey, the method which creates Italian *ricotta;* almost exclusively aged and eaten as *cancoillotte* (qv).

★ *Montrachet* A rather delicious and creamy *chèvre* made in a cylinder about 10cm/4in high and matured only a week or so wrapped in chestnut or vine leaves. A commercial operation. If only fresh goat's milk is used, best from end of spring until autumn.

★ *Morbier* (Franche-Comté, mainly Jura) Also made in the plateaux of Champagne. A fruit of the mountains, a pressed cheese best tasted in spring if you can find one that tray, either in large spoonsful to make a ring (*la Gougère*) or in separate large and small spoonsful to make individual *gougères*. Glaze with beaten egg yolk and bake in a moderate oven (gas 4/180°C/350°) for 20 to 35 minutes, according to size.

Once you have mastered the basic style – and it may be made heavier or lighter – you may like to experiment by adding herbs or spices. I use cumin seeds, which is not an uncommon flavouring in Franche-Comté.

is *artisanale*. A disc of 5 to 8kg/13 to 18lbs – the one with the streak of black soot (from the cauldron) through the middle.

● *Pierre-qui-vire* (Côte-d'Or) Made at a monastery of the same name in St-Léger-Vauban, it is the expected washed-rind disc, only 10cm/4in diameter and on straw. It is stronger in smell and flavour than many such cheeses and is best in summer and autumn. M. Androuet of Paris says it is also eaten fresh after draining.

● *Pourly* (Essert-Yonne) Although aged a month, this cylinder of almost 300g/12oz of *chèvre* is not as pungent or goaty as some smaller or younger such cheeses. Recommended for mutual enjoyment with fine white burgundy.

● *Rouy* (Dijon) A commercial product, and as it is from the north of Burgundy (relatively) it is a washed-rind one, square and boxed; pretty positive flavour and taste. Cow's milk.

● *St-Florentin* (Yonne) Mainly commercial production these days; cow's milk cheese washed with brine, best in summer, autumn and start of winter. Always a most assertive presence on all one's senses.

● *Septmoncel:* variation of name of *Bleu de Gex* .

● *Soumaintrain* (Yonne) Becoming uncommon, it is essentially a farmhouse (original) version of *St-Florentin*. It is considered even higher in flavour and smell; but there is or was a custom for eating them very fresh, so I should, rather, nose around for that version.

● *Tomme de Belley* (Ain) Something to jump at if you find it, not a large tomme but a small brick of *chèvre* or *mi-chèvre* weighing less than 200g/8oz. Medium, nutty flavour. Farmhouse made but less and less so.

● *Vacherin Mont-d'Or AOC* (Joux valleys of Franche-Comté) One of the most important on the AOC list, for it is one of the few genuinely seasonal cheeses, made only in autumn when the herds return from the plateaux of Haut-Doubs. Always circled with a band of spruce and packed in a spruce box, it is recognised by its deeply wrinkled top surface, caused partly by the bottom sticking firmly to the container. Washed regularly with brine, it has distinct odour of fermented milk but a rich, sweet, creamy flavour with just a breath of resin from the spruce. As it is cured from 2–4 months, depending on size, expect it in good condition only from the end of autumn until winter's end. Only the milk of the *montbèliarde* and *pie rouge de l'Est* cows may be used.

● *Vézelay* Farm-produced *chèvre* that is unlikely to stink you out; not dissimilar to *Lormes* (qv).

L·I·Q·U·E·U·R·S

The relative newcomer *cassis*, which is available in several alcoholic strengths, has overshadowed the other fruit-based drinks of the area. There are liqueurs or *crèmes* made true to their flavours in many wine centres. Nuits-St-Georges is very good. Anything made with plums *mirabelle*, *prunelle* or *prunes sauvages* sloe will be terrific in my experience, but it is to the Franche-Comté for something more unusual. Once Pontalier was an important centre for making banned *absinthe*; now gentian is a common flavouring for both aperitif and digestif, and liqueurs or white spirits may be found made from pine, cherries or plums. The wine makers of the Jura also make *marc*, which in turn is mixed with grape juice to make *maquevin*, a *ratafia*; *hypocras* is spiced sweet red wine, a cold sangria in fact.
Sochaux makes well-reputed beer.

PASTRY, PUDDINGS & CONFECTIONERY

The abundance of grain of most types meant that as baking became more sophisticated, Burgundy was always a leader in producing variety in breads and amusing goodies for the end of a meal. The oldest, as in most regions are *galettes, crêpes,* and Burgundian *beignets,* which are not just any old doughnut. Even today the light, deep-fried paste may surround acacia flowers and the honey-muscat flavour of elderflowers *sureau;* although not so popular these days, this once was considered irresistible; it still is in other countries. The most famous of these light, deep-fried balls of batter must be *pets-de-nonne,* which the Francs-Comtois reckon they invented, but so do the Burgundians and several others. The claim is disputed not so much over the undoubted superiority of the recipe but over the wish to bathe in the glory of having invented the name. In case you're not certain, it means nun's farts.

Worth Finding

● *Cacau de Paray-le-Monial* Cherry clafoutis.
● *Cassissines* Small, black-currant-flavoured sweeties from Dijon.
● *Flamussel* Either a sweet omelette with fruit or a sweetened fresh-cheese tart.
● *Gouère* Apple tart.
● *Mias* A local name for fruit tarts.
● *Nonettes* Associated particularly with Dijon, these are iced gingerbread cakes and thus associated with ...
● *Pain d'épices* Common in many parts of France but very much a special association with Franche-Comté and Dijon, although Reims was once almost the sole centre of manufacture. The idea of actually mixing flour with honey apparently came from the Arabs via knights returning from Crusades; the Arabs in turn are thought to have learned it through trading with the Chinese or Mongols. When the Romans made honey cakes, they poured it on to the baking after it was cooked. Spicy but rather dry to many, *pain d'épices* is nice with the touch of *anis* almost compulsory in Burgundy; often includes nuts or dried fruits. Try it cut from a slab in a market, or bought packaged to take home from somewhere famous and grand like Mulot and Petitjean in Dijon, who also sell *cassis* and other liqueurs, plus . . .
● *Rochers de Morvan* Amazingly real-looking marzipan recreations of pebbles. Great to look at, boring to eat.

---

dian *beignets,* which are not just any old doughnut. Even today the light, deep-fried paste may surround acacia flowers and the honey-muscat flavour of elderflowers *sureau;* although not so popular these days, this once was considered irresistible; it still is in other countries. The most famous of these light, deep-fried balls of batter must be *pets-de-nonne,* which the Francs-Comtois reckon they invented, but so

A huge variety of things sweet is offered in the big centres, with Mâcon, Auxerre, Sens, Beaune and Besançon all recommended. As there are eggs, there are meringues and macaroons everywhere and any number of biscuits based on almonds with names that change from centre to centre. Nevers, and others, makes barley sugar *sucre d'orge,* and as *anis* is grown here it's worth looking for the aniseed

sweets of Flavigny, whereas in Autun and other centres of the Morvan you'll find a *pain d'anis.* Apples, pears, Auxerre cherries and other soft summer fruit are served hot and cold in tarts and *crêpes* of various kinds.

BURGUNDY & FRANCHE-COMTE

Bon Marché

Below is a selective list of markets plus some fairs *foires* of special interest. Check with the local S.I. for precise locations and time changes.

YONNE
Aillant-sur-Tholon Tue; **Ancy-le-Franc** Thur; **Arces Dilo** Thur; **Auxerre** Tue, Fri, Sun am; **Avallon** Thur, Sat; **Bléneau** Tue pm; **Brienon-sur-Armançon** Tue, Fri; **Chablis** Sun am; **Champignelles** Thur; **Charny** Tue pm; **Chéroy** Tue; **Courson-les-Carrières** Thur; **Flogny-la-Chapelle** Tue; **Joigny** Wed, Sat; **Migennes** Thur, jumble sale 1st Sun Aug; **Monéteau** Wed; **Pont-sur-Yonne** Wed, Sun; **Rogny** Wed; **Sens** Mon, Fri; **Serbonnes** 23 & 24 Aug; **St-Florentin** Mon, Sat (veg), jumble sale 1st Sun Sept; **St-Julien-du-Sault** Sun; **St-Sauveur-en-Puisaye** Wed; **Tonnerre** Wed, Sat; **Toucy** Sat; **Villeneuve-la-Guyard** Mon; **Villeneuve-l'Archevêque** Sat.

NIÈVRE
Arleuf Fair 17th of month (except Aug.); **La Charité-sur-Lire** Sat; *Prize Poultry Fair Dec;* **Château-Chinon** 2nd Mon each month, 29 Oct; **Corbigny** Fri, 2nd Fri Dec (poultry); **Decize** Fri; **Entrains-sur-Nohain** Wed; **Fours** Farm produce & poultry on Fair Days (see Synd. In); *Turkey fair 2nd Sat Dec;* **Lormes** Thur; **Lucenay-les-Aix** 4th Thur of month, *Poultry, Rabbit, Butter & Egg Fair every 2nd Mon in month;* **Luzy** Fri (poultry); **La Machine** Wed, Sat (veg); **Nevers** daily; **Pouilly-sur-Loire** Fri; **Rouy** Thur (poultry); **St-Amand-en-Puisaye** Mon; **St-Bénin d'Azy** Fair 1st Mon of month; **St-Honoré-les-Bains** Mon, Tue, Thur, Fri during thermal season; **St-Pierre-le-Moutier** Thur, Fri, & 4th Thur; **St-Révérien** Sat, 4th Tue of month; **St-Saulge** Fri (eggs, butter, poultry), 1st Aug Summer Fête, flower float, procession; **Tannay** 4th Mon of month; **Varzy** Thur, *Poultry Market 2nd Thur Dec.*

CÔTE-D'OR
Arnay-le-Duc Thur, 6th day each month exc. Mar & June (7) and Dec (5); **Auxonne,** Wed, Fri; **Beaune** Thur, Sat; **Châtillon-sur-Seine** Sat, Tue (occasional); **Chenove** Wed; **Dijon** daily am, Tue & Fri, Thur; **Les Laumes** Wed; **Marsannay-la-Côte** Thur; **Montbard** Tue, Fri; **Nolay** Mon; **Nuits-St-Georges** Mon, Fri; **Pontailler-sur-Saône** Sat (Fair 4th Sat of month); **Saulieu** Sat; **Semur-en-Auxois** Tue, Thur, Sat; **Seurre** Tue, Fri; **St-Jean-de-Losne** Sat; **Vitteaux** Fair 1st Thur of month.

SAÔNE-ET-LOIRE
Autun Wed, Fri; **Beaurepaire-en-Bresse** Wed; **Bellevesvre** Fri; **Bourbon-Lancy** Sat, Fair Days; **Buffières** Thur; **Buxy** Thur; **Chalon-sur-Saône** Wed, Fri & Sun (poultry); **Charolles** Wed, *Bull Fair Wed before 4th Thur Oct;* **Chauffailles** Mon; **La Clayette** Mon; **Cluny** Fri; **Le Creusot** Tue, Thur, Fri, Sat; **Cuiseaux** Fri, *Chestnut Fair 29 Oct;* **Digoin** Fri, Sun; **Epinac** Sat;

Shopping around in Besançon

Where and when: **Covered market** (daily ex Sun); covered street market (daily ex Mon & Sun); **pl de la Révolution** Tue, Fri, Sat); **Palente** (Tue, Sat); **Chaprais** (Wed); **Clairs-Soleils** (Tue); **St-Claude** (Tue & Sat); **Planoise** (Fri am).

Etang-sur-Arroux *Turkey Fair 1st Mon Dec;* **Joncy** 10 Dec (poultry); **Louhans** Mon; **Lugny** Fri, *Wine Fair 6 Dec;* **Mâcon** Sat, *National Wines of France Fair May 20 (8 days);* **Marcigny** Mon; **Matour** Tue; **Mervans** Fri; **Montceau-les-Mines** Mon, Thur, Sat; **Montchanin** Wed am, Sat pm; **Montpont-en-Bresse** Thur; **Montret** Tue; **Palinges** Fri;

Pierre-de-Bresse Mon; **Romenay** Fri; **Sagy** Thur; **Sanvignes-les-Mines** Fri; **Sennecey-le-Grand** Fri; **Simandre** Wed; **St-Bonnet-de-Joux** Fri; **St-Gengoux-le-National** 1st & 3rd Tue of month; **St-Germain-Du-Plain** Thur; **St-Léger-sur-Dheune** Tue; **St-Martin-en-Bresse** Wed; **St-Pierre-le-Vieux** Thur; **St-Vallier** Wed, Fri; **Tournus** Sat; **Verdun-sur-le-Doubs** Thur.

HAUTE-SAÔNE
Faucogney et la Mer 1st & Thur; **Fougerolles** Fri; **Héricourt** Wed am, Sat pm; **Jussey** Tue; **Lure** Tue; **Melisey** Wed; **Plancher-les-Mines** Fri; **Ronchamp** Sat; **Servance** 1st & 3rd Mon of month; **St-Loup-sur-Semouse** Mon; **St-Sauveur** Sun (Sept), 1st & 3rd Sun (Oct-May); **Vauvillers** 2nd Thur of month; **Villersexel** 1st & 3rd Wed of month.

DOUBS
Arc-et-Senans 4th Wed of month; **Audincourt** Wed & Sat am (Fairs) Spring Market (1 Apr), Jumble sale (29 July); **Baume-les-Dames** 3rd & 4th Thur of month; **Besan-çon** Daily ex Sun; **Colombier-Fontaine** 2nd Wed of month; **Damprichard** Wed, Sat; **Fresches-le-Châtel** Fri; **Mandeure** Sat am, jumble May; **Maiche** Wed, Sat; **Montbéliard** Sat, Fri; **Morteau** Tue, Sat, Fri; **Pontarlier** 1st, 3rd, 5th Thur of month, (Fair 2nd & 4th); **Pont-de-Roide** Fri; **Rougemont** Fri, (Fair 1st & 3rd Fri); **Seloncourt** Fri; **Sochaux** Thur; **St-Hippolyte** 3rd Thur of month.

JURA
Annoire Wed pm; **Arinthod** 1st Fri of month; **Beaufort** Fri; **Bletterans** Tue; **Champagnole** Sat; **Chaumergy** Thur; **Châtillon** 2nd Thur of month; **Clairvaux-les-Lacs** Wed (June, July, Aug), 3rd Wed of month rest of year; **Dole** Tue, Thur, Sat; **Les Hays** Wed am; **Lons-le-Saunier** Thur; **Moirans-en-Montagne** Wed, Fri; **Morez** Sat; **Petit-Noir** Wed am; **Pleure** Tue; **Poligny** Mon, Fri; **Salins-les-Bains** Sat; **Sellières** Wed; **St-Amour** Tue, Sat.

115

Upstart Success

The Charentes' dairying pastures, fat with contented cattle grinding grass into cream for the famous butter of the Deux-Sèvres, are a direct result of the devastation caused by phylloxera. Virtually all of these pastures are the graveyards of vines killed by the pest which did more to change the French way of agriculture than both World Wars. Where Burgundy planted blackcurrants and soft fruits, and the south planted fruit orchards, these western slopes were put to grass, and cattle were brought in from Normandy.

If you have discovered the butters of Normandy and chosen a favourite, you'll have to start again. For, unfair as it may be, there are many who feel the upstart new butter of the Deux-Sèvres to be better and waxier even than that of Normandy. Bocuse does, and so do Air France, who use it exclusively to make their pastries and croissants and cakes. *Beurre d'Echiré* is

unquestionably the best and found everywhere in France; but it has confused the kitchens of the area, for this is traditionally a place of pork fat and walnut oil and goat's milk, from which the cream cannot be separated.

Further south, you can enjoy that butter in more familiar surroundings and more visited areas – Bordeaux and Aquitaine. They were British for centuries, and much of what sustains great parts of the regions remains closely associated with the British way of life – claret in Bordeaux, cognac in Cognac, and holiday homes in the Green, White or Black Périgord of the Dordogne.

Clairette or Claret?

Claret, which is what only the British call their Bordeaux red wines, is an echo of those older kingdoms, when the wine exported was light and clear and called

clairette. It became the generic name for all Bordeaux red wines, but a true *clairette* may still be bought, and drinks delightfully when chilled. I enjoyed it first on a restaurant terrace in Bordeaux with a pretty plateful called *Les Trésors de la Mer* – pieces of the freshest fish from the Atlantic made brighter with tiny cultivated mussels *moules de bouchot* and succulent with fat oysters from Arcachon. It was a boiling hot day and chilled *clairette* was being drunk by almost everyone, seemingly regardless of what they ate.

But it is unfair to think of Bordeaux only in terms of the opportunities she offers for drinking wines you might not find at home. Like all big cities, she does the same for foodlovers. In her famous markets and in the broad, traffic-free streets of the centre you will easily espy

> " In which we...
> ● Meet the pest which made a better butter but confused the kitchens...
> ● Sip a wine we've put out in the cold and collect an abandoned bounty...
> ● Recover the leek and eat flowers in a château...
> ● Buy a 'green chicken', needle some mussels, and discover the truth about lawyers' tongues and the bar...
> ● Meet a rapturous oyster, yellow chickens and the best salty lamb in France...
> ● Learn how to judge a beast on the hoof and which bay to leave...
> ● Share the charm of *sarment,* slice the best of tomatoes and find a *pastis* that you eat...
> ● Go in search of an unapparent royal hare... "

fly-away sweet pastry tarts *croustades* from Gascony, *foie gras* from the Landes, a truly encyclopaedic array of fresh, mature and rotten goat's milk cheeses and, if you look carefully enough, the sweet specialities of Bordeaux itself. You'll also find a fair range of cognacs.

Périgord Harvest

A few hours' drive inland is the Périgord, one of the best known culinary areas of France associated mainly, I suppose, with geese and *foie gras*. For me it is not so much the food of the Dordogne which is the attraction, undoubted though that may be, but the surroundings in which you

can enjoy it. Périgueux, capital of the lush rolling White Périgord, has the most entrancing of old quarters, now marvellously restored to match the scarcely touched 17th-century splendour of Sarlat, the Renaissance queen of the Black Périgord, an area thickly wooded with oak and chestnut, darker and more mysterious as you approach the Gouffre de Padirac and Rocamadour.

There is a certain sadness in the Périgord, but one which is to the advantage of the traveller who has time. For much of it has been deserted by its owners – châteaux, cottages and farmhouses rattle empty in the wind, so you may walk or

ride for miles through their lands. The bonus is their orchards and hedgerows, crammed in their rightful seasons with unwanted baskets of the bounty which made the area famous. Blackberries and sloes, chestnuts and walnuts, greengages and sudden golden walls of *mirabelles* are yours. It makes a lovely afternoon to wander thus, and if you put the ripest fruits into jars with an *eau-de-vie* or some flavourless pure alcohol, sold just for this purpose, you will have souvenirs of the day to enjoy long into the future.

Rightful Seasons

Market days in the connected little squares of Périgueux are Wednesday and Saturday, and here the progress of the seasons and prosperity of the land is chronicled by the produce brought for sale. Autumn and winter are the most fascinating times, for then pearlescent lobes of *foie gras* are displayed naked in the chill air, while strung above them are the red-black-clotted, curling necks and head and crop and lungs of the birds from which they have been cut. I've never seen truffles among the wild mushrooms there during the season, but I'm told you might. One summer I bought my first bottle of walnut oil in that market, stoppered with a cork wrapped in newspaper, so we had to use it before we flew home. Next day was another first: sun-warm slices of tomatoes from Marmande sprinkled with walnut oil. I ate this celestial combination (*at least* as good as *foie gras* and trumpets) on the terrace of the Bellevue Hotel and Restaurant, which looks from a flustering height over the Padirac Gorge to the crankily sited town of Rocamadour.

Vineyard Diplomacy

Yes, I've eaten superbly, but never as when we called at the slip-tiled château of Max and Barbara Freeman. By now they may have restored much more of it, but then (in 1979) they had a long way to go and were living in the basement, which was as big, and as grand as many an 'ordinary' country house. 'We'll have to eat like peasants,' Barbara said, rattling us up truffled *foie gras* she had tinned herself, an omelette of scorzonera flowers, and some chocolates. The bread was thick and chewy rye from a village far enough away to be an expedition, but everything was an expedition from here; any trouble was repaid because the bread lasted so very long. The wine was Pécharmant, a Bergerac from close-by. Max swears the name means 'charming fart', and refers to a time when an aristocratic lady of the court of one or another of the kings called Louis, broke wind rather noticeably whilst touring the vines. Courtly etiquette demanded the gaffe be ignored, but circumstances denied this as a possibility. Diplomatically, the host announced he was charmed and flattered by the 'ill wind' and turned it to good, by declaring that the domaine's name would henceforth enshrine the lady's 'charming fart' . . .

CHARCUTERIE

Charcuterie here is far from exclusive or typical of the region. Certainly, the markets are all packed with *pâtés* and both salted and air-dried parts of pig. The best by far are the local hams, famed in Poitou, but sweeter to my mind in Charente, for there cognac is used in the pickling, as well as herbs and spices.

Rillettes and *rillons* are regularly found; they actually belong to the Loire regions, and to make some proprietorial claim, I suppose, the latter are more likely to be called *grillons*.

The Dordogne is much given to stuffing meats, and so they use their *foie gras* to make *galantines* (cold) and *ballottines* (hot); and as even these are more likely to be made with poultry cannot strictly be called *charcuterie*. Poitou and the Charentes also make the same things, using their own *foie gras*.

My best discovery, mentioned elsewhere, was the *poulet vert* found in Jarnac's Sunday morning market, a *pâté*-type mixture flavoured with every fresh spring green, including sorrel and dandelion, and baked in cabbage leaves; it is called *farci* in Poitou. I took some back in the plane to eat at home with thick slices of charentais ham.

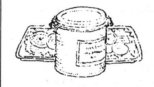

FISH & SHELLFISH

The Atlantic coast of France has a good line in special fish and fish dishes, especially those incorporating the small, sweet, cultivated *moules de bouchot*, and a reputation for a number of fishy things you won't actually find. Caviar is one no-show, although as you doubtless did not expect it, this may not be a shock. Yet the Gironde does welcome sturgeons (called *créat* here) from March to June, when they swim up as far as the headland at Ambès to spawn. For most of this century extremely passable caviar was made from their roe, so much so that Pruniers in Paris, who were responsible for organizing the initial project, were largely supplied from here. Small amounts are *said* to be made today, but the increasing pollution of the river makes this unlikely. Still, the places you might try are Chenac-Saint-Seurin-d'Uzet, Talmont-sur-Gironde, Meschers-sur-Gironde and Mortagne-sur-Gironde, in that order. The end of spring is probably the best time.

The shad *alose* and its superlative roe is best between mid-April and mid-June. The sorrel you so often find in shad, or on it, is said not just to dissolve away most of the bones, but to neutralize some poison. Either there is no poison, or all shad are quickly stuffed with sorrel, for I know of no-one who has died from eating them. This is not true when it comes to lampreys *lamproie,* they of the hideous face and poisonous thread.

Their preparation is so complicated, including the skinning and saving of the blood, and takes so long – at least two days – that few restaurants serve them. Some housewives still make *lamproie à la Bordelaise,* indeed I was given some, thick with the mandatory red wine and local leeks cut to the same size as the steaks of lamprey; but many more do not, or make a slightly easier (and safer) version with eel.

Oysters Galore

You *will* find superlatively cooked fish, especially in La Rochelle, France's second fishing port after Boulogne, and in Bordeaux. For a delicious change, accompany it with a lightly chilled red *clairette.* Marvellous.

On the Charentais coast the most important oyster centre is Marennes, renowned for its *vertes de Marennes, (natives* or *creuses)* which have fattened in the *claires* salt marshes at the mouth of the Seudre River. The centre is unique in France for both breeding and fattening oysters, for the others do just one or the other. La Tremblade is another important centre close by.

The Bay of Arcachon in the Gironde is one of the biggest oyster-growing areas in France, and here as elsewhere pests and disease have all but wiped out the native *plates,* locally called *gravettes.* The prevalence first of the replacement *portugaises* and now of *creuses* or *gigas* from Japan, more suited to cooking, explains why oysters are found so often in hot dishes, on *brochettes,* in stuffings and the like. In many places raw oysters will be accompanied by

---

---

small hot sausages in caul fat *crépinettes,* sometimes also truffled. The combination of oysters and hot sausages is excellent.

Real oysters, or *creuses,* are also offered with lemon wedges or with shallot vinegar. Anybody who actually likes oysters, and who is not simply spending money conspicuously, will add nothing but the merest threat of lemon juice to the raw flesh of an oyster. Anything hot or sharp or acidic obliterates any delicacy or complexity of flavour. You may as well save money and eat something else.

Arcachon and Marennes, which were once famous for making a specially white salt, also rear every other type of shellfish including delicious small clams *palourdes.* The mussels you'll cook yourself in an *éclade* will also turn up as a *mouclade,* richer than simple steamed mussels *(marinière)* through the addition of cream, a *bouquet garni,* garlic with cognac and/or *pineau de Charente.*

Verdun-sur-Mer is well thought of in the Bordelais for its lobsters and crayfish. Fresh cod *cabillaud* is served more often than the salted version and large sardines, often called *Royans* after the town which specializes in them, are eaten grilled, but more often raw, much to the *effroi* or horror of the visitor.

There is excellent variety of freshwater fish here too, including carp from the étang de Cadeuil in Charente, and trout, farmed in most places but excellent from the Candrea at Bergerac. In the Dordogne the eel is well flavoured, but this could be said of the whole region. They are best, though, at their most un-eel-like fry stage, thin threads sizzled in a *friture*.

Regardless of its provenance in the Atlantic or Mediterranean, fish and shellfish here are both likely to be drowned in cream or the rich butter of the Charentes.

MUSSEL BEACH

Whatever else you do in France, make yourself an *éclade*. No restaurant will do it, and if it does it won't be half as much fun. An *éclade* is something for a group or family to prepare; a couple will get more reward for their effort. First, find a beach, then take a large plank of wood and place it firmly in the sand. You can if you like, then coat the board with a thin layer of sticky clay but this is not important. Now you take mussels, which must have been well cleaned and bearded – if they are permanently open they must be discarded. Build a little mound of sand, clay or anything non-flammable in the centre of the board and then start arranging the mussels pointed end up. Lay them as tightly as possible one to the other so they do not open prematurely. Once that is completed, cover the mussels with a thick layer of pine needles and set fire to it. If there is a fig tree about, you might cover the mussels with fig leaves before you strew the needles – not to disguise any nakedness but to make it easier to remove the ashes when the flames have subsided; the leaves add a syrupy flavour too. I suppose that, as long as you have a cache of pine needles, you might enjoy an *éclade* wherever there is a plank and mussels: but it'll never be the same as on a beach. Or as safe.

Whichever letter of the alphabet the month contains, or doesn't, you'll always be able to enjoy oysters *huîtres*. The theory about not eating oysters in summer is not based on any danger to your health but on thoughtfulness for the well-being of the oyster. It can

Two types of oyster are found in France today, the true oyster *ostrea edulis* known as the flat oyster, the *plate, native* or *belon*, and the *creuse*, a Japanese variety *crassostrea gigas*. The *portugaise*, which wasn't even an oyster but a *gryphea*

oysters cannot pivot upon their firmly anchored feet, for how would they know which way to turn? I think, though, we should not begrudge them any pleasure; an oyster's life is a chancy business. Out of a million eggs only a dozen or so will become spats and grow up to equivocate.

SHELL SHOCKS

only breed in summer's soupy-hot water, so you are either eating an oyster that has not yet reproduced (described as 'milky') and are depriving yourself of future enjoyment, or will be presented with a thin, flabby one that has, and deprive yourself of present pleasure.

angulata, and which stepped in earlier this century, when the *natives* failed, has in its turn been virtually wiped out by disease.

The true oyster promiscuously changes from male to female as it matures, some returning to masculinity for refresher periods. It is as well

You are much more likely to be served the *creuse* or *gigas*, first introduced into the Brittany oyster parks in 1974. They are easily recognizable, much longer than *plates*, and have a very crinkled, tough, thick shell, even more so than the *portugaises* you may have learned to identify. The *creuse* does not change sex, and has an even more depressing rate of reproduction. They have quickly become accepted as an excellent alternative to native oysters and develop the same range of flavours and

MEAT, POULTRY & GAME

Classically, Poitou and the Charentes are 'snail country' and the two regions have long-standing agreements to disagree about how snails are best cooked. The *lumas* of Poitou are usually simmered in wine or made into a ragoût. In the Charentes, they do the same to their brown shelled *cagouilles* with perhaps a dash of cognac or, sometimes, of tomato, and serve them hot, as a salad or in an omelette. Ruffec is the place to eat Charentais snails best. The *cagouille* has so dominated life here that the Charentaise have long been called *cagouillards*, for they are considered to have emulated the gastropod's slowness and

delight in privacy. The snails of Cauderan were traditionally eaten in Bordeaux during the first days of Lent, apparently not being considered meat. Of course, the herbicides used in the vineyards have had the same effect as elsewhere and there are fewer genuine local snails and more imported ones.

Poultry here is specially good. In Poitou, Sauzé-Vaussay and Chef-Boutonne rear the almost white poitevin goose and excellent ducks to make the *confits* and *foie gras* more associated with the Dordogne or Gascony. Civray in Vienne makes specially good *pâté de foie gras*. In Charente, Barbezieux raises wonderful

poultry, including turkeys and geese. Flesh from those reared with fattened livers is considered sweeter of flavour. Down in the Landes, St-Sever is the most important meat and poultry production centre, with a market long known for pigs, beef and the famous Landais *poulet jaune*. Bred in Charente-Maritime, the chicks come here at a day old to be raised in the open air for 12 weeks on a diet based on maize. Packaged and numbered individually, tens of thousands are sent to markets and restaurants all over France. St-Gours and St-Vincent-de-Tyrosse produce most. There are plenty of geese, too, but Dax is the biggest centre for *foie gras*. Ducks are slowly taking over from the goose here too, to make a year-round industry, although virtually every market will have fattened goose livers displayed for sale between November and February. If you can buy one vacuum-packed, which is big time in France, it will safely last some time before you get it home.

Perhaps more important than *foie gras* to the average visitor, is the *pré-salé* lamb of Pauillac, an important wine centre 48Km/30miles from Bordeaux. Twice each day the Atlantic tide floods the marshy banks of the Gironde, and spring lamb feeding on the salty grass develops a flavour considered unsurpassed. But as they are eaten very young it needs a good palate to appreciate the delicacy of flavour, and to protect this the meat is often roasted in a crust of breadcrumbs and parsley. Certainly there will be no garlic, onion or shallot used unless summer has truly come

---

appearance, according to where they have been grown to maturity. In Brittany and in Normandy this is done in the mouths of rivers, and these are generally sold as *huîtres* or *creuses/gigas de parc*, and they tend to look yellow to cream. But on the coast of Charente-Maritime and Aquitaine, they are matured in *claires*, old salt marshes, where they feed on an endemic blue algae and turn a variety of shades of green; perversely the algae which allows oysters to develop such a delicate flavour is that which gives a musty taste to tap water.

Oysters are sold according to size, but also according to how they have lived immediately before you bought them.

● *Claires* Are oysters which have spent a rather crowded couple of years in a park, as they all do, then just a month

in a *claire* which allows them merely a breath of special flavour or colour.

● *Fines de claires* The kings and queens of oysters. After the usual two years in a park, they will spend another 18 or 24 months in a *claire*, at only 5 or 6 to the square metre. The effect transforms them almost into another being, with a texture and flavour that makes them the *foie gras* of the sea.

● *Huîtres raptures* are overgrown oysters, rather too daunting to confront when raw, unless you are prepared to chew more than once. Instead, roast them on a barbecue or in a fiery-hot oven, flat side up, until just opening. Quickly pry open fully and tip a little garlic or herb butter onto the just set, warm oyster. Eat with a fork and lots of bread. You can imagine why initiates call them *huîtres raptures*.

and the animal is starting to mature.

Pauillac lamb is often served with potatoes sautéed with strips of black truffle, but I think the fattiness coats the tastebuds and disguises the lamb's sweetness. Other claims along the long coastline to present pré-salé lamb are probably true, for there are pockets of production everywhere. In the Landes, they compete with pré-salé by rearing milk-fed lambs to give extremely pale meat with even more delicacy. Spring in Poitou – the centre for goat-raising – also brings the chance to dine off kid pirot with oseille and vert d'ail, sorrel and green garlic shoots.

Because so much pork is raised for the fine hams of Poitou, there is a wide range of pork dishes offered, some of considerable eccentricity and of little interest to anyone not brought up to be so persuaded; one such example is the poitevin gigourit/tautouillet pig's head cooked with wine and blood . . . I'll say no more, except that you are more likely to find the full range of pork products in autumn. Charente also raises fine pork, which for the most part is presented quite simply, if not being used for unusual dishes. Tripe, more familiar to the visitor, is much esteemed in all this region and may be met in many guises.

There seems no close season for another speciality from the same area, oreilles de veau. But you would have the satisfaction of knowing the ears came from calves of the highest breeding, beasts of either the parthenay or bressuire varieties – both regarded with esteem. Yet your beef talk is more likely to be of the entrecôte bordelaise, grilled over sarments de cabernet cabernet vine shoots (you'll be lucky) and finished with a coating of shallot or bone marrow or both. In Bordeaux itself this often becomes a sauce based on red wine, thought to be a 19th century Parisian 'improvement'. This dish's real ancestor is said to be the rat du chai, rats fattened under the vines and in the wine warehouses, for until recently this was never an area known for edible beef. But once tastes changed universally from rat to beef, it became generally accepted that only a highly unusual local breed was proper, the cattle of Bazas in the Gironde.

Bazadais beef is well worth tracking down. The breed is ancient, the animals grey-coated with flattened but tip-tilted horns, and naturally firm and tender, dark red meat, with rather a lot of highly-flavoured marbling and fat. Castrated before it is a year old, each steer spends three years grazing on grass and then is stabled and fattened on hay, rye, barley and maize. They are never slaughtered until they are five years

Worth Finding

Bifteck poitevin Beef chopped with sorrel and bone marrow. Civet de lièvre Jugged hare. A rich stew of hare which should be thickened with its own blood. Lièvre à la royale, one of the world's best-known least-seen dishes is probably native to one or all of these regions, but Poitou and Périgord seem strongest claimants. It is boned, marinated and stuffed with everything expensive (foie gras, truffles) braised for an extraordinarily long time in wine and finished with cognac and its own blood.
Dindon désossé Boned turkey braised with vegetables and wine.
Foie gras chaud As well as being served in cold slices, fattened liver is freshly baked or fried and served hot, as often as not with grapes and cognac.
Grosse nounou Magnac-sur-Touvre makes this calf's head stuffed with pork and veal, eggs, mushrooms and sometimes truffles and serves it with brains, gherkins and olives!
Poulet à la Niortaise Chicken with fried potatoes and the local rouge de Niort onions.
Salami de palombe Pigeons in red wine sauce. To ensure flavour and tenderness there should be one old pigeon for each young one.
Tourtière A great speciality in Angoulême; chicken and salsify pie; but there is quite a liking for tourtes of other white meats and these will often be called pâté en croûte.

FRUIT & VEGETABLES

old, and the most beautiful are paraded through Bazas each *jeudi gras* (Thursday before Shrove Tuesday). How do you tell a beautiful *bazadais*? It must have a *cul panoramique*, that is horizon-to-horizon hindquarters, for the qualities of the meat are directly proportional to the size. Just a few shops sell guaranteed *bazadais* beef, for the long raising period makes it expensive. Duhayot is the only one in Bordeaux; Messrs Darroman, Bergon, Medail, Beziade and Lafon sell it in Bazas. If you aren't cooking yourself you'll have to rely on restaurateurs. Expensive.

Other than hare *lièvre* there is precious little game nowadays, for the netting and eating of ortolans and other migrating songbirds has been forbidden by the laws of the EEC. Of course, there will always be someone who knows someone who has a brother-in-law ... You may find woodcock *bécasses* or (more likely) pigeons *palombes* and if you do you should be well pleased.

The Périgord reputation for fine food is hardly based on the products found by summer visitors, for it is a region of *confits*, and of every kind of poultry stuffed with enriching livers, sometimes with chestnuts, and sometimes with truffles. Suckling pig is popular and so are *pâtés*, now most likely made from game birds that have been farmed, but better than nothing. Yet heed what I have said elsewhere about the French tendency to use such birds unhung so that there is not enough flavour to perfume the rest of the mixture, thus negating the effort.

It was while dining at Courvoisier's château on the Charente in Jarnac that the point of this book struck me most forcibly. On earlier visits to the region, I had dismissed as fashion, or as outside influence, the appearance of leeks in any recipe – particularly when in such a gastronomic temple as La Rochelle. Leeks are northern, aren't they, and isn't this the area of garlic and shallots? Well, no. Ginette, longtime cook at the château made me realise leeks are important to all the west and much of the south, but are vital foundations of tradition from the Charentes, and in Bordeaux and Cognac especially. The increasingly rare *poireaux des vignes*, strong-tasting wild leeks from the vineyards, at risk, like snails, from insecticide sprays, were the asparagus of the *sabotiers*, the country people. Dishes ranging from the rugged richness of lampreys in red wine or blood, to the delicate seafood *porée* in La Rochelle, would not be possible without the leek. Poitou's leeks, *les jaunes de Poitou*, are highly regarded in Paris. It was from Ginette that I also learned there are three types of bay leaf *laurier* (basically *laurus nobilis*) the *soupe* for savoury foods, the *cerisier* for custards and sweets soufflés and the *fleurier*, just for show. Her locally-produced cookbooks said so, but my horticultural French was not up to pursuing the subject closely. Perhaps by *cerisier* she meant the cherry laurel, *prunus laurocerasus*, the leaves of which have a sour,

cherry-almond flavour.

Légumes du primeur, baby spring vegetables, are grown all through this region, from the Marais of Poitou to the Dordogne (especially green beans *haricots verts*) to Lot-et-Garonne, whence comes one of the best tomatoes in the world, the knobbly giant *marmande*.

All around Marmande the fields positively throb with growth. One of the best ways to see the gardens, the extraordinary orchards of espaliered fruit trees, and the watercress beds rinsed by the Garonne, is to go by train. The line goes through the fields from Bordeaux to the plum orchards of Agen, incidentally traversing the backyards of a number of famous wine châteaus; the views are more fulsome and more interesting than from your car. Simpler domestic gardens have as much to offer in spring; new wild leaves of dandelion or sorrel, and the green shoots of young garlic *aille*. Dandelion *pissenlit* is made into soup. Look hard for *fars* or *farci*, which I have also seen called *poulet vert* (see *Charcuterie*), great with locally cured ham, and asparagus from the Landes.

In autumn, the excitement of the fields focuses on wild mushrooms, *cèpes* particularly, which should appear between September and mid-October. Bordeaux is the place most associated with them, and one of the many bordelais garnishes is based on *cèpes*, here authentically cooked in oil rather than butter.

The major vegetable of the

area is the broad bean *fève*, which you will not need to go out of your way to find. Artichokes *artichauts* are also grown and those of Macau come to market in Bordeaux already stripped of their leaves.

A major key to assessing the extent of local influence on the cooking throughout the area is the inclusion or otherwise of the shallot, for it is the secret of notably superior savour.

Onions are used, of course, notably in one of the oldest of bordelais dishes, *le tourin,* a soup of onions, cooked in fat but not browned, a breath of garlic, thickened with egg yolks and poured over bread. Once he has eaten the bread, a local will pour in a glass of *vin de l'année* creating the *chabrot,* which so unites the people of this region.

Bordeaux likes raw vegetables, too, *carrottes râpées* for instance, and young artichokes with butter and salt. In some families it is only children who eat them cooked. The American habit of eating salads as a first course was early assimilated here, and welcomed by the salad growers north and south. Ruffec, incidentally, has its own variety of curly endive, *chicorée frisée,* and you'll easily find lambs lettuce *mâche, feuilles de chêne* pinkish oak-leaf lettuce and other unusual salads.

Expect, too, the occasional pumpkin *potiron* dish, cardoons *cardons,* delicious small spinach pies (look on stalls in markets) and *mojettes,* yet another type of bean, so named, they say because they look like nuns praying.

Potatoes vary from simply cooked *primeurs* to the indul-

LOCAL PRODUCE

Vegetables

● **Artichoke** *artichaut* Var: *Blanc Hyperois, Chrysanthème Gapean* (violet) The *violet* is the one eaten raw so often	Two seasons, spring and autumn Dep: Charente-Maritime, Gironde, Lot-et-Garonne
● **Asparagus** *asperge blanc*	Mid-July until November Dep: Lot-et-Garonne
● **Aubergine** *aubergine* Var: *Violette de Toulouse* (white flesh) *violette de Barbentane* (green flesh)	Mid-July until November Dep: Lot-et-Garonne
● **Beans** *haricots verts*	June to October Dep: Lot-et-Garonne, Dordogne

Based around Marmande and Villeneuve-sur-Lot, two thirds are for commercial use. Second biggest French producers.

● **Capsicum** *poivrons* Var: *Lamuyo, Esterel*	July to November Dep: Lot-et-Garonne
● **Courgette** *courgette* Var: *Seneca* (under glass, spring and autumn) *Diamant* (open air, main season)	Mid-April until end October Dep: Lot-et-Garonne
● **Cucumber** *concombre*	March until November
● **Mushrooms** *champignons de couche*	Year round Dep: Gironde, Charente, in total about 1000 tonnes a month.
● **Onion** *oignon*	May to September Dep: Lot-et-Garonne
● **Potatoes (new)** *pommes de terre de primeur* Var: *Sirtema, Alcamaria*	May and June Dep: Lot-et-Garonne
● **Tomato** *tomate* Var: *Marmande*	March to November, summer or open-air grown ones Dep: Lot-et-Garonne Dordogne, Gironde.

Lot-et-Garonne is one of the four most important production zones of France, as well as being the home (Marmande) of one of the world's best knobbly tomatoes.

Fruit

● **Apple** *pomme* Var: 5% are *reine des reinettes*	Picked August-October, sold until next April Dep: Dordogne, Gironde, Lot-et-Garonne

Chestnut *marron/châtaigne*	Harvested September-November Dep: Dordogne, Lot-et-Garonne

Marrons have an unsegmented single kernel; *châtaignes* are segmented.

Grapes (table) *raisins* *Black chasselas* is followed by white *muscat*	August until November, peak October Dep: Lot-et-Garonne mainly
Greengage *reine-claude*	July and August Dep: Lot-et-Garonne
Hazelnut *noisette* Var: *Fertile de Coutard*	Harvested September or so, but cobnuts sometimes available earlier Dep: Dordogne, Lot-et-Garonne

Together with the Loiret, the Dordogne is the principal producer.

Kiwifruit *kiwi* Var: *Hayward* (NZ)	November until March Dep: Gironde, Landes, Lot-et-Garonne
Melon *melon* Var: *Charentais*	End June until mid-October Dep: Lot-et-Garonne

Most grown in small family plots, ensuring proper attention

Nectarine *nectarine/brugnon* Var: yellow and white, mainly foreign strains	June until September Dep: Lot-et-Garonne
Peach *pêche* Var: yellow and white mainly foreign	June until September Dep: Lot-et-Garonne
Plum *prune* Var: *prune d'ente*	July onwards for drying Dep: Lot-et-Garonne

Although juicy and sweet, these redskinned and fleshed plums are almost all dried for prunes – see *pruneaux d'Agen*. Dessert plums are grown in Gironde and Dordogne

Strawberry *fraise* Var: *Belrubi* and *Favette* dominate main season	March (forced) until October, peak May and June Dep: Dordogne, Lot-et-Garonne

These are the two biggest production zones in France: 42%. Sometimes the Dordogne has a second crop in September. Centres includes Périgueux, Marmande, Agen.

Walnut *noix* Var: *Grandjean*, native to the Dordogne	Harvested first fortnight in October Dep: Dordogne, Charentes

The Dordogne and Isère (Rhône Valley) are the premier production zones in France.

gence of *pommes de terre Sarladaise*, cooked in goose fat, with or without truffles.

Modern transportation means that the region can share fully the gigantic amount of fruit produced in one part or another. I suppose the most famous of all has to be melons – the *charentais* from the Charentes, the netted oranged-fleshed melon also called a canteloupe. This is grown all over France, sometimes under different names, but it is never better than on its home ground, especially when drenched with *pineau de Charente*. Drenching fruit with wine or spirits is a natural thing to do here. You will find many combinations, and now that the Charentes are investing so heavily to produce wines too good to be distilled for cognac and brandy, there will be more to come.

Bordeaux is specially fond of showing off its fruit bathed in its wines: strawberries are served in real Bergerac and the elegant white peach is complemented with chilled white Bordeaux, a sweeter Sauternes, or the lighter, sharper red *clairette*.

The Dordogne and Périgord areas both produce a fantastic amount of fruit and nuts, and have consequently developed extraordinary ways to enjoy them. Perhaps the most unusual is to split hot *miques* dumplings and to spread them with honey, jam or redcurrant jelly (something the visitor is unlikely to be offered in modern restaurants I reckon). But peaches and pears, apricots and cherries are just as likely to be simply preserved in local cognac, brandy or *pineau,* and served on or with really super ice cream or sorbets. Poitou, incidentally, does a very nice *Louise Bonne* pear, among others. And should you ever tire of spooning up the sumptuous charentais melon in its natural state, Périgueux offers a *confiture de melon* for you to slip into your suitcase. I shouldn't bother with the heart-arresting prices of whole candied melons, for the perfume of the slightly unripe fruit needed for the process rarely overcomes the preservative soup of sugar.

Most of the walnuts and hazelnuts of the Dordogne are pressed into oils which, although meant mainly for salads, I use to flavour butter for spreading on ordinary bread, or actually put into dough with more of the same nuts. These nut and raisin breads, available universally hereabouts and often made with rye *seigle* are utterly addictive and have the special appeal to travellers of lasting a very long time, so are marvellous with cheese and fruit for a lunch when you are en route to or from somewhere. Both these nuts and chestnuts are used for stuffing chocolates or are stuffed themselves. Those which escape either might be crushed into purées or spreads or used to flavour a variety of interesting drinks in which the nuts (or sometimes peach leaves and kernels) have been marinated. Both are excellent ways to take with you two of the best products of these lands.

Don't leave without buying some walnut oil, *huile de noix* so much better for the experience of buying it in the sensitively restored medieval lanes of Périgueux,

CHEESE

Chèvres predominate in this region, particularly in Poitou and the Charentes. Produced both commercially and domestically, they are quite sharp to the tongue.

● *Bougon* A factory-made goat's milk cheese of Poitou with predictable nutty flavour; best spring to autumn.

★ *Caillebotte Caillée* actually means curdled milk. This fresh unsalted cow's milk cheese is made in farms and homes in Poitou, Brittany, Anjou and Maine. It has a mild creamy flavour.

● *Caillebotte d'Aunis* A farm-made sheep's milk from Deux-Sèvres. It is fresh, unsalted and very mild; packed in a wicker or rush basket, often served with fruit. Also made in Charente-Maritime. When moulded and drained it is called *pigouille*

● *Chabichou fermier* Produced only on the occasional farm around Poitiers, a small truncated cone of *chèvre*.

● *Cabrichou laitier* Dairy-produced in Poitou, the Charentes and Touraine, a small truncated cone of *chèvre* with a full flavour and strong smell. Also seen as *cabichou*.

● *Chèvre à la feuille* See *La-Mothe-St-Héray*.

● *Chèvre long* Widely available in Poitou, Charentes and Touraine; a soft *chèvre*.

● *Couhé-Verac* A soft goat's milk cheese, wrapped in plane-tree or chestnut leaves. Weighs about 250 g/8 oz. Best from late spring to early autumn; has a robust flavour. Named after nearest town to its farm-based production.

★ *Echourgnac* Made by Trappists at the monastery of

Echourgnac in the Périgord, a small washed-rind cheese with tiny holes in the body. A mild, fruity flavour.

● *Jonchée Niortaise* Mild and creamy in taste, a very soft fresh goat's milk cheese from around Niort in Poitou; also in the Vendée and Charente. Sometimes called *Parthenay*.

★ *La-Mothe-St-Héray* There is a robust flavour to this small soft goat's milk cheese made at the dairy of La-Mothe-St-Héray whence it takes its name. Also known in Poitou as *Mothais* or *chèvre à la feuille*.

★ *Lusignan* A fresh goat's milk cheese farm-produced in and around Lusignan in Poitou. Weighs about 250 g/8 oz. The cheese used in *tourteau*

Cognac, like so many of the good things in life is the result of tax avoidance. Cognac's wines are always thin and of low value and really too weak to travel. Yet travel they did, by barge down river, and they were taxed willy-nilly on quantity alone. Often the wines didn't survive the journey, or if they did, no-one wanted them at the taxed price. The joint solution was to distill, reducing the volume and increasing the robustness; the rest is history.

The use of 'champagne' in connection with cognac, is a variation of the word for countryside *campagne*, and descriptive of the actual soils in which the essential wines are grown: Grande and Petite Champagne cognacs are considered the best, named because their rough chalk-strewn soil is the same as that of Champagne. Outer areas of *fromagé,* a cheesecake with a blackened upper crust.

● *Pigouille* A fresh creamy *charentais* cheese from the milk of cows, goats or sheep. Packed on straw, and varying in quality and price.

● *Poustagnacq* A fresh sheep's milk cheese from the Landes, best in winter, but sometimes fermented longer in crocks.

★ *Rocamadour* Known also as *cabécou de Rocamadour,* made from sheep's milk in the spring and goat's milk in summer, the latter giving a nutty flavour to this tiny disc of cheese. When aged with wine or spirit in crocks they are called a *picadou.*

● *Ruffec* A richly flavoured goat's milk cheese made in Ruffec and the northern part of Charente. A thick disc; from farms from the end of spring to autumn.

PASTRY, PUDDINGS & CONFECTIONERY

Honey, fruit, wine, cognac and chocolate in one proportion or another, are the traditional bases of sweet eating from Poitou through the Charentes and into the Dordogne. Surprisingly, the unctuous cream and butter of the Deux-Sèvres has not given rise to new creations, but enhances those of other *départements,* so pastries, croissants, *brioches* and the like seem universally to excel. Equally unexpected is the retained taste for baking with maize flour, which long ago replaced the old sweetish standby, millet, (although millet is remembered in the names given to the new versions). The same thing happens in the Limousin and Auvergne.

Fruit of every description is grown locally, and much of it finds its life extended by marriage with cognac, but glitzy packaging makes the coupling too heavy to carry unless you have a car. Fruits in cognac are also very expensive – you are better off buying duty-free liquor and making such treats at home. While in the area, however, eat the fruit fresh with cream, or in *tourtes, tourtières* and *tartes* – the *tarte verte d'Angoulême* breaks fruity ranks by being made from a paste of green almonds.

Beignets doughnuts or shapes of fried, flavoured

---

grape growing for cognac are the *borderies* and the *bois.*

Most of the big cognac houses sell a cognac made only from the Grande Champagne area towards the top of

☆ ☆ ☆ ☆ ☆ ☆ ☆ ☆ ☆ ☆ ☆ ☆ ☆ ☆ ☆ ☆

COGNAC, BRANDY – OR BOTH?

☆ ☆ ☆ ☆ ☆ ☆ ☆ ☆ ☆ ☆ ☆ ☆ ☆ ☆ ☆ ☆

their range. You may also see *fine champagne,* which means a blend of Grande and Petite Champagne cognacs and should not be confused with the *fine* that Frenchmen ask for in bars, which gets them a glass of anonymous firewater.

Be certain you are buying what you think you are . . . for although all cognac is brandy, all brandies are *not* cognac. Only when the word cognac appears on a label can you be guaranteed, by law, that the contents have been distilled from grape juice and that the wording on the label actually means something.

The generally used degrees and styles of cognac are based on age, but the quality depends solely on the blend of distillates used. It is important to know that, in France, the legal minimum age requirements for the levels of quality are lower than they are, say, in Britain. In the UK, three star brandy must be at least three years old, in France only one. At the higher levels (VSOP/VO/- Réserve and Extra/XO/- Napoléon/Vieille Réserve), cognacs will be up to two years younger in France than in Britain.

More unusual, and more accessible pocket-wise, is *pineau de Charente,* one of the few remaining examples of the old *ratafias.* Pineau is made by adding cognac to the freshly-pressed juice of grapes. It can be red, white or rosé and when perfect is delicious, with a clean raisin-like taste, that a few people confuse with simple sweetness. In my opinion it is better than wine or spirit for cooking and well worth taking home.

The museum in Cognac has a display concerned with its eponymous spirit; there is also the Cognac-thèque, dispensing knowledgeable advice, but no samples. Courvoisier have opened an excellent museum under their riverside premises in Jarnac.

dough are pretty common and the much-vaunted *merveilles* are just that. Pancakes are less ubiquitous than elsewhere, although there are *cruchades*, made from a thick batter of maize flour. The macaroons are very good and are the basis of one of the best ever confections made with chocolate, the *Saint-Emilion*.

The almonds which make macaroons also make marzipans *massepain*, often shaped like sardines and *fruits de mer*, and the *nougatine* of Poitiers. Whole almonds are baked into almost impossibly hard and chewy *craquelins* – I like those of Bordeaux. But if you need to keep children, friends or yourself amused in Bordeaux, search in its outstanding pastry shops for *canalles*. They look like tall little *brioches* and are made of maize flour which gives a highly unusual, chewy but open texture. They are recognizable by their coating of rich brown caramel and ridged sides (the *canals*). They seem unique to Bordeaux, and no-one other than natives of that city appears to know them. They travel well, though, so are excellent for picnics or munching *en route*.

Worth Finding

- *Gâteau Landais* See *pastis*.
- *Millassou* Essentially a batter made with maize flour and eggs, baked over grapes which have been soaked in *eau-de-vie* or honey, and especially associated with the Périgord. This is obviously a variation on Limousin's *clafoutis* (or vice versa) and such dishes are made with almost every fruit. *Cajasse* is the same thing, flavoured with dark rum as well. *Millasses* are small tarts of bitter almonds made in Périgueux. *Millas* is an egg custard mixture flavoured with *laurier cerise* and incorporating beaten egg whites.
- *Pastis* More associated with Gascony, but sold in Bordeaux shops as *gâteau landaise*. Consists of folds of paper-thin pastry baptized with cognac or armagnac and baked with butter, sugar and perhaps orange flower water. If there is some layer of fruit, usually apples or prunes, it is a *croustade*.
- *Pruneaux fourrées* To my mind, the only one of the confectionery specialities except for chocolates worth the premium price. They are prunes stuffed with a purée of prunes and almond paste – or variations on this theme. In many places you can buy them singly for a taste of velvety seduction.
- *Tourteau/tourte au fromage* You will have seen this all over France. It looks like a large brioche with a smooth black-charred top. It is a cheesecake from Poitou, made with very freshly curdled goat's cheese.

The drinking dates given below refer to classed growths and the top bourgeois châteaux only. The ordinary AC bordeaux and similar wines, both red and white, are ready for drinking almost immediately. Most experts agree

A DRINKER'S GUIDE

that a good sauternes from a good vintage needs 10 years or more in bottle, and a top white graves at least 8.

The last decade:

1984 A small crop of concentrated though sometimes unbalanced wines, tending to acidity. Drink with care from the late '80s. Sauternes sound but lightweight.

1983 A 'classic' bordeaux year: excellent on every front. For long-term drinking, starting 1990. Sauternes very good indeed.

1982 An extraordinary, exciting and untypical vintage, producing very rich, ripe, heady red wines. Sauternes and white bordeaux less distinguished. For mid- to long-term drinking beginning 1988.

1981 Modest quantity though good quality. Some châteaux much better than others. Drink from mid- to late '80s.

1980 Light, sometimes weak red wines, but good sweet and dry white wines. Drink no until 1990.

1979 Large harvest of average to good wines, red and white. Drink from 1985 onwards

1978 Good, solid, fruity vintage: reds and dry whites better than sauternes. Should last well. Drink from 1986 onwards.

1977 A miserable year: treat with caution. Drink up.

1976 Large harvest of easy-drinking red wines, nearly all ready now. The excellent sweet wines are still young.

1975 Tiny harvest of generally good, though still tannic, red wines. Excellent sweet white wines. More time needed. Drink from 1989 onwards.

1974 Avoid

Previous greats

1970, 1966, 1961, 1953, 1949, 1947, 1945, 1929.

Bon Marché

Below is a selective list of markets plus some fairs *foires* of special interest. Check with the local S.I. for precise locations and time changes.

DEUX-SÈVRES

Ardin Sat; **Argenton Château** Thur; **Le Beugnon** Every 2nd Thur; **Bressuire** Tue; **Brious-sur-Boutonne** Thur; **Champdeniers-St-Denis** Sat; **Chef Boutonne** 1st & 3rd Sat; **Clessé** Sat; **Coulonges-sur-l'Autize** Tue; **La Crèche** Tue; **Lezay** Tue; **Mauléon** Fri; **Melle** Fri; **Niort** Daily, esp. Thur & Sat; **Parthenay** Wed; **Sauzé-Vaussais** Thur; **Secondigny** Mon; **St-Maixent-l'Ecole** Wed; **Thénezay** Sun am; **Thouars** Tue & Fri; **St-Varent** 3rd Sun in month; **Voultegon** Wed.

VIENNE

Angles-sur-l'Anglin Wed, Thur, Sat, 1st Tue of month; **Availles Limouzine** 1st Wed of month; **Bouresse** 1st of month; **Buxerolles** Thur am; **Chatellerault** Tue, Thur, Sat; **Chaunay** Mon; **Chauvigny** Sat; **Civray** Tue; **Coulonges** 29th of month; **L'Isle-Jourdain** 1st Mon of month; **Jaunay Clan** Fri; **Liglet** 2nd of month; **Luchapt** 14th of month; **Lusignan** Wed; **Mirebeau** Wed & Sat am; **Naintré** Sun am; **Poitiers** Daily except Mon; **Pouillé** 1st & 3rd Wed of month; **La Roche-Posay** Daily; **Rouillé** Fri; **St-Jean-de-Sauves** 1st Fri of month; **St-Savin** Fri; **La Trimouille** 8th of month; **Les Trois Moutiers** Sat; **Vendeuvre-du-Poitou** Tue; **Vivonne** Tue & Sat.

CHARENTE-MARITIME

Angoulins Daily; **Aytre** Fri am; **Le-Bois-Plage-en-Ré** Daily (15 June – 15 Sept), Thur (rest of year); **Bourcefranc-le-Chapus** Wed, Fri; **La Brée-less-Bains** Daily; **Château d'Oléron** Daily ex Mon & Sat (Sat June 16 – Sept 15); **Couarde-sur-Mer** Daily (summer); **Dolus d'Oléron** Daily (summer); **La Flotte** Daily; **Jonzac** Tue, Fri; **Marennes** Tue, Fri, Sat; **Mirambeau** Sat; **Montendre** Thur; **Mortagne-sur-Gironde** Thur; **Port-des-Barques**

Daily; **Pons** Wed, Sat; **Rochefort** Sat, Tue, Thur; **La Rochelle** Daily; **Royan** Daily (summer), daily ex Mon rest of year; **Saintes** Daily ex Mon; **Surgères** Tue, Thur, Sat; **St-Denis-d'Oléron** Daily (summer); **St-Genis-de-Saintonge** Fortnightly; St Georges-de-Didonne Daily (summer) daily ex Mon rest of year; **Ste-Marie-de-Ré** Daily; **St Martin-de-Ré** Daily; **St Pierre-d'Oléron** Daily (summer); **St Trojan-les-Bains** Wed, Sat; **Tonnay-Charente** Wed, Sat; **La Tremblade** Sat.

CHARENTE

Aigre Thur; **Angoulême** Daily; **Barbezieux-St-Hilaire** Tue, **Blanzac-Porcheresse** 3rd Sat of month; **Brossac** 2nd & 4th Sat of month; **Chalais** Mon; **Chasseneuil-sur-Bonnieure** Sat; **Châteauneuf-sur-Charente** Tue, Thur, Sat; **Cognac** Daily; **Confolens** Wed & Sat; **La Couronne** Sat; **Jarnac** Daily Mon; **Mansle** 2nd Mon of month; **La Rochefoucauld** Daily; **Rouillac** 27th of month; **Ruffec** Wed & Sat; **St-Michel** Wed, Sat; **St-Séverin** 2nd Tue of month; **Villefagnan** Tue & Fri.

GIRONDE

Ambarès-et-Lagrave Fri am; **Arcachon** Daily; **Audenge** Tue; **Bassens** Sun am; **Bazas** Sat (also Cattle Fair); **Blaye** Wed & Sat; **Bordeaux** Daily except Sun; **Braud-et-St-Louis** Mon, Wed, Fri (15 Mar – Oct), fruit, veg, eggs, poultry; **Cavignac** Thur; **Coutras** Wed & Sat am; **Créon** Wed; **Frontenac** Fri am; **Guitres** *Onion Fair 2nd Wed Sept*; **Langon** Tue, Fri; **Libourne** Tue, Fri, Sun am; **Monségur** Fri am; **Pauillac** Tue, Sat am; **Pellegrue** Wed; **Podensac** Fri; **Pugnac** Wed am; **Reignac** Mon, Wed, Fri (prunes); **La Réole** Wed & Sat; **Sauveterre-de-Guyenne** Tue; **Soulac-sur-Mer** Sat (summer), Thur am (rest of year); **St-André-de-Cubzac** Thur & Sat am; **St Ciers-sur-Gironde** Sun am; **St-Emilion** Sun am; **Ste-Foy La- Grande** Sat am; **St-Loubès** Mon am; **St Médard-**

en-Jalles Sat; **St-Savin** Mon am; **St-Seurin-sur-l'Isle** Sat am; **St-Symphorien** 1st & 3rd Sun of month; **St-Vivien-de-Médoc** Wed; **La Teste** Daily; *Oyster-farming Fair/Exhibition last week July.*

DORDOGNE

Agonac Sun; **Belvès** Sat; **Bergerac** Wed & Sat; **Brantome** Fri; **Le Bugue** Tue, Sat am; **Le Buisson-de-Cadouin** Fri; **Champagnac-de-Belair** Fair 1st Mon of month; **Cogulot** Thur; **Excideuil** Thur; **Eymet** 2nd & 4th Thur of month; **Les Eyzies-de-Tayac Sireuil** Mon; **Lalinde** Thur; **Monpazier** Thur (*Chestnut Market Thur & Sun am Oct – Dec)*; **Montignac** Wed, Sat am; **Montpon Ménestérol** Wed; **Neuvic** Tue, Sat; **Nontron** Sat; **Périgueux** Wed, Sat; **Razac-sur-l'Isle** Sat am; **Rouffignac-St-Cernin-de-Reilhac** Sun; **Serges** 1st & 3rd Thur of month; **St-Astier** Thur; **St-Aulaye** Sat; **Terrasson-la-Villedieu** Daily; **Thenon** Tue; **Thiviers** Sat; **Tocane-St-Apre** Mon; **Vergt** Fri; **Villefranche-du-Périgord** Sat, (*Chestnut Market Sats Oct–Dec).*

LOT-ET-GARONNE

Agen Wed, Sat & Sun am, *Fat Geese Fair 2nd Mon Dec, Ham Fair Mon before Easter*; **Aiguillon** Tue; **Astaffort** Mon; **Cancon** 1st & 3rd Mon; **Casteljaloux** Tue, Sat; **Castillonnès** Tue; **Cocumont** Mon; **Fargues-sur-Ourbise** Mon, Wed, Fri eve; **Fumel** Sun, Tue, Fri; **Houeillès** Wed am; **Labretonie** Mon; **Lauzun** Sat; **Lavardac** Sun am; **Marmande** Mon, Thur, Sat; **Le Mas d'Agenais** 2nd Thur of month; **Miramont-de-Guyenne** Mon; **Monbahus** Sun am, 1st Sat in month (calves, poultry); **Monflanquin** Thur; **Nérac** Sat; **Penne de'Agenais** Sun am; **Port-Ste-Marie** Sat am; **Prayssas** Sun, Tue, Thur (June – Aug 15) (fruit & veg), Daily (Sept – Nov), (Chasselas Grapes); **Sauvetat-de-Savères** Sun (poultry & eggs); **Seyches** Fri; **Tonneins** Wed, Sat am; **Villeneuve-sur-Lot** Tue & Sat; **Villeréal** Sat, 1st & 3rd Mon.

Valleys of Eden

Contrast is an insidious word to a food writer, invidious even, for the frightful ease there is in using it, because it too often accurately describes the experience of a place. Yet, try as I might, I can't think of a better word to describe the singular appeal of Limousin and the Auvergne. In mitigation, there are, at least, lots of different contrasts.

If you know anything about either region, it is probably that they get pretty cold and pretty hot, and can drop from mid-summer to midwinter in a few hours, and that they are high and fairly inaccessible and rather plain in parts, with sheep. That's all true enough and you'll get what you bargained for.

What You Used

The foods thought most 'typical' of these related areas are based on cabbage, on potatoes, chestnuts and pork. They are the thick soup/stews, the *potée auvergnat* and the *bréjaude* or *bréjauda* of Limousin. There are the usual arguments about which should have what, whether leeks and beetroot, or a whole head of a pig, or just this or that salted piece should be there, but these are modern scholarly arguments of little relevance, for such dishes are the basis of the cuisine of every region of France, the sons and daughters of necessity. What you saw was what you used.

But there were definite problems with what you ate with those hearty dishes. The solution here was often that of the Bretons, pancakes of buckwheat *sarrasin/blé noir*. It is basic, rude simple food, packed with calories needed to get you through days of hard work or harsh winter temperatures; thus the surprise of finding, also, associations with some of France's most sophisticated names and products.

Disappearing Table

It had never occurred to me that one of my heroines, Madame de Pompadour, was actually a *marquise* and a *duchesse* of a real place, but Pompadour is in Limousin and her château, much too unfashionably sited for her to have spent much time in it, became a stud farm after her death, and remains so. She would have know well the tapestries made in Aubusson, about 60 km/37 miles away from her château as the crow flies; they would have been used to cut out the draughts and the whispers of the palace, and to make discreet backgrounds for her intriguing *petits soupers*.

Her private dining room in Versailles was no place for servants to overhear gossip and innuendo either. To save their blushes and those of her guests, La Pompadour's table disappeared through the floor after each course, returning when summoned, suitably relaid. But she missed by one year the discovery that made Limoges famous: that in 1765 of kaolin at St-Yrieix-la-Perche and the subsequent founding of the porcelain industry, fashioning tureens and bowls and gold-rimmed services. They would have looked good on that table.

"" In which we ...
- Look at royal hangings and chips off old plates ...
- Identify rude food, and find how Pompadour spared servants from blushing ...
- Discover a thousand-year-old corporation and the meaning of Millevaches ...
- Listen to some very tall stories ...
- Cook famous carrots ...
- Taste what Adam sat on and the mouldy beards bartered for a bride ...
- Fish in the Jordanne, see sizzling springs and a meatloaf crossed with soufflé, taste nutty oils ...
- See the old hams that became an Auvergnat sensation ...
- Cheer the homesick with jellied eels and Yorkshire pud ...
- Find out that life really can be a bowl of cherries ...
- Marvel at the *kamikaze* chestnut that cracks its own shell ...
- Ride to find raspberries, poke about blue cheeses and taste a 2,000-year-old variety ...
- Avoid herbs in innocent guise but look for a cake that commanded the Black Prince's troops ...
- Meet a wine that wants promotion ...
- Discover the water table of the table waters ... ""

Water for Fattening

It was surprising (to me, at least) to find meat, beef in particular, has been important long enough for there to have been a corporation of butchers ever since 930. Since the 17th century *les bouchers* have had also the honour and duty of guarding the safety of all visitors. Incidentally, I'm not sure if the words are related but the verb *limoger* means to dismiss or retire someone. Perhaps being sent to Limoges was once considered a banishment.

They seem to have had plenty to do, these butchers, preparing the flesh of the Limousin cattle of the plateau de Millevaches, which disappointingly doesn't mean thousands of cows but lots of rivers. Indeed there are many, and water in every other form possible, except for thermal spas, which is the prerogative of the Auvergne. The abundance of water makes the Limousin such a green luscious place in summer and the great stretches of thick, green vegetation and trees magnify its reputation for being so sparsely peopled. Of course, the water also nourishes the fruits and nuts of those trees, notably *reines-claudes* in the Corrèze, and makes fat the cherries *cerises* which in turn moisten *clafoutis*.

A Local Technique

The Auvergne, which is the greater part of the Massif Central, is much wilder to see than the Limousin, and full of tall stories. Its *puys* are extinct volcanic cones reaching even higher, but loved quite as much as they are cursed for their inconvenience by Auvergnats. When the days are too hot to bear you can always climb a mountain, and it will be cooler. Where there are mountains there are valleys and plains; thus, although it is true that grazing is sparse on the heights, so that only sheep and goats can be expected to live and lactate, down below are thriving gardens, pastures for dairy cattle, orchards, and farms to rival any. Vichy is a good example of an unappreciated agricultural centre, and is encircled by market gardens *cultures maraichères,* a renowned crop of which is carrots. I can't find anyone who actually knows what has so indelibly linked Vichy and carrots, but I'm quite certain that cooking carrots in bottled Vichy spa water is not the reason. This confusion has arisen because local cooks add a pinch of bicarbonate of soda and of sugar to the saucepan. The slight taste the soda leaves was thought to be from the local mineral water. My opinion is that the fame was originally based on the local technique, either cooking carrots in butter only or in so little water it evaporated to make a thick sauce by the time the carrots were cooked – add butter and chopped parsley, and voilà, Vichy carrots. Of course, any water used may have been from a local spring. . . .

Fantastic Stories

The contrast between what the uninitiated expect and what the locals feel about their country and their food is nowhere better illustrated than in Aigueperse, Puy-de-Dôme. The local view is that this was the very epicentre of the Garden of Eden. Of all the wicked fruits which hung from the trees of Paradise, *pralines* were the favourites of Adam and Eve. One day, God came visiting, and caught them having a right old feast. They apparently heard him coming – thunderbolts I presume – and attempted to dissemble with nonchalant lounging. But God knew better and made Adam stand up, revealing that he had been sitting on a couple. God was so cross he chased them both out of the garden. Much later the confectioners still make a speciality of the forbidden sweets that Adam – not Eve mind you – could not resist. More research required I think. . . .

None is needed into the reputation the locals have for being as canny about money as the Scots. That's a fact. And like the Scots they've gone to make it somewhere else if times have been tough, usually opening small restaurants or shops specializing in the hams and *charcuterie* and excellent cheeses of the Auvergne. Auvergnat shops all over France, particularly in Paris, are always worth a visit.

Tomme incidentally is not a type of cheese, but the local name for cheese, and this is why *tommes* from the same area may be totally different types of cheese.

What each will have in common is a fantastic story woven about it, some curious enough to be true. *Gaperon,* for instance, is a grey half-sphere wrapped in ribbon, made from skimmed milk and flavoured with garlic and black peppercorns. How pale and uninteresting is its modern life in cheese shops around the world compared to its once and proper place in society. *Gaperons* were the conspicuous part of a young girl's dowry, hung outside her parents' house promiscuously to be counted, and allowed to grow beards of mould that dangled a foot or more. If you see lumps of garlicy mould hanging outside the house, and you are a single male, apply within.

Concentrate

There is plenty of confusion about what rightfully belongs to the culinary repertoire of the Limousin and the Auvergne. It's partly a matter of knowing quite where older boundaries, like those of the Aveyron and the Rouergue, belong. Because they *are* central surely it is expected that both regions have invaded and been invaded. Thus *bleu d'Auvergne* is meant to be like the *roquefort* of Aveyron, and *cantal* cheese is mixed into a potato purée *aligot* as carefully as in the Rouergue, and salads are seasoned with nut oils as in the Périgord. But just because you can't find the wines of Chanturgue, don't think chicken cooked in those wines was not the original *coq au vin;* it's simply that the vineyards are no longer with us. In any case, I shouldn't bother too much about the stories you hear, but concentrate instead on what you find. You may be surprised at the contrast. . . .

CHARCUTERIE

As pork features among the many riches of the Auvergne – marginally more than in Limousin – and as the climate is just right, air-dried *charcuterie* is extremely good. All through France you are likely to find stalls of travelling Auvergnats selling their *andouilles,* their air-dried sausages and, even better, the famed hams of the Auvergne; recommended centres of production are Ussel, St-Mathieu, Lezoux and Clermont-Ferrand. As well as the raw, the cooked ones are worth seeking out; in Lezoux, for instance, they are baked in pastry with madeira.

In Rochechouart on *mardi gras* you should find small pies of pork, spices and egg in pastry – a French pork pie. It is slowly being learnt, I believe, that they are good enough to be worth making at other times of the year. *Pâtés* are universally made, but are too strongly flavoured for foreign palates when the local taste for pork liver predominates. Yet all of them are interesting for the variety of herbs and spices of the plateau that might be employed, including juniper. More to the general taste are the large *tourtes*, pastry-covered pies of pork and veal nicely spiced with pepper and cloves. Smaller are *friands sanflorains,* little sausages baked in pastry.

The presence of pigs means black pudding *boudin.* Chestnuts are often included and on a cold day or chilly evening the combination of hot *boudin* and the common Limousin garnish of red cabbage, with or without more chestnuts, is quite wonderfully warming ... even in summer you may need it.

Worth Finding

● *Fricandeau* A *crépine* of pork; chopped, flavoured pork wrapped in caul fat *coiffe*.
● *Farcidure* The name means 'hard stuffing' and these are small dumplings based on buckwheat, a *hachis* of green leaves (like sorrel), and herbs. Sometimes wrapped in cabbage leaves as well.
● *Tripoux* Small cushions of tripe stuffed with boned trotter flesh; they might well be made with mutton rather than pork, but are always flavoured with cloves. Further south they will be called *trénels,* and the exact composition of the stuffing is, naturally, subject to many variations, argument and opinion.

FISH & SHELLFISH

The abundant freshwater fish found in the Limousin and Auvergne is most likely to be served to you in a *friture* almost certainly prepared in butter. Experimenters might dribble in a little nut oil, which is local, or olive oil, which is not. Auvergnat frogs were fattened and taken to 18th-century Paris, so renowned was their succulence, but they are fewer since the swamps of Limagne have been drained for pastureland. What remains – or what are imported – are served as simply as the fish, fried in butter. The mixed freshwater *matelote* based on carp and eels, pike, tench and so on is also made.

The treat to really go for – if you can find them these days – is the local crayfish *écrevisses.* A simple and effective ploy in the Haute Auvergne is to cook them with fresh mint; delicious. Guéret serves them *à la sauce sans nom* – in a nameless sauce.

Pike *brochet* is stuffed and roasted and sometimes made into a *pâté,* a lazy but tastier version of a *quenelle.* You can be fairly certain that trout is wild and local and it will be served classically (*au bleu* if you are lucky), experimentally, or in local tradition, which might include cheese, vermouth or spinach. For the greatest of travelling fishy tales, order local trout in Aurillac – it will have come from the River Jordanne. Brits may welcome the regular appearance of jellied eels *anguilles en gelée.*

MEAT, POULTRY & GAME

Beef, lamb, mutton, veal, pork, turkeys, geese and chickens are all produced in one part or another of the valleys and high pastures of central France. Since the 19th century, Limousin has become the virtual meat factory of France. Its small cattle were primarily kept as workers but have subsequently been bred into the huge modern *limousins* with first-class meat which has changed local cuisine. You'll find many products traditionally made from pork now sweetened and made more sophisticated with veal, or with parts of veal. *Tourtes* are an example.

Lamb and mutton equally thrive on the well-watered heights of the Auvergne, especially in Cantal. In Chaudes-Aigues they have been important far longer than have the pig, but are just one of the claims to fame of this place. It doesn't just have hot springs: the water positively sizzles at over 80°C.

Cantal is also an important centre for raising turkey and geese, and in the north of the region, the Bourbonnais, you'll find a highly reputed race of chickens, the *poulets bourbonnais*. The name usually also indicates the bird will be served in typical sauce of cream and cheese.

Game is here limited and not as important as elsewhere. There is some fame for a method of preparing hare *lièvre en cabessal*, differing from the exalted but complicated *lièvre à la royale* (qv) in the stuffing. You are unlikely to meet either but may find the wild rabbit *lapin de garenne*. In the Auvergne it is more likely you will find boar *sanglier*, sometimes in a *daube* which makes a change from roasts. Partridge *perdrix* (*perdreau* for young birds) is prepared with two of the local favourites – cabbage and lentils.

Some of the most famous dishes of the region were based on such songbirds as the thrush, which were stuffed with *foie gras*; but these may no longer be taken, being protected by the Common Market. The most surprising food fact is that *coq au vin* was first cooked here and was actually called *coq au Chanturgue*; it is deceptive of local restaurateurs to dub it *au Chanturgue*, for this is one of the wines which has all but disappeared as the vineyards have been replaced by pastures.

Chicken will also be found stuffed with chestnuts *à la limousin* or made into a *tourte* or chicken pie. Cherries, too, are combined with poultry. Anne Willan has an excellent recipe for duck with the tart cherries which may be gathered wild in the hedgerows in her book *French Regional Cooking*.

Worth Finding

● *Gigot brayaude* Also called *cassette*. A most famous dish, almost a pot roast really, of leg of lamb cooked in a little wine on a bed of vegetables, potatoes included usually. Gault Millau publish the unresolved question of whether the *gigot* should be stuck with cloves of garlic or larded, but the former was all I found. It should be served with the usual mixture of vegetables in these parts – cabbage, red beans and onions.

● *Mortier*. A casserole from the Auvergne associated with Easter which combines beef or veal with ham and chicken.

● *Pounti* Described almost everywhere as a cross between a meat loaf and a vegetable soufflé, which is about as close as you could hope to get to encapsulating something mixing chopped pork or bacon with eggs, cream, ham and almost any green leaf or herb, plus, sometimes, raisins and prunes. When it includes sorrel or dandelion leaves in spring time, it is a somewhat lighter version of Cognac's *poulet vert* (see **Bordeaux**).

● *Pountari* Not the same as *pounti* but a sort of sausage wrapped in cabbage leaves.

FRUIT & VEGETABLES

If you are of the uninitiated and think of central France, as I once did, as an area of high, dry and scrubby fields nibbled at by scrawny sheep, you will thoroughly enjoy exploring the surprising range of its produce. For in between those plains, and much lower down, rich valleys grow an extraordinary choice of fruit, vegetables and grains.

Auvergne and Le Puy grow everything from *petits pois* to chestnuts, although cabbage and exquisite lentils *lentilles* are the best-known crops, turning up, with beans green, white or red, whatever the season. The blue-green *lentilles de Puy* are protected by an AOC. Limagne and its plain is the most perfect example of the Auvergne's spread of produce. Its wheat fields are bordered by orchards producing sun-ripened apricots and other fruits for the excellent local *confitures*. Look out specially for the strawberries from Courpière, fresh or preserved.

The autumnal debris under chestnut trees is the place to find succulent *cèpes* in autumn. Spring offers the more sophisticated flavours of morels *morilles* and *mousserons*. Both garlic and shallots are important commercial crops in Puy-de-Dôme, but you should particularly plan to stock up on nut oils – either walnut *huile de noix* or exquisite hazelnut oil *huile de noisette*. Both are used to finish the flavour of dishes cooked in pork fats and as the dressing for salads of all kinds. Corrèze (Limousin) grows the most and best nuts,

Worth Finding

- *Criquettes* Potato pancakes, usually flavoured with garlic in the Auvergne.
- *Farinettes* Savoury pancakes usually filled with vegetable mixtures.
- *Aligot* One of the most famous dishes – a purée of mashed potato and fresh cheese (*aligot* is actually the fresh curd of *cantal* cheeses). Also associated with the Rouergue which corresponds to the *département* of Aveyron, just across the border from Cantal.
- *Pastourelle* The best of the many delicious auvergnat salads, dressed with a nut oil, cream, blue cheese, tarragon and chervil.
- *Gâteau de potiron et maïs* A bread/cake of pumpkin and corn meal like that made in the Basque country.
- *Pommes de terre à la guerilla* Potatoes sautéed then grated into milk.
- *Truffado/truffade* Potatoes cooked with cheese, properly *cantal*, and then shaped into cakes and fried.

LOCAL PRODUCE

Vegetables

● **Cabbage** *chou pommé* Var: none French	Autumn and winter Dep: Creuse
● **Shallot** *échalote* Var: *Longue, demi-longue*.	Fresh June/July; available 12 months Dep: Pûy-de-Dome
● **Fruit** **Apples** *pommes* Var: *Reinette blanche* and *grise*	Mainly September to October Dep: Corrèze
● **Chestnut** *marron/châtaigne* Var: *Précoce Migoule* (châtaigne), *Laguepie* eaten fresh; *Dorée de Lyon*	Late autumn early winter Dep: Corrèze
● **Hazelnut** *noisette* Var: none French	July to September, fresh, then dried Dep: Corrèze
● **Plum** *prune* Var: *Reines-claudes, Prune de Vars* (July)	Mid-July to early October Dep: Corrèze
● **Raspberry** *framboise* Var: none French	June and July high season Dep: Corrèze
● **Strawberry** *fraises* Var: *Favette, Belrubi*	Forced start end April. May and June main season Dep: Corrèze
● **Walnut** *noix* Var: *Corne, Marbot*	Harvested September to January Dep: Corrèze

and so may offer marginally better choice.

Limousin was one of the very first areas in France to enjoy the potato, long before Parmentier and the Revolution. Both here and in the Auvergne you'll find some of the most unusual and delicious potato ideas, often mixed with dairy products of one kind or another. Potatoes are creamed to go with salt cod, in pies, in *farcidure*. The *gratin auvergnat* is potatoes mixed with an equal amount of chestnuts.

Chestnuts with red cabbage is a classic Limousin mixture but they are just as often served separately; boiled chestnuts are *boursadas*, when grilled *chauvets*. They are usually the *châtaigne* rather than the *marron* and turn up almost everywhere in simple home cooking; perhaps that is why the *debou ciradour* was developed, which neatly cracks open its own shell.

Limousin is one of the few French regions to grow jerusalem artichokes *topinambours* and of all central France its southern département, Corrèze, has the greatest number of commercial crops – of apple, table plums and greengages, strawberries and raspberries, the biggest of all. Less common fruit includes the sumptuous mulberry *mûre*, which may turn up with saddle of hare *râble de lièvre*. And should you be walking or, blissfully, riding through August woodland or forest you stand well to discover bilberries *myrtilles* or exquisite wild raspberries. With the wine you would, naturally, be carrying, a shady bough and a thou, who'd mind the lack of bread?

CHEESE

The rich pastureland of this region – which includes Cantal, the Aubrac mountains and the *massif* of Auvergne – gives an excellent flavour to the milk of the cows and goats grazing there, in turn producing many excellent cheeses. There is a wide selection of blue cheeses made on mountain farms, including the *bleu d'Auvergne*, the celebrated *fourmes* and many other pressed-uncooked cow's milk cheeses and some fine *chèvres* and *mi-chèvres*.

● *Aligot* (Rouergue) Originating in the mountains of Aubrac, *aligot* is a fresh pressed cheese that has to be eaten within 48 hours of manufacture. Produced by small mountain dairies called *burons* it is slightly sour with a somewhat nutty flavour; used in cooking.

★ *Bleu d'Auvergne AOC* Only created in 1845 by a peasant of the Auvergne who added some of the blue mould he saw on his rye bread to his cheeses and poked them with a needle to ensure the air passages in which the mould might grow. Others in the area followed his example and so was born one of the newest cheeses to be honoured with an AOC. Neither pressed nor cooked, the body should be very evenly moulded with veins, firm to the touch and have a strong smell and full, savoury flavour. It is always wrapped in foil, weighs 2 to 3 kg/4 to 6 lbs (smaller ones 1kg/2¼lb) and can be enjoyed all year round. In effect a cow's milk version of *roquefort*.

● *Bleu de Laqueille* Related to *bleu d'Auvergne*, this soft cow's milk cheese, now produced commercially, was developed about 1850. Foil wrapped, weighing 2kg/5 lb it has a keen smell, definitely savoury flavour and is at its best in summer and autumn after its three month's curing.

● *Bleu de Loudes* Sometimes called *bleu du Velay* although there is another cheese of this name with a higher fat content. This is low fat (25-35%) cow's milk cheese with a savoury flavour similar to many other blue cheeses from small mountain farms in the region.

● *Bleu de Thiézac* Made exclusively by mountain farms in the upper valley of Cère and the Jordanne, a soft cow's milk cheese not unlike *bleu d'Auvergne* although a little less smooth. A savoury flavour, at its best in summer and autumn.

● *Bleu du Velay* A 30-40% fat blue very similar to *bleu de Loudes*.

● *Brique du Forez* Known also as *chèvron d'Ambert* or *cabrion du Forez*. A soft *chèvre* or *mi-chèvre* from the Auvergne, brick-shaped, 300-350 g/12-14 oz, which is cured dry on rye hay for two or three months and eaten summer to autumn. *Chèvres* have a bluish mould exterior; *mi-chèvres* are grey.

★ *Cantal AOC* Known also as *fourme de Cantal* this is one of the most ancient cheeses known, dating back at least 2,000 years. It comes from an area in the volcanic *massif* of the Auvergne where vegetation is luscious and excellent for grazing.

A very large cow's milk cheese – it can weigh between

30 to 45 kg/77-99 lb (although the *cantalet* weighs a mere 10 kg/22 lb) – it is pressed but not cooked and can be eaten young (*le cantal jeune*) or matured (*vieux* – about 4-6 months). With a light grey crust and ivory coloured body it has a mild flavour, comparable to that of a good nutty farm-made cheddar. Made commercially throughout the year it is also produced on mountain farms in the summer. It is used in cooking, in any way a cheddar would be.

● *Cantalon* Produced in most of Auvergne, it is a cow's milk cheese *very* similar to *cantal* but smaller, weighing 4-10 kg/9-22 lb.

● *Chevrotin du bourbonnais* A small truncated cone of goat's milk cheese that receives very little curing – no more than a week or two – and can be eaten fresh and creamy (with sugar if you want) or semi-dry, when it has a nutty flavour.

● *Conne* Known also as *chevrotin de bourbonnais,* a cone of soft goat's milk cheese with a mild, nutty flavour; made close to Moulins, centre of the Bourbonnais in Allier.

● *Coulandon* or *chaucetier* Eaten fresh, this soft cheese from the Allier is rather like fresh *coulommiers* but made from partly skimmed cow's milk.

★ *Fourme d'Ambert or Fourme de Montbrison AOC* The cheese we know probably emerged in the 8th or 9th century, although it has a history that pre-dates the arrival of the Caesars. *Fourme* refers to moulds in which the cheese is made. It is a typical blue pressed uncooked cow's milk cheese but has a rougher, more mould-covered crust than most; it is taller and thin-

ner, too. Produced extensively in the farms and dairies of the Puy-de-Dôme plus some in the neighbouring Loire (Rhône Valley) and five cantons around St-Flour. Although a little salty, it has a smooth fruity flavour. This is Giscard d'Estaing's favourite.

● *Fourme de Pierre-sur Haute* Closely resembling the *fourme d'Ambert*, this blue cheese is made high up in the mountains of Livradois.

● *Fourme de rochefort* Linked with the history of Cantal this is a big cow's milk cheese with a lactic smell and, usually, a tangy flavour. Best summer or autumn.

● *Galette de La Chaise-Dieu* A charming name – *galette* means flat cake and La Chaise-Dieu is the place of origin; thin, farmhouse disc of *chèvre* or *mi-chèvre* with a strongly nutty flavour; sometimes brick-shaped; blue or grey surface moulds.

★ *Gaperon* (or *gapron*) The name is derived from a dialect word *gap* or *gape* meaning buttermilk and it is that, or cow's skimmed milk, that is used to produce this very low-fat cheese. Pressed into a rounded cone shape and uncooked, it is flavoured with garlic and black peppercorns. Light delicious flavour when fresh; used to be aged until a beard grew all over. Once part of a bride's dowry (see p.132).

● *Guéret* A small low fat (10%) cheese from the Creuse made from almost totally skimmed milk may be aged in crocks up to 6 months and even through into winter. Possibly found in markets only. Known also as *geusois* or *coupi*.

★ *Laguiole AOC* Pronounced *laiole*, this is a large cheese related to the *cantal* but with

an even herbier flavour, the cows grazing on pastures rich in thyme, fennel, gentian and broom in the Aubrac mountains. It is made only from raw full milk; pressed but not cooked, made in mountain *burons* or creameries. Also known as *Laguiole-Aubrac* or *fourme de Laguiole* it is best eaten after it has been cured at least 5 months.

● *Murol* Produced in small factories in and around Murol; a milk-flavoured cow's milk washed-rind disc.

● *Pouligny-St-Pierre AOC* This full-cream goat's milk cheese gets its special savour from the wide-range of grasses and plants available to the short-haired goats in the pastures around Pouligny-St-Pierre. The cheese is at its best from April to October. Has a definite earthy taste; traditionally eaten only with dry white wines, usually a sauvignon from Touraine or Berry, or a white chenin.

● *Rigotte de Pelussin* (Pelussin-Auvergne) A small soft *chèvre* or *mi-chèvre* made in farms or small traditional dairies. A slightly nutty taste, best enjoyed between late spring and autumn.

★ *St-Nectaire AOC* An outstanding cheese of great antiquity – Louis XIV was fond of it. It's a pressed cow's milk cheese, made in farms and dairies in a large area of south-west Puy-de-Dôme and the north of Cantal. The crust is brine-washed during curing to encourage moulds varying in colour from white to red and violet. Best eaten in summer and autumn; often used in cooking, this semi-soft cheese should have a light mushroom smell and sweet but rounded flavour.

LIMOUSIN & THE AUVERGNE

★ *Salers* or *fourme de Salers AOC* Cheese which obtains its characteristic savour from the fragrant grasses, bushes and berries (including bilberries) that the cows feed upon in Cantal and its surroundings.

Made from raw, full-cream cow's milk it has an earthy flavour that strengthens with age – matured for 3-12 months.

● *Tomme de Brach* Related to fresh-drained *roquefort*

cheeses this *tomme* from the Corrèze is made from sheep's milk but has no internal veining. Best in spring and summer it has a distinct sheep smell and strong taste; mainly farm-produced.

BOTTLING IT UP

Nowhere else in the world are mineral waters consumed in such quantity and treated with such reverence as in France. The French drink some 300 billion litres of *eau minérale naturelle* each year, believing it to be an important aid to health, beauty and above all *le foie*.

All bottled waters are highly regulated by the French government which has put them into three distinct classes. Bottom of the league is *eau de table* (table water) which can come from either a public or a private supply, but it must be drinkable and contain a certain number of mineral salts. *Eau de source* (spring water) must be of a specified origin and be drinkable in its natural state. A spring water gains the accolade of *eau minérale naturelle* if it is found by the National Academy of Medicine to be positively good for you, and can therefore be used therapeutically. Such is the French attitude to mineral waters, doctors study their different properties during training and can forbid or recommend different brands according to their minerals.

According to law, mineral water must be bottled as it emerges from the ground,

without any sterilization – in other words it reaches the public in its natural pure state. All aspects of collection, bottling and protection from pollution are subject to the most stringent checks and standards. Some mineral waters carry a *d'intérêt public* seal of approval, meaning the spring and surrounding land are even further safeguarded. Differing tastes come from mineral salts naturally present in the water and usually waters such as *Evian* and *Perrier* are lower in minerals than brands such as *Vichy*, which has a more distinctive taste. Sparkling waters get their sparkle from carbon dioxide, found under carbonate rocks, which may be collected separately at the spring and re-injected at bottling. Only *Badoit* has not been re-injected, amongst sparkling waters.

These are the most famous waters from France's 1200 mineral springs and 100 spas.
● *Badoit* Medium-strength flavour with a natural, light sparkle. Licenced in 1838, it was the first mineral water to be bottled and sold commercially for mass consumption. The source is St-Galmier in the Loire Valley, the spring

emerging on the edge of Monts du Lyonnais. Recommended for nervous disorders. Much the most fashionable in France; because the bubbles are smaller and more elegant?
● *Contrex* A still water with an earthy taste. The source was discovered in 1760, 383 m/1,148 ft above sea level in the Faucille mountain range, near the French-German border. Contrex has a high calcium sulphate content, and is popular with dieters because of its diuretic properties.
● *Evian* A light, still water and the biggest selling bottled water in the world. The source is the water and the snow falling on the French Alps, which eventually collect in a deep bed formed in sands of glacial origin, natually protected by two thick layers of clay. The average time it takes to filter through the sands is thought to be 15 years. Low in sodium and nitrate, it has diuretic properties, and being particularly pure is recommended by French doctors for kidney diseases, arthritis and gout.
● *Perrier* Naturally highly carbonated and pure, and the most popular imported mineral water in America. The source was a resting place for Hannibal and the site of roman baths in the 1st century AD. Its name comes from Dr Perrier, who sold the spring at the turn of the century to A.W. St John

• *Vachard* Made only in farms in the Dore mountains this is a 20cm/8in disc of pressed uncooked cow's milk cheese. It is perhaps the ancestor of Louis XIV's choice, *St-Nectaire* (qv), but is stronger.

Harmsworth, brother of the Fleet Street tycoon Lord Northcliffe. Harmsworth gave to Perrier its distinctive Indian-club-shaped bottle and coined the slogan *Perrier – le champagne des eaux de table*. Its effervescence comes from gases trapped by volcanic eruptions deep beneath the earth's surface, which travel up through porous limestone to mix with the water. The carbonated water collects in a basin of white sand topped with sand and gravel, which acts as a natural filter. Over 360 million bottles of Perrier are sold each year.

• *Vichy Celestins* Still water with a slightly salty taste, high mineral content and naturally mildly carbonated. Its source is one of four springs bubbling out of Vichy, including Puits Carré, the hottest spring which emerges at 42.5°C and is used for baths. The Vichy resort was originally built by Julius Caesar and rebuilt several times, lastly by Napoléon III.

• *Vittel* A still water with moderate mineral content, collected from springs discovered by the Romans. The spa specializes in kidney troubles and blood pressure.

• *Volvic* Still water, low in minerals. The source is a valley in the Auvergne, filled over thousands of years with layers of volcanic rock, which filter the water. Volvic has a perfectly balanced pH (7.0), making it a popular water for skincare.

PASTRIES, PUDDINGS & CONFECTIONERY

Best known of the edible sweet delights of central France is the *clafoutis*, usually asociated etymologically only with Limousin, but commonly made throughout the Auvergne too, particularly in Allier. Often called other names – *millat, milla, mias millard* and *tuillard* (Vichy) – but essentially a good old-fashioned baked batter pudding, classically containing fresh unpitted black cherries, but just as often you'll find grapes, plums or redcurrants. Today's freedom of culinary interpretation means one might come to you thicker, thinner or in some other way different from what you expect – if it includes black rum, so much the better. Clermont-Ferrand has had a sugar refinery of sorts since the 18th century and as this began processing only cane from the Caribbean, rum was bound to turn up. Cognac or *kirsch* are just as likely to be used.

Clermont has actually been famous for sweetness more than 400 years, preserving with honey local apricots and angelica *angélique* and making superior fruit pastes and jams, or *confitures* which are noticeably thinner and runnier than a British jam or American preserve. Many other centres do the same admirably, notably Riom. But for locals with aspirations, sugar was used to sweeten the same batter as a *clafoutis*, a ritzy alternatve to the natural sweetness of fruit; this sweet, baked pancake is the *flognarde* or *flaugnard*, and really

only worth ordering if it is to be doused in the region's fruity alcohols, or covered with fresh fruit and cream.

The cold nights of the central plateau are perfect for producing crisp apples and voluptuous pears. Everyone makes tarts and flans (with cherries or chestnuts too) and you may also find covered pies of apple paste or *sucre de pommes*, something the Americans make and call apple butter or apple cheese. In puff pastry, like turnovers, these are often called *chaussons*. Even better are cakes made with unusual local varieties of pear; *gargouillau* is the best known of these. *Piquenchagne* or *picanchagne* and *le poirat* are also pear pies or cakes, sometimes in combination with walnut.

With chestnuts and hazelnuts growing here and almonds from the south easily available, you'll find *nougatines* (Saint-Pourçain), marzipan, macaroons and the like. The barley grown here but used for maltings in northern breweries makes a famous barley sugar *sucre d'orge* in Vichy. The *noisettes* of Aubusson are little cakes flavoured with hazelnuts. A reminder of

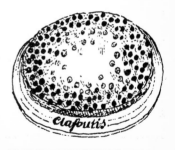

Clafoutis

Better Batter Puddings

the occasional harshness of the climate is seen in the use of the reliable buckwheat crop, here often called *sarrasin* rather than *blé noir*, and used in pancakes *galettes*, called *galetons* in Haute Vienne and *tourtons* in Corrèze. Rye flour *farine de seigle* is used for *bourioles,* a yeasted pancake.

In a sublime confluence of indulgences, Royat makes what many feel are among the best if not actually *the* best chocolates in the world using the fruits and liqueurs of the surrounding countryside. Make sure you go there, and

make sure you have plenty of money. Good barley sugar *sucres d'orge*, glacé fruits and fruit pastes, too.

There is but one caveat for the sweet of tooth. The herbs grown here extensively for medical use flavour many innocent-looking pastilles. Some are distinctly unusual! Stick to names you recognize, or to other chocolates, like the *palets d'or* of Moulins, or move on to *fouasses*. These are also called *pompe*, and like *fougasse* and *pompe* of Provence are sweetened dough spiked with glacé fruits.

The clafoutis of Limousin is typical of many ancient puddings throughout Europe based on pouring a sweet batter onto fruit then baking the mixture. Ripe cherries feature in the best known version, but any fruit can be used; the mixture may be enlivened by rum, cognac or other spirits and you can use your favourite pancake batter.

For a more spectacular effect, pour oil or butter into the baking dish and heat to piping hot. Add fruit, heat well in the oven then pour batter over it and pop it immediately into a very hot oven. It will rise to the occasion like a Yorkshire pudding and can be taken directly to the table.

From the Bourbonnais in northwest Auvergne comes the related *gargouillau*, based on an unusual pear and blackcurrant combination and a rich batter mix with single cream.

Mix together a couple of eggs, 75g/3oz sugar, 25g/1oz flour and 300ml/½ pint cream into a liquid paste. Peel and chop half a dozen pears and mix into the paste with a few ounces of blackcurrants. Pour into a buttered pie dish and bake until set (about half and hour). Serve warm, with more cream, of course. You might find it easier to manage in individual ramekins.

A DRINKER'S GUIDE

The Auvergne uses its many wild herbs to make liqueurs and aperitif drinks. *Verveine, gentiane,* sloe *prunelle* are found beside more familiar flavour, raspberry *framboise* and strawberry *fraise*. Le Puy's *Verveine de Velay*, green or yellow, is best known and there is a juniper-flavoured *genièvre* and an unexpected *mandarine*. You may see lots of barley growing but once it is malted it is shipped off to the brewers of the north.

Don't miss the under-rated wines of St-Pourçain-sur-Soule from the Allier, ready to be promoted from VDQS to AOC. And in between meals you might like to try the beer of Clermont.

Bon Marché

Below is a selective list of markets plus some fairs *foires* of special interest. Check with the local S.I. for precise locations and time changes.

HAUTE-VIENNE

Aixe-sur-Vienne Sat, Sun; **Ambazac** Thur; **Bellac** Wed, Fri, **Châteauneuf-la-Forêt** Last Sat in month; **Châteauponsac** Sun; **Coussac Bonneval** 3rd Thur in month; **Eymoutiers** Sun, 1st & 3rd Thur (except May, Sept & Oct); **Limoges** Daily; **Magnac-Laval** 8th Jan, April, Dec, 22nd other months; **Nantiat** Fri, **Rochechouart** Tue, Thur, Sat; **St-Junien** Daily; **St-Léonard de Noblat** Sat; **St-Paul** Tue before Mardi Gras; **St-Yrieix-la-Perche** Sat.

CREUSE

Aubusson Sat; **Auzances** Tue; **Bonnat** Wed; **Bourganeuf** Wed; **Chénérailles** 5th & 20th each month, 2nd Sun May & Oct (poultry); **Gouzon** Tue; **Le Grand Bourg** 2nd & 17th of month; **Guéret** Sat; **Jouillat** Thur; **Moutier-Malcard** Sat; **Nouziers** Sat; **Peyrat-la-Nonière** Sat; **La Souterraine** Thur, Sat; **St-Étienne de Fursac** 5th & 19th of month; **St-Marc-à-Loubaud** *Sheep Fair 25 Aug*; **St-Pierre Bellevue** *Lamb Fair 4th Sept*; **Vallière** Thur.

CORRÈZE

Allassac Daily; **Arnac Pompadour** Tue, Thur, Sat; **Beaulieu-sur-Dordogne** Sat; **Brive-la-Gaillard** Sat, Tue, Thur; **Chamboulive** Sat; **Donzenac** Thur, Sun; **Lubersac** Summer Fête (flower procession) Sun after Aug 15; **Marcillac-la-Croisille** 14th & 26th each month; **Neuvic** Wed; **Objat** Daily (summer), Wed, Fri, Sun rest of year. Lamb Fair 4th Mon Jan; **Treignac** 6th & 22nd of each month; **Ussel** Sat & Wed; **Uzerche** 20th of each month.

ALLIER

Bourbon-Larchambault Wed; **Cerilly** Thur am; **Cosne d'Allier** Tue (2nd Tue poultry); **Coulanges** Thur; **Lurcy-Levis** Mon, *Poultry Fair 4th Mon Oct*; **Marillat-en-Combraille** Thur (poultry); **Mayet-de-Montagne** Mon; **Montluçon** Tue, Wed, Thur, Fri, Sat; **Moulins** Fri; **Néris-les-Banis** Thur; **Neuilly-le-Réal** Thur; **St-Pourçain-sur-Sioule** Sat; **Varennes-sur-Allier** Mon; **Vichy** Wed.

PUY-DE-DÔME

Aigueperse Tue; **Ambert** 1st & 3rd Thur of month; **Les Ancizes Comps** Wed; **Ardes** 2nd & 4th Mon; **Arlanc** 2nd & 4th Mon; **La Bourboule** Sat; daily in summer; **Brassac-les-Mines** Sun am; **Chatel-Guyon** Fri; **Clermont-Ferrand** Mon; **Combronde** Every 2nd Mon; **Cournon d'Auvergne** Thur; **Courpière** Every 2nd Tue; **Cunlhat** Wed; **Issoire** Sat; **Maringues** Thur (farmyard produce); **Menat** Wed; **Messeix** Thur; **Olliergues** Sat;

AOC

This means *appellation d'origine contrôlée*. It is awarded to cheese and other foodstuffs by the same body that awards *AOC* to wine.

An AOC guarantees by law that specific conditions regarding the area of growth, the manufacturing technique, the animal from which the food came, its composition, physical aspect and specific attributes are all met.

AOCs are most often awarded to cheeses (see **Cheese** sections) but have also been given to poultry (*poulets de Bresse*), walnuts from Grenoble, Chasselas grapes, certain types of olives, two kinds of potato, some Golden Delicious apples, and lentils from Puy. Always worth buying.

Picherande *Cheese Market* every fortnight from 10 Jan; **Puy-Guillaume** Wed; **Randan** Fri; **Riom** Sat; **Sauxillanges** Tues; **St-Alyre-d'Arlanc** 2nd & 4th Sun; **St-Dier-d'Auvergne** Thur; **St-Donat** Every other Sat (pigs, cheese); **St-Genès Champespe** Thur (cheese); **St-Gervais d'Auvergne** 2nd Mon of month; **Thiers** Sun; **Vernet-la-Varenne** 1st & 3rd Mon; **Vic-le-Comte** Thur.

CANTAL

Allanche Tue; **Aurillac** Wed, Sat, Fair days; **Chaudes-Aigues** Mon; **Condat** Tue; **Lacapelle-Barrès** 1st Mon of month; **Laroquebrou** 2nd Fri of month (and 4th Fri in summer); **Marcenat** Thur; **Massiac** Every 2nd Tue; **Mauriac** Tue, Fri; **Maurs** Thur; **Marat** Fri; **Neussargues-Moissac** Fri fortnightly; **Neuvéglise** every 2nd month; **Pierrefort** Wed; **Riom-iès-Montagnes** Sat; **St-Flour** Mon fortnightly; *Wool Market last Sat June*; **Trizac** Tue (summer) every 2nd Tue (rest of year).

HAUTE-LOIRE

Allègre Wed; **Alleyras** Mon, Wed; **Bas-en-Basset** Wed; **Blesle** Thur; **Brioude** Sat (Pig market 1st & 3rd Sat); **Champagnac-le-Vieux** Fri; **Costaros** Mon; **Craponne-sur-Arzon** Sat; **Fay-sur-Lignon** Wed; **Landos** Tue; Langeac Tue; **Lavoute-Chilhac** Sun; **Lempdes** Tue; **Loudes** 1st & 3rd Tue of month; **Mazet St-Voy** Thur; **Le Monastier-sur-Gazeille** Tue; **Monistrol-sur-Loire** Mon; **Paulhaguet** Mon; **Pradelles** Sun; **Le-Puy** Wed, Fri, **Retournac** Wed; **Saugues** Fri, Mon (calves); **Solignac-sur-Loire** Tue; **St-Didier-en-Velay** Wed; **St-Front** Fri; **St-Julien Chapteuil** Mon; **St-Just Malmont** 1st & 3rd Thur of month; **St Paulien** 2nd & 4th Tue of month; **Ste-Sigolène** Tue; **Vorey** Sun; **Yssingeaux** Thur.

A Christian in the Lyons Den

Many offer to teach you to cook in France, but few do it as well as American Aileen Martin and her French husband, Chef Jean Berrard, at *Moule Martin,* just above Annecy. Madame Berrard believes food must be relevant, used to enhance experience rather than to fuel you for it. Her classes often start by driving down to the markets of Annecy and handing each student a different shopping list. One must buy flowers and ground almonds, another is sent to find *lavaret* or *lotte du lac,* another for local peaches and a chicken from Bresse, another for oil from Nyons and olives from Nice, walnuts from Grenoble or cheese from Franche-Comté. It's a marvellous way to bring any place into focus, for once you are looking for something specific, you see everything else as well, instead of it all passing you by in an agreeable but incoherent haze.

This is also the best way to use the information in this book; decide on something that specially interests you – seasonal, basic or frivolous – before you wander in a market or village centre and you'll see more than you imagined possible.

It is a strange grouping, these three *départements,* each highly distinctive and ranging from the highest heights to the most fertile valleys. If there is a link to be found other than that of geography it must be the individuality each has retained, and that's why I so much like driving east towards the mountains once I've touched base in a few centres along the Rhône.

Princely Gratins

The Dauphiné makes no culinary bones about taking exactly what it wants from neighbouring styles of food, particularly claiming as its own the *gratins* of Provence

and the Languedoc; but in return it usually makes them more interesting. The most famous, and often shamefully abused is *gratin dauphinoise,* a dish of sliced potatoes baked in a thin layer with rich milk; eggs and a little *gruyère* are sometimes added but not authentically, and onion has no place at all.

If the sheer simplicity of that surprises you, so will the tremendous variety of other *gratins.* Most are of vegetables, and late in the year there will be a *gratin* of cardoons *cardons* and of wild mushrooms, of tripe or of pumpkin *potiron* and, during summer, of soft fruits and of pears. Some of these will be topped with a little sauce, some with breadcrumbs, and there will be cream, eggs and perhaps almonds on the fruit versions but hardly ever a sight of that bane of good taste, a thick blanket of bubbling grated cheese thrown over the top.

> ## In which we...
> ● Shop for our lessons and find gratification in gratins...
> ● Follow a liqueur to Spain and back and worship a new monarchy...
> ● Smell a sensation and meet the *mères* who made their own...
> ● Look for a faded reputation but revel in *charcuterie*...
> ● Enjoy undiluted pork liver, meet the unusual fish of Annecy and learn which frogs have fat legs...
> ● Trace the source of the essential crayfish...
> ● Go nuts in Grenoble, even though they do not, and visit the potato's first French home...
> ● Discuss an unfair cushion, sip a protected vermouth and buy the cherriest Kirsch of all...
> ● Discover that mountain hare can be good for you...
> ● Glissade seamlessly from silk to glacé fruit...
> ● Pine for honey *bonbons* and find which cheese is the perkiest...

Missing the Point

On the border of Isère and the Rhône is Vienne, once the seat of a local lord, the Dauphin of the Viennois, the childless last of whom agreed to cede his lands to the then king of France, Charles V if his title remained as that of the heir to the throne. It was centuries before Vienne had another hereditary monarchy, but after World War I, the family Point came and took over *La Pyramide* restaurant. First they, then their son Fernand, turned this into one of the most influential restaurants France has ever known, brilliantly executing or reinterpreting classics of the kitchen and creating new ones, inspiring the careers of dozens of modern luminaries – and there is the rub. *La Pyramide*, the pride and joy of the Points, unwittingly also opened a Pandora's box, which led to the modern school of sensation, where everything goes with everything, particularly if it hasn't been done before – a school in fact that misses the Point.

Feeling Better?

The Dauphiné actually makes more wine than the Rhône Valley but is more famous for one of the world's best-known liqueurs, Chartreuse. It is a drink that encourages mental images of monks macerating herbs and flowers and barks in cellars, guarding ancient secret formulae and methods unchanged for centuries – but the monasteries of France have been remarkably less secure than in Protestant countries. They were stripped of their possessions during the Revolution but allowed to return in 1816, about which time many of the liqueur-making houses went into serious production of what had previously been medicinal brews. In 1903 many were expelled again, including all of the Carthusians who began making Chartreuse at Tarragona in Spain, this explaining the version still made there. In 1940 all was forgiven again and, with new premises, Chartreuse of green and yellow has been making you feel better, or worse, ever since.

In a perverse settlement of the debt to other *départements* for borrowing their

RHÔNE, SAVOIE & THE DAUPHINE

styles, the Dauphiné makes a great deal of walnut oil, but sends most of it away, for there they consider it much too strong a flavour, although upwardly-mobile restaurants will have followed the fashion for it.

Savoie Fare

Immediately north and somewhat higher is Savoie. Long independent, then part of the Italian conglomeration, it became French only after a referendum in 1860. *Gratins* have crept this far north, but the difference in geography also means more dairying and more cheese; here the common *gratin savoyard* actually mixes potato with cheese and moistens both with stock, usually of veal or beef. In autumn wild mushrooms are layered between the cheesy potatoes, great for the potatoes, dreadful for the mushrooms, and marvellous without the cheese.

Among the cultivated and wild fruit and vegetables which flourish so wonderfully in the valleys of Savoie you find many wheat fields, the grains of which are usually used for making pastas. An older crop is red peppers which, cooked, peeled and served in oil, have been associated with the region for centuries, as has a special liking for nutmeg as a seasoning, particularly suited to the milk, cream and butter made and used so lavishly. But for me the greatest seasoning found here is not imported from some far-off hot country but dug from its own damp earth – the white truffle.

The white truffle season is

shorter and earlier that that of the black one – from October to the first snows of December – but it repays by many times any trouble or expense you may incur. For a start, even a rank amateur can know in a second if it is a real *tuber magnatum* or one of the lesser white truffles. Real ones have a scent that knocks you for six, reeking sweetly of vice and irresistibly savoury for its insinuating promise of new sensation.

There is excitement to be garnered even if you are not interested in *that* sort of thing, for you never risk wasting money on a white truffle that has had its flavour cooked out of it – it is always eaten raw. And best of all, although it is arrestingly expensive it is sliced so tissue-thin over dishes, and in such small quantity, that your pocket would be silly to complain. No better cushion for shavings of white truffle has been found than egg dishes or a real, runny risotto.

A Lesser Example

The south of the Rhône merges so easily into Provence that there is confusion about what belongs to which, for both olive and almond grow there, and glacé fruits and *marrons glacés* are prepared on either side of the border. Of course these are modern borders, but this goes only a short way to explaining the old arguments over which town from which province invented, say, *caillettes*.

My interest though lies in the north, in Lyon, which is translated into English by adding a letter to make it

Lyons. For me, this is the centre of a more modern argument, that of deciding if it really deserves its reputation as one of the great culinary centres of France, indeed of the world.

The Rhône and the Saône which converge here, and its central geographical location, certainly have given Lyon access to the best of the produce of surrounding regions. It once was capital of the Burgundians and has such historical links with Beaujolais that its wines are said to be the third river of Lyon. But access to good produce is no guarantee of universal excellence, as many a Briton will testify. I think the trap fallen into has been to judge all of Lyon by the few, a lesser example of the world judging French food by the standard and style of *haute cuisine*.

Certainly there are now some sensational places to eat in Lyon and its environs, glittering with names internationally famous, and Lyon has served some famous banquets in its time. And there does seem to have been a Golden Age, the age of the *mères*, which began in the second half of the 19th century. Coinciding with more interest in leisure time and competition for its trade, a number of wine traders and bars started to offer a continuous choice of snacks and simple bourgeois food in the same way the *brasseries* of the north had always done. It naturally fell to the wives, the *mères* to do the cooking, which gradually took over in importance from the wine. These small places are, or were, the *bouchots* of which

CHARCUTERIE

so much has been written. But the *mères* who did so well are well dead, and the *bouchots* have been translated into hamburger and fast food centres, no more startling an advance than the *bouchots* first were. Lyon is resting on a reputation for accessible, honest food that only existed for some 50 years or so. Before then she had had little praise from travellers, and since then somewhat less if you read reviews of unstarred restaurants.

If you go to Lyon confident of its expertise and excitement you may be denied pleasure. It is a big city, with all the modern big-city hunger for change and novelty. Once you have eaten in one of the famous or recommended restaurants you are on your own. Personally I have eaten badly more often and more reliably so in Lyon than anywhere else in France, and had service so grossly rude on the Place Bellecour that I endured the wait of one hour for my order to be taken in a half-empty restaurant simply for the thrill of a good story. Be suspicious, do your homework and appear knowledgeable and confident.

One of the most French things you can do is to go to Lyon for lunch from Paris on the wonderful TGV trains, and at least you will arrive. If you drive into Lyon you may not eat at all, for the traffic system is such that I once drove around the centre for an hour without discovering the way in. Perhaps it was one more warning, and Christians should have nothing to do with Lyons . . .

Lyon is the centre of a gigantic commercial *charcuterie*-making operation, with a range of products exported nationally and internationally. Modern techniques, refrigeration and humidity control mean any product of the pig, whether native to valley or mountain top, can be made. Thus in Lyon, and in most contiguous places, the *charcuterie* enthusiast will have a choice unmatched elsewhere. You will also see both in town and country signs exhorting busi-

Worth Finding

● *Andouilles/andouillettes:* these are not unexpected – but the comments of long-reigning mayor Edouard Heriot are. He's supposed to have said that only two things left a bad taste in the mouth, politics and *andouillettes*. In Lyon they are often made with veal intestines rather than pork.

● *Caillettes* Liver-based baked dish with spinach or chard. It's common in Provence but also found in the Dauphiné, Drôme and Ardèche. Indeed, Aubenas claims to have invented it. The only way I know to enjoy pork liver relatively undiluted.

● *Cervelas* The same fine-fleshed, fat sausage found elsewhere in France, once made with brains. Today, very likely to be studded with truffles and pistachios; certainly so in Grenoble. Unlike the German *cervelat*, which is a slicing sausage, this is to be served hot. If you are buying them to cook yourself, older ones will be better value, for what truffle content there is will have had time to perfume the pork somewhat.

● *Farçon* A large *cervelas* made in Montélimar.

● *Jésus de Lyon:* an air-dried salami, one of many of this name. Fat and tapering and tied with strings. The coarsely chopped flesh and fat indicates a sweet flavour.

● *Rose/rosette de Lyon* One of the biggest of air-dried salami-type sausages, made of pure pork, chopped and stuffed into the final length of a pig's large intestine. Some say it is so called because this length is always rosy pink colour, others more vociferous declare it simply describes the appearance of the puckered and tied sphincter (if it is left attached).

● *Saucisses de Lyon* There are two sausages of this name, and confusion is not uncommon. One is a long air-dried sausage, the other a boiling (fresh) sausage. This latter is more common and used for the region's famous sausage dishes – with hot potato salad in *brioche* etc. It is little different from, and may be called, garlic sausage *saucisse à l'ail*.

● *Roulade de tête de porc* Salted pig's head cooked whole, boned and rolled. If it is *pistachée,* it may be studded with pistachio nuts, or with whole cloves of cooked garlic, which would indicate some influence of the Languedoc.

● *Sabodet* A boiling sausage for eating hot, made from pig's head and rind and shaped like a *sabot* clog.

ness, sincere signs earnestly protesting that a local shop's *jambonneau, saucissons* and *cervelas* are veritably of their own manufacture. If the claim seems possible look also for the genuine things from nearby regions, *judru* from the Jura, *Jésus de Morteau* smoked over pine and juniper, hams from Burgundy's Morvan, or, more unusual, smoked hams from Celliers or Taninges in Savoie. The herb and pepper wrapped air-dried sausages associated with Provence are made here too, and will be none the worse for that. Some villages make whole boned hams with a dried herb coating – delicious and now being commercialized in Feillens (Bresse). The herb flavoured sausages of Annecy are called *pormoniers.*

Commercialism, mainly of the best kind, is such that in Lyon I tend to forget any quest for local foods. As in Paris, I take advantage of tasting and learning about whatever looks good or sounds familiar and profit from the rare chance to compare, surely the greatest reward of travelling.

FISH & SHELLFISH

Freshwater fish – and what is done with it – is fairly predictable in the Lyonnais and the Rhône Valley.

Carp, perch, tench etc are served in many a guise, but down the Rhône Valley you might find rather more of the *friture,* an incursion from the south or west but done in butter rather than olive oil. *Pauchouse* – a fish stew – invades the north from Burgundy, then reverts to the more usual name of *matelote.*

In Lyon, fish are kept alive and healthy in great freshwater tanks through which the Rhône and Saône flow ceaselessly. You will undoubtedly be offered *quenelles de brochet,* which translate somewhat boringly as pike dumplings, or poached fish cakes. They are a purée of pike, eggs and something farinaceous, and should be light, sweet and delicate. Too often the farinacea dominate, through heavy hand or light mind. When they are good, *quenelles* count mainly for praise upon the technique which has made them light; when they are bad they are even more boring. If it is the flavour of pike you are after, I suggest pike roasted, or with some cream-based sauce. Of course, it might be that *quenelle* lovers are more enamoured of the *sauce Nantua* which regally accompanies them.

Sauce Nantua is based on the essence of *écrevisses,* the freshwater crayfish which abound in the rivers of Savoie and the Dauphiné quite as much as they do in Franche-Comté. *Écrevisses* come gratinéed, stock made from their

shells is used to flavour mousses of chicken livers in the Bugey, *beurre d'écrevisses* accompanies poultry from Bresse, and enriches *sauce Nantua.* Various manufacturers in the puddles of industry which surround Lyon pack *quenelles* and *sauce Nantua* into tins, sometimes under the banner of one of the region's master chefs. These are quite good enough to serve at home.

Deep in the lakes of Léman and Annecy, there are types of salmon rarely found elsewhere. The finest fleshed is the *omble chevalier* char not unfamiliar to determined fish enthusiasts (I have eaten one in Sweden). More unusual are the white-fleshed *lavaret,* the *fera,* and, in December only, the *gravenche;* any of these may be stuffed or, if your visit coincides with the seasons, served in sauces of cream perfumed with *morilles* or *cèpes.* The *lotte des lacs* is a burbot, but tastes rather different from those of the river; as well as firm white flesh, which is often filleted and fried as though perch, it has a specially succulent liver served as a separate speciality. On the shores of Lake Léman, where trout weighing 15kg/34lb have been landed, there is a *soupe aux poissons.*

In the parts of the Bresse which fall into this region, frogs are excellent and are gratinéed or poached in cream and wine; and eels, although becoming less common, should be offered in stews or in *pâtés.* Incidentally, if your frogs' legs seem particularly plump and rounded they are most probably imported.

MEAT, POULTRY & GAME

The chickens and turkeys of Bresse belong as much to this region as to Burgundy geographically. Anyway, Lyon has always exploited its crossroads position and called many things from neighbouring regions its own; *charollais* beef is one, which is grilled as often as it is cooked in wine; along the banks of the Rhône and in the Dauphiné local beef is cooked slowly in a *daube*.

Pork rules as a fresh meat. Like beef, it's usually found served fairly plainly cooked, and onions and potatoes are usually on the plate too. This can be assured with *cochonnailles* – the boiled head, trotters and odd other pieces of pig served with onion sauce and the ubiquitous hot potato salad. In Savoie you might be offered pork cutlets with cooked pears, which is a far better idea.

Savoie is also where you're more likely to meet local lamb, its sweetbreads, brains or liver. Veal, a speciality of the Dauphiné is sometimes served with ham and cheese, or with vegetables and fresh chestnuts – *à l'aixoise* – but always delicious with cream and wild mushrooms. These are the best ways to enjoy local poultry too. In the Dauphiné look for the turkeys of Cremieu. Lyon and its *mères* are jointly credited with a number of chicken dishes of world renown. The one always mentioned is *en demi-deuil* (half mourning), with slices of truffle stuck under half its skin; frankly you can't expect to find it easily, it will be very expensive, and unless fresh truffles are used and have

been allowed to sit under the skin for 24 hours the exercise is one of inconspicuous consumption. When you are in the region look to chicken with cream, with vinegar *au vinaigre* or anything with mushrooms, cultivated or wild. Sometimes it will be as well to go for a simple roast of *poulet de Bresse*, a casserole or some version of *coq au vin*. At least you will be spending your money on the quality of the chicken rather than risking it on a *soi-disant* truffle.

What game there is comes from Burgundy or the Alps where it is mainly feathered – partridge, quail, pheasant, woodcock, *perdreau, caille, faisan, bécasse*. Even if killed on the wing they may well have been bred on farms, and so the likelihood of their flesh

having been affected by a few weeks' freedom and a wild diet of mountain herbs and berries is largely fanciful. Much of the game bird crop goes into making *pâtés,* which suffer from the French habit of not hanging game for enough time to allow any development of flavour, and of expecting the roasted flesh of a bird to retain any of its native savour when layered and baked in a rich *farce* of pork and veal. If you like *pâté* I suggest you slice into the rougher, more robust *pâtés campagnards*.

Wild rabbit *lapin* or *lapereaux de la garenne* is recommended if it is from Monteynard but the hare *lièvre* is what excites those with a yen for really fulsome flavour. Some would say that *civet de lièvre,* hare cooked in wine and finished with cream and its own blood, was born in the mountains of Savoie.

Worth Finding

● *Boeuf à la moelle* grilled steak with bone marrow.

● *Boeuf* (or *grillade*) *marinière* A provençal-influenced dish, said once to have been the mainstay of the sailors from that region who traded along the Rhône by barge: beef flavoured with onions, vinegar and the anchovies without which they would not leave home. Probably first made from the horses which had pulled their barges north against the river's flow. So much for hard work.....

● *Defarde* A stew of lamb's intestines and trotters, like an unravelled *pieds et paquets*.

● *Poularde en vessie* Chicken baked in a pig's bladder. I've

heard that it isn't that different when done in aluminium foil, for the theory is the same; I hope this is calming rather than inflammatory information for those enthusiasts who may worry their butchers at home for a pig's bladder.

● *Tabliers de sapeur* Beef tripe cooked, then cut into squares, egged and breaded, grilled, then served with garlic butter or a souped up mayonnaise; fancifully reckoned to look like the leather apron sappers wore to protect their uniforms. Like sausages, a snack or first course rather than a main meal; but modern lunchtime customs may differ.

FRUIT & VEGETABLES

The sweet natural rewards for those who wander from summer's beaten tracks and into Savoie are myriad. For hence come some of France's best strawberries and most of her raspberries. Pears are fabulous, and the apples aren't bad. Cherries and plums are harvested and if you literally leave even these untouristy roads there are wild berries – cherries *merises* and strawberries *fraises des bois* to gather yourself. Closer to beaten tracks, Vienne has long been renowned for its cherries.

The Dauphiné matches this abundance with its walnuts *noix de Grenoble,* honoured with an AOC and savoured throughout the world. They are candied, made into cakes, put into *brioche* mixtures called fanciful things by every village *pâtissier.* Nuts which don't make the grade are pressed to make walnut oil *huile de noix,* but this is little used by the Dauphinoises, who consider it indigestible. Silly them. Just over the *département*'s border, Briançon (Hautes-Alpes) makes an even rarer culinary almond oil. In the south both the Ardèche and Drôme produce excellent chestnuts, and make *marrons glacés* and sugar-preserved fruits of all kinds, an *artisanale* tradition that became commercialized when the silk industry was snagged in the 1880s.

The Ardèche can claim, but doesn't do it loudly, to be the first place in France to grow the potato. In 1540 a Franciscan monk from Toledo planted some in St-Alban-

LOCAL PRODUCE

Vegetables

● **Courgettes** *courgettes* Var: *Seneca* (under glass spring and autumn) *Diamant* (open air, main season)	Mid-April to end November Dep: Drôme, Rhône, Ain
● **Garlic** *ail* Var: white: *Thermidrôme, Messidrôme, Blanc de Lomagne* pink: *Rosé d'Italie, Rosé du Var, Fructidor.* violet: *Rosé de lautrec, Germidor*	Harvested June and July but younger and earlier often too. Dep: Rhône

Fruit

● **Apple** *pomme* Var: *Reinettes, Reine des reinettes*	Harvested July to September Dep: Drôme, Ardèche, Rhône, Isère, Savoie.
● **Apricot** *abricot* Var: *Bergeron, Polonais (Orange de Provence)*	Mid-June until August 18th Dep: Drôme, Ardèche, Rhône
● **Cherries** *cerises* Var: *Bigarreau, Moreau, Reverchon*	June until mid-July Dep: Drôme, Ardèche, Rhône
● **Chestnuts** *marrons/ châtaigne (marrons* have only 1 kernel in each shell)	September until end November Dep: Ardèche
● **Currants, black** *cassis* **Currants, red** *groseilles*	July 8th – 20th July 8th – 20th
● **Grapes** *raisins* Var: among many, *Chasselas* and *Muscat.*	*September and October Dep: Drôme, Ardèche*
● **Greengage** *reine-claude*	Early August for 6 weeks
● **Kiwifruit** *kiwi* Var: *Hayward* (NZ)	November through to March Dep: SE corner of Drôme
● **Melon** *melon* ● **Nectarine** *nectarine/ brugnon* Var: white: *Fuzalode,* yellow: mainly American strains	July until mid-September June-ish until start September Dep: Rhône, Ardèche, Isère
● **Walnuts** *noix*	September to November Dep: Isère, Drôme
● **Peach** *pêche* Var: mainly yellow american strains: white *Amsden*	*Early July to October Dep: Rhône, Drôme, Ardèche, Isère*
● **Pear** *poire* Var: *Guyot, Williams; Louise-Bonne d'Avranches*	Early July to end October Dep: Rhône, Drôme, Ardèche, Isère
● **Raspberries** *framboise*	June to end October Dep: Rhône, Ardèche, Hte-Savoie, Drôme, Isère, in that order

The most important area; most varieties grown are British and most of the crop is used for syrup, *confitures* and so on.

d'Aÿ. In 1585 the *truffole* (one of many names celebrating it as a truffle for everyday use) was already a commercial crop and by the early years of the 17th century the Dauphiné and the Auvergne had adopted it.

Drôme and the Dauphiné both sport the white oaks associated with the presence of black truffles, but Savoie is the place for the lesser known but infinitely more aromatic white truffle. If you buy a whole one fresh, store it airtight and cushioned with rice grains to protect it all round. Back home, keep it in a covered bowl with eggs for a couple of days, then make scrambled eggs with unsalted butter and cream.

Wild mushrooms are specially good in the mountains, too, both the *morilles* and delicate *mousserons* of spring and the hunkier *cèpes* of autumn. Enjoy them simply – in omelettes, with artichokes or in cream by themselves or with the exceptional poultry or fish. Local stories of poaching across borders, of the skullduggery of this or that mushroom collector make excellent *digestifs*.

In general the range of vegetables used is a bit more adventurous than many areas. The cardoon *cardon* is a feature of late summer, served with bone marrow *moelle*. Marrow *courge* is made into soups with cream or served *au gratin*.

The great plains which lie among the mountains and gorges of eastern France grow a great variety of cereals, much of the wheat used to make pasta *pâtes alimentaires*.

It is not fair to think of Lyon and its region as living permanently on a cushion of frying onions (the white ones from Roanne are said to be best). The Île-Barbe has supplied wonderful salads for countless centuries. Ampuis would easily satiate you with her apricots alone. Nonetheless few would disagree that to eat a *galette lyonnaise*, a fritter of potato and onion, is about as accurate a picture of the foundations of the region's food as you could hope to get.

GLACÉ FRUITS

AND MARRONS GLACÉS

Ardèche (Rhône) and Vaucluse, (Provence), are the most important French centres for preserving fruit and chestnuts in sugar syrup. Privas and Aubenas are particularly famous for their *marrons glacés* which used to be very much *artisanale*, with many small private manufacturers; but after the silk industry's crisis in the 1880s Privas in particular began larger scale manufacture in central factories.

Glacé chestnuts can be made only from *marrons*, the chestnuts that have a single kernel in the shell; those with more kernels are *châtaignes* and these are broken up for use in confectionery and tinned purées of chestnut, plain or vanilla flavour. *Marrons glacés* are specially expensive because of the twin difficulty of peeling

the skin and the extreme delicacy of the nut once it has been lightly cooked, a process fruits do not need. Look for *marrons brisés* the broken ones, at a cheaper rate. Good for putting into desserts.

Fruits for processing are usually picked before they are fully ripe (one reason they often have so little flavour), then waxed and stored in brine until needed. After washing, stalking or pitting, they are soaked in increasingly stronger sugar solutions, vanilla-flavoured in the case of the poached chestnuts. Once saturated, fruit is given an outer coating of sugar which is quickly baked on to form a shiny, preservative outer coating.

Apt (Vaucluse) is an important centre for crystallizing fruits and from Collobrières

(Var) come *marrons glacés*, but many small family confectioners *confiseurs* will make their own. The most famous, and hardly small, is Aubers in Nice with an extraordinary range. But think before you splurge; many glacé fruits are dreadfully disappointing, retaining little recognizable flavour. Tiny *poires Williams*, apricots *abricots* and mandarines *mandarines* are best, I reckon, and the preserved figs *figues* of Grasse are worth the investment – for real swank you can even buy whole melons or pineapples complete with their leaves. Watermelon *pastèque* is an example of a fruit that offers more than it delivers – you are better off looking for jams *confitures* and other sweet spreads of individuality, such as that of aubergine.

CHEESE

There is a marvellous assortment of cheeses on offer in this area, many of them domestically produced. In the mountains of Savoie there are countless varieties of grey *tomme* and many *chèvres* and *mi-chèvres* to be found. And of course this is the home of the so-called prince of *gruyères* – *Beaufort.*

★ *Abondance* Also known as *tomme d'Abondance* Made from partly skimmed milk up in the mountain chalets of the Abondance valley and the surrounding valleys of the Drasnes. Weighing from 5-15kg/11-33lb. with the usual greyish rind of these *tommes,* it has a creamy taste that varies from subtle to rich. They are best eaten in summer and autumn.

● *Arômes au gêne de marc, Rigottes, St-Marcellins, pélardons* or *picodons* Cured in fermenting *marc:* bigger ones are even more strongly flavoured.

● *Arômes de Lyon* Like *Arômes au gêne du marc* but cured in crocks of white wine.

★ *Beaufort AOC* Called the prince of *gruyères* by Brillat-Savarin, this member of the *gruyère* family is produced in the high Alpine regions of Savoie in small dairies and alpine chalets. Made from raw cow's milk, notably from the *tarines* breed, these large discs can weigh anything from 20-70kg/50-157lb. Usually matured for 6 months it is best eaten at any time except autumn. The surface should be smooth and brown with reddish tints. Fruity to the nose, the flavour has the expected nuttiness associated with this type of cheese.

● *Beaumont* Related to all the *Saint-Paulin* cheeses this commercially made cow's milk cheese is disc-shaped with a light yellow rind, possesses a mild creamy flavour and is best eaten in summer and autumn.

● *Bleu de Ste-Foy* A lightly pressed blue cheese mostly made in the farms and mountain chalets in and around Ste-Foy. It is flat and cylindrical in shape, weighs 2–3kg/4½–6½lb and has a savoury flavour.

★ *Bleu de Sassenage* Mentioned more than 300 years ago by Olivier de Serres this cow's milk *bleu* is still made in traditional dairies in Le-Villard-de-Lans (the Dauphiné) and the neighbouring plateaux of Vercors. Weighing 5–6kg/11–13lb it is matured for 2 or 3 months. Best eaten in summer and autumn. Light coloured with little smell and a savoury taste.

● *Bleu de Tignes* Best in summer and autumn, a lightly pressed blue of cow's milk made in a flat cylinder and tasting, well, like a blue cheese. Also known as *tignard.*

● *Bressan* A domestically produced *chèvre* or *mi-chèvre* – small truncated cone in shape. Soft with a light goat smell and flavour ranging between savoury and extremely fruity, good summer and autumn.

● *Cervelle de Canut* A mixture of beaten fresh curds, garlic, herbs, vinegar wine and oil, aged a little then served as *hors d'oeuvre* or dessert; also called *claqueret Lyonnais.*

● *Chambarand* Made in the traditional way by monks (it is also known as *trappiste de Chambarand*) this is a small washed-rind disc made with cow's milk; mild, creamy flavour.

● *Chevrotin d' Aravis* A mild flavoured *chèvre* or *mi-chèvre* made in chalets in the massif of Aravis. Matured for 2 months and best eaten in summer and autumn.

● *Chèvrine de Lenta* Only available in Bonneval (Savoie) this chalet-produced pressed cheese with a sharp flavour is made from the milk of goats grazing on summer pastures over 2,000m/6,000ft around Bonneval-sur-Arc or Lenta. Best eaten in summer.

● *Claqueret Lyonnais* See *Cervelle de Canut.*

★ *Colombière* A washed-rind cow's milk cheese related to *reblochon, colombière* is produced exclusively by farms in the *massif* of the same name. A 600g/1½lb disc with pink-white rind, it has a mild flavour.

● *Fondu au marc* Also known as *fondu au raisin,* a factory-produced cheese with a rind of toasted grape-pips.

● *Grataron d'Arèches* A 200g/8oz *chèvre* made in the mountain chalets of the Doron valley in Beaufort. With a strong tangy flavour. *Hauteluce* is similar.

★ *Persillé d'Aravis* Very unusual for a *chèvre* in that it is a pressed blue cheese. Made in farms and chalets of the *massif* of Aravis (Savoie) with a savoury flavour best enjoyed in summer and autumn. Known also as *grand-bornand* and *persillé de Thones.* Weighs about 2lb/1kg.

● *Persillé du Mont-Cenis* (Termignon-Savoie) Summer pasturing giving the highest quality milk from cows and goats makes the best of these large blue-veined cheeses. Matured for 3 months. Very strong flavour.

• *Picadon de l'Ardèche* or *Picadon de la Drôme AOC.* Its name is a provençal word meaning to prick or sting. This goat cheese from the mountains of the Ardèche and Drôme (but also the Dauphiné) has a history that stretches back for centuries. In this region goat's milk was the only type available but because goats do not give milk during winter, these full-cream cheeses were also matured for use as a staple food. Shaped to a small flat disc, the cheese has a white mould or a reddish washed-rind appearance. If it is labelled *affiné méthode Dieulefit* it means that it has been matured at least a month to give a more pronounced flavour. Really at their best from late summer to autumn.

★ *Reblochon AOC* A fascinating cheese from Haute-Savoie known since at least the 14th century. Dairy farmers would not milk the cows dry when the steward came to check the yield but once he had gone the high-fat second milking was used to make this special cheese which was the perk or *rebloche* of the job. Made from full-cream raw milk the cheese is gently pressed but non-cooked, and has a washed rind and pinkish-white skin. It generally weighs just over 500g/1lb and is always sold in a wooden box. At its best in summer and autumn, it should have a slightly dank smell but a creamy delicate flavour that leaves a pleasant hazelnut aftertaste.

• *St-Marcellin* Once produced on farms from pure goat's milk, this small (75mm/3in) disc of soft mild cheese is now made commercially only from cow's milk, a few goat farms still produce the original *chèvre.*(Known also as *Tomme de St-Marcellin*). Although 50% fat content, a clear bite of acidity balances this; thin blue-grey rind.

• *Tamié* A rather 'farmy' washed rind cow's milk cheese made by monks in Tamié (Savoie).

• *Tarare* A high fat (75%) triple cream cow's milk cheese from the Lyonnais.

• *Tommes des Allues* Domestically produced on the pastures of Miribel (Savoie); a pressed goat's milk cheese, fairly large, 3–4kg/7–9lb, really eaten only in autumn after the 2 month curing period of milk from summer's pastures.

• *Tomme de Savoie* Produced by farms, *fruitières* and factories this is the best known *tomme*. A low-fat (20–40%) cow's milk cheese with grey rind and mild nutty taste. Usually weighing between 2–3kg/4–7lb it can be enjoyed from the end of spring through to autumn. Variations are enormous, from use of skim or low-fat milk to simple changes of name – *tomme de Belleville, boudane* etc. Often marinated in *marc.*

• *Vacherin d'Abondance* Related to the Swiss *vacherins* of the Joux Valley this soft, mild-flavoured cheese with washed rind, is shaped like a thick pancake; usually best in late autumn and winter, from the controlled richness of stall-fed cattle's milk.

• *Vacherin des Aillons* A soft cow's milk cheese similar to *vacherin des Bauges.*

• *Vacherin des Bauges* An ancient cheese dating back to the Middle Ages before *fruitières* and cooperatives existed, when mountain dwellers made only small cheeses and did not yet know how to prepare cooked ones. Farm produced, it is a thick pancake of washed-rind cheese made from cow's milk. Best eaten at the end of autumn and in winter, it is packaged with a strip of bark. It savours of resin and has a creamy taste.

LIQUEURS

Chambéry makes the only vermouth in France to have an *appellation*; wonderfully dry and herby; Dolin is the best-known shipper in Britain and the U.S., but there are others.

It also makes the less well-known Chambéryzette, a vermouth flavoured with wild strawberries *fraises des bois*, which is said not to last very long in the bottle. *Génépy* made throughout the area is not unrelated to vermouth, being a maceration of mountain herbs in alcohol; you should also find cherry liqueur *liqueur de cerises* or *de merises* if the cherries are wild. These fruits may also be found as *cerise sauvage*, and the kirsch made from them in Allevard is probably the best you'll ever taste.

Le Grand-Lemps makes a liqueur of originality but far less so than Voiron, where you find the modern distillery and caves of Grande-Chartreuse; so you can see the old ones at Fourvoirie. You can visit every day except Sundays and holy days.

Less exciting perhaps, but more generally useful, might be the knowledge that Savoie also makes rather good cider from its apples.

PASTRIES, PUDDINGS & CONFECTIONERY

The abundance of fruit and nuts means you can expect even more of the *tartes* so associated with France. In high summer the *pâtisseries* who make their own ice creams and sorbets really go to town. Many of them will also make small quantities of *confitures*, too – runnier than our jams but very true to flavour.

As the almonds of Drôme and the south are so near, macaroons and marzipan-based cakes and confectionery predominate; the *pain de Châtillon* alone is different, for this is a macaroon brightened with saffron.

Chocolate is as good in the scintillating air of Savoie and the Dauphiné as in the sparkle of Lyon's boutiques. Chambéry makes particularly marvellous liqueur-flavoured chocolate truffles. Chartreuse flavours *bonbons*; so do local raspberries, and aromatic honeys. Mégève honey was famed well before her winter slopes became smart, and most Dauphiné varieties are very fine. The dark honey of pine *sapin* is the most aromatic, the wild flower ones vary from strong to delicate. Chamonix makes terrific *bonbons* from its honey.

Worth Finding

- *Bugnes* Specially big doughnuts or *beignets* seen mainly on festivals and holidays.
- *Gâteau Savoie* Associated specially with St-Genix-sur-Guiers, a large *brioche*-type cake incorporating *praliné*, as far as I can determine.
- *Matefaims* Spelt many ways, but meaning 'appetite killers'; very big pancakes to fill up with at the end of a sparing meal, or if made savoury, at the start of, or instead of one. Found mainly in the Savoie in this region, but elsewhere in France too.
- *Pognes* In most places a large crown of sweetened *brioche* baked with a fruit topping which, once autumn comes, may be exchanged for *courge* marrow, of all things. In the Dauphiné, a *pogne* is more likely to be an open tart, albeit with the same variation of topping.

A DRINKER'S GUIDE

The wines of Savoie are not built for a long life, and should be drunk as young as possible. The drinking dates shown below refer to the *good* wines of the Northern Rhône. Ordinary Rhône wines are for drinking within 2 or 3 years of the vintage. See also **Provence** *Drinker's Guide*.

The Last Decade
1984 Only average. Hermitage a little better than Côte Rotie. Drink from the late 80s.
1983 Wonderful. Hermitage has the edge on Côte Rotie. Both must wait until the year 2000.
1982 Very good, very rich. Another wait until the year 2000.
1981 Poor, whites better than reds. Drink from now on with caution.
1980 Average to good. Drinking well from the late 80s.
1979 Good Hermitage, though light wines elsewhere. Hermitage to keep into the 90s, the others to drink from now on.
1978 A wonderful year. Drink from the mid 90s, but be prepared to wait longer.

1977 Poor. Drink up or, better still, avoid altogether.
1976 A good vintage, developing rapidly. Drink from now on.

1974 Large crop of patchy wines. Drink up.

Previous greats
1970, 1969, 1966, 1961 and 1959 were all excellent, and would still be interesting. Older wines like **1952, 1942** or **1929** should certainly be tried if you get the opportunity, but expect to pay quite highly for the privilege.

Bon Marché

Below is a selective list of markets plus some fairs *foires* of special interest. Check with the local S.I. for precise locations and time changes.

AIN
Bellegarde-sur-Valserine Mon, Tue; **Belley** Sat; **Bourg-en-Bresse** Wed, Sat, *Poultry Fair 3rd Sat Dec;* **Brenod** Tue; **Champagne-en-Valronmey** Thur; **Châtillon-sur-Chalaronne** Sat; **Collonges** Tue; **Culoz** Wed; **Gex** Mon, Thur; **Lagnieu** Mon; **Montrevel-en-Bresse** Tue; **Nantua** Sat; **Oyonnax** Mon, Thur, Sat; **Pont-de-Vaux** Wed; **St-Denis-en-Bugey** Sat; **St-Etienne-du-Bois** Mon; **St-Laurent-sur-Saône** Sat; **Vonnas** Thur.

RHÔNE
Belleville Tue; **Bessenay** Thur, Daily Fruit Market (early am) May-July; **Bron** Daily (Sun am) jumble sale 13 May; **Caluire-et-Cuire** Thur, Sat am; **Chambest-Longessaigne** Wed, Sat am; **Condrieu** Daily Fruit Market (May-Oct); **Cours-la-Ville** Mon, Wed, Sat; **Fontaines-sur-Saône** Wed & Thur, am; **Givors** Tue am, Wed, Fri & Sun am; **Grigny** Thur & Tue; **Haute-Rivoire** Thur pm; **Irigny** Thur am, Wed & Sat pm; **Lyon** Daily; **Meyzieu** Wed & Sat; **La Mulatière** Tue & Fri; **Neuville-sur-Saône** Wed; **Oullins** Tue, Sun am; **Rillieux-la-Pape-Crepieux** Sat am, Sun, Wed, Fri am; **Sérézin du Rhône** Tue pm; **Ste-Foy-les-Lyon** Tue, Wed, Thur, Sat (all am); **St-Laurent-de-Chamousset** Mon; **St-Martin-en-Haut** Mon; **St-Priest** Tue, Wed am, Thur, Fri, Sun am; **Thurins** Thur; **Valsonne** Wed; **Vénissieux** Tue, Wed, Thur, Fri, Sat, Sun; **Villeurbanne** Daily except Mon.

LOIRE
Ambierle Thur; **Balbigny** Mon; **Belmont-de-la-Loire** Tue; **Boen** Thur; **Bourg Argental** Thur, Sun; **Chambon-Feugerolles** Mon, Wed, Fri, Sun; **Charlieu** Sat, Silk Market 2nd Sun Sept; **Chazelles-sur-Lyon** Tue, Fri, Sat; **Feurs** Tue; **Firminy** Tue, Thur,

Sat, Sun; **Maclas** Thur; **Montbrison** Sat, Tue June-Oct; **Montrond-les-Bains** Thur; **Neulise** Tue; **Noiretable** Sat, Wed; **La Pacaudière** Sat, Wed; **Pelussin** Sat, Sun; **Rive-de-Gier** Tue, Fri; **Roanne** Tue, Fri, Sun; **Roche-la-Molière** Wed & Sat; **Sorbiers** Fri; **Sury-le-Comtal** Wed; **St.-Bonnet-leChâteau** Fri; **St-Chamond** Sat, Tue, Thur, Sun; **St Etienne** Mon & Fri, Sat (summer); **St-Galmier** Mon; **St-Georges-en-Couzan** Wed; **St-Germain-Lespinasse** Thur, 1st, 2nd, 3rd Wed; **St-Jean-Soleymieux** Tue; **St-Just-en-Chevalet** Thur; **St-Just-St-Rambert** Thur, Sun; **St-Martin-d'Estréaux** Thur; **St-Priest-la-Prugne** Mon; **St Romain-le-Puy** Fri; **St-Symphorien-de-Lay** Thur; **La Talaudière** Tue; **Veauche** Wed, Fri, Sat; **Villars** Thur.

ARDÈCHE
Annonay Wed, Sat; **Aubenas** Sat, Wed in chestnut season; **Bourg St-Andéol** Wed; **Burzet** Wed, Sun; **Cheylard** Wed; **Chomerac** Thur; **Coucouron** Wed; **Joyeuse** Mon, Wed, Fri, *Chestnut market Sat from 1st Oct, Grape market daily;* **Lamastre** Tue; **Largentière** Tue; **Montpezat-sous-Bauzon** Thur; **Le Pouzin** Tue; **Privas** Wed, Sat; **Satillieu** Tue; **Serrières** Fri; **Ste-Eulalie** *Violet Fair Sun after 12 July;* **St-Felicien** Fri; **St-Martial** Thur; **St-Péray** Wed, daily fruit market May-Sept; **St-Pierreville** Thur during chestnut season; **Tournon** Sat; **Vals-les-Bains** Sun, Thur in summer; **Vernoux-en-Vivarais** Thur, *Chestnut Market during season* (no fixed days); **Villeneuve-de-Berg** Wed.

DRÔME
Anneyron Tue; **Bourg-de-Péage** Mon, Fri, Sat, Sun am; **Buis-les-Baronnies** Daily (during cherry and apricot season), Wed & Sun (during olive season); **Châteauneuf-de-Galaure** Wed; **Claveyson** *Asparagus Market* Mon, Wed (15th April-15th July), *Leeks Oct to 15th April;* **Crest** Wed, Sat; **Die** Sat; **Dieulefit** Fri; **Donzère** Sat; **Le Grand Serre** Tue; **Hauterives** Tue; **Livron-sur**

Drôme Tue, Sat; **Montélimar** Wed, Thur, Fri, Sat; **La-Motte-Chalancon** Wed; **Nyons** Daily; **Pierrelatte** Fri; **Portes-les-Valence** Mon, Thur am; **Romans-sur-Isère** Tue, Wed, Fri, Sat, Sun; **Saillans** Sun; **St-Paul Trois Châteaux** Tue; **St-Rambert d'Albon** Fri, **St-Sorlin-en-Valloire** Mon; **Tain-l'Hermitage** Sat, Daily 31 May-Aug (fruit & veg); **Valence** Daily except Sun.

HAUTE-SAVOIE
Annecy Tue, Wed, Sat, Sun am; **Boege** Tue am; **Bonneville** Tue, Fri; **Chamonix-Mont-Blanc** Sat am; **Evian-les-Bains** Tue, Fri; **Faverges** Wed; **Le Grand Bornand** Tue; **Les Houches** Mon; **La Roche-sur-Foron** Thur am; **Rumilly** Thur am; **Sallanches** Sat; **Samdens** Wed am; **St-Gervais-les-Bains** Thur am; **St Jeoire** Fri; **Taninges** Thur am; **Thones** Tue; **Thorens Glières** Wed; **Viuz-en-Sallaz** Mon am.

SAVOIE
Aiguebelle Tue; **Albens** Fri; **Albertville** Thur; **Bourg-St-Maurice** Sat; **Bozel** Sat; **Chambéry** Daily; **La Chambre** Thur; **Le Chatelard** Mon; **Les Echelles** Tue; **Lescheraines** Fri; **Modane** Thur; **Montmélian** Mon; **Moutiers** Tue; **Novalaise** Thur; **Le-Pont-de-Beauvoisin** Mon; **La Rochette** Wed; **St-Béron** Wed; **St-Genix-sur-Guiers** Wed; **St-Jean-de-Maurienne** Sat; **St-Pierre-d'Albigny** Wed; **Ugine** Sat, Wed am; **Yenne** Tue.

ISÈRE
Beaurepaire Wed; **Bourg d'Oisans** Sat; **Bourgoin Jallieu** Thur; **Brignoud** Tue, Sat; **Chasse-sur-Rhône** Thur; **Cote-St-André** Thur; **Cremieu** Wed; **Domène** Thur; **Le Grand Lemps** Tue, Fri; **Grenoble** Tue, Fri; **Moirans** Sat; **La Motte-d'Aveillans** Wed; **La-Mure-d'Isère** Mon; **Pontcharra** Thur; **Pont-de-Beauvoisin** Mon; **St-Jean de Bournay** Mon; **St Marcellin** Tue, Fri, Sat; **La-Tour-du-Pin** Tue, Sat; **Vienne** Sat; **Virieu** Fri; **Viriville** Tue & Sat; **Vizille** Tue; **Voiron** Wed.

Southern Comforts

This is an enormous region, sprawling eastwards from the very bottom of the French Atlantic coast to just short of Marseilles, bounded to the south by the Pyrénées and to the north by the towns of Agen, Cahors, Rodez. It was to Gascony that I wanted to go, but to find Gascony these days needs determination and the very oldest map you can lay hands on. Officially it doesn't exist: and neither does the Quercy, the Rouergue, the Comté de Foix, and other places which people think they live in, and talk about, and travel to and from. They've all become part of modern *départements*. Thus once you determine where Gascony might be, you find it spilling into all kinds

of administratively untidy areas, into Aquitaine in the west and the Languedoc in the east – and isn't there also something called the Midi down here? Indeed there is, and to add confusion it *is* in the middle, even though that's not what it means; Midi actually means 'towards the South' or 'south facing'. Notwithstanding, Gascony was where I wanted to go, so I headed for Auch, home of d'Artagnan the musketeer and vaunted as the capital of Gascony.

Spring Relief

It was spring and I first took a train from Bordeaux, speeding comfortably through the backyards of vineyards where activity was

just starting, through the market gardens of Marmande where tomatoes were growing plump under plastic cloches, and alighting in Agen where the plums were just about to burst on the boughs. I was on my way to the *Hôtel de France* in Auch to visit M. André Daguin and his wife and to see what the market had to offer.

André Daguin had fascinating stories to tell of the Gascony of only a few decades ago – of how he saw neither milk nor cheese as a child and cannot take either now. Cattle were used solely for ploughing. Even goat's milk and its cheeses were something developed over the last 20 years. The food of the Gascon was simple and by

> In which we ...
>
> ● Shop for garlic tops and a soldier's line up ...
> ● Discuss the future under canvas and find food fairs with musketeers and Spanish music ...
> ● Smell violets and find what should be a sausage in Toulouse ...
> ● Put trout under a *blanquette* and enjoy the influence of Basques and Catalans from over the border ...
> ● Don't avoid a horse's foot, find recipes on your fish ...
> ● Discover what is supreme about fattened ducks, and where musketeers make policeman's eyes pop ...
> ● Brew up some snails and find God in velvet trousers ...
> ● Count the cloves not the kernels ...
> ● Taste a chartered cheese and a cake with wings, that sounds like stew ...
> ● Discover where fruit and nut cases really feel *chez soi* ...

today's standards dangerously high in protein, fat and salt. Goose, duck and pork were the basis – hot in *confits* in winter, cold *confit* in summer, fresh sometimes, or a mixture of salt and fresh in *garbure* or, sometimes, in certain versions of *cassoulet*. The greatest portion of produce grown was, and still is, destined for sale elsewhere, or to feed the livestock, hence the fields respectively of rape and of maize.

But then, as now, spring always brought goodies to relieve a monotonous diet. Mme. Daguin took me to inspect the market.

When we walked across the Place de la République to the cathedral about which the market is set, I was expecting great stacked stalls. There were some, selling early strawberries which hit you at a hundred paces with their syrup sweet perfume, even so early in the morning. But this was not an organized commercial market, this was a meeting place for people young and old who had come to town for the day with a bundle of what they thought might make a franc or two; it was a chance to

escape the thrall of the land and gossip a little.

It was the posies of flowers I noticed first, small knots of blue and gold, yellow, white and violet, laid in bright buttons under a few garlands of lilac or branches of other blossom, gathered you imagined while hurrying for the bus. Most of the vegetables and salads I was looking at had not been bundled. They were so few they were simply spread flat on scraps of newspaper or on brown paper bags which had been split and opened. Garlic tops *aillet* and wild leeks *poireaux de vignes* lined up like soldiers for inspection, with cabbage shoots and ordinary leeks; later in the year cabbage flowers would be offered, to boil and eat with vinegar and oil. The variety of salad stuffs, and the eating of it, is only a few decades old, again the results of wars and immigration. This time it is the Italians, who are indeed everywhere but who have generally added little to what they found, with one small exception. You find marvellous pizzas, but they are now becoming a national dish of France.

'Whither Foie-Gras?'

A further reason for being in Gascony in spring or early summer (and even pretty landscape needs brightening with activity and noise sometimes) is the *foires,* fairs agricultural and cultural that combine modern technology with fun-fairs, fireworks and serious panel discussions under canvas, such as 'Whither *foie gras?'* – it's true, I went to one in Castelsarrasin. There's generally a gastronomic stand or tent, to taste the wines or to eat local prunes and cakes, or even to talk to small producers of *foie gras* and *charcuterie*, which is the most interesting experience of all. (The wine, incidentally, is more worth tasting than ever before, now the growers are turning towards controlled, low-temperature fermentation and producing delightfully clean and elegant wines). *Foires aux Bandas* include roving bands of brass and percussion, *Bandas et Pañas,* clearly with musical roots in Spain.

The *Foire d'Auch* lasts from the first week in April to the first week of May; in smaller places it may be just for a day, but there will be one somewhere almost every weekend, until it's too hot.

Having found some of Gascony, it was by train again, to Toulouse, middle of the Midi. Here you may eat violets, and are reminded of it in every shop selling sweetness of one kind or another. It is strange to be famous for both chunky sausages and violets, but Toulouse is, and violet essence is available in chocolates, bonbons, even in liqueur for the rugged individualist.

The Midi has only one highway of note, few railway lines and produce which lends itself to the attentions of such creators as the 14 chefs of *La Ronde des Mousquetaires.* You'll certainly come back with something to think about – I'm still thinking about *foie gras* steamed with scallops . . . and what you do with violet liqueur after you have sniffed it once? . . . .

CHARCUTERIE

The pigs, the food they eat and the climate combine throughout Gascony and the south to make excellent *charcuterie* of all kinds, although *pâtés* are less common than salted, preserved products. Between the Cévennes and the Cerdagne ranges of Languedoc particularly, air-dried sausages are marvellous. So, too, are the *jambons crus*, notably from the Black Mountain area close to Toulouse and from Ariège. Buy sausages from the mountains; the labels will say *fabrication montagnarde, séchage naturel à 850 m d'altitude,* for instance.

As well as the raw hams enjoyed at the start of meals (often with the local figs or, in the spring, with radishes or young, raw broad beans *fèves*), equivalents to our bacon are common. *Oeufs à la causalade* (Ariège) is simply eggs and bacon. Breakfast by any other name . . .

Black puddings *boudins* are common and in Béziers they contain pine kernels, whereas

THE
Cassoulet War

Only the very wise or the very foolish should dare any attempt conspicuously to be knowledgeable in France about *cassoulet*; even worse is to voice a preference for one version over another, or to declare which is the original. For these are questions that divide towns and villages, even – it is said – families. There are three main protagonists; Castelnaudary (Aude) Carcassonne (Aude) and Toulouse (Hte-Garonne). All three present the same base as Castelnaudary, which *seems* to have the best claim as originator: white haricot beans with pork rind, garlic, a *little* onion with clove, a little carrot, a little bay, thyme and parsley. Other parts of the pig, salted or otherwise, are added from time to time, place to place. Carcassonne adds lamb or mutton, sometimes even partridge (but you'd be

lucky); Toulouse, the most complicated version, adds mutton or lamb, too, plus its famed chunky sausage and preserved goose *confit d'oie* or *confit de canard*. These are but guidelines, and the basis of the conflicts.

None of the additions is as important as the basic treatment of the beans. They must be well soaked, which starts germination and sweetens each bean. And the cooking must be long and slow enough to blend the flavours, reducing the cooking liquid (water) to voluptuousness but retaining the shape and texture of the beans. It is common to sprinkle the top of the cooked *cassoulet* with breadcrumbs and once these have crispened to stir them in and let another crust form. This can be done less dramatically and without adding the crumbs, simply by removing the top of the con-the *boutifarces* of Roussillon include bacon and herbs. *Galabart* indicates a particularly large black pudding and *melsat* a white pudding based on pork rather than poultry. In Aspet, the end of the pig's intestine is used to make a giant air-dried sausage the *marinoun* holding 2-3kg/4-6lb pork when first made; it is the same idea as the *rose de Lyon* (See **Rhône, Savoie & the Dauphiné**).

The most famous product, and one you are more likely to find and afford than the *foie gras* variation, is the *saucisse de Toulouse*. To be worthy of the name, such sausages must first be made only with back fat, neither too firm nor too soft. The flesh and fat must be cut into large pieces by knife; small pieces or machine-cutting might lead to a texture that will break or split. The pepper must be a mixture of two-thirds finely ground and one-third whole grains, and the mixture must sit 48 hours before being put into skins. If they are served *à la languedocienne* they are rolled into a spiral, sautéed in good fat with garlic and herbs and served with tomato, parsley and capers.

FISH & SHELLFISH

There is a certain amount of freshwater fish in Gascony (pike, perch, tench, some *écrevisses* and *truites des gaves* in the Pyrénéean streams) but they are not really important. The rivers Garonne, Ariège, Tarn and Aude contain much the same population. In Limoux trout is served like veal in a *blanquette* – in this case not just a white wine sauce but a sauce made with *blanquette de Limoux*, the local sparkling white wine. In Uzès (Gard) trout and other such fish are braised in sorrel *oseille* for a summer dish. In the northern Pays Basque the River Adour still attracts salmon, one of the few in France with a run big enough to justify the expectations of being served a local salmon.

For sea fish the west of Gascony – Gers, Hautes-Pyrénées and the Midi – rely on ports such as St-Jean-de-Luz for deliveries. The haul includes delicious fresh tuna *thon,* gurnard *grondin* and hake *merluche/merluz*. This last is a great local favourite cooked *à la koskena* with peas, potatoes and asparagus, sometimes given the Spanish name *salsa verde*.

It's a different story down east, where warmwater fish, shellfish and crustacea come directly from the Mediterranean coast of Languedoc-Roussillon to the ports and markets. As the Languedocians were always more interested in the land than the sea, much of the business of catching and eating fish has a Spanish or Catalan flavour as it was the

tainer. Needless to say, there are strong arguments for allowing anything from seven crusts to form to none at all. When Gault Millau interviewed chefs for a modern view only a third felt it at all necessary, and then only once; yet they also said it should be done twice for holidays and three times for weddings . . .

It's considered that only an earthenware container allows a *cassoulet* to cook at the low temperature and slow speed that guarantees results. And thus Castelnaudary's claim to be originator of the dish, for closeby is the town of Issel and since time unknown its potters have made the *cassole d'Issel* for baking slow stews.

In those villages and establishments who want to avoid the battle about which or who is right, there are variations of the basic idea under other names, notably *estouffat*, and other words like that, indicating a dish of local origin cooked very slowly. Some of these, as in Montauban, may contain that upstart new arrival, the tomato (horror!). But tomato's acid sharpness balances the richness for the uneducated palate of those from outside the area or who are foreigners. When I make dishes of this sort I also use more herbs and take advantage of the extraordinary effect red wine has on beans (improving even baked beans from a tin). Whatever your version, the inclusion of goose fat *gras d'oie* adds marvellous velvety flavour and texture; you can buy it in tins. The real problem with *cassoulet* is that it is murderously unsuited to summer eating, and you are ill-advised if recommended to do so unless there is an unseasonal plunge of temperature. Yet in the Hte-Garonne, you might go for *mongetado,* local beans cooked with onions and pork rinds, considerably lighter than a *cassoulet*.

A *cassolette* incidentally, is not a lesser, lighter or smaller version, but an indication that you are to get a small helping of something savoury or sweet in a small dish of the same name.

men from over the border who did most of the fishing.

Sète is by far the most important port with Port-Vendres, almost on the Spanish border, the centre for sardines and anchovies. This is one of the best areas in the world for these two fish and for other 'blue' fish including mackerel; this is often presented under a *nom de guerre* such as *grillade du golfe*. You'll look in vain here for the *cassoulet* – fish and fishy things from the sea are the greatest attraction. And the biggest is oysters.

The *parcs conchylicoles* oyster beds of the Étang de Thau (Hérault) were farmed by the Romans but then ignored until the 1930s. The oysters of Bouzigues are considered the best and have the special advantage of being in season year round. Among the oysters, you may note the occasional presence of a *pied de cheval*, horse's foot, named for its size and shape. I'd love to hear of someone who has actually tried one.

Clams *palourdes* are also grown and mussels are cultivated on loosely woven nets then eaten raw with a thread of vinegar and chopped shallots. But they'll also be eaten *à la brochette, à la marinière* or stuffed *à la Sétoise* with sausagemeat then braised with tomatoes, shallot, garlic and olive oil.

The mussel season is June to September, so summer visitors can spend no better balmy evening than in the company of a raw seafood platter raised high in the middle of their table, glittering dully with ice-cubes, sporting a strand or two of seaweed, and smelling of the sea.

Worth Finding

Almost all the information about fish types given under **Provence** is also relevant to the Mediterranean coast of this area.

● *Alevins d'anguille* Elvers, thin and nutty; what Australasians understand by whitebait and absolutely scrumptious.

● *Brandade de morue* Sort of mayonnaise of salt cod and olive oil and milk. An acquired taste, which I haven't, although amateurs reckon little pots sold in supermarkets are more innocuous, and useful as a picnic spread 'dotted with *harissa* sauce and new garlic'.

● *Bourride* Said actually to have originated in Sète, it differs from *bouillabaise* by using only firm white fish, notably conger eel *baudroie* and bass *loup*. Narbonne makes one just with cuttlefish *seiche*, and Agde just with conger, which other centres copy. If someone suggests something of a crustacean nature is added, refuse and enjoy them separately. Like a classic *bourride* these variations are all served over toasted bread and thickened with *aioli* garlic mayonnaise.

● *Bouillinado* Another fish stew, from Bacares, which combines fish with potatoes and pimentos, Catalan style.

● *Civet de langoustes* This delicious crustacean is thus named when cooked with white wine, usually a Banyuls, tomato, shallots, garlic and ham.

● *Langouste à la Sétoise* Perhaps the real origin of the dratted *américaine/amoricaine* dish, incorporating brandy, tomatoes, etc (see **Brittany**).

● *Lamproie en matelote* The fast disappearing lampreys, cooked with their own blood, but only in spring; if the cook is from Bordeaux, much use should be made of leeks – lucky that, for Perpignan has its own variety, with tiny leaves.

● *Tielle Sétoise* A fishy cornish pasty. Mine was squid or cuttlefish with tomatoes and perhaps other seafood.

● *Ttoro* also *Thoro* A Basque version of *bouillabaisse*. Avoid paying too much for one that includes crustacea which never survive the boiling. Originally used the water left from boiling salt cod, I have read, but doubt – why would fishermen have such a thing aboard their vessel? The major difference from *bouillabaisse* is the inclusion of hake – *colin* usually but *merluche/merluza* locally – or its head at least – gurnard *grondin* and of course sweet and hot peppers. Ciboure and St-Jean-de-Luz make the best, probably.

● *Thon* Fresh tuna, excellent on Atlantic coast usually sautéed or grilled and served in or accompanied by tomatoes and red peppers.

● *Tripes de thon* I'm beginning to think this is the marine version of a literary joke. Said to be a dish of cooked tuna tripes (intestines for the confused) simmered in sea water and white wine, dashed with *eau-de-vie*, thickened with flour and eaten very hot BUT only at sea on the fishing boats of the men from Palavas-les-Flots and Agde. Can *you* find anyone who will actually let you taste it, rather than merely talk about it?

MEAT, POULTRY & GAME

In Sète, keep an eye out for the *cigale de mer* (literally sea cicada). This extraordinary creature, a flat lobster, looks like a huge woodlouse before cooking turns it red, and is said to make a chirruping like a cricket; it is exquisitely sweet. All along the coast the sardines, anchovies, mackerel and tuna are superb and *sèche*, spelt *seiche* everywhere else, which is cuttlefish, is served with a *rouille* garlic mayonnaise with hot red pepper. You might find saffron included in fish dishes, especially soupy ones, and plainly-cooked fish is likely to be basted with one of the many local vermouths; in Agde they use it in their *bouillabaisse*.

Early in summer, enjoy some of the best anchovies in the world; later they'll be sold rock-salted, and the friend who told of his purchase in Coullioure said 'every last fish in the bag tasted of fresh anchovy instead of the smear-on pizza taste.' *Anchoïade*, the garlic, oil and anchovy paste is used a lot in *amuse-gueules* appetizers.

The *bouillabaisse, bourride* and *soupe de poissons* found along the provençal coast prevail here too with variations, but the amazing southern preoccupation with salted fish from the north is now mercifully on the wane.

Locally caught tuna *thon rouge* or *thounina* (dialect) is only a fifth of the size of the deepwater type and makes an interesting change from the red mullet *rouget*, bream *daurade*, sea bass *bar*, crabs, eels *anguilles*, whiting *merlan* and the rest. A tip for the self-catering: fishmongers wrap your purchases in paper printed with good recipes.

Things have changed on the plates of Gascony and Languedoc-Roussillon quite as much as they have on the land, where vineyards are turning into apple orchards. For although still a food to be reckoned with, the goose is no longer sole queen of cuisine; her consort regnant is the duck. But it's her own fault. As explained in the section on *foie gras*, the duck is far more biddable than the goose, reproduces more often and is thus more profitable. Its fattened livers *foie gras de canard* are generally considered superior in flavour and appearance. The lesser amount of flesh a duck presents, is a lesser degree of trouble to sell. But there is plenty of it, hence the emergence, in the last 15 years or so of the *magret* or *maigret de canard* (the former is dialect), essentially a boneless *suprême* of duck breast. The *magret* should properly only be the breast of a duck fattened for its liver. For, eccentrically, such ducks present a thinner breast than usual with less fat, too. But this is generally misunderstood and now any old duck breast might be called a *magret*. More duck means more preserved duck *confit de canard* too, and thus once-goosed dishes are now ducked. Everywhere, chefs are exercising themselves to make more of this bounty, particularly in combination with summer's superb vegetables and salads.

Chickens and turkeys, too, are part of the edible birdlife of the area, with Gascon turkeys well prized throughout France. One of the most interesting poultry dishes is *alicot/ailcuit*, chicken giblets cooked with potato, carrot and garlic, but the best version is made with turkey (giblets are *gesiers* and really real recipes should include the wings, *ailerons,* explaining the name). When you are in the Rouergue/Aveyron, beware of confusing this with *aligot,* which is a purée of potatoes and cheese. All poultry goes with almost anything and so almost every part of a bird may be stuffed with or served with any combination of olives, raisins, nuts, chestnuts, prunes and bitter oranges. They may be spit-roasted with a garlic *croûton* in the gullet, or roasted or boiled as *poulet farcie au pot*.

In the area abutting the Agenais (Lot-et-Garonne) there is much acclaim given to *oie farcie aux pruneaux* goose stuffed with prunes. As it takes four days to make properly, you'd be better of looking for stuffed goose neck *cou d'oie farci*, a sort of sausage.

Many ancient and honourable dishes are disappearing, in many cases in pursuit of a less fatty diet, but just as often because they take too long to cook. *Cassoulets* will flourish for some time I expect and so will the main beanless, long cooked stew of mixed meats, the famous *garbure* of Gascony. Three or four different parts of different animals cooked slowly with vegetables (*gerbe* means a bunch or bundle of them), with cabbage added at an earlier or later stage according to your sophistication, is fast becoming a special occasion dish rather

★ ★ ★ ★ FOIE GRAS & FOIE GRAS DE CANARD ★ ★ ★ ★

Because geese are so relentlessly independent, and refuse to breed more than once a year, the season for fresh fattened goose livers only starts in early winter, with a peak coinciding with demand at Christmas time. But demand is now so great throughout the year that most *foie gras* served in France, especially in summer's tourist season, must be imported from Eastern Europe and Israel.

Today, though, it is *foie gras de canard* you are more likely to meet, and this fattened duck liver is also more likely to be made in France. The emergence and current domination of ducks' livers is largely due to the passion of one man, André Daguin of *Hôtel de France* in Auch, once capital of Gascony. Over 20 years ago he realized it was only the hot Gascon summers that prevented *foie gras de canard* being available all year. Ducks are bred year-round for the table, but no-one ever fattened them in summer's months, for the birds could not be kept in good enough condition. By constructing cool pens protected from the sun, and by using refrigeration, a virtually new industry has been born. Those who have been privileged enough to compare geese and duck livers invariably prefer that of duck, for it is richer and more complex. From the cook's point of view, ducks' livers are less likely to explode in cooking or to breakdown into an expensive pool of liquid fat.

Foie gras is specially important to two main areas, the contiguous zones of Gascony, Landes and the Dordogne,and in Alsace, with Strasbourg as the centre. The major difference between the products of the two areas is that in the north, the livers are mixed with spices and gently massaged and moulded to encourage voluptuousness; in the south they are not man-handled, and if there is any flavouring it is likely to be that of armagnac.

Although it will never be cheap, you are best advised to start your experience of eating *foie gras* in a restaurant. More than ever serve it cold as a first course, or include it freshly cooked on a warm salad *salade tiède* as a first course. At the Château de Montreuil I've eaten it on a bed of *mâche* lamb's lettuce, in Alsace stuffed into a pheasant breast. In the Languedoc it might be baked in pastry or lightly fried with grapes in a traditional kitchen, but M. Daguin serves it with scallops or salts it and serves it raw.

You will argue for days about the correct accompaniment for *foie gras;* it is an argument complicated by the fact that until early this century, *foie gras* was always served at the end of the meal, when there were dessert wines about. Thus even when ordering it as a first course, a luscious, chilled sauterne is often chosen, but it must be one which is balanced by a little acidity (don't say I said so but Austrian dessert wines are cheaper and more balanced than many French styles). White burgundy, an Alsatian *vendange tardive,* red wine, amontillados, madeira, Madiran and champagne all have their advocates.

If you want to bring *foie gras* home, resist canned livers of any type, for the best flavour comes only from cooking at low temperatures; those required properly to sterilize canned goods are far too high. In any case, if you look at the label, you are invariably not buying goose liver but some mixture with pork and/or other fats. Those with a ludicrous 1% or so of truffles are even less value for money. As a Christmas or other treat, buy only *demi* or *semi-conserves,* sometimes called *mi-cuit,* which are always in glass and have a life of several months under refrigeration. They are as good as anything you will prepare yourself, and as cooked *foie gras* improves with age you can pack some into your suitcase or carry-on bag with confidence.

These days you can more readily buy raw *foie gras* or *foie gras de canard* in vacuum-sealed packs – I have done so in the *Marché aux Grand'Hommes* in Bordeaux. This is by far the cheapest source, and is safe to transport without refrigeration. Incidentally you cannot judge the quality of a fattened liver by its colour. The introduction of the yellow hybrid corn to replace the old white type means yellow flesh and fat, which can disguise defects.

In Gascony, the Landes and the Périgord, keep your eyes open for farms which will welcome you to see how *foie gras* is made. In Gascony there will be more chances than anywhere else because *foie gras de canard* is made all year round. Look for signs saying *gavage,* the term for force feeding, if that is what you want to see, or *dégustation* if you would rather concentrate on tasting the finished product.

Home Confits

A *confit* is any fatty meat pickled with salt then preserved in fat, usually more of its own, traditionally prepared in autumn to store protein for winter. *Confits* of goose, or of duck, used to be the most common, usually only the legs and thighs, but now the greater number of ducks being bred for making *foie gras* in Gascony mean both that duck predominates there, and that breasts are preserved too.

The process is simple and easy to do at home. The meat is covered with salt and left to pickle lightly for a day or so according to taste. Some flavouring is usually included, too—bay, peppercorns, that sort of thing. Once the unabsorbed salt has been brushed away, the meat is cooked gently to render most of its own fat, then covered completely with fat and cooked until falling from the bone. Ideally goose is cooked in goose fat, duck in duck and so on. Pork pieces are also preserved, and in some cases, chicken *poulet en confit*. Once packed in the cooking fat, it must mature at least a week before being eaten, but is usually kept much longer when, like anything salted it will slowly harden, and the fat may develop a taint: this is more likely if the preserving fat is being used for a second or third time. When served, *confits* are heated in the fat so any pieces of skin crispen up again. They are usually served with potatoes sliced thinly and browned in the same fat, although this is being changed by thoughtful French chefs who may serve them shaved thinly onto salads as a first course.

than a family staple. The new musketeers of Gascony, *La Ronde des Mousquetaires,* an association of the best chefs, made *garbure* for several hundreds of journalists and dignitaries in Auch's magnificent Corn Market. The chefs' modern lighter touch made it thoroughly delicious and there was an enjoyable *frisson* waiting in line as you spied a choice piece of chicken, for instance, and hoped it would still be there when you were.

not want-not custom called *faire chabrot* practised here.

Sheep are better equipped than cattle or pigs to graze on such stubby plains as the Causses. Uzès and Quercy are also important centres. *Mouton* might actually *be* mutton rather than lamb, and thus able to survive being cooked in rich *daubes* or *civets*, roasted with juniper *genièvre* or served with the extraordinary concoction of Toulouse, *cité rose* or *aux briques*, a mix-

Worth Finding

• *Cabassol* The head, caul and feet of a lamb stewed together, flavoured with ham and vegetables. The tongue, ears, brain and jaw muscles are the good bits. Head for Lodève (Hérault) or Requista (Aveyron) – at *mardi gras* particularly – if you *really* want to try it.
• *Gasconnade* A *gigot* of lamb flavoured with garlic and anchovy, which I have never understood or enjoyed, even though the idea sounds right.
• *Menouls* Also *trénels*. There are two versions; the simple one cooks mutton *tripes*, stomachs, for 6 or 7 hours with herbs and vegetables until the fat is 'perfumed and unctuous', tasting like *le Bondieu en culottes de velours*

God in velvet breeches as it slips down your throat – well, that's what they say . . . a more complicated version wraps pieces of mutton tripe around ham and cooks it in tomato and white wine.
• *Mouton en pistache* In this region *en pistache* usually means studded with whole cloves of garlic. This is supposed to have 50 of them in a shoulder or leg of lamb which is then braised with wine and vegetables; it might be served with beans, when it becomes a southern cousin of *gigot à la bretonne*.
• *Pastis* You are unlikely ever to be served this amazing thing; a sort of perpetual casserole to which wine is constantly added – for months!

Even in the spring evening, balmy rather than summer sultry, eyes were popping and foreheads sopping. A policeman said the temptation to eat too much of it, resisted by few, was why he ate *garbure* only rarely. We were served it all in one plate, but properly the broth and the meat and vegetables should be separate, with the last of the broth mixed with wine, the waste-

ture of black pudding, sausage, preserved duck, tomato and garlic. They do things with mutton tripes, too, like *tripoux* (see **Limousin & the Auvergne**) and *manouls,* and with lambs' head *cabassol*.

Daubes of beef are associated with Albi and Carcassonne, but veal is more common these days, perhaps with a lemon sauce or with green olives. Those of

GASCONY & THE SOUTH

advanced culinary theory will appreciate the knowledge that even in France some things cannot be called anything French; bulls' testicles become a distinctly Spanish *criadillas* when served in Nîmes.

There is little game to speak of, although there once was, especially around Narbonne, but it was senselessly double-decimated between the two wars by literal overkill and insensitive husbanding. There was even a type of mountain goat, the *isard* in the Comté de Foix (Ariège): the small game birds, ortolans, thrush, warblers *becfigues* and so on are now protected by EEC regulations. Some hare, wild rabbit *lapin de la garenne,* pigeons and partridge *perdreau* is all that is left now. It is really worth ordering one if it is from the Foix, for the flesh tends to be perfumed by its heady diet of lavender, juniper and thyme. *À la catalane* should mean it is accompanied by a sharp sauce of bitter oranges.

A *cargolade* is more easily found, a sort of brew-up of snails in white wine or snails grilled *en masse.* In the Languedoc more than anywhere else in France snails are served in ways more interesting than with butter and too much garlic; the best are those which include nut oil or nuts, which underpin the nuttiness of a good snail: *à la gayouparde, Sommiéroise* or *Lodévoise; à la Narbonnaise* mixes mayonnaise with almond milk.

Pork is most likely to be used for *charcuterie,* or included in the many mixed-meat dishes; but suckling pig is often enjoyed at special occasions.

FRUIT & VEGETABLES

Garlic haters, go home. This is the heart of garlic growing and eating, with Tarn probaby the place where more is used than any other part of France. Known also as *aulx* rather than *ail,* it's used in more interesting ways, too. When I poked around the market in Auch on Saturday morning, I discovered *aillet* (sometimes *aillé*) the green shoots of young garlic, used as we would chives or spring onions. It was also the only place I found genuine wild leeks *poireaux des vignes* offered, too – I would have given anything for a kitchen to play in that day.

Generally Gascony and its near neighbours prefer to use

LOCAL GUIDE

Vegetables

● **Artichoke** *artichaut*
Var: *Violet de Gapeau*

March to June and October to December.
Dep: Pyrénées-Orientales, Vallée de la Garonne.

● **Asparagus** *asperge*
Var: White and green*

Early March to mid-June.
Dep: Garde, Hérault, Aude, Pyrénées-Orientales.

One of the most important areas in France; some primeurs are forced for mid-February. In France *green asparagus is still two-thirds white.

● **Aubergine** *aubergine*
Var: West: *Violette de Toulouse* (white fresh); East: *Violette de Varbentanne* (green flesh)

End May to mid-November.
Dep: Gard, Tarn-et-Garonne.

● **Capsicum** *poivrons*
Var: *Lamuyo, Esterel*

June to early November, but later in south west.
Dep: Gard, Tarn-et-Garonne, Pyrénées-Atlantiques.

● **Cauliflower** *choufleur*
Var: *boule de neige, Erfut, Rex Aramon, Brio, Claudia.*

October until January 15th
Dep: Gard.

● **Celery** *céléri branche*

Peak in October.
Dep: Pyrénées-Orientales, Hte-Garonne.

Second biggest producer after the Loire.

● **Garlic** *ail*
Var: white: *Messidrôme, Thermidrôme, Blanc de lomange,* pink: *Fructidor, Rosé d'Italie, du Var, de Lautrec,* violet: *Germidour, Cadours.*

July and first fortnight of August.
Dep: Tarn-et-Garonne, Gers, then Tarn, Hte-Garonne.

The principal French production zones; the relatively uncommercialized garlic of Quercy, which includes some of Tarn-et-Garonne and some of the Lot is considered the sweetest and the least likely to be bitter in cooking. In addition to the amount grown in domestic gardens, each French person buys an extra 800g/2lb a year. France imports more garlic from South America than it exports to European markets.

cloves of garlic whole rather than chopped or crushed. This is flagged by the use of *pistache* in descriptions of dishes, sometimes meaning the cloves have been stuck into, say, a leg of lamb, or used in a *daube* or *ragoût,* as the *ragoût de mouton* of the Haute Garonne, also called *cassoulet Luchonnais.* If the cloves are just lightly crushed in their skins, the eventual flavour is relatively subtle, and if the cloves have cooked long enough their flesh will have melted into a buttery sweetness that is beguiling, addictive, unlike garlic, and hell the next day.

The extraordinary range of vegetables grown from the Atlantic to the Mediterranean find themselves in an even bigger range of soups and stews, generally heartier than you would imagine such a climate would indicate. These are mainly winter dishes but in summer at midday the locals rely upon the equally numberless variations of salad as a mainstay, albeit with a little *confit de canard.* *Salade de Cévennes* is nicer than the Waldorf, with which it has affinities; it is diced potato, celery and walnuts. In Languedoc or Roussillon you will be more likely to be offered the green olives of Lucques or the longer, more savoury black *picholines.* And the bread is guaranteed to be good and honest, and interesting, for cereals have been a major crop for centuries. Early in the 19th century, Tarn and Haute-Garonne made quite a lot of wine, but now vineyards are being converted to orchards. Many look to the Golden Delicious for their future prosperity, but no apple can thrive without cold nights to develop texture and skin colour. Some growers who have seen, and tasted, the better crisper apples being developed elsewhere in the world are now turning to the vines of the kiwifruit, the monkey peach from the Yangtze Valley, perfected by New Zealand.

Millet used to be a staple used for the porridge-like *bouillie* or *millas,* but it has been replaced, even though the name has not, by corn from America. The use of corn for human food is considered eccentric in most of France. Most of the corn is not sweet, but grown for the sustenance of the huge population of animals and poultry. The great mesh-sided stores of dried corn-cobs seen everywhere are as nourishing a sight for the culinary traveller as the reality of cornfed chicken or tur-

● **Leek** *poireau*	Mainly autumn/winter Dep: Hte-Garonne, Tar-et-Garonne.
● **Lettuce** *laitue* Var: white and green cabbage varieties plus icebergs, batavia, curly endive etc.	Open-air: November until March. Covered: December until March. Dep: Pyrénées-Orientales, Gard, Hte-Garonne.

The Pyrénées-Orientales produce 40% of winter lettuce and 65% of *scarole,* (frisée etc).

● **Onion** *oignon*	End March until September. Dep: Hérault, Gard.
● **Short day onions** *Oignons de jours courts*	Ready from end of May to end of July
● **Parsley** *persil* Var: *Le Commun* (most perfumed); *Frisé* (crinklier). Over 25% of French producton.	Year round. Dep: Pyrénées-Orientales.
● **Potatoes** (new) *pommes de terre de primeur*	End May to end July Dep: Gard, Pyrénées-Orientales, Hérault, Pyrénées-Atlantiques.
● **Tomato** *tomate* Var: *Beefsteak*	East: End April until start December. West: Gard, Hérault, Pyrénées-Orientales, Tarn-et-Garonne.

Gard is a most important centre, but Pyrénées-Orientales are first on the market with quantity, in May. As well as growing an average of 2kg per head, the French buy 8.5kg/2llb of tomatoes a head per year.

● **Turnip** *navet* Var: long: *Nantais, Croissy, Milan.* flat: *de Nancy, de Saint-Benoît, Jaune boule d'or*	September until April. Dep: Gard, Hérault, Lozère, Hte-Garonne.

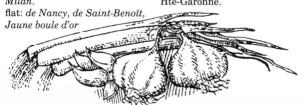

key on the plate. There is some little local complaint, for the yellow hybrid variety most commonly sown is not considered to produce such delicately-flavoured flesh as the old but less prolific white corn, which gave also a less startling colour to flesh and fat.

Pumpkin is another delicious vegetable often given only to animals but here commonly used to advantage; in the Pays Basque there is a delicious pumpkin bread, easily spotted for its warmth of colour and recommended for its amicability of flavour. Its combination of pumpkin, corn meal and dark rum owes nothing to local tradition, however, for all three are from the New World, and are more likely to have crossed the border from Spain.

The vegetables associated in the northern European mind with the Midi—aubergines, tomatoes, courgettes, beans, artichokes and the like—are all here, of course, and constantly being used in more ways than with oil and garlic. The courgette flower will be stuffed, the aubergine combined with wild mushrooms in Nîmes. The *cèpe* might be found solo in a *daube* of distinction, but there is more to wild mushrooms than that. The Béarn, for instance, has a wide range of wild mushrooms in the valleys of Aspe and Ossau. As well as *cèpes* there will be the slightly earlier *oronges,* an edible amanite of which the *oronges des Césars* is the best, and the *psalliotes des prés*, related to and almost the same as the cultivated variety, and also including *champignon rosé*, with a pinky-brown, scaled skin which I bought in August

LOCAL PRODUCE

Fruit

● **Almonds** *amandes* Var: mainly introduced	Green: June/July Main harvest: August to October. Dep: Hérault, Aude, Hte-Garonne, Pyrénées-Orientales.
● **Apple** *pomme* Var: *Reine des reinettes*	East: July/August. West: September/October. Dep: Hérault, Gard, Hte-Garonne, Tarn, Tarn-et-Garonne, Lot, Gers, Ariège.
● **Apricot** *abricot* Var: *Rouge du Roussillon, Rouge de Rivesaltes, Précoce de Boulbon.*	Early June until early August. Dep: Pyrénées-Orientales, Gard.

The Pyrénées-Orientales is as important as the Drôme as a premier production zone, but crops 10–20 days earlier, peaking about the end of June.

● **Cherries** *cerises* Var: *Bigarreau, rouge et blanc, Berlat*	Mid-May to end June. Dep: Gard, Hérault, Pyrénées-Orientales, Tarn-et-Garonne, Aveyron.

● Céret (Pyrénées-Orientales) is usually the earliest place to harvest followed by the Gard. Remoulins and St-Quentin are important centres.

● **Chestnuts** *châtaignes*	Harvest begins September. Dep: Lot, Hte-Garonne.
● **Grapes** *raisins* Var: *Lavallée, Cardinal, Chasselas, Muscat; Chasselas de Moissac* are AOC.	East: August until November West: September until December. Dep: Gard, Hérault, Tarn-et-Garonne.
● **Greengages** *reines-claudes* Various varieties over season	July until October. Dep: Tarn-et-Garonne, Gers, Lot.
● **Hazelnuts** *noisettes* Var: *Fertile de Coutard*	Harvest starts Steptember Dep: Hte-Garonne.

Green hazelnuts, cob nuts, are often available earlier for snacking.

in Toulon's Cours Lafayette market; they have a richer, stronger flavour and keep their shape and texture remarkably well in cooking. If you are in the south in spring, you might be rewarded instead with *mousserons* or the crinkly topped *morilles*. Like *cèpes*, they are equally wonderful dried.

Lentils are a favourite in the Lozère through the proximity of the Auvergne, but the most unusual vegetable must

be the salsify *salsifis* which is fried and sweetened before serving.

Béarn, and the valleys behind the coasts of the Pays Basque grow a remarkable range of vegetables; the latter being the centre for the cultivation of several varieties of red pepper, sweetish or hottish, which dominate the cooking and condiments of the area. Esplette is the centre of the business of sun-drying and selling them. A naive belief

• **Kiwifruit** *kiwi* Var: *Hayward* (NZ)	December until April. Dep: Tarn-et-Garonne, Hte-Garonne, Tarn, Pyrénées-Atlantiques.
• **Melon** *melon* Var: types of *Charentais*	June until mid-October. Dep: Tarn-et-Garonne, Gers, Lot.

Accounts for 30% of French crop, often sold under name of production area but all are charentais; much of the production is on a small scale to protect quality.

• **Nectarines** *nectarine/ brugnon* Var: *Fuzalode* (white – mid July) Yellow ones are American strains.	End May until end August. Dep: Pyrénées-Orientales, Gard, Tarn-et-Garonne, Hte-Garonne.

More than half of the French crop comes from the Pyrénées-Orientales; vallées de la Salanque, de la Têt, du Tech: Perpignan is an important market for them. Moissac, Montauban and Toulouse are important centres, too. *Nectarines* have a free stone; *brugnons* do not.

• **Peach** *pêche* Var: *Genadix* 4 & 7 old white; rest of white, and yellow-fleshed are American.	June until early September. Dep: Pyrénées-Orientales, Gard, Hérault, Tarn-et-Garonne, Hte-Garonne.

Pyrénées-Orientales and Gard produce about 50% the nation's crop, with continuously extended season as new strains are included.

• **Pear** *poire* Var: *Williams, Guyot, Beurré hardy, Passe-Crassane* (winter)	Mid-July to mid-September Dep: Tarn-et-Garonne, Gard, Hte-Garonne.
• **Plums** *prune* Var: *Prune d'ente*	June to September Dep: Tarn-et-Garonne, Gers, Lot, Gard.

Hugh production almost exclusively for processing of one sort or another; but delicious fresh if you have the chance.

• **Strawberries** *fraises*	April/June and mid-August/October. Dep: Tarn-et-Garonne, Gers, Hte-Garonne, Lot.
• **Walnuts** *noix* Var: *Grandjean marbot*	Harvest starts in September Dep: Lot

...hat the rest of France was as ortunate in the bounty of heir horticultural harvests as is home in the Vicomté de Béarn is what I think led Henri IV to promote the belief hat each family might aspire o a weekly *poule au pot*.

Potatoes, yet another mport from the Americas, are ombined there with peppers nd as throughout the region oth with the traditional cooking media of pork fat and oil, nd in combined olive oil and butter, too. In north Languedoc, *criquettes* are potato and garlic pancakes. In Ciboure, potatoes are puréed with beans, garlic, olives and shallots to make the distinctive *purée Ciboure*. Marjoram *marjolaine* is used in the southwest, for stuffing peppers or with masses of parsley in soups. Parsley is the most common garnish, *persillade*. The proximity of the Spanish border explains the regular but not common use of saffron.

CHEESE

Although the range of cheese made locally is not enormous it covers a wide spectrum. The greatest opportunity offered is to compare *roquefort* cheeses, for some will have more veins, some less, some will be fresher, some more aged. A gentle stroll through a market or along a village street will offer a choice you will never find back home. Look, too for the plain soft sheep's milk cheese in cartons; if you can keep it chilled it is a delicious, but somewhat startling spread for picnics.

Take the plunge and try other local blue cheeses, too, made with cow's milk. Lovers of goat's milk cheese will find *cabécous*, but my favourite is *bethmale*.

• *Amou* A west-Gascon farm-made sheeps' milk cheese (45% fat) in the shape of a thick disc, cured for 2–6 months, thus mild to sharp, may be used in cooking. Fragile golden rind, lightly oiled.

• *Ardi Gasna* Basque for 'local cheese'; this is a nutty flavoured sheep's milk cheese made in the mountain farms of the Pays Basque. Used in cooking and sometimes eaten when a little mouldy. Best end of spring to autumn.

★ *Bleu des Causses AOC* Clearly related to *bleu d'Auvergne* geographically and in culinary terms. Made for centuries; now produced commercially (although cured in natural caves) it is a non-cooked non-pressed blue cheese with moderate veining. Eaten all year, although a winter cheese (whiter and dryer than a summer one) has a more vigorous flavour. Adds savour to pasta and potatoes and, oddly enough, to grilled meats or the juices of roast beef and other meats. Production in Lot, Aveyron, Lozère, Gard and Hérault, an area which includes, but is bigger than, Les Causses.

★ *Bethmale* (Ariège) A large disc of cows' milk cheese made in the Comté de Foix. At its best in spring and summer it has a haunting flavour becoming sharp. Really wonderful. Phillipe Olivier in Boulogne has found someone who makes *artisanale* cheeses.

● *Bleu du Quercy* Commercially-produced blue closely related to *blue d'Auvergne* (45% fat); a soft blue with strong smell and positive savoury flavour. From Figeac area particularly: best in autumn and winter.

● *Bossons macérés* Look for this home-produced cheese only in small markets. Produced by macerating dry *Tommes de chèvre* in a mixture of white wine, olive oil and *marc:* a local *fromage fort*, in fact.

● *Cabécou d'Entraygues* Made on farms around Entraygues-sur-Truyère and the immediate area in the Aveyron, these are very small discs of *chèvre* or *mi-chèvre* with a mild to nutty flavour. *Cabécou* is a generic name for a group of small *chèvres* of this type derived from the word for goat in Languedoc patois – *cabre*.

● *Cierp de Luchon* Also known as *bethmale*.

● *Esbareich* A large flattened loaf of sheep's milk cheese made in the mountain cottages of the Pays Basque, it has a mild flavour becoming stronger as the cheese matures (2–6 months). Grate like *parmesan* when mature.

● *Iraty* Another Basque cheese, this time from the Basse Navar. Made in mountain homes from a mix of sheep's and cow's milk. A large flattened loaf with washed-rind and strong flavour variable according to exact mixture of milks used.

● *Livernon* (Quercy) A soft goat's milk cheese, also called *cabécou de Livernon*.

● *Montségur* Relatively new, very bland washed-rind cheese made commercially of pasteurized cow's milk down in the Pyrénées of the Ariège.

● *Les Orrys* (Ariège) Named after a mountain village in the Comté de Foix, a large flat cylinder of cow's milk cheese, pressed and uncooked with a fairly strong flavour. Often used grated on food.

★ *Ossau - iraty - brébis - pyrénées (Pays Basque and Béarn) AOC* Remarkable cheeses that are made from the milk of two types of sheep: *manech* and *basco-béarnaises.* Lightly pressed with a dry brushed crust that may vary from a yellow-orange to grey, a creamy white body and rich earthy flavour. Best from late spring to the end of autumn. The hot curd is broken up by whisking, then the cheeses are hand-shaped, treated with *gros sel*, and matured about 3 months in a humid atmosphere at less than 12°.

● *Pélardon des Cévennes Pélardon* is the generic name for several cheeses of this type – small soft *chèvre* with a nutty flavour.

● *Passe l'an* (Montauban Languedoc) A large very hard cheese with a low fat content (28–32%) cured for at least 2 years; it not surprisingly has as distinct flavour; a commercial attempt to imitate Italian

grana cheeses; mainly used as such.

● *Picodon de St-Agrève* St-Agrève is the place to buy this rich nutty small disc of *chèvre* although it is also found in the Cévennes. Best in summer and autumn.

● *Picadou* A very powerful small cheese, wrapped in leaves; made from sheep's or goat's milk; called *cabécou* when cured in crocks.

● *Rogeret des Cévennes* (Languedoc) Small goat's milk cheese, red, blue rind and a keen nutty flavour. Made around Lamastre.

★ *Roquefort AOC* In 1411 Charles VI signed a charter giving the inhabitants of Roquefort-sur-Soulzon the

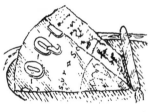

monopoly on making this the best-known of all blue cheeses. Made only with full, raw sheep's milk, each cheese is turned 5 times a day while it drains, after which it is placed for at least 3 months in the famous natural caves of Roquefort-sur-Soulzon, known also as the caves of Cambalou but called *cabanes* (huts) by the local workers. Their humid air contains natural moulds and forms a unique microclimate in which this cheese is matured. It has a sticky surface, white unevenly veined body (it crumbles easily) and an incomparably rich flavour, both savoury and salty. It must be left to reach room temperature – wrapped – before eating, and can be enjoyed all the year round.

PASTRIES, PUDDINGS & CONFECTIONERY

In Castelsarrasin, there was a man selling *gâteau à la broche,* like the german *baumkuchen;* batter is dribbled onto a slowly turning skewer over a fire until the layers build up into a cake; a bit dry. There was also a *gâteau de noix* with chocolate icing and a rich stuffing of nuts and honey, packed on wooden slats. It lasted some days in my suitcase. Back home the rich, rather short crust and filling were excellent. The manufacturer, *La Coupiagasse,* based in Coupiac, makes a wide range of broadly authentic baked goods.

The word *pastis* is complicated in Gascony. It is used both for its constantly refreshed stew, and for a dessert creation found in the Landes and most places south of Bordeaux, yet made with a paper-thin pastry related only to the *strudel* leaves of Austria and to the *phyllo* pastry of Greece and the lands of Islam. Leaves of the lightly vanilla-flavoured pastry are torn raggedly, perfumed with armagnac and orangeflower water then folded twice, piled with lumps of butter into a baking dish and baked into *un gâteau qui a des ailes* a cake with wings. *La croustade* is the same wondrous pastry, which should look as fine as a bridal veil before it is baked, but adds layers of apple or plum and sugar. Anyone you see walking on tip-toe while balancing a cakebox on Sundays, is almost certainly carrying a *pastis* or *croustade* from the pastry shop to grace a family lunch.

Castelnaudary and other places follow the example of the Ardèche by making crystallized fruits, but Toulouse, capital of the Midi, does it to violets. Indeed her violets flavour bonbons and fill chocolates – even perfume a liqueur. A more universal flavour perhaps is liquorice *réglisse* and Uzès is the French liquorice capital, producing more than half of all that's consumed. There is a fine range of liquorice confectionery (*bou d'Zan* particularly) but the major part of the crop goes into *pastis* aperitif drinks such as Ricard.

But if ever there was a home for fruit-and-nut cases, this is it. In the south-east corner, the Pyrénées-Orientales produce France's best apricots plus excelling peaches and raspberries. The Agenais grows its famed plums for the world's best prunes, often still dried in old-fashioned prune ovens by the orchards. *Prureaux fourré,* prunes stuffed with a paste of almonds and themselves taste too wonderful to imagine. From old and new orchards in the west and east tumble barrelsful of greengages, apples (although frankly the area is too hot to expect much quality) and pears, often found happily relaxed in armagnac. Preserved fruits in sugar, alcohol, or both, are common throughout the region. In Gascony, fruits are poached with spices in red wine; on the Côte Vermeuil – Perpignan and thereabouts – fruit is more likely to be served fresh, mixed in a salad and all the

THE PIES
•
OF PÉZANAS
•

When Clive of India escaped from the heat of battle and business for the winter of 1766 to stay in the Château de Larzac, near Pézanas, he brought with him both Indian servants and a taste for sweet mincemeat pies. It is commonly written in France that these pies of chopped mutton, sugar and lemon peel were invented by, or an ethnic speciality of, the Indians, but they are simply a rare survival of the original pies of this sort brought back to Europe from Araby by the Crusaders.

Pézanas still bakes them according to what is said to be the original recipe: four parts of brown sugar, two of minced mutton, one of mutton fat, one of beef suet, ideally from veal kidneys, and some grated lemon peel – all baked in an elegant French version of a hot-water crust. Béziers has its own version, but it is considered impolite, i.e. dangerous, to be heard comparing the two. They may sold as *pâtés de viande sucrée* or *de Pézanas/Béziers.* In Béziers, other, simpler fillings may be used including fish. In Nîmes, there are *pâtés de mouton.*

more welcome on your plate for its customary slurp of Banyuls wine.

Preserved or fresh fruit, and the syrupy jams *confitures* made from them, adorn thick pancakes *pannequets,* or are dipped in batter and deep-fried, *beignets*. I specially liked the sudden appearance here of the blood-juiced pomegranate *grenadier* and the sensuously perfumed quince *coing,* normally more associated with the preserves of Spain and Portugal. Thin, lacy-edged pancakes *crêpes en l'air* are mixed with eggs and water and fried only in lard, then basted with a fruit *eau-de-vie.*

Walnuts, hazelnuts, almonds and pine-nuts from the tall parasol pines of the coast, *noix, noisettes, amandes*

and *pignons*, add snap, crunch and richness to a huge variety of nibbles and cakes. A great speciality of the Pays Basque, *turrones* or *tourons,* of Spanish birth, are almond-nougat loaves stuffed with these local nuts and other fillings. Nuts go also into the *nougat* of Limoux and the richer, darker *nougat noir* you'll specially find in Perpignan. *Rosquillas* is an almond cake from Rou-

ssillon: and *gimblettes* and *petitsjeans* are almond biscuits, ideal for nibbling with a glass of wine.

Less publicized than its peppers is the excellent Basque summer crop of figs, plums, table grapes and, best of all, cherries. If you miss the season do not fret, for the sensational chocolate-makers have combined them with their product for centuries.

Worth Finding

- *Coques* A *brioche* studded with angelica *angelique.*
- *Flônes* Associated with the marvellously-named town of Ste-Affrique, these are made from the whey of sheep's milk, thickened with egg yolks and flavoured with orangeflower water.
- *Nênes* Again something to find in Ste-Affrique, this is an aniseed cake.
- *Pinus* Small anise cakes from Lunel.

Some think armagnac inferior to cognac. Its bouquet is earthier, more obvious, less subtle, they say. But it's important to realize that the two brandies aim at completely different styles: the best cognacs seem to capture the soul of the grapes from which they were made; Armagnac's rich flavour reflects the *soil* on which its grapes were grown.

Many of the largest armagnac producers are partly (or wholly) owned by cognac houses and the differences are sometimes blurred. This is a pity because armagnac has a strong character of its own. The traditional still, the *alambic armagnacais,* is mainly responsible. Distilled only once, armagnac thus retains many of the volatile flavouring components that are lost in the second distillation that cognacs endure.

Armagnac is essentially a region of small producers, many of whom sell direct to the public. At most roadside shops, farms and market stalls you may taste first.

Within the region, the best confusingly comes from Lower Armagnac Bas-Armagnac, while most of the lesser stuff that finishes up inside expensive bottles of fruit in armagnac comes from Upper Armagnac, Haut-Armagnac. In between comes Ténarèze, which produces a lighter style of spirit.

Armagnac

THE SPIRIT OF THE SOIL

When you find single vintage armagancs on sale, remember the oldest lose much of their character as they age, as well as being horrifyingly expensive.

There are two mixed drinks you will find regularly: *floc* is grapejuice and armagnac; a *pousse-rapière* is armagnac with orange and a sparkling white wine.

Bon Marché

Below is a selective list of markets plus some fairs *foires* of special interest. Check with the local S.I. for precise locations and time changes.

LANDES
Aire sur l'Adour Tue; **Capbreton** Wed; **Dax** Fri, Sat; **Gabarret** Wed; **Geaune** Thur; **Hagetmau** Wed; **Labouheyre** Thur; **Mont-de-Marsan** Tue; **Montfort-en-Chalosse** Wed; **Peyrehorade** Wed; **Pouillon** Thur; **Roquefort** Sat; **Sabres** Sun; **Soustons** Mon.

PYRÉNÉES-ATLANTIQUES
Artix Wed; **Bayonne** Tue, Thur, Sat *Charcuterie and Ham Fair Wed, Thur, Fri of Holy Week*; **Bedous** Thur; **Biarritz** Daily; **Hendaye** Wed, Sat; **Laruns** Sat; **Mauléon Soule** Tue; **Monein** Mon, Thur May-Oct (Fruit & Veg); *Cattle Fair 7 Oct*; **Navarrenx** Tue; **Nay-Bourdettes** Tue; **Oloron-Ste-Marie** Tue, Sun am; **Ossès** Thur am (Mar-April), every 2nd Thur rest of year; **Pau** Daily, Mon (Poultry, cattle, foie gras & chestnuts Oct-Feb); **Salies-de-Béarn** Daily; **St-Jean-de-Luz** Tue & Fri.

HAUTES-PYRÉNÉES
Argelès Gazost Tue; **Arreau** Thur; **Bagnères-de-Bigorre** Sat; **Maubourguet** Tue (veg, poultry, rabbits); **Pierrefitte-Nestalas** Sat; **Sarrancolin** Tue; **St-Lary-Soulan** Sat; **St-Pé-de-Bigorre** Wed; **Trie-sur-Baise** Tue; **Tarbes** Thur; **Vieille-Aure** Tue.

GERS
Aignan Mon; **Auch** Wed, Thur, Sat; **Beaumarchés** Mon am; **Cazaubon** Fri pm, Sat am; **Condom** Wed; **Eauze** Thur; **Gimont** Wed; **L'Isle-Jourdain** Sat; **Lectoure** Fri; **Marciac** Wed; **Miélan** Thur; **Mirande** Mon; **Plaisance** Thur; **Riscle** Fri.

TARN-ET-GARONNE
Beaumont-de-Lomagne *Garlic Market Tue, Turkey & Capon Fair Sat*, **Castelsarrasin** Thur, *Poultry Show Thur before Christmas*; **Grisolles** Wed; **Lafrançaise** Wed; **Molières** Tue;

Montauban Sat; **Montech** Tue; **St-Antonin-Noble-Val** Sun am; **St-Nicholas-de-la-Grave** Mon.

LOT
Bretenoux Sat; **Cahors** Wed, Sat; **Castelnau-Montratier** Tue & Thur, Sun (20 June onwards); **Figeac** Sat; **Lalbenque** *Truffle Market Mon (Dec-Mar 20)*; **Mayrinhac-Lentour** Mon, Wed, Fri (plums); **Souillac** Mon, Wed, Fri; **St-Céré** Sat.

AVEYRON
Decazeville Fri, Sat; **Entraygues-sur-Truyère** Fri; **Laguiole** Sat (May & June); **Macrillac-Vallon** Sun; **Millau** Mon, Wed, Fri; **Najac** Fri, *Ham Fair 4 Mar, April, May 20 April*; **Rignac** Wed; **Rodez** Wed, Fri, Sat; **St-Affrique** Tue, Thur & Sat.

TARN
Albi Sat, 2nd & 4th Tue; **Castres** Thur, Sat, Mon (Cattle); **Gaillac** Fri; **Graulhet** Thur; **Labastide Rouairoux** Thur, Sun; **Lautrec** Fri; **Lavaur** Sat; **Lisle-sur-Tarn** Sun; **Mazamet** Tue, Sat, Sun.

HAUTE-GARONNE
Auterive Fri; **Bessières** Mon; **Cintegabelle** Tue; **Cugnaux** Sat; **Grenade** Sat; **L'Isle-en-Dodon** Sat, Tue (Poultry); **Lanta** Sat; **Lévignac** Tue; **Montastruc-la-Conseillère** Sat (eggs & poultry); **Montesquieu-Volvestre** Tue; **Montréjeau** Mon; **Muret** Tue, Sat; **Ramonville-St-Agne** Wed; **Toulouse** Daily ex Mon *Garlic Fair 24 Aug, 15 Oct.*

ARIÈGE
Ax-les-Thermes Tue, Thur, Sat; **Daumazan-sur-Arize** 1st Fri of month (Poultry Market retail 11.30-12); **Foix** Wed, Fri; **Laroque-d'Olmes** Thur, Sat; **Lavelanet** Wed, Fri; **Mazères** Thur; **Mirepoix** Thur, Sat (veg); **Pamiers** Tue, Thur, Sat; **St-Girons** Sat am; **Seix** Thur.

PYRÉNÉES-ORIENTALES
Banguls-sur-Mer Tue, Thur, Sun am; **Le Boulou** Thur; **Cerbère** Daily am Wed; **Collioure** Sun am; **Estagel** Daily ex Sun; **Ille-sur-Têt** Daily ex Sun; **Maury**

Daily ex Sun; **Millas** Tue, Thur; **Port Vendres** Sat; **Perpignan** Daily; **Prades** Tue.

AUDE
Carcassonne Daily; **Castelnaudary** Mon; **Chalabre** Sat; **Labastide-d'Anjou** Thur, Sat; **Lézignan-Corbières** Wed; **Limoux** Tue, Fri; **Narbonne** Thur, *Languedoc Exhibition May.*

HÉRAULT
Agde Thur; **Balaruc-les-Bains** Tue, Fri; **Bédarieux** Mon; **Bessan** Tue, Sun; **Béziers** Fri; **Cazouls-les-Beziers** Tue; **Florensac** Tue; **Ganges** Tue, Fri; **Lamalou-les-Bains** Tue; **Marseillan** Tue; **Montagnac** Fri; **Montpellier** Tue (Wine); **Palavaz-les-Flots** Sun; **Pézenas** Sat; **Pomérols** Mon.

GARD
Beaucaire *Olive Market Thur & Sun (Oct-Dec)*; **Beauvoisin** Daily; **Bessèges** Thur; **Calvisson** *Grape Market Aug Truffle Market Tue Nov-March*; **Clarenzac** *Olive Market Wed & Sat Oct 5-end of harvest, Grape Market daily in season*; **Congénies** *Olive Market Tue & Fri* (Sept-Jan); **Connaux** Daily (April-June) **Jonquières-et-St-Vincent** Fri (fish), Sun am; cherries May-15 June, grapes Aug-15 Sept; **Les Mages** Fri; **Marguerittes** Mon, Tue, Thur, Fri (olives); **Meynes** Daily, (asparagus, fruit April - June); **Montfrin** Tue, daily (fruit & veg May-Jan); **Nîmes** Daily; **Redessan** April-June (cherries), July-Sept (grapes); **Rochefort-du-Gard** *Late Tomato Market 2/3 times a week 20 Sept-1 Dec*; **St-Gervasy** *Asparagus Market April-June* **St-Jean-du-Gard** Tue, Sat (summer); **Uzès** Sat; **Vers-Pont-du-Gard** Mon, Wed, Fri, *Cherry Market daily in season.*

LOZÈRE
Aumont Aubrac Fri (May); **Barre des-Cévennes** Sat; **Berc** Thur; **La Bastide-Puylaurent** Wed; **Le Bleymard** Sat; **La Candurgue** Tue; **Chanac** Thur; **Florac** Mon & Fri; **Ispagnac** Tue & Sun; **Malzieu-Ville** Sat; **Marvejols** Sat; **Meyrueis** Thur, Sat; **Nasbinals** Tue.

Servants of the Sun

The French say the Mediterranean ends where the olive trees stop growing. But when I drive south, I reverse that. For me the Mediterranean starts where I see my first grove of olive trees. They are a sure sign that wines have changed to pink, olive oil is replacing butter and pork fat, and a more masterful southern sun commands a veritable cornucopia of fruits, flowers and vegetables to swell and to sweeten.

Luscious Preserves

Between those first ancient signposts and the first sight of the Mediterranean, the wild scrubland of the *garrigue* partners voluptuous manicured fields to become both herb garden and perfumery. Almond trees succour pastry chefs and confectioners. Bees buzz honey from lavender and mountain flowers, from jasmine and orange blossom,

honey which once preserved the luscious glacé fruits of Apt but now drenches cakes and pastries or makes the black nougat *nougat noir* of Montélimar and St-Tropez. In summer there will be wild raspberries, in spring wild asparagus and mushrooms to join *limaçons,* snails to be cooked and sucked directly from their shells, and in winter black truffles, if you know where to look. And then, affirmation that I've arrived, the fish, noticeably better in the cooler weather, but always welcome for its colour and freshness and unfamiliar flavours.

Bruised by the sun and battered on her leading edge by tourism, the south of France is pictured by many an enthusiastic eater as an Elizabeth David chapter come to life, redolent of garlic and tomatoes, of dishes robust with olive oil and summer's herbs. The reality is often startling in its

subtlety, restrained and simple.

The Best Place to Drink

In culinary terms, there were three areas of Provence until rail and irrigation canals began to give some sense of unity. Down by the Mediterranean, which was clean enough to swim in only when fashion dictated you did not, they ate well, of fish.

Because there were fishing boats and a tradition of trade with other coasts of the Mediterranean, olive oil was imported for repacking: in such ports, as Nice or Aigues-Mortes (when it was on the sea), taste was developed for the basil and pine-nuts of Genoa, oranges from Majorca, the pastas of the Maghreb and Southern Italy, and for the cloves and cinnamon which came west through Venice.

Behind the coast the swallows swoop over the

> In which we ...
> ● Find more water than we thought and little places in the country – with bread for dinner ...
> ● Return to the village baker with leftovers ...
> ● Discover the mistake of modern chefs – and how not to recognize onions ...
> ● Consider who sells the most authentic food ...
> ● Give some *pâtés* the bird, find a saltwater caviare, the best hay in France and the laws which inhibit restaurants ...
> ● Eat a provençal truffle under the moon and meet a kissing cousin ...
> ● Find capers being cut in bottles, get an earful of puddings, and cook for a village lunch ...
> ● Visit the three wise virgins who look after their oil, and enumerate a Christmas pudding ...

orange-pantiled villages of valleys and small plains where garlic, chard, chick peas, peaches and cherries grew. This was the best place to drink, too, for vines are jollied by the sun into producing lakes of wine with high alcohol levels. 'Here, m'sieu,' I was often told, 'we are servants of the sun. It is too hot to grow elegant white wines, too hot to drink heavier red wines. We had to choose grapes that would yield us a rosé wine, to be

drunk cool with whatever we were eating'.

Further inland, past the sere *garrigue* of scrub and pebble, where the hills begin to swell into the mountains which will eventually become Alps, olive trees rule, deep-rooted on fragile terraces constructed to conserve what little top-soil has accumulated over the centuries. Olive trees also serve to protect smaller crops and shade the goats, sheep and few chickens needed for

protein. Cattle were virtually unknown in Provence until after the World War I – there was little pasture for them to graze on and even less for them to drink.

A Place in the Country

Surprisingly, there is plenty of water throughout the area, for it is one great drain for the snows of the Alps. But it is not widespread, or flowing in a tracery of rivers and rivulets. It is not close to the surface, and worse, it is rarely where you would choose both to live and garden ... in Provence it was almost unknown, historically, to live where your food grew, and it is thus that there are only rare examples of great country houses or estates here. Any travellers' tales of luscious profusion are based on the gardens fed directly by the Rhône, the Durance or few other rivers.

The labouring men and women who were the backbone of Provence built a society which relied on 'little places in the country' – *cabanons*. Groups of families would first settle in a place with freshwater springs that was also easy to protect with fortifications, hence the great number of hilltop villages, each with central wells fed by the even higher Alps. From this fortified family retreat you had regularly to journey to your parcel of agricultural land, often far enough away to require you to shelter in your *cabanon* several nights, and to carry with you what you expected to eat or drink. The simplicity of bread scraped with garlic and dribbled with his own oil was all a tired man could bring himself to prepare. The luckier might add a salted anchovy or two to make *anchoïade* but all would have wine.

Great Civilizations

Once back in the village, you enjoyed the convenience of a central baker, whose large bread ovens would cook the dishes impossible to handle over the open fires of a provençal kitchen, common still in many a tall, village house. The baker would, for instance, cook and brown the stuffed, olive-oil bathed vegetables – the *gratins* and *farcis* which were the canny country way to use up leftover pieces of treasured meat from the spit.

Essentially, the people of the south traditionally relied on the same three products that had sustained and encouraged the growth of the great civilizations of the Mediterranean – the olives, wheat and wine the Romans had perfected for them. For those with no fish, there was a little cheese and milk from sheep and goats, but not until the tomato arrived from the New World – only in the 19th century – was there any degree of culinary unity in the area.

A Surprise to Visitors

It is a fascinating exercise to ask old people what they consider the real tastes of the south to be. Universally, they will first indicate spit-roasted game and birds, for the south was once crammed with game and songbirds. But just as frosts regularly murder the olives, forests have burned and suffocated their

inhabitants, and as food the fat songbirds are now forbidden by EEC law. *Brouillard,* scrambled eggs thick with black truffles, is another nomination, and so, less surprisingly, are the sharp tangs of thyme and of summer savory *sarriette,* and most older housewives maintain that today's chefs and cooks use too many herbs and that, properly, none should be recognizable in a finished dish, not even onion.

When you discover the living food of the south it is unlikely to be where you thought it might be. If, as seems fair to me, it is food based solely on the wide range of fresh *local* produce then the galaxy of innovative starred chefs – Vergé at *Mougins,* Maximin in Nice, Oulthier in *La Napoule,* for instance – may well be more provençal than the auberges

you seek so diligently in the countryside; almost 70 per cent of French frozen vegetables is used in such small places, and their aubergines and garlic, cucumbers and tomatoes – even their oils and olives – have come from North Africa because they are cheaper. The food is not necessarily less good, it simply isn't provençal.

The real food of the south is warmer and more subtle than the dry land or the million-dollar excess of hamburgers, pizza and chips of the coast, and the wine will be smoother and more sophisticated. Today there will be butter and cream and oils other than olive. Be prepared to be seduced, but beware, for the sun-ripe nectarine on a roadside stall is probably from an American tree, and the luscious tomatoes from Spain . . .

STAGES DE CUISINE PROVENÇALE

Over in the Var, there's a school with no lecturer that happens in a karate club's hall in La Roquebrussane, the hometown of Reboul, author of one of the bibles of provençal food (*La Cuisinière Provençale*, 1895).

Here local housewives cook with your assistance and you learn at their apron strings, as they did from their mothers. Many of the recipes aren't provençal, some aren't authentic – but it's a terrifically entertaining way to spend a morning, and you'll learn buckets if your French is good enough. The small cost includes lunch (three course menu), prepared during the morning and upon which most of the villagers descend like vultures. With the long tables, local wine and some homemade *vin cuit* or *vin d'oranges* as an aperitif, it's the closest you'll ever be to village life.

This remarkable experience is yours for a whole week once a month from February to November, but only on Wednesdays during August. For details, contact the energetic Madame Caulet (whose husband is the local doctor), Chemin de la Palun, 83136 La Roquebrussane, Tel: (94) 86 93 36.

CHARCUTERIE

Although many a southern family was once sustained by a pig or two in the yard, I cannot think pigs have ever been as important here as in other regions, and thus you will find true local *charcuterie* difficult to identify. Most pork seems to have been converted into salted products and then used in cooking, so any *saucisson sec* you find is likely to have come in from the southwest, from the Lyonnais, or, if you are lucky, from the chestnut-fed porkers of Corsica.

Generally, what *charcuterie* Provence made had two distinguishing features: it was stored in oil and more commonly contained blanched greens, chard or spinach –

and, naturally, herbs. Such a mixture of pork and greens is *caillettes,* which is likely to be served to you often. The air-dried *saucisson* which has endured is from Arles.

Both the Camargue and the uplands of Provence are spoken of as producing excellent air-dried hams. Worth looking for, but be wary in any place that does not look as though it caters only for locals.

Worth Finding

● *Caillettes* (also *gayettes*) Meatballs of chopped pork liver or slices of liver plus blanched chard or spinach, flavoured with herbs, baked in a terrine and eaten cold.
● *Saucisson d'Arles* Air-dried sausage made traditionally from 75% pork and 25% beef from the nearby Camargue. Distinctive flavour comes from the *lardons* included, from the quality of the natural gut used and its spicing with whole black pepper-corns, paprika and garlic. Much is still made authentically, and hung to ripen in *séchoir.*
● *Pâté de merles* blackbirds or *de grives* thrushes Their manufacture is now forbidden, though you will still be able to taste these *pâtés* from tins. Worth doing once, but even the whole birds preserved in a *farce* taste only of the pork which surrounds them. I suspect the only way to enjoy such flesh is spit-roasted.

The Herbs of Provence

The most successful indigenous plants of the south of France are those which meet the challenge of the sun with glossy reflective leaves, deep roots and a protective vapour of aromatic oils: sweet herbs. Once you reach the south, herbs are likely to be uppermost in your mind, but don't expect them to be uppermost in flavouring your food, for the authentic way to use herbs here is with great restraint, so that they add savour without an independent obtrusive presence.

The mixture of herbs sold as *herbes de Provence* is nice, and it is useful, but do not be misled by the inclusion of lavender or lavender flowers. Lavender is used, exceptionally, to flavour some sweets and a liqueur, but its

inclusion in this herb mixture is to disguise the low quality of the other ingredients.

Basil is very popular but apart from its role in *pistou*, a version of the Genoese *pesto* that you particularly find in Nice, it had no part in provençal food until the past few decades. Like saffron in Marseilles it is not native and came back with sailing and fishing fleets – and remained in port. Chervil, coriander, tarragon, fennel, marjoram, oregano, parsley and sage are mainly commercial crops. Chives are grown too, but rarely used as they are considered 'northern'; the exceptions are the *nouvelle* restaurants which stupidly put them on course after course thus swamping what delicate flavour there might have once been there.

But just as drinkers can follow wine routes, any eater can ramble to find the true

herbes of Provence, particularly by following the ancient walking paths to and from the hill towns, or, my favourite, from Peillon to Peille; you'll find beds of thyme and field thyme *serpolet/farigoule* (some restaurants now perfume sauces just with the blossoms), rosemary *romarin*, bay and juniper. Most specially provençal is summer savory, *sarriette*, also known as donkey's pepper *poivre d'âne/ pèbre d'ai*. It grows only in the foothills and mountains and thus does not belong to coastal recipes; it is particularly liked, and good with, rabbit and hare. Bottles of herb-flavoured oils and vinegars are hardly authentic, but are interesting additives to a cook's repertoire; much better to make your own by macerating herbs you have picked in oil you have bought direct from the press.

FISH & SHELLFISH

The arc of Mediterranean from Spain's Costa Brava to the Côte d'Azur is one of the most important areas in the world for anchovies; they're just as good as sardines when young, but by the time July comes, housewives along the coast know they are good for salting and *pissaladière,* a type of local pizza, or *anchoïade.*

In today's world, there's no longer need to come south to eat these and other well-known specialities – red and grey mullet, bream, mussels, conger, sea bass or langoustines. Instead you should look for different ways of enjoying them or, better, discover something you can't get back home. Try the mussels of Marseilles with saffron and rice from the Camargue, the raw, iodine-perfumed pulp inside potato-shaped *violets* in Toulon, the *telline* a sort of clam of the Camargue or the famed, rich stew *catigau* of Martigue's freshwater eel. Look, too, for grilled gurnard *grondin,* or fresh tuna, or *rascasse,* a basic ingredient of *bouillabaisse,* served with capers, an important local flavouring. Best for firm, sweet flesh, in my view, is the *chapon.*

There is one essential rule for enjoying Mediterranean fish – they should live in water but die in oil, olive oil. Fennel, bay and lemon are the most authentic flavourings with chopped, mixed parsley and garlic, and perhaps onion coming next. Tomato is used mainly for colour except in the Camargue.

FISHY TREATS
• • • •

Self-catering in villas is one of the best ways to give yourself fishy treats. Once you've exhausted the familiar, here are some of the unfamiliar you might like to bring home from the market; sometimes you'll see them in restaurants, and you'll encourage the others by ordering them.

Clams *clovisses* or *palourdes* and limpets *patelles* may be found raw on platters of seafood. Sea urchins *oursins* provide a rich roe, but *favouilles* are small crabs and some people eat them all. *Seiche, supion, muscardins* and *poulpe* are all local names for types of cephalod or squid-octopus related things. The *spinard* and the *esquinade* (especially associated with Nice) are spider-crabs, the former being rather giant-sized and more difficult to eat than the latter, and thus usually cheaper; both might be served with a vinaigrette rather than mayonnaise. More daring are sea anemones *orties* which should stripped of their tentacles, marinated in vinegar, cooked in oil and served with lemon or in omelettes and fritters.

Poutine is the fry or *alevins* of sardines (although some local fishermen disagree with this) and used like whitebait. But before they become *poutine*, the eggs can be found attached to the shaded side of rocks close to the shore between April and July. Easily collected now you know where to look, they are skinned gently then fried in olive oil, a provençal saltwater caviare.

Best of all is the *saupe*, a pale yellowish fish with brilliant golden stripes, sometimes sold as *fausse* (false) *daurade* sea bream. It is generally despised, for dining exclusively on seaweed it is thought to develop a pronounced flavour. The trick is to scrape away the black lining of the gut cavity. Then, baked with a splash of white wine, *saupe* rewards you by being *le seul poisson avec un vrai goût de la mer* – the only fish with a true taste of the sea. I've tried it – it's true.

BOUILLABAISSE

This is a saffron and oil-rich fish stew, originating in Marseilles. The name supposedly comes from the French words for 'to boil' and 'to lower': for once the cauldron had boiled it was taken from the heat.

There is no common consensus about the recipe except that it must not be served with 'eyes' of oil on the surface indicating the mixture had not been boiled to emulsify the oil with the other liquids, and that fennel and saffron are essential. You may find grudging agreement that the dish should include at least some *rascasse, chapon, galinette*, a little *congre*, perhaps some *rouget* and some *St-Pierre*. But opinions divide furiously on whether there should be shellfish or crustaceans.

Remembering this was originally a hearty meal created to reward fishermen at the end of their toil, it is difficult to emulate its manufacture properly on shore. The sailors threw 'one for the pot' into the cauldron as they fished; and as the fish sat with some olive oil, and some fennel, some herbs and onion, there was an exchange of flavours as they marinated in juices of their own creation. This marinating of the ingredients seems authentically to be more important than precisely which fish are included and in what proportion. Cooking over a wood fire, so that a flavour of smoke is absorbed, is largely a thing of the past, but wondrous it must have been, from reports.

Once marinated, the *bouillabaisse* is boiled, and in today's more sophisticated times, finer-fleshed fish are added last: the broth and fish are served separately. To be honest, the fish is almost always overcooked (paying for a *bouillabaisse* that includes lobster is lunacy) and few people who have a palate order it twice.

The Toulonnais version always includes mussels and potatoes, the ingredients about which locals argue most. Although now common, it is not correct to accompany the dish with *rouille* as this properly belongs to *bourride*.

MEAT, POULTRY & GAME

The south of France has never been a place for large grazing animals, neither cattle nor horses. Even though there were and are domestic pigs, most of the flesh eaten regularly was game, game birds or songbirds.

Real treats came from domestic animals, the most important being sheep. From the highlands, down to the plains, you'll find herds of sheep everywhere. The sheep of Provence have been famed for the succulence of their flesh for centuries, and historically, many of the most envied *daubes* or stews of the area are properly based on lamb or mutton. It could never be claimed that these specialities were staples, except perhaps for the *pieds et paquets* of Marseilles; most ewes were kept exclusively for milk, to make into such fresh cheeses as *brousses*. When they were past that, the flesh was of little use even to themselves. Male lambs invariably found themselves welcomed directly on to the spit, for the *gigot* of Easter, which is universal still.

There are two distinct types of lamb or mutton to look for. The sheep from Sisteron, fed on the mountain herbs and grasses of the uplands, and those from the commune of Arles, largest in France, especially from Nîmes and the plains of the Camargue to the west and of Alpilles and the Cau to the east. Arlésien grass and hay *foin* is so fragrant that such culinary luminaries as Gault Millau have long suggested it should be granted a protective AOC rating! It gives flesh such flavour that the *pré-salé* animals of the north are rendered effete and bland by comparison – or so any red-blooded Arlésien will argue!

Goats are kept for milk, cheese and meat, but they are much less important than sheep. Uncontrolled shooting for sport and ill-advised culling to protect crops means you'll be lucky to be served local game anywhere but private homes, yet if you are well inland in late summer, autumn or winter, who knows? Shooting parties are back as the forests refill with animals after the decimation of recent forest fires. There are

Worth Finding

- *Alouettes sans têtes* What we call beef or veal olives – thin slices of meat wrapped around a stuffing and braised. Also known as *paupiettes*.
- *Boeuf en daube* See *Daube*.
- *Broufade* A piquant local type of stew marinated like a *daube* but using rather more vinegar, plus those local standbys, anchovies and capers.
- *Canard aux olives* Duck with olives. The olives are usually blanched and added towards the end of the cooking and so do not add much to the basis of the dish, but delicious nonetheless. Lamb with olives is better.
- *Civet* A stew or *daube*, ideally of game, in which the blood is used as a thickener; but this is rare these days.
- *Daube* A stew, usually of beef nowadays, cooked very slowly in locally made earthenware pot called a *daubière*. A *daube* would traditionally be cooked overnight in the kitchen fire's ashes, thus an authentic *daube* must be cooked long and slow. The cooking method explains why they were often only eaten cold, in their own jelly, the next day. The meat must always marinate a while in vinegar and oil. Fresh herbs, salt pork, a little onion and some garlic are the basic flavourings and red, white or rosé wine added to the cooking later. Root vegetables or leeks have no place in a proper *daube*, but some orange peel is a common provençal addition. Some old recipes also include a few cloves and a piece of cinnamon. Wild mushrooms might be added, fresh or dried, if available. Beef being fairly recent down here, the *daube* you find in Avignon made with mutton or lamb is more likely to be authentic.
- *Escargots à la suçarelle* or *limaces/limaçons* A small white provençal snail (not a *petit-gris*). Part of the shell is cut off so when served with a spicy stew of tomatoes and sausage, you can pick them up one by one and suck them; also known as *à l'arlésienne*.
- *Estouffade* A type of pot roast of a piece of meat with herbs and other aromatics; the container is, properly, hermetically sealed; also called *étuvée*.
- *Lapin à la sarriette* Rabbit is popular in many ways but the most typical is rabbit braised in wine with savory.
- *Pieds et paquets* or *Pied-paquet* Sheep's feet cooked with tied packets of tripe. Don't leave Marseilles without eating them at least once.
- *Râble de lièvre* Saddle of hare, most often flavoured with juniper berries.

certainly enough wild boar *sangliers* about Draguignan and Brignoles to be a threat to the young shoots of the vines, a favourite snack. One nameless restaurant did serve me a *pâté de sanglier,* but it was apparently illegal to do so. Extraordinarily, laws of hygiene prohibit restaurateurs dealing directly with small producers of specialist products and then selling them. But wild rabbit *lapin de la garenne* or, closer to the coast, *farigoulette* if it has dined upon wild thyme, and hare *lièvre* flavoured with local juniper berries are commonly offered on menus; hare from Ventoux is recommended. Poultry does not thrive here, but some ducks do, and get served with green olives. Quails *caille*, to be spit roast or barbecued in vine leaves, and guinea fowl *pintadeau* are farmed here and there; some turkey too.

Travellers in the Camargue, are the only ones likely to try local beef, usually charcoal grilled. The flesh of the bulls of the Camargue is well reputed, but as the ritual bullring fights do not end in the animal's death, this is harder to test.

The real glory of the meat here is less what it is than how it is prepared, cooked very long and very slowly, with a piece of orange peel to blend the herbs and wine, and to add a haunting tang. These are the *daubes, estouffades, civets* and *broufades* which never seem quite right in summer, but which make being here in autumn or winter so very rewarding.

The tree that will not die

If you cut me, you make me more beautiful.
If you pull me out, you hurt me
Only if you destroy me completely do I die.
Provençal Proverb

The gnarled olive tree – its leaves symbolic of peace and love, its fruits of resurrection and renewal, its oil used for baptisms – thrives only on a narrow border of sea-lapped land. It can't grow at heights and won't grow far inland. It is the touchstone of provençal life, and the oil mill, unchanged in its function, remains essential to everyday life.

The olive tree's reputation is based on its reliability, for nothing short of dynamite can guarantee the death of one. Even the disastrous snows of 1985 will have killed the trees only above the ground. Already new shoots will be growing.

Both green and black olives come from the same tree, for green olives are simply unripe ones. Some varieties are good both green and ripe, others better as one or the other. Green olives are usually gathered about the end of August for by autumn the fruit will be turning violet. The finest black olives are only truly ripe in the coldest months of winter and their harvest can be a raw, chill task. The less common wrinkled olives are the raisins of the olive world, left on the trees until the new season's sun begins to dessicate them and concentrate their flavour.

The *Lucques* and *Nyons* are considered the *grandes dames* of olives, but there is also the *manzanille*, the *sevillane*, the *turquoise, sigoise, pansue* and *royale, tanche, aglandau, cayon...* the list is as long as for any other fruit. The markets of Nîmes are an important centre for stuffed green olives; Nyons and Carpentras for black ones in brine. Menton olives grow especially big and make a luscious oil.

Green Olives

● *La Picholine* Small, elongated and pointed. Fine, savoury flesh proportionately generous for size of stone. It keeps a long time in brine and is harvested in October in the Gard, Hérault, Bouches-du-Rhône and Pyrénées-Orientales.
● *La Lucques* Elongated, rather curved, pointed tip; sometimes dented in the curve. The fine flesh parts easily from the small stone. Gathered in October in Hérault and Aude.
● *La Salonenque* Pear-shaped, but usually broken for use in cooking, where the slight bitterness it retains is welcome. Harvested in September and October in Bouches-du-Rhône.

Black Olives

● *Nyons* or *Tanches* Round, heart-shaped with large stone and superb flesh. It ripens first to a violet colour and then deepens to a rich plum-black. Fully ripe in December and January in Drôme and Vaucluse.
● *Le Cailletier* or *Olives de Nice* A little olive with shining black skin, rarely seen outside Provence. Very perfumed flavour and the proper one to use in Niçoise cooking. Ripe in February or March and grown only in the Alpes-Maritimes.

PROVENCE
FRUIT & VEGETABLES

In Aix-en-Provence there were golden courgette flowers to stuff and steam or fry, in Cannes Old Town armsful of fresh herbs to take as gifts; in Nice in mid-summer early *champignons rosés,* a rich wild mushroom from the woods, marvellous to find for it keeps its texture and shape when cooked; outside the walls of Aigues-Mortes in the Camargue there were barrels and buckets and tins and jars of green and black and violet olives each differently flavoured and marinated, first to sample and then to copy in the jars in the boot of my car; in Les Arcs tiny new broad beans *fèves* were to eat raw, dipped into grated *parmesan* as the Romans did, and in the square of Méounes fragile stems of wild asparagus – this is how many of my memories of Provence start, with the specialities I bought from its markets. The most vivid are of a Sunday morning spent in the gigantic ribbon of stalls along the Cours Lafayette in Toulon, where I discovered stall after stall of white peaches and nectarines *nectarines* or *brugnons blancs* (if there is a cling-stone), fruit I thought came only in tins at Christmas time. Two days earlier I had been honoured, given a lustrous black provençal truffle by the woman who had first found it. I wanted to eat it in Provence and to prepare a meal of local produce to enhance and surround it.

That night, with the moon hung full above the vineyards we ate under a bay tree. The peaches and nectarines were sliced, dribbled with raspber-

ry vinegar (an old thing here, where raspberries still grow wild), topped with mint and served on slices of the sweetest air-dried ham there is, from Corsica. Then I cooked fresh noodles, made with local wheat, and bought in Toulon's covered market. The night before we had eaten quail barbecued in vine leaves, one of the few culinary uses for the leaves here; the birds' bones had been making a rich, dramatically reduced stock while I shopped. Half the truffle perspired its fragrance into this sauce for hours, and now I

sliced the rest into the sauce too and, as its perfume ballooned, poured it warm, but not hot onto the pasta. Then a salad, with raw plum tomatoes for the first time, and a little *brousse,* a little more wine from our friends from Domaine de Chaberts ... it had been a perfect provençal meal, and day. And the only time I have enjoyed (or detected?) the flavour of black truffle ...

But only in the last 25 years, with the coming of irrigation canals, has the south become a garden of orchards

- **Courgette** *courgette* — Mid-May to September.
Dep: Bouches-du-Rhône,
Vaucluse, Var, Alpes-Maritimes
Bouches-du-Rhône produce almost 25% of national crop.

- **Garlic** *ail* — Harvested mid-July to mid-
Var: *Rose du Var,* August.
d'Italie, Fructidor, Rosé Dep: Vaucluse, Bouches-du-Rhône
de Lautrec
Vaucluse is one of the top three production zones. Provençal
garlic is generally smaller-bulbed than that of Drôme and the
Rhône valley. Cavaillon specialises in fresh garlic, Aix-
en-Provence in dried. Vaucluse specialises in white garlic,
Bouches-du-Rhône in white and pink varieties.

- **Lettuces** *laitue/* — All year, except summer.
chicorée Dep: Bouches-du-Rhône, Alpes-
Var: every conceivable Maritimes, Vaucluse
type.
Bouches-du-Rhône is second biggest producer after the Pyrénées-
Orientales; the Alpes-Maritimes are in the second rung.

- **Onion** *oignon* — Mid-May to mid-September.
Var: various Dep: Bouches-du-Rhône, Vaucluse
The region around Aubagne (Bouches-du-Rhône) is the most
important for white onions. Fresh ones will appear as early as
spring. Cavaillon, Avignon are major market centres.

- **Shallot** *échalote* — Fresh June to August or so
Var: various Dep: Vaucluse, Bouches-du-Rhône
Not a major crop locally but the long, wine-streaked shallots
found here are considered the sweetest and most succulent of any.

- **Turnips** *navets* — October through to April
Dep: Bouches-du-Rhône, Vaucluse
Two of the four most important zones in France.

- **Tomato** *tomate* — April to November: open-air from
Var: different every year end June only.
Dep: Vaucluse, Bouches-du-Rhône
Almost 40% of all French tomatoes are grown here.

sweet with the perfume of apricots in Vaucluse, with cherries in Olargues and Remoulins. There had been some, and perfumed violet figs and melons in Cavaillon – but now everything can grow, and flourish. The paradox is that this fertility cannot fully be exploited, either to service the local tourism or France itself, for what is not flourishing is agriculture. Most of the land remains divided into small jealously held family plots, so the benefits of modern bulk harvesting and handling procedures cannot be used to make prices competitive. Although the area exports internally most of the apples, pears, courgettes, spinach, cherries, apricots, parsley, peaches and figs grown in France it does not dominate the market; the local tourist industry largely feeds it fodder with fruit and vegetables imported more cheaply from North Africa and Spain and Italy.

A complication for the visitor wishing to luxuriate in the produce of the south is that many varieties – sometimes the best – aren't French in origin. Most yellow peaches and nectarines, most cherries and many soft fruits are American or Canadian strains. But a judicious peek at the boxes or the price labels will usually tell you the variety, so you can pick French varieties and that's why these are the only ones listed in this book.

The dearth of meat in the south meant historically that once you had nibbled on almonds and olives, vegetable dishes absolutely dominated first and main courses, in soups and in stews like *ratatouille,* in *gratins* and in *farcis* of courgettes, aubergine and, latterly, tomatoes. The equal paucity of ovens in most houses meant that fruit, fresh or dried, was and is the most common way to end a meal.

A summer vegetable I recommend you try is Swiss chard or silver beet *blette,* like a tastier spinach but with a broad white stalk that is often cooked and eaten separately in a sauce or *gratin,* but is sweet enough to slice thinly when raw into a salad; especially look for sweet tarts of *blette* leaves *tarte aux blettes.* This is the kissing cousin of an old British dish, made with spinach and sometimes called Florentine Tart which was popular from the time of the Crusaders right up to until late 19th century. Later in the year, cardoons *cardons,* a member of the thistle family, become so important to some families that Christmas is not complete without a *gratin* of them.

Not unexpectedly the EEC is having its effect in Provence and there is the common battle about which varieties of which may be grown. But the

PROVENCE

most startling sight in the new provençal agriculture was self-generated, in the Camargue. It had been simply swampy and unproductive, but wildly beautiful with its white horses and wild bulls and sensational birdlife. Now areas are being semi-drained and used to grow rice. It's not the best rice in the world, but perfectly useable, and after a few year's production, each paddy field is further drained and turned into orchard, garden or pasture. It's a bit hard on the succulent eels that liked the Camargue the way it was, but once they have been simmered to the local taste, the flavour of the Camargue's rice is the perfect though poignant partner.

LOCAL PRODUCE
Fruit

● **Apples** *pommes* — Mid-July to November
Var: *Reine de Reinettes* — Dep: Vaucluse, Bouches-du-Rhône
(best in August)
Much of the product is the dratted Golden Delicious, but some Granny Smith is grown in Bouches-du-Rhône and Vaucluse, which together produce about 20% of French apples.

● **Apricot** *abricot* — End July to mid-August
Var: *Hatif Colomer, Orange de Provence, Luizet, Rouget de Sernhac, Bergeron* — Dep: Vaucluse, Bouche-du-Rhône

● **Cherries** *cerises* — Mid-May to early July.
Var: *Bigarreau, Coeur de Pigeon, Napoléon* — Dep: Vaucluse, Bouches-du-Rhône, Var
Vaucluse produces almost 25% of the national crop. Most varieties are not native. Biggest centres include Carpentras, Cavaillon, Châteaurenard, St-Didier and Vallegregues.

● **Grapes** *raisins* — August to October, with later and earlier crops.
Var: Black: *Livan, Alphonse Lavalle, Muscat de Hambourg, Ribou.* — Dep: Vaucluse, Bouches-du-Rhône, Var
White: *Gros Vert, Dattier de Beyrouth, Chasselas.*

Melon *melon* — May until October with peak July to mid-September.
Var: *Charentais, Galia, Ogen,* Honeydew and new types. — Dep: Vaucluse, Bouches-du-Rhône

Worth Finding

● *Aïgo boulido* Garlic-flavoured stock (often just water boiled with garlic in it) served over oil-soaked bread, either as a light supper or, often, as a quasi-medicine.
● *Artichauts à la barigoule* Can be one of two dishes, both based on very young spring artichokes. They are either stuffed with, among other things, a special local mushroom called *barigoule* or simply braised in wine and oil with a garlic and parsley stuffing.
● *Caviar Niçois* A purée of anchovy fillets, black olives, garlic, thyme, mustard and oil – clearly a relation of *tapénade* (qv).
● *Farcis* Stuffed vegetables cooked in oil. The fillings were always based on *restes*

(leftovers) and may still be, so only buy from what seems to be a reputable and busy shop.
● *Pan bagna* or *bagnat* Speciality of Nice originally but now universal; indispensible for picnics. Split long or short bread roll, sprinkle with olive oil, fill with mixed salad, leave to marinate.
● *Pissaladière* Although tempting to call it the pizza of Provence, it isn't quite right. Topping should consist of onion purée cooked in olive oil, flavoured with anchovies and a few olives. Any other additions, especially tomato, makes it a pizza.
● *Pistou* Provençal *pesto* made with a paste of basil, garlic, sharp cheese and olive oil and used in a bean soup.
● *Ratatouille/ratatouia* Essentially a stew of summer vegetables in olive oil (with

no other liquid), made with whatever vegetables are most abundant. Aubergines, tomatoes, courgettes, red and green peppers, lots of good oil and garlic are the basics, plus some onion. Herbs are not traditional or necessary if you have been generous with the oil. If you make some and it really needs a lift, basil works. And if you want to keep it for a while, you must boil it up 24 hours after you make it or it will ferment.
● *Salade Niçoise* Apparently not mentioned by any of the old food writers, which probably explains the many variations. Gault Millau nevertheless think it is established enough to say the real one is made from the following: segments (*never* slices), of tomato, radish, peppers, broad beans, onion, black

● **Nectarines** *nectarine/ brugnon*
Var: *Fuzalode* (white); yellow are all American varieties.

Mid-July to mid-August.
Dep: Bouches-du-Rhône, Vaucluse, Corsica

Crau et Contat, Châteaurenard, Senas and Salon are the centres in Bouches-du-Rhône, Cavaillon and Carpentras in Vaucluse. Basically similar, *nectarines* differ from *brugnons* by having a free stone.

● **Peach** *pêche*
Var: White: *Genadix;* Yellow: all imported varieties.

June to early September.
Dep: Bouches-du-Rhône, Vaucluse, Var

Avignon is one of the biggest centres

● **Pear** *poire*
Var: *Guyots, Williams, Alexandrine Douillard,* plus some winter pears – *Passe-Crassane*

Peaks July to September but continues until end November.
Dep: Bouches-du-Rhône, Vaucluse, Alpes-Maritime

Bouches-du-Rhône grows almost 20% of French pears.

● **Plums** *prune*
Var: all yellow or green- types generally French

Red fleshed Italian variety starts with July.
Japanese varieties ripen about June 15th and other types continue until early August.

Vaucluse and the two other *départements* produce almost half the national crop.

● **Strawberries** *fraises*
Var: *Fayette, Belrubi*

Approx: March to May
Dep: Vaucluse, Bouches-du-Rhône

olives, garlic, anchovies and a dressing made of olive oil and pounded anchovies. Modern versions seems to substitute green beans for the broad variety and tuna fish is a common addition, which is welcome if it is of a worthwhile quality.

● *Sauce poivrade* Sharp pepper/shallot sauce with an effective amount of vinegar; for *brochettes,* game etc. Once thickened with blood.

● *Tarte aux blettes* An important relic of the past, a sweetened but still rather savoury open tart based on *blettes* (chard or silver beet) or spinach. Here it is flavoured with sugar, currants, pine-nuts and spices, sometimes set in an egg custard to bind it. Very Middle Eastern but traditional here for aeons. Savoury French versions include anchovies and olives.

● *Tapénade* Something else called 'poor man's caviar', but actually made more like Gentlemen's Relish. Although some sources say it is timelessly ancient, the much respected J-B Reboul says (on page 71 of *La Cuisinière Provençale*) that it was invented by 'our friend Meynier at the Maison *Doré* in Marseille' . . .

Tapéno is the Provençal dialect word for capers, for *tapénade* turns out to be not so much a purée of black olives but one of capers and olives. Olives, capers, anchovies and olive oil are the basics, but marinated tuna, lemon juice, and even English mustard are included in seemingly authentic recipes. It is used as a dip or a spread and is good with hard-boiled eggs.

On Christmas Eve in Provence *les treize desserts* are arranged on a table with *le pain Calendal,* a big round wheat-flour loaf, surrounded by 12 smaller ones representing the apostles and decorated with berries and bay leaves. The casual visitor is unlikely to be invited to share this family tradition, but it makes fascinating reading, for it is a summary of the most common ways to end provençal meals throughout the year.

★ **La Pompe** A fairly dry orange or lemon flavoured bread; dipped into *vin cuit* it swells or *pompes*. Its provençal name is *lou Gibassie*.

LES TREIZE DESSERTS

★ **Nougats** All varieties including *pistachio pistache* and pine-nut *pignon*.
★ **Les Quatre Mendiants** Raisins *raisins secs*, peeled almonds, dried figs and walnuts, indicating the mendicant orders of the Dominicans, Carmelites, Fransiscans and Augustines respectively.
★ **Dates** *dattes*
★ **Mandarin oranges** *mandarines*
★ **Oranges** *oranges*
★ **Grapes** *raisins*
★ **Melon** *melon*
★ **Chestnuts** *marrons/ chataignes* Often roasted.
★ **Apples** *pommes*
★ **Pears** *poires*
★ **Prunes** *pruneaux*
★ **Quince jelly** *gelée* or *pâte de coings* Usually homemade but also from *pâtisseries*.

CHEESE

With one rare exception all provençal cheeses are variations of the one style, a small, round, white, sometimes crumbly, fresh cheese called a *brousse*. It is mainly made with sheep's milk but it might be made with goat's milk. The creamy freshness should outbalance any 'sheep' taste. It is sometimes mixed with fresh or stewed fruit or perfumed with orangeflower water to be used as a dessert cheese.

These dessert cheeses go perfectly well with a chilled, dry provençal rosé wine; in fact, I don't think red or white wines match them at all. *Brousses* are best in autumn and winter; *banon* (see below) all year depending on which animal is lactating.

● *Banon* The best known version of *brousse* is this commercially-produced cheese. Small, clear-flavoured and wrapped in chestnut leaves, it is mainly made in the *départements* of Isère, Drôme and Vaucluse. I like it slightly chilled which complements the clean, lactic flavour. When mixed or coated with summer savory it will be called a *poivre d'ai* or a *pèbre d'âne* which are local names, meaning 'donkey's pepper' (these versions are not wrapped in leaves). Look carefully when you buy a *banon*, for the time-honoured tradition of making cheese with whatever milk was closest, persists. Thus you will find them made with cow's milk, sheep's or goat's milk, or any combination.

★ *Brousse du Roue* Made on the Roue peninsula; *Brousse de la Vésubie* in the Comté de Nice.

Olive oil is one of the world's marvels. The best requires no processing other than cold-pressing and will last for years in a cool, dark place. The great stone storage tanks of the old oil mills needed only to be drained annually, to different day's pressing and each one will taste a little different.

The Three Virgins

The word virgin or *vierge* indicates the oil has been obtained only by mechanical

● *Vierge, vierge courante or semi-fine* Excellent quality, but with an acidity of up to 3%.

Huiles d'olives raffinées is oil made by refining virgin oil that originally had an unattractive taste or too high an

OLIVE OIL

remove any debris which may have settled, for the oil to last another year...

French olive oil has a lower acid content that that of other countries, but within each grade there will be enormous variations of flavour depending on the exact mixture of olives used, how ripe they were, even the temperature on the day they were picked. When you visit an oil mill on a quiet day, ask if you can sample the oil from several of the storage tanks. Each will be a pressing, and that it has not been subsequently treated in any way. The insignia 'Huile de Provence' is a guarantee of quality. In terms of quality it is generally considered that the lower the acid content the better.

There are three types:

● *Vierge extra* Irreproachable quality and flavour, and guaranteed not to have an acidity of more than 1%.

● *Vierge fine* Equally irreproachable, but with an acidity of 1½%.

acidity. *Huile d'olives pures* is made by mixing virgin oil and refined oil, sometimes called Riviera oil.

Buying Olive Oil

Whenever you are in the south you won't be too far a drive from an oil mill, although they are by no means as common as winemakers. You'll easily be able to find their locations from tourist offices, but real enthusiasts should know that the oil of La Lucques, around the

- *Sarriette* A very creamy, commercially-manufactured cheese, flavoured with savory. Other equally large cheeses for cutting on deli counters are made with a provençal tag or flavour, and most are a double-cream or triple-cream type, so they go off quickly. Great for picnics, of course.

★ *Tomme de Camargue* (also called *tomme Arlésienne* or *tomme Gardien*) Lightly pressed sheep's milk cheese flavoured with ground thyme. Some cheesophiles like the sheepier taste it develops when it is more aged.

corner in Languedoc, is considered to be among the best.

Ets. Roger Michel is at Opio, straight up the D4 from Antibes passing through Biot (where you can see and buy the famous handblown glassware). There, at the 15th-century mill, you'll also find other regional products.

Much further west there are five mills north of Marseilles on either side of the A7. Closest is at La Fare-les-Oliviers, where local olives, *aglandaus* and *saurines*, combine to make a very individual oil. You might also go to Maussane-les-Alpilles, Mouriès, Beaumes-de-Venise and, perhaps best of all, Les Barronnies at Nyons.

But before you go visit the *Musée de l'Olivier* in the château of Cagnes-sur-Mer. Or if you are in Provence during late July or August, head for Ampus to visit the fascinating private, free museum of M. and Mme Martin, on the place de la Mairie. Open every afternoon during that time, it explains everything – history, culture, cultivation, olive pickling, oil pressing – even soap making.

PASTRIES, PUDDINGS & CONFECTIONERY

To call puddings in the south of France a bit of a pig's ear is no insult. As there were few ovens in private houses, any cooked sweetness had to be deep-fried. Almost the only

kind were pieces of flat dough shaped like an ear, *oreillettes*; they were often flavoured with a orangeflower water.

In any traditional house fresh and dried fruit and nuts are still the most common way to end meals, although on Sundays you will find bought ice creams or sorbet and the ubiquitous *crème caramel* or *îles flottantes*, clouds of poached meringue afloat in a sea of custard *crème anglaise* and topped with caramelized sugar. Expensive or 'modern' restaurants will probably offer a *gratin* of seasonal fruits

in a light sauce of eggs and ground almonds.

Where apples and pears and quinces *coings* grow medieval tastes often prevail; quinces especially might be rolled in

Worth Finding

- *Calissons d'Aix* Iced lozenges of ground almonds and puréed crystallized fruits, usually melon, and enjoyed since the 13th century. In Aix-en-Provence, Bicheron at 32 Cours Mirabeau makes them on the premises. Take a fat purse.
- *Fougasse/fougassette* Essentially a loaf of bread, flattish with holes in it so it is somewhat ladder shaped. Sometimes a *fougasse* will have the fruit or some nuts, but the word seems used as freely as *quiche*.
- *Nougat blanc* and *noir* White nougat, especially associated with Montélimar is basically sugar syrup and

egg whites and may have come inland from Marseilles. Nuts and glacé fruits of every kind may be included. Much better though is one you cannot often find outside the province, *nougat noir* black nougat. Based on honey made darker and richer with the addition of caramelized sugar, it is usually filled with chunks of toasted almond. Marseilles, Draguignan and St-Tropez are noted centres.
- *Panisses* A common way of using flour of ground chickpeas *pois-chiches*, mixed with milk and butter, moulded into shape and deep-fried.
- *Socca* Pancakes of chickpea flour, popular along the coast.

honey or sugar and baked in dough.

The cookery school I found in La Roquebrussane teaches a number of sweet dishes, based on the almond... baked pears stuffed with a macaroon mixture, orange-flavoured *barquettes* from Nîmes, biscuits flavoured with anise seed, a lemon flan, and green figs baked with rum and served with cream. They are certainly more appealing than the peeled and baked broad beans which once joined your sweet store of raisins and almonds.

TRUFFLING MATTERS

Yes, I was surprised to find truffles in Provence too, so thought if this section appeared here, instead of in the Dordogne, it might fire your imagination rather more, and be more likely to help stop you wasting money.

The essential information about black truffles *tuber melanosporum* is this – those in tins and glass jars are less than a pale shadow of themselves, like tinned *foie gras* the fabled elegance of flavour is destroyed by the preserving process. They are just not worth the outlay. Some which are semi-preserved in small glass jars, often privately, are marginally better for having been exposed to lesser heats. Don't expect culinary fireworks if you've bought, or used, the equivalent of damp squibs. In addition, the flavouring action of black truffles is a mysterious process, acting more as an enzymic catalyst, it *must* both be raw and sit in the food for some time if you are to get any result, or be gently poached or baked at lowish temperature to be enjoyed by itself in generous amounts. It is mere posturing to slice canned truffle over something and to serve it straight away. You may as well slice a black olive or some dyed gelatine – some places do. And if all that weren't enough to put you off, there are black truffles and lesser black truffles, and only the expert can really tell whether the warty black thing offered you is worth the money – there's no way your nose alone can do the job.

The truffle's widespread home ground is around the roots of certain white oak trees, truffle oaks *chênes blancs truffés*, in an area around the edge of the Massif Central, roughly southwards from the Dordogne then swinging in a curve through upper Languedoc and Provence and up the Rhône Valley and into parts of Alsace. Opinions clash over whether there are varieties of black truffles or whether like other natural products, some are good and some are better; hence the arguments over the merits of truffles from this or that area. Yet often the reason for disappointment is the method of preservation.

Down the ages, the truffle harvest has swung slowly through a pattern of paucity or plenty; right now it is paucity. Only 50 years ago it was common to harvest 50kg/ 112lb a day (!) in Provence, and to buy a fistful for a few francs. Thus there are many folk memories of grating them thickly into omelettes or eggs scrambled in olive oil *brouillard*, but only after the truffle had sat with the eggs for 24 hours to perfume them. Poached or baked truffles were sliced thickly into potato salads, and on Christmas Day into salads of wild leaves *salade sauvage*. They were lavished raw into *pâté* mixtures, left uncooked overnight, chopped into the stuffings of game birds or sliced into matchsticks and poked under the skin of a *gigot* of lamb instead of garlic. You could even eat them whole, roasted in ashes.

The biggest stupidity of the truffle business is that they are in greatest demand for Christmas, when they are actually at their least interesting and barely ripe. The season begins in mid-November or so and continues until the middle of February, when they are ripest, most flavoursome – and cheapest. In most places, trained pigs or dogs are used to find the truffles, which may be as much as a foot underground; but most country folk out walking in likely spots will be seen tapping the ground with a stick as they walk *towards* the sun. Once the light glitters on a disturbed swarm of tiny transparent flies, they've found a truffle.

Throughout the season, truffles straight from the ground might turn up at any market; but there are recognized truffle centres. If you go, expect little of the exuberance of the usual market. Nothing happens until an agreed time, often as late as 10.30. Until then most vendors will sit silently with pathetic ragged bundles, feigning disinterest. At a given sign, often a bell, their black diamonds will be revealed. If you have advice or nerve, you'll certainly save money on one hand, and by using fresh truffle will get far better value on the other. Carry them sealed in a jar full of rice, which prevents any damage, and keep them cool and dark and they'll last a few days easily. But if you are in a truffle area for some time, you may like to take the astonishing advice of some of the older inhabitants of the hill towns of the Var. They, traditionalists to a man, are now brushing and cleaning their truffles, wrapping them in foil – and deep freezing them. They are as good as fresh if defrosted rather quickly in warm olive oil.

The far more fragrant, reliable and more expensive

white truffle *tuber magnatum* is, strangely, more accessible in its short season, from October until the first snows of December. This is because it is always eaten raw, shaved thinly over eggs or rice or hot *brioche*, for instance, and thus you pay only for what you eat. White truffles are found in Savoie, especially around Chambéry.

Happy truffling. But if in doubt, go for the chocolate ones.

Truffling Centres

These are some of the centres where the best of the best black truffles are collected:

Hindisheim (Bas-Rhin), the best Alsatian centre: **Belley** in the Bugey (Ain): **Digne** (Basse-Alpes): **Bordeaux** (Drôme): **Grillon** (Vaucluse): **Montségur-sur-Lauzon** (Drôme): **Valréas** (Vaucluse): **Riez** (Basse-Alpes): **Montagnac** (Hérault): **Trèves** (Gard): **Brive-la-Gaillarde** (Corrèze): **Cahors** in the Quercy (Lot): **Thiviers** (Dordogne): **Sault** (Vaucluse): **Sarlat** (Dordogne): **Périgueux** (Dordogne). The best Périgord truffles are thought to come from the Black Périgord, with those from Sarlat perhaps the very best.

Major Truffle Markets

In the Ardèche: **Bourg-Saint-Andéol;** in the Drôme: **Pierrelatte, Buis-les-Baronnies** and **St-Paul-Trois-Châteaux;** in Vaucluse: **Valréas, Carpentras** and **Orange;** in the Gard: **Uzès.**

There is a Truffle Museum at **Sorges,** which is between the truffling centres of Thiviers and Périgueux, and an experimental truffle farm near **Coly.**

A DRINKER'S GUIDE

In general, all the wines of Provence are at their best at 2 or 3 years old. Wines older than 5 years are unlikely to please.

Vintages don't generally differ greatly from one another in Provence. Such differences as there are will be reflected in the *Drinker's Guide* for the southern part of the Rhône: adjacent to Provence, it enjoys much the same sort of climate.

Ordinary Rhône wines are for relatively speedy drinking. Only the traditionally made, old-style Châteauneuf-du-Papes and the best Gigondas need ageing. It is dates for these that are given below.

The last decade

1984 Smallish vintage because of heavy losses in the Grenache crop. Whites are fresh and good, reds should be ready by 1990.
1983 Another vintage affected by a low Grenache harvest. Best reds will keep until 1994.
1982 Unlike the Northern Rhône, not a very successful vintage. Hot weather during picking meant many wines taste jammy, and will not survive for long. Drink by 1988.
1981 The very best wines need another 10 years.
1980 Best Châteauneufs are still very tannic. Gigondas more approachable. Drink these from 1989 on.
1979 Traditional Châteauneufs still need another 8 years, but everything else is drinking very well.
1978 Wonderful vintage for both Châteauneuf and Gigondas. Best still need 10 years.
1977 Pleasant, light vintage which needs drinking up.
1976 Gigondas need drink-

ing up. Best Châteauneufs will still be good drinking for 2 or 3 years.
1975 Avoid.
1974 Only if recommended.

Previous greats
Traditionally made Châteauneuf *can* develop increasingly complex flavours as it ages. Years worth trying are **1972, 1971, 1969, 1967, 1966** and **1961.**

PASTIS, VERMOUTHS AND LIQUEURS

A number of Provence's other alcoholic drinks are first-rate. The suburb of Ste-Martine in Marseilles is the home of *Ricard pastis*, which differs from the Parisian anise drinks such as Pernod in that it is based on liquorice. If you want to drink it *à la marseillaise* you should add 5 times as much water.

Marseilles is also the home of France's second most important vermouth, *Noilly Prat*. Unusually, it is matured by exposing it to the sun and sea breezes in barrels, which contributes to its aroma and salty tang. It is the finest vermouth for cooking.

Wine-based aperitifs abound. They may be flavoured with fruit, nuts or herbs: In Forcalquier *Rinquinquin* is made with peaches and peach leaves, others are made with nuts, Colignac with quince. In many of the houses I visited, liqueurs had been made by macerating herbs in alcohol – in Ampus I was offered a pungent verbena version. There is also *vin cuit*, not wine at all, but boiled down grape juice and *vin d'oranges*, oranges macerated in red wine with added spirit. And somewhere, someone makes a lavender liqueur, which is said to make a sensational sorbet. Let me know if you find it.

Bon Marché

Below is a selective list of markets plus some fairs *foires* of special interest. Check with the local S.I. for precise locations and time changes.

VAUCLUSE

Apt Sat; **Avignon** Daily ex Mon; **Bédarrides** Mon; **Bollene** Mon, daily (March-Oct); **Cadenet** Mon; **Carpentras** Daily (April-Nov), Fri (Winter), (Vine plants, truffles, game); **Cavaillon** Daily; **Courthézon** Fri, Sun am; **Entraigues-sur-Sorgues** Wed; **Grillon** *Truffle Market Mon Nov-Mar; Melon Market daily 10th Aug-Sept;* **Lauris** Mon am, daily 15 Sept-15 Nov; **Malaucène** Wed, daily May-June asparagus & cherries etc; **Mondragon** Tue; **Monteux** Daily; **Orange** Daily (15 May-15 Oct), Mon, Wed, Fri (fruit & veg) Thur (poultry) 15 Oct-15 April,) **Pernes-les-Fontaines** Sat am; **Pertuis** Fri, daily 10 June-31 Aug; **Piolenc** Mon am; **Le Pontet** Thur am; **Sault** Wed; **Sorgues** Daily (eve), (May & June cherries and veg), Sun; **Ste-Cécile-les-Vignes** Sat am; **St-Didier** Daily 10 May-30 June (cherries), 25 Aug-30 Oct (grapes); **St-Saturnin-les-Avignon** Mon; **Le-Thor** *Grape Market daily Aug-Oct;* **La-Tour-d'Aigues** Tue; **Vasion-la-Romaine** Tue; **Valréas** Wed am, Mon, Wed, Fri & Sat pm, April-June; **Védène** Tue; **Visan** Fri.

BOUCHES-DU-RHÔNE

Aix-en-Provence Tue, Thur, Sat; **Arles** Wed, Sat, Tue, Thur, Sat; **Aubagne** Daily; **Châteauneuf-les-Martigues** Weekly; **Châteaurenard** Daily; **Fos-sur-Mer-Pal** Wed, Sat; **Istres** Daily in harvest time, Tue, Thur, Sat other months; **Mallemort** Fri; **Marseille** Daily; **Martigues** Thur, Sat, Sun; **Peyrolles-en-Provence** Wed, daily April-June; **Port-de-Bouc** Daily; **Port-St-Louis-du-Rhône** Daily; **Rognonas** Daily; **La Rogue d'Anthéron**

Daily June, Mon, Wed, Fri rest of year; **Salon-de-Provence** Wed; **St-Rémy-de-Provence** Wed, Sat; **Tarascon** Daily; **Trets** Daily ex Mon.

VAR

Aups Wed & Sat am; **Barjols** Tue, Thur, Sat; **Brignoles** Sat; **Callas** Thur & Sat; **Collobrières** Thur & Sun; **Cuers** Fri am; **Draguignan** Wed, Sat am, Junk Fair 4 days in 2nd half Feb; **Flayosc** Mon; **Fréjus** Daily; **Gonfaron** Thur am; **Hyères** Daily am, **Le Lavandou** Thur am; **Lorgues** Tue am; **Le Luc** Fri am;

ALL THE FUN OF THE FOIRE

The French hold *foires* on saint's days, holy days, public holidays, at the change of season and at the drop of a hat. Virtually no animal or edible plant glides *foire*less through life – look out for the Charolles Bull Fair, a chance to see *charollais* beef on the hoof. Most towns and large villages have an annual foire to celebrate their own continued existence. The *Syndicat d'Initiative* will give you information on these. Easter and Whitsun (*Pâcques* and *Pentecôte*) are especially good for fairs: look our for them on *Jeudi Gras,* the Thursday before Shrove Tuesday (*Mardi Gras*), *Jeudi Saint,* Maundy Thursday, and *Dimanche des Rameaux* Palm Sunday.

Méounes-les-Montrieux Thur am; **Ollioules** Mon, Wed & Fri; **Pignans** Thur am; **Le Pradet** Fri am; **Rians** Fri am; **Salernes** Wed & Sun am; **Le Seyne-sur-Mer** Daily; **Signes** Thur am; **Six-Fours-les-Plages** Tue, Thur am, Sat; **Solliès Pont** Wed am; **St-Maximin-la-Ste-Baume** Wed; **St-Raphaël** Daily; **St-Tropez** Tue, Sat; **Toulon** Daily (ex Mon 15 Sept-15 Mar); **La-Valette-du-Var** Daily am; **Vidauban** Wed, Sun am.

ALPES-MARITIMES

Antibes Daily; **Breil-sur-Roya** *Olive Fair mid July & 19 Oct;* **Cagnes-sur-Mer** Daily; **Le Cannet** Daily; **Cannes** Daily; **Le Colle-sur-Loup** Wed, Fri; **Grasse** Daily; **Guillaumes** Sun, daily in summer; **Menton** Daily, *Lemon Fair end Feb;* **Nice** Daily; **Puget-Théniers** Sun; **Roquesteron** Wed, Sun; **St-Etienne de Tinée** Sun am, Mon (18 Nov-25 Dec); **St-Sauveur-sur-Tinée** Tue; **Valbonne** *Grape Fair 4 Feb;* **Vence** Daily; **Villars-sur-Var** Sun.

ALPES-DE-HAUTE-PROVENCE

Barcelonnette Wed, Sat; **Castellane** Wed, Sat; **Château-Arnoux** Tue, Wed, Fri, Sun; **Digne** Wed, Sat, *Lavender Fair 26 Aug-3 Sept;* Entrevaux Fri, Sun; **Forcalguier** Mon; **Manosque** Sat; **Moustiers-Ste-Marie** Fri; **Riez** 2nd Sat of month, *Truffle Fair Wed & Sat am Nov-Feb;* Seyne-les-Alpes Tue, Fri; **Sisteron** Wed, Sat; **Valensole** 2nd Wed of month.

HAUTES-ALPES

Abriès Wed; **Briançon** Wed & Thur; **Chorges** Thur; **Embrun** Sat; **Gap** Wed, Thur & Sat; **Guillestre** Mon; **Laragne-Montéglin** Thur; **Rosans** Wed (15 June-15 Sept); **Serres** Sat; **St-Bonnet-en-Champsaur** Mon; **Veynes** Thur.

Index

INDEX

INDEX

INDEX